Ethical Choices

*An Introduction to Moral Philosophy
with Cases*

Ethical Choices

An Introduction to Moral Philosophy with Cases

RICHARD BURNOR
Felician University

YVONNE RALEY

SECOND EDITION

New York   Oxford

OXFORD UNIVERSITY PRESS

Oxford University Press is a department of the University of Oxford. It furthers the University's
objective of excellence in research, scholarship, and education by publishing worldwide. Oxford is a
registered trade mark of Oxford University Press in the UK and certain other countries.

Published in the United States of America by Oxford University Press
198 Madison Avenue, New York, NY 10016, United States of America.

Library of Congress Cataloging-in-Publication Data

Names: Burnor, Richard, author. | Raley, Yvonne, author.
Title: Ethical choices : an introduction to moral philosophy with cases /
   Richard Burnor, Felician College, Yvonne Raley, Felician College.
Description: Second [edition]. | New York : Oxford University Press, 2017.
Identifiers: LCCN 2016049781| ISBN 9780190464509 (student edition) | ISBN
   9780190464516 (instructor's edition) | ISBN 9780190464530 (course website)
   | ISBN 9780190464547 (instructor's manual (arc))
Subjects: LCSH: Ethics—Textbooks. | Ethical problems—Textbooks.
Classification: LCC BJ1012 .B755 2017 | DDC 170—dc23
   LC record available at https://lccn.loc.gov/2016049781

9 8 7 6 5 4
Printed by Webcom Inc., Canada

To the reader, whose intrinsic moral worth has been and continues to be our most important reason for writing this book.

BRIEF CONTENTS

CONTENTS

PREFACE

TO THE READER

We are pleased to be able to offer the second edition of *Ethical Choices* to both students and the general reader. In preparing this new edition, we have worked to preserve and improve upon what many reviewers have considered to be the special strengths of the book.

Many parts of ethics are not exactly easy to understand, but we haven't wanted to add to your difficulties by poor writing. By adopting a deliberately informal style and conversational tone, we have sought to make this book clear, readable, and accessible regardless of whether or not you've previously studied ethics or philosophy. Since we don't want you to feel that ethics is tedious, we have shortened unduly long sentences, removed jargon, and reduced the number of technical terms. Ideally, our hope is that when you read this book, your experience will be something like having a pleasant conversation with an especially intriguing friend.

This book differs from most ethics introductions in several useful and appealing ways. Most of all, we intend this book to make ethics *engaging* for you. Not surprisingly, *we* find ethics captivating; we'd very much like you to find it so as well. Achieving this, it seems to us, requires that we relate ethical topics to your own life, experiences, and interests. For instance, each chapter includes at least one opening narrative or scenario meant to grab your attention, boost your interest in what follows, and illustrate what the chapter is about. Some of these stories are true; others are at least true to life; they often portray quite ordinary and everyday experiences. To further engage you in your ethics reading, each chapter is also followed by a number of practical cases. Again, many of these portray actual situations; all of them invite you to discover how ethical theory can apply directly to moral problems. Most of these cases are not about global or national policy issues; instead, they describe problems and issues that you can probably relate to in your own life. It's gratifying to us that, after examining a particular case, students have sometimes told us that they've just gone through a similar experience themselves.

To aid you further in your study of ethics, we have included a number of helps:

- Immediately following this Preface are the *Guidelines for a Case Study Analysis*. These propose a set of steps to follow as you analyze a case or even work through a personal moral problem. These are also discussed more informally in the last section of the book.
- Important terms appear throughout the book in boldface where they are first presented and explained. These "technical" terms will often be used again. Master these, as they are essential to your "internalizing" concepts and ideas you need to fully understand ethics.
- Each section of each chapter is usually followed by a set of questions *For Discussion*. Whether instructors select any of these as class discussion topics, you can consider how you would answer them for yourself. This will help you think more deeply about that section's material; it may also reveal how that material relates to other issues that interest you.
- Each section is also followed by a brief *Summary*; whenever the section introduces important terms, there is a list of *Key Terms* together with their definitions as well. Both can help you reinforce your understanding of what you've just read; they can also be very useful for doing a quick review of that section and of essential terms and concepts.
- At the end of each chapter, you will find another set of questions labeled *Chapter Assignment Questions*. These are more comprehensive than the questions *For Discussion* but can serve several of the same purposes.
- Every chapter includes a collection of *Additional Resources*. Some of these are links to short YouTube-type presentations on parts of that chapter. Others take you to an interesting video clip or trailer relating to that chapter's topics. A number are links to original works referred to in the chapter.
- Be sure to refer often to the book's detailed Table of Contents and its Index; both can help you find material you need to look at or want to review.
- There is a glossary near the end of the book. This can serve as your first resource for reviewing and further clarifying the meanings of important terms.
- A website has been set up specifically for this book. The site provides several additional tools: (a) outlines of each chapter, (b) flashcards for learning key terms, (c) practice quiz questions, (d) PowerPoint presentations of each chapter's material, and so on.

Do check out these helps for yourself. Also, thumb through the book to see how it's laid out, where you can find help, and how you can best use everything it makes available to you. We think that many of these things can benefit you greatly.

Our best wishes are with you as you start your discovery of what the ancient, fascinating, urgent, and dynamic field of ethics is about!

TO THE INSTRUCTOR

This book is primarily intended to serve as an introduction to ethics for college students who don't have much familiarity with ethics or philosophy. (It can also serve as a handy review text for more advanced students and even for graduate students.) It provides a survey of major ethical theories and perspectives that we think is highly accessible even as it remains philosophically accurate and also attempts to stay up to date. The book's underlying theme is that of *choices*. It invites readers to rationally evaluate a wide range of ethical perspectives, theories, and insights and to decide which they find to be the most compelling. It also encourages readers to *apply* what ethics has to offer to a variety of moral problems as well as to their own moral predicaments. What particularly sets this book apart from other ethics texts is its large number of student-relevant "real-life" cases, which can be used to help students make the transition from theory to application. In addition, each chapter includes at least one illustrative story or scenario (usually in its opening section) to pique the reader's interest and set the stage for what follows.

This book takes the approach that has worked best with our students. We particularly aim at presenting ethics so that it will resonate with the experiences, beliefs, and thinking of today's post-modern-minded students. For instance, it has become increasingly clear that teaching can be more effective when supplemented or even largely replaced by relevant stories and narratives that have affective as well as cognitive force.[1] To use the text to best promote the reader's engagement and understanding, therefore, we urge you to make systematic use of the book's case studies. We also suggest that you draw upon the many narratives appearing in most chapters—along with the accompanying *For Discussion* questions—to jump-start class discussions. These will not only engage your students but also provide valuable opportunities for you to interject comments and even "mini-lectures" about the material. If you feel even bolder, you might try teaching primarily through class discussions that afford you plenty of opportunities to correct, reinforce, and extend what students have previously read in the text. We have provided the *For Discussion* questions as suggestive starting points for leading such discussions.

There are several things to mention about the book's cases. First, a few case discussions introduce material not presented in the main text (e.g., "Just War Theory," "Locke and Load"). These allow you to take your students to a deeper level in thinking about issues raised by those particular cases. Second, cases have been deliberately matched to particular theories, chapter by chapter. Nevertheless, this does *not* preclude using one chapter's cases with another chapter's material.

---

[1] Joanna Szurmak and Mindy Thuna, "Tell Me a Story: The Use of Narrative as a Tool for Instruction," paper presented at the annual conference of the Association of College and Research Libraries in Indianapolis, Indiana, April 10, 2013, accessed October 2, 2016, http://www.ala.org/acrl/sites/ala.org.acrl/files/content/conferences/confsandpreconfs/2013/papers/SzurmakThuna_TellMe.pdf. Philosophical pioneers in the instructional use of stories include Kieran Egan and Gareth Matthews, among many others. Several other relevant resources are available online.

In fact, many cases may be effectively used with several different theories. The book's online website (see more in the following discussion) offers additional suggestions for pairing cases to chapters and theories. Third, the cases following each chapter proceed (more or less) from shorter and simpler cases to more challenging and multi-faceted ones. Next, each case is followed by a collection of *Thought Questions*. Many of these provide opportunities for applying the concepts and theory introduced in the chapter to that case. Others extend or even challenge the theories. To encourage the comparison of different accounts, some allude to previous theories as well. All of these questions are designed to inspire students to think beyond their initial or "gut" reactions and to develop more carefully considered and defensible viewpoints of their own. We have made no attempt to limit case problems to the easy or uncontroversial. As in real life, many of the problems raised by the cases pose challenging moral dilemmas that admit to having no straightforward moral answer.

The *Guidelines for a Case Study Analysis* immediately follows this preface; you may want your students to follow these guidelines in doing their case analyses. If you'd rather they not take such a formal approach, you might assign just selected parts of the guidelines to ensure some structure to student analyses, or you might use them simply as a source of ideas when you create your own assignments. We have found the guidelines to be helpful to our students; nevertheless, they may also be completely ignored. None of the book's cases explicitly requires their use.

If you have used the first edition of this book, you will find that we have preserved and even added to its pedagogical tools. Many of these have just been mentioned or are discussed in the part of this preface directed to the reader. In addition, note that you can refer to each section's *Summary* and *Key Terms* to determine or remind yourself what that section covers. Further, you should know that each section's *For Discussion* questions tend to be informal and personal; the more substantive *Chapter Assignment Questions*, meanwhile, can be used for assignments or to suggest assignment ideas. Further, you may find that some of the *Additional Resources* include videos and other types of presentations that might usefully supplement your classes.

Depending on the chapter, these might include videos or movie trailers related to the chapter's material, short presentations of portions of that chapter's material, other texts that also cover the chapter's material particularly well, or, when available, links to relevant online primary sources in ethics (e.g., Plato's *Republic* or Hobbes's *Leviathan*). You might want to use some of the primary source links to have students do readings in the original works (without having them buy a supplementary text). All of these resources enable readers to pursue many topics more fully as they wish.

As many reviewers approved of the text's organization, we have largely preserved that while adding some additional flexibility. On the most local level, each chapter still divides into clearly delineated sections. You may thus assign readings by section, or you might assign students to read only certain sections rather than an entire chapter. Sections that go beyond essential material or that are more specialized or advanced are also still marked (by ** in their headings). These may be excluded from a course without jeopardizing student understanding of later sections or chapters.

On a more global level, the book discusses more theories and cases than most courses can accommodate. It thus allows considerable leeway in what topics you want to include in a course. Most chapters are fairly self-contained, though some unavoidably must refer to preceding material. When such references are made, the relevant chapter and section is identified. This not only helps in reviewing earlier material but also allows you to entirely skip an earlier chapter and then assign one of that chapter's sections as background for a topic introduced in a later chapter. Several chapters may simply be skipped entirely. Chapters that seem more discretionary include Chapter Five: Moral Psychology and Egoism; Chapter Seven: Consequentialist Ethics: Rule Utilitarianism; Chapter Nine: Natural Law Theory; Ten: Social Contracts and Rights; Twelve: Feminism and Care Ethics; and Chapter Thirteen: Ethics and Religion. Another chapter you might elect to skip is Chapter Three: Personal Autonomy and Moral Agency, although some of this must be covered if you wish to include Chapter Fourteen's §II: Medical Ethics: Futility, since the latter relies heavily on concepts of autonomy and agency. A knowledgeable instructor can also present many of the chapters in different orders with relatively little inconvenience.

CHANGES IN THE SECOND EDITION

The book has been completely overhauled stylistically in an effort to simplify and streamline the presentation, to reduce the number of "key terms" and other technical jargon, to standardize terminology, and to achieve a friendlier conversational tone. Occasional corrections have also been made (e.g., the discussion of Kant and absolutism has been corrected and further elaborated). Besides these, a number of other quite substantial changes have been made:

- **Changes in organization:**
  - Material from the previous Chapters One, Two, and Five has been rearranged, simplified, and consolidated into Chapters One and Four. Chapter One now begins with values, which we think provides a more intuitive route to understanding morality and ethics; our characterization of moral claims and an expanded discussion of moral thinking then appears in Chapter Four.
  - The chapter on Moral Relativism (Chapter Two) now precedes the chapter on Personal Autonomy and Moral Agency (Chapter Three).
  - The previous Chapter Six on egoism has been removed, though some material from that chapter has been incorporated in the new Chapters

Five and Six. This change connects egoism to related topics in moral psychology rather than to consequentialist theories in general.

○ The previous edition's chapter on natural law and natural rights has been divided into separate chapters. The new Chapter Nine is devoted exclusively to natural law theory; the new Chapter Ten treats rights more comprehensively as part of its exposition of social contract theory.

- **Additional content:**
  ○ Added to the generalist, principle-based pattern of "moral reasoning" of the previous edition is a contrasting particularist pattern of "moral reflection." See the new Chapter Four, which now presents both patterns of moral thinking.
  ○ A largely new Chapter Five explores major themes in moral psychology, some of which is related to ethical and psychological egoism.
  ○ The largely new Chapter Ten, Social Contracts and Rights, presents the social contract theories of Locke, Hobbes, and Rawls while also expanding the previous edition's presentation of rights.
  ○ A synopsis of feminist ethics and its development has been added to Chapter Twelve, Feminism and Care Ethics.
  ○ A largely new final Chapter Fourteen, Pluralism in Theoretical and Applied Ethics, has been added. This chapter revises the previous edition's presentation of ethical pluralism and adds three major new sections in applied ethics: §II Medical Ethics: Futility, §III Environmental Ethics: Anthropocentrism and Ecocentrism, §IV Business Ethics: Whistle-Blowing. The chapter closes with a revised section that discusses the application of ethics to one's personal life.

- **Added pedagogical tools:**
  ○ Sixteen new cases have been written for this edition, making for fifty-seven cases total. Most of the previous cases have also been updated to reflect more recent developments; a few have been dropped, and a few have been altered significantly (e.g., "Guess Who's Not Coming for Dinner," "Climate Change and Oil").
  ○ Each chapter section is now accompanied by a set of *For Discussion* questions.
  ○ A glossary of terms is now included at the end of the book.

A Companion Website at www.oup.com/us/burnor is available. This provides several resources for both students and instructors. Besides what is previously mentioned in "To the Reader", instructors will also find sets of quiz questions, suggestions for alternate uses of the cases, and an additional applied ethics chapter on moral responsibilities toward future generations. More cases may be added from time to time.

ACKNOWLEDGMENTS

Our special thanks go to Robert Miller, Donald Casey, Irfan Khawaja, George Abaunza, and Vicky Burnor as well as to the many students, colleagues, and reviewers who provided suggestions, corrections, and criticisms of the many drafts that have ultimately culminated in this book. For their invaluable reviews, we would especially like to thank Mark Alfano, Australian Catholic University; Luke Amentas, Kingsborough Community College, CUNY; Christopher Baker, Armstrong State University; Kate Bednar, University of Kansas; Jason Borenstein, Georgia Institute of Technology; Julien M. Farland, Anna Maria College; Bob Fischer, Texas State University; Dana R. Flint, The Lincoln University; Lisa Jorgensen, Vanier College; Shawn McKinney, Hillsborough Community College; Christian Perring, St. John's University; Peter Simpson, The Graduate Center, CUNY; Daniel Star, Boston University; Peter B. Trumbull, Madison College; Bas van der Vossen, University of North Carolina, Greensboro; Andrea Veltman, James Madison University; and Julius L. Wynn, St. Petersburg College. Finally, we thank Felician University for its funding and support of this project over many years and in many ways.

GUIDELINES FOR A CASE STUDY ANALYSIS

A case study analysis provides a powerful tool for sorting through and resolving an ethical problem, regardless of its specific subject. A complete case analysis consists of the following five steps:

1. Summarize the main problem and its setting.

What are the essential elements of the situation, and what is the ethical problem at issue? Summarize the case in your own words, writing as though you were explaining it to someone who is not familiar with it. Some helpful questions: Who are the key players? Who is affected by the outcome? Are there other important facts that are being assumed and left unstated? While your summary need not be exhaustive, it should identify the salient facts for your reader. Be careful not to alter the facts of the case.

2. List possible ways of responding to the problem.

What are the possible responses to the problem; that is, in what ways might a person (or a society) act if faced with the problem? List and briefly explain those that seem most likely (both good and bad). Include the actual responses made by those portrayed in the case itself. While some responses may be obvious, others may require you to think more carefully and creatively. Don't neglect either! Also, be certain that you include the response that you actually think is best—what you ultimately will defend as right.

3. Identify moral principles and theories that most directly apply to the case.

Some ethical principles may be obvious, others may not be. Be careful, however, to include only *moral* principles so that you don't confuse your analysis with legal or other types of non-moral principles. Don't formulate principles so that they are not strictly true. Especially identify principles that support your responses in part 2.

In most cases, you will also want to show how various ethical theories relate to the case. This can often be done simply by stating a theory's essential idea as a fundamental principle (e.g., "Always act so as to maximize the resulting overall utility" or "Never treat a person as a means only").

4. Identify and justify the one response that you think is morally best.

Justifying your chosen response from out of the possible responses (listed in part 2) requires you to provide moral *arguments* in support of your response. Use the pattern of moral reasoning, or moral reflection, or both (see Chapter Four, §IV, §V). Try to offer the most compelling arguments you can. These arguments should incorporate ethical theory as well.

5. Explain why the other possible responses are not as acceptable.

A person who argues for his own view is merely biased. Moral thinking requires you to also see a problem from the perspective of others. Thus, your analysis should also address the most important remaining responses (from part 2), explaining why each is morally less desirable than your response in part 4. In arguing against other responses, you don't have to show that they are all *wrong*; only that your response is better justified than any of the others.

PART I

✦

Introduction:
Theory and Practice

What use is ethics—the study of morality? If you're hoping for ethics to increase your paycheck, sell a product, or get a new job, you should probably look elsewhere.[1] Still, this hardly means that ethics has no practical value. Ethics has to do with desperately important practical matters, including many our society struggles with: questions about genetic engineering, drone strikes, stockpiling and using weapons of mass destruction, fair taxation, campaign finance, and a host of social justice issues. It's no accident that ethical theorists have often led the vanguard in achieving moral reforms. For instance, the nineteenth-century utilitarians deliberately formulated their theory to correct abuses in the criminal justice system of their time.

Yet ethics is not just essential for handling major social problems. The study of morality is important because morality itself is important. Without any functional morality, society would not even be possible. Imagine that no one bothered about the moral duty of truthfulness. Business and government would collapse since no agreement could be depended upon. Education and the news would become useless since their accuracy could not be trusted. Science would whither to mere "politics" and opinion. Even families and friendships would suffer since these require that we be truthful with each other.

Morality is not only essential to the *possibility* of human society but also to the *quality* of our lives. Imagine living in a world where morality has eroded to such

---

[1] Although businesses are increasingly discovering that morally right business practice—going beyond just the law's requirements—makes for successful business.

a point that crimes have tripled, political and business abuses rock the economy many times a year, and even everyday life is much more dangerous and violent. In the words of the seventeenth- century philosopher, Thomas Hobbes, life in such a world would be "solitary, poor, nasty, brutish, and short."[2] Since morality is so important, its study and analysis—namely, ethics—is important as well.

Both morality and ethics impact our personal lives—every time we get angry at another driver, are hurt by someone, make a commitment to a friend, or sign a document. They have this sort of living practicality because they expose the tension between what *is* and what *ought to be*, a tension we encounter daily. Studying ethics can aid us in dealing with this tension by helping us better understand what distinguishes right and wrong, how to think through moral problems, and how to address moral conflicts (among other things).

More profoundly, morality and ethics relate to the most important responsibility each of us has in life: the formation of our selves. Every choice we make contributes toward producing the moral personality that will define us in the next moment. As the twentieth-century existentialists emphasized, this power of choice—especially of moral choice—is an awesome responsibility.

In Plato's *Republic*, Socrates and his friends grapple with what they believe to be a central question of our existence: Why should I try to live a moral life? They fully recognize that moral living doesn't always advance a person's short-term interests. As their discussion draws to a close, however, Socrates forcefully summarizes a remarkable conclusion: only the morally just person can find happiness in this life. Only the moral woman or man can achieve fulfillment as a human being *right now*. Those who neglect the moral good life will inevitably be beset with internal and external conflicts that will lead to an incomplete, debased, and frustrated existence.

If our fulfillment and well-being as persons depends so much upon the moral quality of our lives, then we each have pressing work to do. We need to do all we can to establish a satisfactory moral life for ourselves. But how do we do this? It would certainly help if we could have some account of what makes something just, good, or right in the first place. For that matter, it wouldn't hurt if we could also be assured that there even *are* such things as the morally good and right.

Ethics addresses these concerns, primarily by developing ethical *theories*— accounts meant to explain what makes something morally good or right. These accounts tend to agree regarding much of the practical moral guidance they offer. They also differ and even conflict with each other in significant ways, but this should not be viewed as a serious drawback. It's partly because of these conflicts, in fact, that ethics yields such a diverse set of moral perspectives and insights. These, in turn, can contribute markedly to our moral understanding as well as to guiding our moral choices.

---

[2]Thomas Hobbes, *The Leviathan* (public domain, 1660), accessed August 18, 2016, http://socserv2.socsci.mcmaster.ca/econ/ugcm/3ll3/hobbes/Leviathan.pdf, 78.

The study of ethics is also deeply absorbing in itself. In pursuing this study, however, it's important that we keep our balance. As Aristotle warns us, many get so caught up in the *study* of ethics that they forget the importance of simply *living* morally. The ultimate practicality of ethics, then, is available only to those who actually *apply* it. It would be hard to put this better than Aristotle himself does in his *Nicomachean Ethics*:[3]

> But most people do not do these [things], but take refuge in theory and think they are being philosophers and will become good in this way, behaving some-what like patients who listen attentively to their doctors, but do none of the things they are ordered to do. As the latter will not be made well in body by such a course of treatment, the former will not be made well in soul by such a course of philosophy. . . .

*   *   *

This book provides a wide-ranging introduction to ethics, including a survey of several major ethical theories. To understand those theories, it is helpful to first address some of the key concepts and distinctions that pertain to the moral realm. This is done in Part I, which also provides some direction for thinking about moral problems. Part I also explores a few important preliminary matters—about ourselves as moral beings, about the relationship between morality and culture, and about how people actually think and act when facing moral problems.[4]

---

[3] Aristotle, *Nichomachean Ethics*, trans. W. D. Ross, Book II, chapter 4, accessed August 8, 2016, http://classics.mit.edu/Aristotle/nicomachaen.4.iv.html.

[4] The Part I "preliminaries" belong to a field called "meta-ethics," which addresses issues having to do with the possibility, nature, and application of ethical theories.

CHAPTER ONE

Ethics and Values

I. EXTRAORDINARY AND ORDINARY MORALS

Glaucon, one of those who discusses the moral life with Socrates in Plato's *Republic* (See the introduction to Part I), worries that people might often be better off if they just did whatever they wanted rather than try to act morally. He relates a Greek myth to explain his doubts:

> Gyges was a shepherd in the service of the king of Lydia; there was a great storm, and an earthquake made an opening in the earth at the place where he was feeding his flock. Amazed at the sight, he descended into the opening, where, among other marvels, he beheld a hollow brazen horse, having doors, at which he stooping and looking in saw a dead body of stature, as appeared to him, more than human, and having nothing on but a gold ring; this he took from the finger of the dead and re-ascended.[1]

Later, while sitting among the shepherds with the ring on his finger, Gyges happens to turn the ring inward and is amazed to find that he has become invisible. Turning the ring back outward, he reappears. Having confirmed that the ring always works this way, he quickly makes his plans. He travels to the king's court and uses the ring to secretly find and seduce the queen. He and the queen then kill the king. Gyges takes control of the kingdom and ends up enjoying great power and wealth—all thanks to the ring's magic.

For a seemingly ordinary guy, Gyges sure goes off the deep end! Obviously, he takes an actively immoral turn once he finds the ring. Glaucon relates this story because he can see no reason to live morally other than because society forces us to. As soon as society's power of law and punishment is removed, "No man would keep his hands off what was not his own when he could safely take what he liked . . . wherever any one thinks that he can safely be unjust, there he

---

[1]Plato, *The Republic: Book II*, trans. Benjamin Jowett (Public Domain, 360 BCE), accessed August 31, 2016, http://classics.mit.edu/Plato/republic.3.ii.html.

is unjust. . . . "[2] Glaucon's view seems supported by recent meltdowns in business and government. Businesses usually follow the letter of the law, but some business people still look for ways to "stretch" the law whenever they can. Since it's often easy to hide one's actions, people in government have also committed wrongs: lying, spying on allies and citizens, and discriminating against certain groups, for instance.

Are these sorts of moral breakdowns only committed by those on the sleazier side of humanity? After all, similar invisibility tools have appeared since Plato—for example, the Ring in the *Lord of the Rings* and Harry Potter's invisibility cloak. In *these* stories, the characters apply the power of invisibility for good. Though none of this is reality, the comparison does reveal something about human nature. Specifically, people use the capabilities they have—whether actual (strength, talents, knowledge) or magical (rings and cloaks)—to pursue their own goals and values. Clearly Gyges's values were not admirable. The same may be said of some people in business and government. Others, meanwhile, want their lives and actions to achieve some lasting good. To get more personal—how about *you?* Would your actions tend to be more moral or immoral if you could "get away" with doing certain things?

We've been assuming that we all know what "moral" means. But the term is used in several different ways. *Morals* often refer to what a person, group, or society believes people should or should not do: "Drinking goes against my morals;" "Some countries' morals are stricter than others." *Morals* may also refer to a concept of *objective* right and wrong (what holds independently of people's feelings and beliefs): "Murdering an innocent human being simply is wrong." Describing something as *moral,* meanwhile, typically says that thing *is* good or *is* right: "John is a very moral person;" "Lying is immoral." To add to the confusion, *morals* and *moral* are often used interchangeably with *ethics* and *ethical.* Although this book occasionally uses these terms in each of these ways, it will most often use "moral" and "morality" objectively, as something that holds regardless of people's beliefs.

Next, we can divide the moral realm into two major (but interconnected) parts: that which is good or bad (discussed in ethics as *value theory*) and that which is right or wrong (discussed in ethics as *deontic theory*). **Good** and **bad** have to do with *values*—properties of things or people. A medical procedure might be good because it can save lives; a person, meanwhile, can be honest or dishonest, generous or selfish. Thus, Glaucon's ultimate question is one about values: What good is a moral life? **Right** and **wrong,** meanwhile, describe what we should *do.* Gyges's later actions, for instance, are *wrong.*

We should also mention a few things the moral is *not.* Although laws often require us to do morally right things, the moral is not the same thing as the law. Nor does it have much to do with what may be *prudent*—that is, what is in our own interest. Furthermore, while religions often have substantial moral components, morality is distinct from religion and religious teachings.

---

[2]Ibid.

To further establish your intuitions about what morality involves, here are a few illustrations of moral issues as they might arise in everyday life:

- While renewing your driver's license, you are asked if you'd like to be designated as an organ donor. There is, in fact, a serious shortage of organs, and many die as they wait for a needed organ to become available. Do you have a moral duty to become an organ donor?
- You like to play a "first-person shooter" computer game in your spare time.[3] Lately, this has become a bit of an obsession—you even dreamed last night about taking down sharpshooters in a dark tunnel. You also think your five-year-old brother is playing the game on the sly. Although it has all seemed harmless, you now are feeling a little uncomfortable with how the game is affecting you and your brother. Should you change your pastime?
- At the store where you work, you notice Bill, one of the employees, stealing small amounts of money from the cash register. Bill is always lots of fun—your job would be pretty unpleasant without him. He's also a friend—in fact, he helped get you your job. But the store manager, having recently noticed cash shortages now for several days, has threatened that no one will get an end-of-month bonus if the shortages continue. Should you report Bill to the manager?

Finally, let's return to the notion of *ethics*. Ethics is concerned with both the morally good and right and with explaining what makes things good or right (among other things). Ethics is *about* the moral realm of thought, action, and experience. Roughly speaking, we can describe **ethics** as *the systemic and reasoned study of moral right and wrong, good and bad, including the principles and claims that employ these concepts.* Just as we refer to *the natural world* or *the natural realm* as including everything that science studies, we can usefully think of *the moral realm* as including everything that ethics studies.

Rest assured that we will discuss and develop these ideas much further in the remainder of Part I (Chapters One and Four).

For Discussion

1. *What are your reactions to the Gyges story? How do you think people would act (including yourself) if they found such a ring?*
2. *Compare the Gyges story to the* Lord of the Rings *or* Harry Potter *stories. Which story most accurately depicts human nature?*
3. *Consider one of the moral problems mentioned in the Part I Introduction. How do you think we as a society should respond to that problem? Why?*
4. *Considering the organ donation, gaming, or stealing cases, what do you think should be done? Why?*

---

[3]In first-person shooter games, the computer portrays the player as a character under attack in an evil world. The goal is to stay alive while shooting as many enemies as possible.

Summary

Ethics tries to answer questions like "Are there reasons for doing what is morally right?" "Can we know what is morally right? How?" "What makes something good or right in the first place?" The terms "ethical" and "moral" are often used interchangeably, but it can be helpful to think of ethics as studying the moral. Ethics has two major branches: one is about moral values (good/bad) and the other has to do with moral actions (right/wrong).

Key Terms

- **Ethics:** *the systemic and reasoned study of moral right and wrong, good and bad, together with the claims that employ these concepts.*
- **Good and bad:** *have to do with values.*
- **Right and wrong:** *have to do with actions*

II. THE NATURE OF VALUES

What is *really* important to you? What do you live for? What guides your decisions, plans, and projects? People give many different answers to these kinds of questions. Still, certain answers surface again and again: friendship, love, family, faith, self-determination, health, happiness.

These are called *values*—and we build our lives upon them. Since our **values** represent what is most important to us, most of our choices attempt to promote these values in our lives. We see this with Gyges—once he finds the ring, it immediately becomes clear that Gyges's greatly values pleasure, power, and wealth. He doesn't seem to place much value on honesty, loyalty, or even life. In contrast, Frodo in the *Lord of the Rings* most values friendship, kindness, and responsibility as evidenced by his closeness to Gandalf and the other Hobbits, his kindnesses toward Gollum, and his commitment to destroy the Ring whatever the cost. Especially as he matures, Harry's uses of the cloak indicate his values of friendship, loyalty, and family.

Values are **normative**: they belong to some *standard* or *norm* by which other things are to be evaluated. Saying that a road is no good appeals to a standard about what roads should be like. By describing Jeff as honest, I am saying that he measures up to a high standard of truth-telling. In telling a patient that he has a poor heart, the doctor compares the patient's heart to normal, functional hearts. Each of these *value claims*—statements that ascribe values (positive or negative) to things—refers to some standard and evaluates a thing relative to that standard.

Several interesting things can be said about values. As we've discussed, we usually act in keeping with our values.[4] But this idea can be taken further. If

---

[4] My showing respect toward others is in keeping with my valuing persons, but my respect is an aspect of the act itself, not a result. No commitment to consequentialism is intended here.

something is genuinely valuable, then you presumably *ought* to act to promote that good. Thus, genuine values support—and explain—what we should do. If health is genuinely important in itself, then you *ought* to do what preserves and improves your health. If living a sedentary life is *bad* for you, then you *should* exercise—in fact, you have a *responsibility* to exercise. If friendship is a genuine good, then you should cultivate relationships by being friendly toward others, sharing interests, and spending time with them. Values call for action.

Claims or statements that tell us what we should or should not do, how we ought or ought not to act, are also normative. Each inherits its normativity from the value that supports it and so appeals to the standard that value belongs to. "Should" and "ought" claims are called *prescriptive claims* - they prescribe or prohibit specific things. "People shouldn't lie" prohibits lying; "You ought to attend that lecture" or simply "Attend that lecture" tells you to do something. In sum, values are normative and are used in value claims; they also support prescriptive claims, which are also normative. The two kinds of normative claims—value and prescriptive claims—need to be carefully distinguished from mere *descriptive claims*.

A *descriptive claim* asserts something about how the world *is*, not how it *should* be. The distinction is quite important—for, as we are all aware, the way things are is not always the way they should be. Descriptive claims don't appeal to any standard and they don't evaluate; they simply describe: "Jeff is six feet tall," "I used to hate broccoli," "Over a billion people will remain in desperate poverty this coming year," and even "If everyone did what is right, the world would be a happier place."[5] Regardless of their differences, these are *all* descriptive claims.

Next, it may seem that values are things a person either just has or doesn't have—and when people disagree, it's because they have different values. However, people tend to share most values. Where they differ is not so much in *which* values they have but in the *importance* they assign to each. If you are asked what you value most, you might say that personal loyalty is especially important. Another person might say that he most respects being open and telling the truth. Both of you almost certainly value the other's main value as well but to a different degree. Given that difference, you will sometimes act differently from each other—even in very similar situations. In the cash register story, you might feel that you must remain loyal to Bill and so should not report him—though loyalty might also require you to confront him for his own good. The other person—even if he stands in the same relationship with Bill—would probably report him.

For Discussion

1. *Given how you act, what values are most important to you?*
2. *Provide several additional examples of value claims, prescriptive claims, and descriptive claims.*

---

[5] This *mentions* the morally right, but merely describes (correctly or not) the result of everyone acting rightly. This claim does not say, by itself, that everyone *should* act rightly.

3. *What values support the prescriptive claims you thought of for question 2?*
4. *Explain how the values of safety, friendship, education, income, pleasure, and love can each support prescriptive claims.*

Summary

Values are things we consider important, things we usually try to achieve and maintain. Our values drive most of our choices and actions. While people share most values, people may place differing degrees of importance on those values. Values are normative: they belong to some norm or standard. Values support prescriptive claims (which are also normative) because we usually should act in keeping with important values. Normative claims, meanwhile, must be distinguished from descriptive claims. Roughly, descriptive claims talk about the world as it is; normative claims about how it should be.

Key Terms

- **Value** claims: *These ascribe values (positive or negative) to things on the basis of some standard.*
- **Normative** claims: *Appeal to some norm or standard; must be either value claims or prescriptive claims.*
- **Prescriptive** claims: *These say how we should act: what we should or should not, ought or ought not do.*
- **Descriptive** claims: *These say how the world is (was or will be) and even how the world could be but not how it should be.*

III. MORAL VS. NON-MORAL VALUES

So far, we have not limited our illustrations to just moral claims. *Moral* claims are only one of several different kinds of normative claims. Like other normative claims, *moral* claims (whether prescriptive or value) appeal to some standard. The standard in this case is a **moral standard**—a comprehensive set of foundational moral values (or sometimes, of foundational moral prescriptions) together with all that can be derived from these. *Moral* value claims evaluate people in moral terms. We might call someone a "good person," meaning she acts in morally right ways most of the time. We describe murderers as "bad," emphasizing their glaring moral failings. We can also describe people by particular moral traits (e.g., as loyal, caring, dishonest, or selfish). Moral value claims nearly always ascribe some value, good or bad, to *persons* or their personal characters. *Moral* prescriptive claims, meanwhile, talk about the rightness or wrongness *of actions*. Some examples:

- Workers ought to accurately report their income when filling out IRS form 1040. (prescriptive)
- Gyges stopped acting decently and became an extremely vicious person. (value)
- No one should physically injure another person. (prescriptive)

- It's a good thing for people to be generous. (value)
- It was right for you to tell him that. (prescriptive)

It's worth pausing here to make a useful distinction. In our terminology, every claim or statement (value, prescriptive, or descriptive) that is true *holds* for everyone. This simply means that it's true; it doesn't mean that I believe it or even know about it. Unfortunately, there are many truths I don't know and many more I don't believe. Even when a claim *holds* for me and everyone, however, it may not *apply* to me. To apply, it must call for some response—often some action. Thus, true moral claims, unless specifically addressed to just some person(s), *hold* for all, but they don't necessarily *apply* to everyone in every circumstance.[6] For instance, the prescriptive claim about reporting income on form 1040 *holds* for all U.S. citizens but only *applies* to citizens who are required to file form 1040. Likewise, the prescription about not injuring others holds for everyone but can't very readily apply to someone who is completely alone.

To make the nature of morals and morality clearer, it will help to distinguish the **moral realm** from other normative "realms" that have their own standards and give rise to their own value or prescriptive claims.[7]

The **realm of etiquette** has to do with what is acceptable social behavior. It refers to values such as being "well-mannered" at the table, "polite" at social events, "proper" at weddings and other formal occasions, "courteous" in driving, and even "decent" when texting or emailing. Values like these in turn yield normative claims of etiquette:

- Kevin shouldn't noisily slurp his soup. (prescriptive)
- Everyone in that family is polite. (value)

Etiquette develops, in part, from practical considerations like efficiency, safety, and hygiene. For instance, all human societies have rules about meeting people—probably because our determining if the other is a friend or foe can be very important. Etiquette also forbids talking with your mouth full, no doubt because of the inevitable loss of clarity and the inconveniences of food falling out. Etiquette is also a matter of convention, and cultures often differ over what they consider acceptable. The values of etiquette for a particular culture make up that culture's standard of etiquette. Being conventional, however, doesn't diminish etiquette's importance. Etiquette plays a central role in achieving smooth social interaction and avoiding unnecessary conflicts.

Although it is normative, etiquette doesn't overlap a great deal with morality. I am not a moral failure because I am bad-mannered or impolite. Nevertheless, etiquette—being impolite or discourteous, say—can have moral implications. In such cases, the breach of etiquette itself is not usually a moral wrong but is a

---

[6]Moral claims hold for all if they are universalizable; see Chapter Five, §III.

[7]There are other types of normative values as well, including aesthetic values (e.g., *well-designed, balanced*) and certain professional values (*confidentiality, dependability*).

means to committing a moral wrong (e.g., expressing an insult). Etiquette becomes a moral issue when there is an accompanying *intent* to offend or demean the other person. Without such intent, the very same act might merely be embarrassing. Thus, the values of etiquette must be distinguished from moral values.

The **realm of law:** Law resembles the moral realm more closely than any other. Both moral and legal standards prohibit murder and stealing, for example. In fact, most moral values are mirrored by legal values; for example, justice and equality are both moral and legal values in our society. There may also be a moral duty to obey most (but not necessarily all) laws. Despite their close relationship, however, law and morality differ in important ways. Laws are created by civil authority; without such authority, there can be no laws. Furthermore, laws only *hold* in certain jurisdictions; for instance, some Texas laws don't hold in Indiana, and some U.S. laws don't hold in Britain. In addition, laws come into and go out of existence at definite times; moral values and prescriptions appear much more timeless. Even where the law normally does *not* hold, furthermore, moral values still do: honesty between family members remains morally important even though the law only rarely reaches into homes. Also, there are important legal prescriptions that have no moral basis. For instance, in the following pairs, neither claim is *morally* preferable to its alternative:

- (a) All drivers should stay on the right side of the street. (b) All drivers should stay on the left side of the street. (It depends on the laws of the particular country.)
- (a) No one may use a registered trademark that has been renewed within the past ten years. (b) No one may use a registered trademark that has been renewed within the past twelve years. (The number of years is partly arbitrary.)

Most important, it is possible for laws to be immoral. Laws establishing apartheid or slavery, for instance, violate basic moral rights. It can even become one's moral duty to violate such laws. In any case, it should be clear that laws and morality differ.

The **prudential realm:** There is another wide range of normative values that differ from moral values. Prudential values include *what is in our self-interest and what contributes to our well-being*—what would be *prudent*. Health, personal safety, and a decent education are all good for us. Thus, these prudential values support corresponding prudential prescriptions:

- Everyone should brush their teeth daily.
- People shouldn't associate with shady characters in dark alleys.
- If Sandra wants to make it safely home in the heavy rain, she should slow down.
- If you want to do well in your new job, you should ask questions.

Since our interests are often too obvious to be worth mentioning, many prudential claims are expressed as simple prescriptions as in the examples about brushing teeth and avoiding dark alleys. Everyone recognizes that it's in their interest to take care of their teeth and avoid getting mugged. Other sorts of actions, meanwhile, are called for only under certain circumstances. For this reason, prudential claims are *best* expressed in an "if/then" (*conditional*) form: "*If* you want to do well in your new job, *then* you should ask questions." Stated this way, prudential claims prescribe something (asking questions) that would be wise to do *if* our circumstances make the corresponding value or goal (doing well in a new job) relevant to our self-interest. For those who don't have a new job, or any job at all, this prescription wouldn't apply. Likewise, if Sandra isn't driving through a downpour, she may not need to drive as slowly. That's why it's best to formulate prudential claims as conditionals; while the complete conditionals typically *hold* generally, their prescriptive parts don't always *apply* to everyone. *That* depends on whether or not a person shares the conditional statement's other part—its value or goal. Of course, it's also true that if you don't want healthy teeth, then you don't have any reason to brush daily. Since nearly everyone wants healthy teeth, we don't normally bother adding "*if you want healthy teeth*"; that "goes without saying." Whether full expressed or not, therefore, complete prudential claims are, strictly, conditionals.

In response to the Gyges story, Plato argues that living a moral life actually *is* in a person's best interests, just like the saying "Honesty is the best policy" suggests that it is prudent to practice honesty. Nevertheless, specific moral acts do sometimes work to our disadvantage. Telling the truth or protecting a threatened child *can* put us at risk and even cause us personal harm. Thus, we can't take moral claims to be automatically prudential. Further, many prudential claims are clearly *not* moral claims (e.g., while brushing my teeth tonight is certainly prudent, I'm not acting immorally if I skip tonight's brushing).

For Discussion

1. *Think of other familiar claims that belong to the realms of etiquette, law, or the prudential.*
2. *Dividing into small groups, have each group work through about ten values from the Values Exercise at the end of the chapter. Share and defend your categorization of each value.*
3. *Think of other prudential claims that are stated incompletely (i.e., they just state the prescription). Restate these claims in their complete if/then form.*

Summary

Values, along with the value claims and prescriptive claims they support, make up several distinct normative realms, including the moral, etiquette, laws, and the prudential. The bases of law and etiquette are social and conventional; the prudential primarily reflects human needs and interests; the moral seems to go deeper—perhaps being rooted in human nature itself. While these realms—particularly the moral and legal— share many claims, they differ not only in their bases but also in their functions.

Key Terms

- **Moral standard:** *a comprehensive set of moral values along with the value and prescriptive claims these values support.*
- **Moral realm:** *applying "moral" in one of its senses, this is the subject matter of ethics. This realm includes everything that relates to people's moral beliefs and practices.*
- **Realm of etiquette:** *based in practical considerations and social convention, etiquette typically varies somewhat from culture to culture.*
- **Realm of law:** *created by civil authority, laws exist and apply at definite times and places. Many, but not all, laws reflect moral claims.*
- **Prudential realm:** *prudential claims are best expressed in an "if/then" (conditional) form: if some value or goal is important and relevant to your circumstances, then you ought to act in a certain way. Prudential claims usually hold for all but apply depending on one's circumstances.*

IV. FOUNDATIONAL AND INSTRUMENTAL VALUES

Values belong to law, morality, and other normative realms. But values can also be distinguished in another way. We value some things for their own sake; we value other things because they help us attain something else. Some things we value for both reasons.

A value that is desirable in itself is a **foundational value**. The idea is that certain goods are intrinsically or essentially valuable: they have worth in themselves and do not depend upon other values for their worth. Pleasure, happiness, and love are often cited as examples of foundational values. For instance, we seem to value pleasure for its own sake—it's intrinsically desirable. A more controversial example is life. It certainly seems that life has value in itself. Still, some claim that it isn't *mere* life that is worth having but only a meaningful or happy life.

Other things have no real worth in themselves, although they may be exceedingly useful for attaining something we do value. The clearest example of such a *purely* **instrumental value** is paper money. Money is useful for obtaining other things we desire, but it's nearly worthless in itself. What good would a suitcase of money be on a deserted island? Likewise, an academic degree is valuable as a means to attaining recognition and employment; a driver's license has value because it gives the holder a legal right to drive. Instrumental values are *derived* values—their worth derives from the value of things they can help us obtain. By themselves, however, purely instrumental values are largely worthless.

Some values may be both foundational and instrumental—health and knowledge, for instance. Without decent health, it's difficult to attain most other goods in life. Although health thus has instrumental value, it arguably also has foundational value—being a good thing in itself regardless of what else it makes possible. The same may be said of knowledge, which clearly is instrumental for attaining all kinds of goods but may also be desirable purely for its own sake.

Deciding on questions about foundational value can be difficult. Although many people consider health and knowledge foundational, others see no value to either beyond the advantages they can enable us to obtain. *Mere* health or *mere* knowledge may be no good whatsoever. In any case, one thing seems clear: while there are plenty of instrumental values, there are far fewer foundational values. Foundational values may be quite rare. In fact, some theorists say there is only *one* foundational value or good, but which value that is remains a matter of sharp disagreement.

For Discussion

1. *A car has instrumental value. What things is a car valuable for attaining?*
2. *Are health and knowledge foundational, instrumental, or both?*
3. *What is happiness? Is it a purely foundational value?*

Summary

We can characterize values as foundational, instrumental, or both. Foundational values have value purely in themselves; instrumental values derive their value from what they can obtain. Some values are both foundational and instrumental. Foundational values are rare, although they are particularly important.

Key Terms

- **Foundational values:** *things that are intrinsically valuable in themselves; foundational values are not derived.*
- **Instrumental values:** *things that are useful for attaining something else of value. A purely instrumental value has no genuine worth in itself.*

V. EXPLANATION AND FOUNDATIONAL VALUES

Although most values are instrumental, it is not possible for *all* values to be instrumental. Instrumental values must derive their worth from something else; if nothing had foundational value, there would be nothing to give instrumental values *their* worth. It follows that all instrumental values ultimately derive their worth from foundational values. Furthermore, the worth of any instrumental value is *explained* by the foundational values from which it derives. If life has foundational value, then anything that maintains, promotes, or makes life possible also obtains value. Food, clothing, and shelter do these things, so their instrumental value is explained by (and derived from) the value of life. Likewise, since money is an effective means of obtaining food, clothing, and shelter, its instrumental value is explained by its ability to serve *these* values, which in turn serve the foundational value of life. Foundational values explain and support all other values.

As previously seen, values also support and explain prescriptive claims. The reverse, meanwhile, is not generally true. It's natural enough to say that an individual ought to study hard because she values doing well in a class. Also, it's reasonable to conclude that we ought to respect persons because persons are valuable. But the reverse of these doesn't seem to work. It is not very enlightening to suggest that doing well in class has value because one ought to study hard or that people are valuable because we should respect them. Typically, prescriptive claims don't do much to explain *why* things have value.

Foundational values can thus explain other value claims and prescriptive claims. But since *all* moral claims are either value or prescriptive claims, it follows that we should be able to explain *all* moral claims by appealing to some set of foundational values. Putting this another way, we should be able to consolidate the entire moral realm by showing how its claims can all be derived from certain foundational values. Since there aren't many foundational values, this should greatly simplify the moral realm. This is what an **ethical theory** usually attempts to do—to explain every claim of morality based upon just one or a few foundational values.

The moral realm could derive from a small foundation of values in either of two ways.

- *Appealing to foundational moral values:* One way would derive all moral claims from foundational *moral* values. One important instance of this approach is *virtue ethics,* which bases the moral realm upon a small set of foundational moral values called *virtues.* A virtue is a good character trait, like honesty or loyalty, that persons can have. Like any values, virtues in turn support prescriptive claims: if something is a virtue, then we *ought* to act in keeping with it. Thus, the virtue of honesty supports the prescription, "A person should tell the truth." Loyalty, meanwhile, supports the claim that Gyges should not have betrayed and murdered the king. In this way, virtues serve as the foundational *moral* values upon which the rest of morality is based.

Other ethical theories also appeal to foundational moral values for their bases. There is an important drawback, however: because these theories *start* with moral values as their base, they cannot explain *everything* that belongs within the moral realm. In particular, they cannot explain the moral good of these foundational values *themselves.* Leaving certain moral values unexplained can be somewhat unsatisfying.

- *Appealing to foundational non-moral values:* The alternative is to base the moral realm upon one or more foundational *non-moral* value(s). This opens the door to a wider range of bases since non-moral values can include anything we might consider desirable. Further, grounding morality to something *external* to it allows *everything* in the moral realm to be explained— even the most basic moral values. The drawback is that we might wonder how values *unrelated* to morality could shed light on the nature of morality!

Several important moral traditions have nevertheless taken this approach. To get a better sense of how this could work, let's examine the tradition called **hedonism,** which claims that there is just *one* foundational value: pleasure (or happiness). Everything else has value only to the degree it derives its worth from this value. All other values are thus merely instrumental. Furthermore, since pleasure is valuable, it is our responsibility to maintain and promote this value in our own lives and in the lives of everyone else. We also ought to oppose whatever leads to suffering, since suffering diminishes pleasure. Building on these general prescriptive claims, hedonists attempt to derive—and so to explain—the entire moral realm on the basis of the one non-moral value of pleasure.

Hedonism has psychological appeal, for we all seek pleasure and happiness while we strive to avoid pain. In addition, we clearly desire many things either because they bring us pleasure or help us avoid pain. We eat because we enjoy it and because it can become painful not to. We also eat to stay alive, which is obviously needed to enjoy any pleasures at all. We work perhaps because we enjoy our work but also because it provides means to a comfortable rather than unpleasant existence. We even undergo painful experiences (e.g., various medical treatments) to avoid greater suffering later. People doing morally right things also commonly promote overall pleasure or happiness, while wrongdoing often causes pain. It thus seems a small step to infer that anything that promotes pleasure must be morally right whereas anything that leads to pain is wrong.

* * *

There are many ingenious ways of explaining and basing the moral realm upon foundational values—moral or non-moral. While each generates important theoretical problems, each also has its distinctive merits, and each furnishes valuable ethical insights. Much of the fascination and challenge of ethics arises from the attempt to counter the problems while still benefiting from the insights each way has to offer.

For Discussion

1. *Which approach do you think is better: basing the moral realm on foundational moral values or on foundational non-moral values? Why?*
2. *Do you think that hedonism could adequately serve as a basis for an ethical theory? Explain.*

Summary

Instrumental values derive from and are explained by more foundational values. Prescriptive claims can also be derived from and explained by foundational values. Thus, we may be able to explain all moral claims by showing how they can be derived from one or more foundational values. One way to do this is to ground morality upon moral values, as virtue ethics does, though this doesn't explain what makes these values morally good. Another way grounds moral claims upon non-moral values, as hedonism does, using the non-moral foundational value of pleasure. But we might wonder how a non-moral value could be the basis for morality.

Key Terms

- **Ethical theories:** *typically attempt to explain every claim of morality by just one or a few foundational values.*

- **Hedonism:** *an ethical tradition that maintains that there is just one foundational good: pleasure (or happiness).*

Chapter Assignment Questions

1. *Describe some moral problems you have found yourself in. What did you do?*
2. *What do you hope to gain from your study of ethics? Where do you think it will be most useful to you?*
3. *Plato argues that living a moral life is in a person's best interests. Argue both for and against this claim. Does this force you to rethink what our "best interests" actually are?*
4. *§II maintains that "If everyone did what is right, the world would be a happier place" is a descriptive claim. Explain in your own words why it is descriptive and not normative.*
5. *Can you think of a situation in which obeying the law or acting prudently apparently has priority over any moral obligation(s) relevant to that situation? If so, can this be explained by appealing to some yet deeper moral claim?*
6. *Do you think that health is both a foundational and an instrumental value? How about knowledge? Explain.*
7. *Suppose you value earning a good grade in a course. Trace the grade's instrumental value all the way to some foundational value (e.g., happiness).*
8. *Aristotle suggested that the only foundational value is happiness. Does this seem true?*
9. *If you were constructing an ethical theory, what value(s) would you base your theory upon?*

Additional Resources

"Plato: Ethics—The Ring of Gyges." Great Philosophers. Accessed September 2, 2016. http://oregonstate.edu/instruct/phl201/modules/Philosophers/Plato/plato_dialogue_the_ring_of_gyges.html.

Pojman, Louis P. and James Fieser. *Ethics: Discovering Right and Wrong.* 6th ed. Belmont, CA: Wadsworth Publishing Company, 2008, chapter 4.

Schiffman, Kelley. "Intrinsic and Instrumental Values." Khan Academy. Accessed September 2, 2016. https://www.khanacademy.org/partner-content/wi-phi/critical-thinking/v/intrinsic-extrinsic-value. This video discusses the distinction between instrumental and "intrinsic" values (which we call "foundational values").

Schiffman, Kelley. "Normative and Descriptive Claims." Khan Academy. Accessed September 2, 2016. https://www.khanacademy.org/partner-content/wi-phi/critical-thinking/v/normative-and-descriptive-claims. This video explains differences between normative and descriptive statements.

Schroeder, Mark. "Value Theory." In *The Stanford Encyclopedia of Philosophy* (Fall 2016 Edition), edited by Edward N. Zalta. Accessed September 2, 2016. http://plato.stanford.edu/archives/fall2016/entries/value-theory/.

Taylor, Richard. *Good and Evil.* Amherst, NY: Prometheus Books, 2000. The chapters "Good and Evil" and "The Common Good" provide a nice, nontechnical presentation that parallels much of this chapter.

Traer, Robert. "Right and Good." Doing Ethics. Copyright © 2007. Accessed September 2, 2016. http://doingethics.com/DEE/dee%20ch1/right.good.htm. This article discusses the right versus the good.

"UCB Phil 160: Ring of Gyres Presentation," https://www.youtube.com/watch?v=4qjGp6TWqe4. This video is an illustrated telling of "The Ring of Gyges," with *Lord of the Rings* overtones.

Values Exercise

1. Consider the following values. (a) Which are purely foundational, which purely instrumental, and which are both? (b) Briefly explain what each value means and identify its one or two (if more than one seems to apply) most appropriate categories:

   M: moral   **PRU**: prudential   **E**: etiquette   **L**: legal   **O**: other
   For any value you label (O), try to explain the category you have in mind.

BENEVOLENCE	KNOWLEDGE
CAREER	LEISURE
CARING	LOYALTY
CLEANLINESS	LOVE
COMFORT	MARRIAGE
COMPETITION	NATURE
COOPERATION	PERSONAL AUTONOMY
EDUCATION	PLEASURE
EFFICIENCY	POLITENESS
EQUALITY	POWER
FAMILY	RESPONSIBILITY
FRIENDSHIP	RELIGION OR FAITH
HAPPINESS	RESPECT
HEALTH	SOCIAL FREEDOM
HELPING OTHERS	SPIRITUALITY
HONESTY	TRUST
JUSTICE AND FAIRNESS	TRUTH
KINDNESS	WEALTH

2. List the three values (not necessarily moral or from the list in question 1) that you consider most important. What prescriptive claims does each value support?

3. Honestly assess yourself: do you truly live by the values you've identified as most important to you? Why or why not?

4. Have you learned anything important about yourself from this values exercise?

Case 1

Breastfeeding in Public

Jessica, twenty-six, has just started back at college. Because her college offers great child services during class times, she brings her six-month-old with her each class day. One afternoon, as she sits in the cafeteria studying before her class, her baby starts crying. After a quick glance at her watch, Jessica unbuttons her shirt, exposes her breast, and begins to feed Joseph, who gurgles happily.

Two male students are sitting nearby. One notices Jessica and starts staring. Laughing uncomfortably, he gestures toward her to his friend. Another woman catches their reactions. "Leave her alone," she tells the two guys. "Breastfeeding is

Continued

Case 1 *(Continued)*

totally natural and good for the baby." One of the guys answers in Jessica's hearing, "Maybe so, but this is public. Must I put up with some woman showing her breast in front of me while I'm trying to eat? That's just more than I need to see. She shouldn't make the rest of us uncomfortable in a public cafeteria; she ought to go somewhere private for that. Aren't there any rules here?"

THOUGHT QUESTIONS

1. In most places in the United States women may legally breast feed in public. At work, they are also supposed to be allowed adequate time to breast feed. What do you think of these laws? Are they morally justified?
2. Does Jessica have a natural moral right to breast feed wherever she needs to? Are there any places where women should not do this?
3. Would you be uncomfortable if a woman started breast feeding in front of you? Do you think it is too private? What values come into play in this case? Do you think breast feeding in public is bad etiquette?
4. If you witnessed the two guys' behavior, would you interfere? If so, whose side would you take? What would you say and why?
5. In most Islamic countries, public breast feeding would be unthinkable. How much do you think culture and religion influence people's thinking and values on this?

Case 2

The Real Price of Coffee

According to the National Coffee Association, half of all Americans drink coffee every day.[8] Young adults average 3.2 cups of coffee per day. Most of this coffee is produced in developing nations, yet less than 10% of its annual yield goes back to the farmers.[9] Much of the rest ends up in the pockets of the companies that process, package, and sell it, such as Kraft (Maxwell House), Proctor and Gamble (Folgers), and Nestlé (Nescafé). The low return on their investment is devastating for farmers in developing nations like Ethiopia, Kenya, Guatemala, and Nicaragua, among others, where poverty is widespread and coffee plantations are a critical source of income. In Columbia, some coffee farmers have converted their farms to opium farms, which bring them a better income.

The coffee industry's practices don't just hurt the farmers. Rather than using the traditional method of growing coffee in shade, most coffee today is grown in full sun to increase yield. This has brought on the destruction of tropical rainforests and a tremendous loss of biodiversity. According to Equator Coffee Roasters,

Continued

---

[8]"National Coffee Drinking Trends," National Coffee Association, accessed August 31, 2016, http://www.ncausa.org/Industry-Resources/Market-Research/National-Coffee-Drinking-Trends-Report.

[9]Brian C. Howard, "Grounds for Change," *E: The Environmental Magazine* (November/December 2005): 26–37. Most of following information is taken from this article.

Case 2 (*Continued*)

full-sun coffee production is "the second leading cause of rainforest destruction."[10] Furthermore, trees left for shade could provide additional income for coffee farmers by producing fruit, avocados, and wood; the ground underneath the coffee plants could also be used to grow vegetables and herbs.

Full-sun plantations also lack the natural fertilizers provided by plants and the natural pest control provided by rainforest animals. Thus, the coffee plants require chemical fertilizers and pesticides. These plantations are also prone to flooding and erosion, both of which could be avoided if the coffee plants were nestled between larger trees. Runoff from chemical fertilizers and pesticides pollute the surrounding rivers. The chemicals also harm farm workers, who often cannot read and so cannot follow the instructions for using the chemicals. Sometimes the workers don't even have the protective gear needed to guard them from chemical poisoning.

Birds are another casualty of the full-sun method. More than 150 bird species thrive in the rainforest of a traditional coffee plantation—over twenty times the number living on full-sun farms. Some species have declined by as much as 70%.

Many of these effects could be avoided if consumers would look for "eco-labels," which can inform them about the coffee they buy. Consumers should particularly look for the label "organic," which assures them that the coffee has been shade grown with few if any pesticides. A New York advocacy group, the Rainforest Alliance, also certifies coffee. It prohibits certain chemicals, requires that water and biodiversity be protected, and ensures that farmers plant new trees. One farmer says that following the Rainforest Alliance principles is "helping him farm in balance with nature, and greatly improve worker productivity and morale."[11] Consumers can also look for the fair-trade label, which guarantees farmers a certain minimum price for their coffee; a portion of the profits is also reinvested into their community.

According to the National Coffee Association, younger consumers are becoming both more aware and more concerned about the sustainability of coffee production. Yet, overall awareness of the ways it affects the world remains limited.

THOUGHT QUESTIONS

1. Is this a moral or economic issue? Could it be both? What are some of the most important values involved here? Do you consider any of this case's non-moral values to be more important than its moral values? Why or why not?
2. Does the fact that this issue involves *international* trade affect this case? How?
3. U.S. workers would never be allowed exposure to the kinds of risks these foreign workers are exposed to. Nor would any U.S. worker be paid so little. Is such exposure and low pay nevertheless morally OK for workers of other countries?

---

[10]Ibid., 30.

[11]Brian C. Howard, "What Do All Those Labels Mean?" *E: The Environmental Magazine*, (November/December 2005): 37.

4. To what degree should the rest of the world take action against farming practices like these, which can harm farmers, others in the area (e.g., by chemical poisoning), and the environment? Formulate some moral claims supporting your view.

Case 3

Jurassic Kitty: Should I Clone My Cat?

In the past twenty years, the idea of pet cloning has moved from "rare freak show" to a fairly lucrative business venture. For about $50,000, you can get a copy cat, and for $100,000, a copy dog.[12]

Aside from being profitable, is kitty cloning ethical? Let's first look at what cloning actually is. A "clone" is a genetic copy of a living organism. We routinely clone plants when we cut off a shoot from one to grow another. But that method doesn't work for animals. Instead, scientists create a genetically identical twin by transferring a cell nucleus from the body of one animal into the egg of another, a process called "nuclear transfer."[13] The resulting embryo is implanted into the womb of a host animal, which will, with luck, carry the clone to term. Beginning with Dolly the sheep in 1996, sixteen different mammalian species have been cloned so far, but science is far from even attempting to clone a human being.

The idea of cloning a departed pet should perhaps give one pause. Isn't a pet supposed to be irreplaceable, special, one of a kind? As it turns out, that remains the case even when cloning is done: only 99.8% of the animal's DNA is reproduced in the cloning process—the rest comes from the host egg. Given that the genetic difference between us and a chimpanzee amounts to less than 1%, the 0.2% genetic difference between a cat and its copycat could still be significant. Also, the copycat would gestate in a different kitty womb, thus introducing additional dissimilarities; the surrogate mom's health and nutrition can also affect the clone's coat pattern. Finally, the copycat would grow up in a different environment, possibly also making its personality different.

Adding it all up, the copycat and the original probably wouldn't be so much alike after all. Further, the cloning process is fraught with technical difficulties: fewer than 10% of the implanted eggs result in live births, and many clones die shortly afterward. Clones that survive can have genetic abnormalities. Meanwhile, there are thousands and thousands of animals in shelters waiting to go to a good home.

Although there clearly are more constructive ways to spend $50,000, there's another and more serious implication of animal cloning. As biodiversity steadily decreases because of our irreverent—and sometimes downright ruthless—expansion of our human habitat, some scientists see cloning as a way to preserve endangered species. In line with this, the Audubon Center for Research of Endangered Species

Continued

---

[12]David Warmflash, "Miss Your Deceased Dog? Pet Cloning Dips Below $100,000," *Genetic Literacy Project*, August 21, 2015, accessed August 31, 2016, http://www.geneticliteracyproject.org/2015/08/21/miss-deceased-dog-pet-cloning-dips-100000/.

[13]For further reading on the science of cloning and its difficulties, see Jose Cibelli, "A Decade of Cloning Mystique," *Science Magazine* (May 18, 2007).

Case 3 (*Continued*)

cloned a small African wildcat called Ditteaux (faux French for "ditto") in 2003. Thinking on a much larger scale, Japanese scientists are working to resurrect the long-extinct woolly mammoth—so far without success. The San Diego gene bank has frozen samples of over 450 different animal species. One day, this "Frozen Zoo," as it's sometimes called, may be the last best hope for those species' preservation.

THOUGHT QUESTIONS

1. What moral and non-moral values seem relevant to this case? Which of these are most important?

2. What moral and non-moral prescriptive claims seem relevant to this case? Which of this case's facts (which descriptive claims) are most relevant to deciding whether pet cloning is ethical or not?

3. What moral and non-moral values apply to cloning endangered species but not pets? How important is the value of biodiversity? Is it important enough to make this sort of cloning morally acceptable or even our moral duty?

4. We don't know what effects our resurrecting an extinct species would have on existing species. For example, what might happen if we resurrected an extinct insect species that has no natural predator today? What problems do such concerns suggest for our trying to restore extinct species?

5. What issues are raised by the idea of cloning a human being?

Case 4

Sex Selection

It isn't science fiction any longer, and it's already practiced in the United States and many other countries: you can now select your child's sex. How does it work? The most common technique is preimplantation genetic diagnosis (PGD). PGD involves genetic screening of embryos (a technique originally developed to screen for genetic diseases). The embryos are created via in vitro fertilization (IVF), and only the embryos of the "desired" sex are implanted in the uterus. The remaining embryos may then be destroyed.

Clinics that currently offer sex selection advertise it as a way of "family balancing." If a family already has a child of one sex, they can deliberately choose to have a child of the opposite sex to "balance" out their family. For instance, Sharla and Shane Miller of Gillette, Wyoming, already had three boys: Anthony, Ashton, and Alec. Both grew up in families having more boys than girls. They initially looked into adopting a girl but then found a Web site that mentioned PGD. For $18,000, the chances of getting a girl were almost 100%. They opted for the procedure, and in November 2003 Sharla was implanted with two female embryos (identical twins).[14] CBS News reported that twin girls were born in July of 2004. Both were healthy.

Continued

---

[14]Claudia Kalb *et al.*, "Science: Brave New Babies," *Newsweek*, February 2, 2004.

Case 4 (*Continued*)

One worry often raised about sex selection is that its widespread use could create the opposite of balance: too many boys or too many girls, depending on existing cultural preferences. The University of Illinois at Chicago released the results of a survey in 2005 that appear to counter this worry. The survey, administered to 561 women being treated for infertility, showed that if sex selection were free, 41% of these women would take advantage of it. More important, the study showed that parents without children did not prefer one sex over the other.[15]

However, the study was carried out with a fairly small set of United States women (presumably all from the Chicago area), so we shouldn't generalize too much from these results. In particular, the results are not likely to carry over to women in countries where there is a strong cultural preference for one sex.

The Canadian Medical Association Journal says that we can expect 10% to 20% more adult males in the next twenty years in China and India due to the excessive use of sex selection.[16] This bias is because a family must either provide an expensive dowry for their daughters or provide continued support for those who remain unmarried and stay with their families. Currently, the most prevalent method for sex selection is the already disconcerting practice of selective abortion. On the other hand, as PGD becomes more available and less expensive, it may only add to the gender imbalance in these countries and the world.

THOUGHT QUESTIONS

1. List some reasons a couple might have for choosing their next child's sex, considering parents in both the United States and in other countries (e.g., China or India). What value and prescriptive claims seem to be most relevant to people making such choices?
2. Do you think that parents who would like to choose the gender of their child are motivated by appropriate or inappropriate values?
3. Which of the relevant values are moral values and which are non-moral? Which are foundational, and which are instrumental?
4. Suppose a family maintains that they can't afford the dowry for a daughter, and so, for their own welfare, they must select for a male child. What do you think of this argument?
5. Do you think that it was morally OK for the Millers to choose the sex of their twins? What are your reasons?

---

[15]Among other places, this information is available at Sherri McGinnis Gonzalez, "Sex Selection Popular Among Infertile Women," *Medical News Today,* accessed August 31, 2016, http://www.eurekalert.org/pub_releases/2005-03/uoia-ssp031005.php.

[16]"The Impact of Sex Selection in China, India and South Korea," *ScienceDaily*, March 15, 2011, accessed August 31, 2016, http://www.sciencedaily.com/releases/2011/03/110314132244.htm.

CHAPTER TWO

Moral Relativism

I. INTRODUCTION

"No, Madame may not drive this way," explained the officer who, with the nicest smile, had just waived them to a stop. Alison looked at her husband, Dave, sitting beside her in the car, who just shrugged. They had recently arrived in this town for the next leg of their tour of the world's more exotic spots. "But you just let another car go by you a minute before," Alison said, turning back to the policeman. "Don't much speak English," the policeman said, "but cannot drive this road." Dave and Alison stared at the man, who was smiling still more broadly than before. "I cannot let drive. I sometimes only let officials." Dave continued staring for a moment and suddenly gave Alison a knowing look. Pulling out his passport, he placed a five pound note on top. "Oh, then, it's OK," he said to the officer, "we are visiting officials. Here, see my papers." Reaching in front of Alison and over to the window, he carelessly dropped the money out the window while holding open his passport. The policeman swiftly caught the fluttering money, pocketed it, and glanced for a moment at the passport. Then, still smiling, he stepped back and waved. "Good, Madame. You are official. You have right this way," he said, not giving them a further glance. Alison drove a mile and then shot a curious look at her husband. "When in Rome, do as the Romans do," he said, forcing a little laugh. "And just how much do you think we should act like Romans, anyhow?" Alison retorted. "Live and let live," Dave muttered. "Let's just forget about it." "But I don't like that sort of thing, and I hate to waste the money," Alison said, more heatedly than she intended. As an afterthought, she added, "You know, Dave, men in this culture may have several wives. I wouldn't be surprised if that policeman has a couple. And I didn't care for the way he looked at me. I hope you won't tell me that polygamy's OK too!" Trying to laugh it off, Dave commented "Well, my dear, it has its attractions." "That," Alison spat out as she floored the accelerator, "is *not* funny."

* * *

25

People don't always live by the same moral principles. When we compare societies, we find a range of moral beliefs and practices. In Alison and Dave's situation, perhaps the officer's action was in keeping with his society's customs. If so, could that make bribery morally right in his society? If bribery can be morally right in some societies, then why do so many—like this friendly policeman—still avoid any open acknowledgement of the practice? And what about polygamy? Although monogamous marriage is the law in most western countries, polygamy has been the practice of much of the world for thousands of years. But which is *right*—monogamous or polygamous marriage? Does this question even make sense, or is morality simply a matter of what most people in a society accept?

For Discussion

1. *Even if this officer's society accepts bribery, suppose Dave's does not. Does this make it morally right or wrong for Dave to bribe the man?*
2. *Which is morally better: monogamy or polygamy? Is this just your society's view, or can you provide reasons for your position?*
3. *The text asks why bribes are seldom acknowledged even in places they are widely used. How do you answer this?*

II. THREE VIEWS OF ETHICS

Our everyday use of moral principles (e.g., "Keep your promises," "Do not kill") strongly suggests that we take them to hold for everyone—that they are universal. In fact, the very notion of a moral *principle* is that it holds *in general*. It further seems that the same *moral standard* (see Chapter One, §III)—consisting of *all* that determines moral good or bad, right or wrong—must hold for everyone. Nevertheless, this view—*moral objectivism*—has been challenged by an influential alternative called *moral relativism*. There are two types of relativism that many people identify with today: popular relativism and subjective relativism (more simply, *relativism* and *subjectivism*, with both being opposed to *objectivism*).[1] Let's start with some definitions of each.

- **Objectivism:** *There is only one universal moral standard.*[2] That standard—based on objective moral facts—consists of moral values and principles that hold universally: for all people and all societies.
- **(Popular) Relativism:** *There can be different moral standards for different societies.* Each standard—based on that society's moral beliefs and practices—consists of moral values and principles that hold for *all* members of that *particular* society.

---

[1]There are much more sophisticated versions of relativism, which lie beyond the scope of this text (but see section VII). We will limit ourselves mainly to these two popular versions.

[2]*Objectivism* in ethics, and as we will use this term, is *not* related to Ayn Rand's philosophy of objectivism.

- **Subjectivism:** *There can be different moral standards for different persons.* Each standard—based on that person's moral beliefs and practices at a given time—consists of the moral values and principles that hold for that person at that time.

It's important to understand what each of these views is about. *None* of them is talking about principles from other normative realms (e.g., from law or etiquette, which unquestionably vary across societies). Rather, each is talking exclusively about *moral* principles and values. Nor are any of them concerned with the rich diversity in the institutions, dress, religious beliefs, and *non-normative* values that distinguish various cultural traditions. Next, these three views are completely distinct: each rules out the others. Finally, these views are *meta-ethical:* none takes any stand on what actually *is* right or wrong (e.g., on the morality of lying or polygamy) but are about ethics itself.[3]

Let's start with objectivism, the claim that there is only one valid moral standard that holds for all human beings. Differences between cultures make no difference to the moral principles and values people ought to live by. Even if a society's moral *beliefs* and *practices* are not the same as those of other societies, the same moral values, rights, and obligations hold for them as for everyone else. There is one universal moral standard, regardless of what anyone believes or practices.

Objectivism *does not* mean that people must all act exactly the same way no matter what the *circumstances* are at the time. Given objectivism, the very same moral principles can lead to different obligations in different situations. For instance, suppose that the objective moral standard entails that lying is wrong and that human life has great moral value. It would follow that everyone normally has a duty to tell the truth and avoid harming others. But in a situation where telling the truth would lead to someone's death, objectivism could require that we *lie* rather than risk someone's life. Objectivism is binding upon all but need not be morally rigid—it can still adjust to circumstances.

Next, what is relativism? Popular moral relativism denies the universality of moral standards. Instead, it maintains that there can be different but equally valid moral standards for different cultures or social groups. It *does* insist, however, that *all* who belong to a given group are bound to their group's moral standard whether or not they agree with its values and principles. What *actually is* right for everyone in that society is what the majority of that society accepts as right.

Subjectivism, finally, takes relativism even further, maintaining that there can be different but equally valid moral standards for different persons even within the same society. Thus, there's no guarantee that the moral standards for any two people will match, nor is there any guarantee that a person's present moral

---

[3]The choice between these three options must be made before we can do ethics, since two of these views make much of ethics nearly impossible.

principles will be the same a year from now. Subjectivism makes moral standards entirely dependent on each individual (a subject) at any given time.

What do you think of these alternatives? Again, only one can be correct since each rules out the other. Interestingly, even people who *think* of themselves as relativists or subjectivists still commonly adopt objectivism as their perspective when a moral issue affects them. Our task now is to determine—on rational grounds— which of these views is most plausible.

For Discussion

1. *How much are your moral beliefs the products of your culture and society? Which ones are?*
2. *Do you disagree with any particular moral belief or practice that is widely accepted by your society?*

Summary
There are three important views regarding moral standards: (a) There is only one universal objective moral standard that holds for all (objectivism); (b) there can be different moral standards for different societies, depending on each society's moral beliefs and practices (relativism); or (c) there can be different moral standards for different persons, depending on each person's own moral beliefs and practices (subjectivism). Only one of these views can be correct, but one must be.

Key Terms
- **Moral standard:** *consists of all moral principles and values that dictate what is morally good or bad, right or wrong.*
- **Objectivism:** *maintains that there can only be one universal moral standard.*
- **Relativism:** *maintains that there can be different moral standards for different societies.*
- **Subjectivism:** *maintains that there can be different moral standards for different persons.*

III.** EVALUATING SUBJECTIVISM

People often talk as though morality is a personal matter that depends solely on our own personal views. People often *do* have different beliefs and opinions about moral issues. It may even be that a person can feel so strongly about something being wrong that this actually makes it wrong for that person. For instance, some are persuaded that drinking is morally wrong. Because drinking violates that person's conscience, it may *be* wrong for *that* person to drink, although it might not be wrong for anyone else. For those with sensitive consciences, the requirements of morality could be more stringent than for others.

Still, it doesn't follow that just *any* moral principle can vary from one person to another. For one thing, mere differences of opinion cannot show that moral principles themselves also vary between people. Some people's opinions might simply be mistaken. Further, could it really be wrong for me to lie or commit murder but not for you?

To appreciate the implications of subjectivism, imagine that you have been standing in line at the theater. Suddenly, a strange man steps into the line right in front of you. How would you react? You would certainly object—telling him that he has no right to cut in front of so many people and that he should go to the end of the line. You might add that it's not fair for him to cut in line when no one else has.

Note a few things about this very natural reaction. First, you are making *moral* claims here about fairness, rights, and what this man *ought* to do. In making these claims, you imply that the same obligations or rights hold for him no less than for everybody else. Moreover, you seem to assume that he—along with everyone else—already knows these things. All of this is part of the intuition that the same moral principles hold for everyone.

The man now makes an extraordinary reply: "I'm sorry," he says politely, "for I see that the fairness and rights you have just appealed to must hold for you. Perhaps they hold for other people here as well. You have my sincere sympathy, for I can imagine how inconvenient these principles of yours must be—I bet you've been standing here for some time, right? What you must understand, however, is that these principles don't happen to hold for me. Each of us is bound by our own set of moral principles, you know. You have a principle of fairness; fortunately for me, I do not. Please don't misunderstand; I always do my best to live an upright and moral life, and if fairness *were* one of my principles, I wouldn't dream of cutting in front of you! However, it's *not* one of my principles, and so I am perfectly within my rights to cut in front of you. As you probably didn't realize this when you started complaining, I assure you that I take no offense. I hope we've now cleared up this little misunderstanding. By the way, can you step back a little? You're crowding me."

This is the speech of a subjectivist. Would you stand for it? None of us really believes for a moment that this argument has any legitimacy.

There's a deeper reason for rejecting subjectivism. Since it insists that each person can have a different moral standard, you can never assume that any moral principle that holds for you also holds for others. This would work against one of morality's primary functions—to regulate how individuals relate *to each other*. How could morality fulfill this function if different principles held for different persons? People stand in lines because they accept the same principles of fairness. Eliminate that shared acceptance and you will instead find mobs and fights at the theaters! More important, without that shared acceptance, the value of fairness itself loses meaning, just as a dollar bill could no longer stand for anything if its value were to change from person to person. This is what subjectivism does to moral principles. Instead of giving us a different version of morality, it gives us something very close to no morality at all.

What about differences in personal conscience? Many would agree that if drinking a beer would violate someone's conscience, then it would be wrong for that person to drink a beer. But it's also tempting to say that if drinking a beer isn't *really* wrong for people in general, then it isn't *really* wrong even for that person. The wrong arises, not because he drinks a beer, but because he violates his conscience. In any case, we don't need subjectivism to handle matters of moral conscience. Both objectivism and relativism can also acknowledge the moral impact of conscience. Specifically, each could include the moral principle: "When a person feels strongly that some kind of act is morally wrong, then *that* person commits a moral wrong by acting that way." If this way of handling conscience is satisfactory, then there's no good reason to accept subjectivism.

For Discussion

1. *Do you think that if someone strongly feels something is wrong as a matter of conscience, then it is wrong for them? Explain.*
2. *Does the way you'd react to the man cutting in front of you show that you don't really accept subjectivism? How?*

Summary

Subjectivism can create conflicts with our strongest moral intuitions (e.g., the fairness of standing in lines). Worse, subjectivism effectively negates one of morality's most important functions. Although differences in conscience might seem to support subjectivism, these can be accommodated by both relativism and objectivism. Subjectivism does not look like an acceptable account of morality.

IV. SUPPORTING POPULAR RELATIVISM

Let's now turn to relativism. The following argument captures much of what persuades many people to favor relativism.

1. Different societies exhibit differences in particular moral beliefs and practices.
2. The moral standard that holds for a society is determined by the moral beliefs and practices most widely accepted in that society.

Thus: Different moral standards hold for different societies; that is, relativism is true.

Looking at the first premise, it seems undeniable that societies sometimes believe different things to be morally right or wrong. One famous story compares the ancient Callatian practice of cannibalizing their dead with the Greek preference for cremation. Although both societies were comfortable with their own practices, each found the other's practice utterly repugnant. Within our own society, there are vehement disagreements about abortion. We also see that while some cultures practice polygamy, others consider it immoral. Given these differences in what people think is right or wrong, mustn't we conclude that moral principles vary across social groups?

Although societies' particular moral beliefs and practices often differ, it's not so clear that they always differ over the underlying moral principles they accept. The disagreement about funeral practices, for instance, can be explained by appealing to differing beliefs about death. The Callatians apparently believed that ingesting the dead person's flesh allows the deceased a continuing life in the living person.[4] Given such a belief, cannibalism certainly *does* serve as a powerful expression of caring for the dead. The Greeks apparently held that only cremation could keep the body from suffering corruption; they also may have viewed "living" fire as the most fitting way to release the spirit from the dead body. Given *these* beliefs, cremation likewise appears to be a reasonable way to show respect for the dead. While the Greeks and Callatians differed regarding the descriptive claims they accepted about death (see Chapter One, §II), they both agreed to the same underlying moral principle: we ought to honor the dead. Their apparent moral disagreement thus turns out to be over their beliefs about death, not over moral principles.

What about our society's division over abortion? Even here, there is more agreement over fundamental moral issues than first appears. Very few "pro-choicers" would accept the killing of an innocent human being, for instance. Nor would many "pro-lifers" dismiss the right to control (usually) our own bodies. Given this widespread acceptance of both principles, what's the dividing issue? The differences, once again, are usually over how people answer questions like "When do human beings first come into existence?" or "Is the fetus part of the woman's body?" Although people's answers have extremely important moral implications, they are not, in themselves, actual disagreements over any moral principles.[5]

It is thus a mistake to conclude that different moral principles must hold simply because societies differ in their moral practices and beliefs. Accepting different descriptive claims of how the world *is* can lead to very different moral conclusions about what is right, even when we start with the same moral principles. Cultural history strongly indicates that peoples of very different races, languages, and cultures (e.g., compare ancient China with present-day America) have still been amazingly alike in their moral beliefs.

Nevertheless, it cannot be denied that sometimes there are actual differences over moral principles. Polygamists differ from monogamists over at least one of the moral principles defining marriage. Let's grant Premise 1, therefore, with the understanding that differences over moral principles are not necessarily widespread.

---

[4] Joseph Rickaby, S.J., *Moral Philosophy: Ethics, Deontology and Natural Law* (London: Longmans, Green & Co., 1918), accessed August 31, 2016, http://www.nd.edu/Departments/Maritain/etext/moral108.htm, ch. 8, sect. 2.

[5] An exception is Judith Jarvis Thomson's qualification of the principle regarding letting an innocent person die, illustrated by her violin player thought experiment. See Judith Jarvis Thomson, "A Defense of Abortion," *Philosophy & Public Affairs*, 1.1 (Fall 1971).

Does this make relativism true? Not yet, because so far we only have differences in what societies *accept*. Relativism makes the stronger claim that there can be moral differences in what *actually holds* for different societies. What people accept and what actually holds can be very different! To establish relativism, therefore, we must proceed to Premise 2 and show that what holds for a society is *determined* by the beliefs and practices of that society.

What is curious about Premise 2 is that what holds in the world normally does *not* depend on what people accept or believe. In fact, what we normally want is exactly the opposite—for our beliefs to depend on what holds true about the world. Consider the following argument.[6]

1. Different societies have accepted different views about the earth's shape (e.g., that it is flat or that it is round).
2. The *actual* shape of the earth for a given society is determined by the view about the earth that is most widely *accepted* in that society.

Thus: The earth has different shapes for different societies; its shape is relative.

This would mean that the earth actually *was* flat for medieval Europeans; if they sailed too far, they would have fallen off the edge. But this is absurd; it's obvious that people's beliefs about the earth cannot determine what actually holds true about the earth. More generally, even widespread acceptance does not ensure truth, and claims like Premise 2 (going back to the moral argument) are usually not true. Unless a relativist can provide some special reason for thinking Premise 2 is true in the case of morality, we have no reason to accept moral relativism as true.

Pressing a little further, if the widespread acceptance of a moral principle *could* make it true, then we'd be driven to the surprising conclusion that no society's majority *could ever be mistaken* about anything moral. Since the majority determines what is moral, the majority has moral infallibility![7] But we know societies can make mistakes about all sorts of matters, including morals. One such moral error was America's widespread acceptance of slavery less than two centuries ago.

We thus have reason to reject Premise 2 of the relativist argument, which in turn undermines the argument itself. However, this only shows that we have no compelling reasons *in support* of relativism. This doesn't prove it false. Thus, we must next turn to arguments that have been advanced *against* relativism.

For Discussion

1. *Suppose an ideological/religious group of terrorists believe that they should kill anyone belonging to an "inferior" ethnic group. Is this an instance of a genuine relativistic moral principle? Why or why not?*

---

[6]This comparison is also made by James Rachels and Stuart Rachels, *The Elements of Moral Philosophy*, 6th ed. (Boston: McGraw–Hill Higher Education, 2009), section 2.3

[7]This point is made by Rachels and Rachels, *Moral Philosophy*.

2. *If different societies do have different moral beliefs and practices, why doesn't it follow that different moral standards hold for each?*

3. *If you don't think the flat earth argument is a good analogy to relativism, why not? What is the actual point being made by this analogy?*

Summary

Those attracted to moral relativism often maintain that different societies have different moral beliefs and practices. But these differences often derive from differences in how people view the world rather than from different moral principles. Furthermore, even if we grant that societies do accept different moral principles, it doesn't follow that different moral principles hold for these societies. Thus, we have no good reason at this point for accepting relativism.

V. AGAINST RELATIVISM

There are several arguments against relativism. Those we will examine all employ the same strategy. Each begins with the supposition that relativism *is* true. Each then shows how something unacceptable follows from that supposition. Because relativism leads us to something unacceptable, it then concludes that the cause of this result is relativism. In short, each argument indicates that we should reject relativism because our accepting it would commit us to something unacceptable. Here are four important arguments against relativism.

1. Making anything right: In keeping with the strategy just described, we look at what would follow if relativism *were* true—if a society's actual moral standard were determined by that society's beliefs and practices. Consider southern America in the early nineteenth century. That society had a distinctive culture with its own characteristic beliefs, values, and practices, including slavery. Now, if relativism is true, then the widespread acceptance of slavery *was* morally right for *that* society. This isn't simply saying that they believed in it; it's saying that the institution of slavery was morally acceptable according to the *moral standard* that *held for them*. But how can we grant that the enslavement, exploitation, abuse, and even murder of people of one particular race could *ever* have been morally right? This flies in the face of our deepest, clearest, and most widely held moral intuitions. There are matters in morality we might be mistaken about but surely not about slavery being wrong. Since this is the case, we shouldn't abandon such a strong moral intuition for the sake of some theory. Rather, we should reject that theory—relativism. Since relativism allows for slavery to have been morally right, there must be something wrong with relativism.

Tragically, there are many more examples of a similar nature. For instance, some cultures considered it morally acceptable for families to abandon infant girls to their deaths, since marrying a daughter was costly and a girl couldn't help support the family like a boy could. Then there's the long history of genocides up through the present day, including the Nazi murder of Jews, Gypsies, and mentally disabled.

Assuming that we react to these examples with moral dismay, that gives us reason to reject relativism, which must *approve* such practices as being morally *right* for those cultures and societies. Nevertheless, the problem here is not just that relativism must approve of certain practices that we find horrific. The bigger problem is that relativism opens the door to *any practice* being morally right—human sacrifice, torture, child prostitution, or whatever. All that's needed is for a practice to be widely accepted within some society. But this is something we clearly cannot accept. If there's a morality at all, then it cannot be that absolutely *anything* could count as morally right. Thus, relativism must not be correct.

2. Moral Reformers: Of course, not everyone in these cultural groups has supported slavery, infanticide, genocide, and the like. There have always been some who've actively opposed their society's immoral practices. Abolitionists like William Lloyd Garrison denounced American slavery, and Martin Luther King Jr. fought segregation. Such people are **moral reformers**—people who oppose, on moral grounds, some of their society's beliefs and practices. Rather than approving of such moral visionaries, however, relativism condemns them. For relativism, after all, the moral *right* depends on the majority view of a society. Since reformers *oppose* the majority view, relativism must judge them to be in the *wrong*. Many of the people we most admire—Martin Luther King Jr., Confucius, Jesus, Socrates, and others—should therefore be placed among history's morally *worst* people, given relativism. Surely this is unacceptable.

3. Moral Progress: Moral reformers call upon a society to change its beliefs and practices—to make moral *progress*. "Making progress" means moving closer toward what the relevant standard says is best. But first, the possibility of moral progress requires that there *be* some objective moral standard toward which a society can progress. This is exactly what relativism denies. Second, relativism says that a society's moral standard is what *that* society believes and practices. Thus, changing these things can never count as progress for that would be to abandon the very practices required by that society's moral standard.

Relativism precludes the very *idea* of a society making moral progress: the notion simply *makes no sense.*[8] But this can't be right: it's not unintelligible to say that our society has made moral progress by coming to oppose racial discrimination. Even if a KKK member, say, refuses to call this progress, she must still grant that the claim makes sense so she can argue against it. Since it *does* make sense to speak of a society making moral progress by becoming fairer, more just, or morally better, relativism is mistaken.

4. Social Groups: Relativism says that your morality is that of the social group you belong to. Which social group, then, determines your moral standard? If you were an eighteenth-century Yavapai brave living in what is now Arizona, that question would be easy to answer. But you are not, and this question is vastly more difficult to

---

[8]One could make sense of a *part* of society "making progress" by coming closer to what the majority of that society already accepts. But this is not what we mean in talking about a society making moral progress

answer in our twenty-first-century society. Although the Yavapai no doubt shared a well-defined set of moral beliefs and practices, it's no longer true that any single set of beliefs or practices neatly characterizes our whole society today. Imagine an American citizen who is a card-carrying union member as well as the child of Catholic parents who came into New York twenty years ago from Mozambique. What social group does this person belong to? Arguably, she is Catholic: does that put her under the moral standard of the world's Catholics? Or should it be just that of American Catholics? Being a labor union member, she may well be a Democrat: is *that* her morality-determining social group instead? Suppose this person also preserves many of the values and practices of her Maravi ancestors. Does this make her moral standard that of the Maravis? What if Maravi moral values and beliefs conflict with those of most other twenty-first-century Americans or with Catholicism?

It's quite common for a person today to belong to several distinct social/cultural groups, each group being distinguished by different values, beliefs, and practices. Which social group defines that person's morality? There's no good reason to pick one group over any of the others. Since this is true of *most* people in modern societies, relativism can't assign any definite standard to most people. Either *no* moral standard holds for them or several distinct standards (which may conflict) must all hold at once. Another possibility is that the Maravi–female–Catholic–union member counts as a subgroup consisting of herself. But this solution turns relativism into subjectivism, which we have already rejected. In sum, if relativism were true, then the moral standards for many people in today's complex world would be undetermined. This provides yet another reason for rejecting relativism.

For Discussion
1. *Name some of today's moral reformers, or describe where you think our society is either making moral progress or is morally regressing.*
2. *What practice(s) in your society would you want to reform?*
3. *What distinct social groups do you identify with? Do these groups differ in any moral beliefs and practices?*

Summary
There are several serious objections to relativism. First, relativism can allow any immoral practice—like slavery, discrimination, and genocide—to qualify as morally right. Second, it counts history's greatest moral reformers among the worst people who have ever lived. Third, relativism can make no sense of moral progress. Fourth, relativism seems unable to determine what moral standard holds for most people in today's complex societies.

Key Terms
  • **Moral reformers:** *persons who, on moral grounds, work to change some of their own society's accepted beliefs and practices*

VI. A MATTER OF TOLERANCE

One more argument—intended to support relativism—needs to be considered. We will call this the *argument from tolerance*. This intriguing argument maintains not merely that relativism is true, but that we are *morally bound* to accept it.

Again, relativism asserts that each society can have its own unique moral standard since there is no universal standard. No particular standard can be viewed as better or worse, morally speaking, than any other. It follows that no society's moral standard can be judged by any other society's standard. But this, relativists say, is the essence of **tolerance**—the moral value that obligates us to respect the moral beliefs and practices of other people regardless of how we feel about them. Since relativism rules out the possibility of judging any moral standard, it arguably supports tolerance. Since objectivism does *not* rule our judging particular moral standards (any can be evaluated by the one objective standard), objectivism apparently conflicts with tolerance. Since tolerance is so important, we *ought* to accept relativism rather than objectivism:

1. The important moral value of tolerance requires that we respect the beliefs and practices of other societies.
2. Relativism rules out the possibility of judging any particular society's standard to be better or worse than others; objectivism allows for this.
3. Judging a group's moral beliefs and practices is not compatible with respecting their beliefs and practices.

Thus: we must accept relativism and reject objectivism.

How compelling is this argument? To start, Premise 2 is made true by the meanings of relativism and objectivism. We may also agree with the relativist's claim, in Premise 1, that tolerance is morally important. This is not to say that *only* tolerance is important or that it is *the most important* moral value. It simply is of great moral importance.

Finally, Premise 3 attempts to specify the sorts of behavior tolerance requires. It is certainly true that in respecting other peoples we must tolerate their cultures, beliefs, and practices. We may not attempt to destroy a society or its culture simply because it's different. But does it follow that no one should even *disagree* with another society's views or offer them *reasons* for thinking that different beliefs or practices are more defensible? No. In fact, engaging people in reasoned moral dialogue is one important way to *show respect* toward them. Imagine leaving a primitive tribesman ignorant about the dangers of drinking contaminated water. This doesn't show him respect; instead, it *disrespects* his value as a person, unnecessarily abandoning him to sickness or death. But the same can be said regarding a society's harmful moral beliefs and practices.[9] Tolerance is not compatible with

------

[9]For instance, consider harms caused by a society that sees no need to help an injured child, that finds nothing wrong with a sexual assault, or that practices discrimination.

an effort to annihilate another society, but it is perfectly compatible with criticism and reasoned arguments that support moral judgments. These considerations undermine the argument's claim in Premise 3. But Premise 3 is essential to the argument successfully supporting relativism.

The argument from tolerance is, therefore, unsound. But there is an even clearer objection. We can get at it in either of two ways. First, consider how we understand the principle of tolerance. We take it for granted that tolerance extends to *all* persons—that *everyone* should be tolerant and respectful toward others. After all, if tolerance did not ensure equal respect for all, then there would be little point to championing tolerance. But this amounts to treating tolerance as an *objective* moral value, holding universally. Since relativism rejects objectivism, relativism precludes exactly what we want—a universal value of tolerance.

The same point can be made another way. Given relativism, a society's standard depends on what its people accept. Because our society widely accepts tolerance, we are bound to act in tolerance. But what holds for one society need not hold for others. In fact, there's no guarantee (given relativism) that tolerance will be a moral obligation elsewhere. Suppose that there's a social group whose people are strongly committed to *intolerance,* who consider it their moral obligation to do everything possible to destroy individuals or peoples with whom they disagree. Relativism, given its own position, must then acknowledge the moral legitimacy of these people's intolerance no less that it acknowledges tolerance in other groups. But this shows that relativism is just as capable of supporting intolerance as it is of supporting tolerance.

Clearly, then, relativism is no special friend of tolerance. But what about objectivism—doesn't that still conflict with tolerance, as the relativist has suggested? It seems not. For one thing, objectivism gives no society a license to carry out acts of moral imperialism upon another society. In fact, given that tolerance is objective, such acts would be forbidden by tolerance. Further, objectivism says nothing about *our* particular beliefs and practices being the *right* ones. Objectivism offers nothing to support the moral conceit that *we*—or any other particular society—have exclusive access to the true moral standard. Finally, we have seen that we *must* accept objectivism if we want to treat tolerance as a universal value. Ironically, then, the relativist's argument from tolerance turns on its head. We must accept objectivism to support tolerance; we must reject relativism because it undercuts tolerance.

For Discussion

1. *What does tolerance mean to you? Do you agree with the text's discussion of tolerance and its limitations?*
2. *Suppose your neighbor often locks his young child in a closet and then leaves the house for hours at a time. How tolerant should you be about this? Explain.*
3. *The Hindu practice of suttee—burning the widow to death on the funeral pyre of her deceased husband—began to be banned by Europeans in the early nineteenth century. Was this ban an act of intolerance by the Europeans?*

Summary
It may initially seem that relativism supports the principle of tolerance because it forbids one social group to judge the moral standard of another. However, the principle of tolerance is usually understood as holding universally, which is not allowed by relativism. Further, relativism supports intolerance just as readily as tolerance. Genuine support for tolerance can be found only in objectivism.

Key Terms
- **Tolerance:** *requires that we respect the moral beliefs and practices of others but doesn't preclude rational disagreement or even taking action in certain cases.*

VII.** CAN RELATIVISM SUPPLY WHAT OBJECTIVISM CANNOT?

Moral relativism—at least the popular version—has a great deal against it. While this version is unacceptable, more sophisticated versions of relativism do not so readily fall prey to the previous objections. One such version is David Wong's **"pluralistic relativism."**[10]

Wong's view grants that while there can be different valid moral standards for different societies, it's still not possible for just *anything* to be morally right. Every valid standard must include the same core of objective moral requirements—requirements, for instance, that rule out torturing someone merely on a whim. Although this moral core must be part of every moral standard (the objective part), that core alone can never provide a completely adequate moral standard. Any society's standard must also add certain less crucial moral claims reflecting the particular moral practices and institutions of that society (the relative part). Thus, there can be many equally valid or legitimate moral standards, all sharing the same objective core, but differing in other respects. How great can these differences be? Wong thinks that although moral standards probably all share most of their foundational moral values, they often differ in how they prioritize those values. For instance, one society might give greater value to kindness than to honesty; a second society might reverse these priorities. The former society would probably treat lying with greater leniency than the latter.

Wong's limited relativism certainly deserves consideration. Yet we might still ask if we need even this milder form of relativism to accommodate the differences Wong is concerned about. We have already seen how personal differences in conscience might be brought under objectivism simply by adding an objective principle that people should not violate their own consciences. Paralleling this, could objectivism grant each society its own distinctive "social conscience" and then add

---

[10]David B. Wong, *Natural Moralities: A Defense of Pluralistic Relativism* (Oxford: Oxford University Press, 2006); David B. Wong, *Moral Relativity* (Berkeley: University of California Press, 1984).

the objective principle that no people in any given society should ever violate their society's social conscience? This seems a promising alternative, although those sympathetic to Wong would no doubt reply that this strategy could never sufficiently explain all the important moral differences that exist between societies

For Discussion

1. What moral values and principles should be included in Wong's common moral core for all societies?
2. What sorts of things might be included in your society's social conscience?

Summary

There are more sophisticated versions of relativism than the popular version we have considered in most of this chapter. For instance, Wong's limited relativism suggests that although societies may differ regarding how they prioritize moral values, all societies share a common core of foundational values and principles. This account avoids allowing just anything to count as morally acceptable but still allows for several different but equally true moral standards.

Key Terms

- **Pluralistic relativism:** maintains that different societies can have different but equally valid moral standards, though all share a common moral core.

Pluralism the belief that people of all races, classes religious beliefs

Chapter Assignment Questions

1. What do people mean when they say things like "That may be true for you (or that *should* may hold for you), but it isn't true (or doesn't hold) for me?" *be able to*
2. In your own words, explain the four objections to relativism regarding (a) making *get* anything right, (b) reformers, (c) moral progress, and (d) social groups. *along*
3. Our society has recently come to accept "gay marriage," but even just a few decades ago, this was opposed by most people in our society. Does this represent a *on* genuine change in morality or merely a change in belief and/or practice? *equal*
4. Explain why the principle of tolerance can be supported by objectivism but not *footing* by relativism. *in a*
5. ** Do you agree with Wong that some mild form of relativism is necessary or do you agree with the text's argument that objectivism can handle Wong's concerns? *in a diverse*
6. ** The United States has recently used torture on suspected terrorists for the *diverse* sake of national security. Many other countries condemn this. Is the United *society* States simply in the wrong about this, or is this an example of Wong's differing priorities?

Additional Resources

"All Is Not Relative." Ethics Unwrapped. Accessed September 2, 2016. http://ethicsunwrapped. utexas.edu/video/relative. This video is a helpful discussion of relativism, with interviews,

n. However, stop watching when "pluralism" is mentioned at about eight minutes; is used differently than in this text and will be confusing.

James. "Subjectivism." In *Companion to Ethics*, edited by Peter Singer. Oxford: Blackwell Publishers, 1993.

Rachels, James and Stuart Rachels. *The Elements of Moral Philosophy*. 6th ed. Boston: McGraw–Hill Higher Education, 2009. See the chapters "The Challenge of Cultural Relativism" and "Subjectivism in Ethics."

Singer, Peter, ed. *A Companion to Ethics*. Oxford: Blackwell Publishers, 1993.

Wong, David. "Relativism." In *Companion to Ethics*, edited by Peter Singer. Oxford: Blackwell Publishers, 1993.

Case 1

Arranged Marriage

Emma's co-worker, Sukrita, tells Emma that she has fallen in love with an American man. But her parents, who are strict Hindus, do not support love-matches. They have already engaged a marriage broker in India who has found several suitable candidates for Sukrita to meet. They are urging her to go with them to Jaipur to meet these young men. Sukrita's parents explain that they want what's best for Sukrita, and they feel that she will be better off with a man that fits her culture and values. They make it clear that they won't force Sukrita to choose any specific man, but her choice must be from the Indian men the marriage broker has found. Sukrita asks Emma for advice.

THOUGHT QUESTIONS

1. List some cultural principles that Sukrita would probably consider in her decision.
2. Sukrita has adopted some American values. What are these? Do they conflict with her parents' values? How so? Which ought to take precedence?
3. What objective moral values seem to relate to this case?
4. If you were Emma, what would you advise Sukrita to do? Why?

Case 2

Female Genital Mutilation

The practice of female genital mutilation (FGM), sometimes called female circumcision, is still widespread in many African countries. The procedure is most commonly carried out on young women who are about to be married. Because the procedure involves removing the clitoris, it greatly reduces the amount of sexual pleasure a woman experiences during intercourse and so is thought to help ensure the woman's faithfulness to her husband. As may be imagined, the procedure can be exceedingly painful. Although it may be carried out using modern surgical techniques in a clean environment, it is also often done by a relative with knives, razor blades, or even sharp rocks. Many women suffer infection, bleeding, and other complications; some die as a result. It is estimated that between 100 million

Continued

Case 2 (Continued)

and 140 million young women have received FGM to date; in Africa about three million girls are at potential risk for FGM each year. In January of 2008, the United Nations issued a statement in support of abandoning the procedure.[11]

Fauziya Kassindja, a young woman from Togo, Africa, was one of the few women in her society who expected to escape the ritual, called *kakiya* in her country.[12] Fauziya's father was a businessman who, contra to cultural norms in Togo, thought that his daughters should choose for themselves the kind of life they would lead. He sent them to school, and he protected them from kakiya. In 1994, however, when Fauziya was just seventeen, her father died and his sister moved in with them. She soon had it arranged that Fauziya would be married to a forty-five-year-old man and undergo FGM. Because Fauziya, her sister, and her mother objected, it was quietly arranged for Fauziya to be smuggled out of Togo to neighboring Ghana. Using a false passport, she then flew to Germany and on to the United States. Upon her arrival at Newark Airport, Fauziya applied for asylum on the basis of her father's death and her desire to avoid being married against her will. At the time, she did not mention FGM because her English was limited and she was too embarrassed. She was told that a judge's decision would be required to grant her asylum and that in the meantime she would have to either return to Togo or Germany or go to prison. Fauziya chose prison. She was stripped, chained, and taken to a detention center. Later, she was transferred to a regular prison, where she was held for over seventeen months.

Eventually, Layli Miller Bashir, Fauziya's lawyer, presented her case before an immigrations judge, who denied Fauziya asylum. At that point, the case was brought to the attention of the international news media, and the *New York Times* featured the story on its front page. Thirteen days later, Fauziya was released and granted asylum and now resides in the United States. Fauziya was the first woman to receive asylum for FGM in the United States, thus making it possible for other women to obtain asylum for the same reason. As a result of the international uproar over FGM, several African countries have since ruled FGM to be illegal, including Togo, Fauziya's home country. There is evidence, however, that FGM continues to be quietly practiced in these countries—and even (much less often) in the United States.

THOUGHT QUESTIONS

1. Should Fauziya have stayed in Togo and accepted her county's cultural practices? Why or why not?
2. Do you think that there is an objective basis from which we can derive a moral standard? If so, how could we go about convincing people in, say, Togo to apply this standard to FGM without our improperly interfering in that society's cultural values?
3. Can you find any basis for morally justifying the practice of FGM? Are there any objective moral values or principles that may support it?

---

[11]These facts are obtained from the *World Health Organization*, Fact Sheet No. 241, May 2008.

[12]This story is taken from the book by Fauziya Kassindja, Layli Miller Bashir, and Gini Kopecky, *Do They Hear When You Cry?* (New York: Bantam Books, 1999)

4. Give some reasons against FGM. (Your reasons need not be only moral.)
5. Could a society's cultural approval of FGM ever make such a practice morally right or even the moral duty of women in that society? Tie your response in with the discussions of relativism and objectivism.

Case 3

Religious Exemption and the Death of Matthew Swan[13]

If relativism is correct, then what is right is whatever a society or culture takes to be right. The terms "society" and "culture" are somewhat vague, however, since distinct social groups can include religious communities, for instance, as well as countries or cultural communities. This makes it possible for moral standards to vary not just from country to country but also from one religious group to another even within a single country.

For example, according to the teachings of *Church of Christ, Scientist*, illness is caused by sin and can only be healed by prayer. Ordinary physicians do not actually heal disease but merely relieve its symptoms. Seeking medical care is considered morally wrong because it amounts to a sinful rejection of faith in God. Instead, Christian Scientists may only consult Christian Science Practitioners—people specially approved by the Church of Christ, Scientist. The only exception is that anyone may set a broken bone, since this is not an illness. Christian Scientists are not the only group forbidding various types of medical care. In the United States, there are groups that oppose all medical care and only practice faith healing.

For some members of these groups, the consequences have been devastating. Douglas and Rita Swan had been Christian Scientists all their lives and so knew little of even basic medicine. In 1977, their only son, sixteen-month-old Matthew, developed a high fever. The Christian Science practitioners maintained that Matthew was being made sick by the negative feelings of his parents and that prayer was needed to cure him. When Matthew didn't get better, Douglas and Rita considered going to a doctor, but according to Rita Swan, they "were terrified that the doctor wouldn't be able to treat the disease, . . . and then we'd have no way to resume the Christian Science healing. Thus, if we made the wrong decision, we could find ourselves bereft of help from both medical science and God."[14] After twelve days, a practitioner suggested to the Swans that Matthew had a broken bone, which allowed them to go to a doctor. They did so immediately. In the hospital, Matthew was diagnosed with meningitis, which is very serious but can be treated effectively with antibiotics if diagnosed early enough. Unfortunately, it was not early enough for Matthew, and he died in the hospital after receiving intensive care for a week. The Swans left the Christian Science church. In 1983, they founded *Children's Health Care Is a Legal Duty* (CHILD), an organization designed to protect children from "religion-based medical neglect."[15]

The Swans are not the only ones whose religious adherence cost them the life of their child. About 170 child deaths related to faith healing have been reported over the past twenty-five years. More recently, Neil Beagley died in 2008 of complications from a

Continued

---

[13]Rita Swan, "When Faith Fails Children," *Humanist*, (November/December 2000): 11–16. Unless otherwise noted, information about this case is taken from this article.

[14]Swan, "When Faith Fails Children," 11–16.

[15]CHILD, Inc., accessed August 31, 2016, http://www.childrenshealthcare.org.

Case 3 (*Continued*)

urinary tract blockage.[16] Neil died surrounded by his family and a number of members of his church. His parents were tried and convicted for criminally negligent homicide.

Parents cannot normally be prosecuted in such cases, however, because of religious exemption laws, which, in effect, hold members of certain religious communities to different laws. Such laws provide special exemptions to child-abuse and neglect laws, allowing parents to refuse medical treatment for their children on religious grounds. Over forty U.S. states have some such laws. In states without religious exemptions, these kinds of cases may be treated as manslaughter or criminal mistreatment. Even in exemption states, parents who do not practice an exempt religion *are* subject to legal prosecution for failing to seek medical attention for their seriously sick children. In effect, then, the law establishes different standards regarding a parent's responsibilities towards their child and when medical treatment is required. These standards depend on the community one belongs to.

THOUGHT QUESTIONS

1. If there were no religious exemption, how would that have affected the Swans?
2. Do you think a religious community constitutes a distinct social group for relativism?
3. From a relativist perspective, could a Christian Scientist oppose the moral values of his or her religion? Why or why not?
4. Parents have a moral responsibility to do what is best for their children, which includes availing themselves of needed medical treatment for a sick child. Christian Scientists also seem to have a moral responsibility to follow the beliefs and teaching of their church, which forbids their use of modern medicine. An *American* Christian Scientist belongs to both groups. When an American Christian Science parent has a seriously sick child, which set of responsibilities applies?
5. Do you think that the Swans and the Beagleys should have sought medical attention for their children? Do the deaths of their children raise any problems for relativism?
6. Is it morally justifiable to have religious-exemption laws, allowing parents to refuse medical care for their children? Tie your response in with the discussion of relativism.

Case 4

Women in the Middle East[17]

Many religious and cultural traditions set different standards of behavior for men and women. For example, in many Islamic cultures women must veil themselves— a requirement that does not apply to men. Islamic scholars say that the stricture to

Continued

---

[16]Ibid.

[17]Much of the material for this case was obtained from the book by Geraldine Brooks, *Nine Parts of Desire: The Hidden World of Islamic Women*, (New York: Anchor Books, 1995). Amnesty International is also a good source of information regarding the treatment of women in the Middle East.

Case 4 (*Continued*)

wear the veil comes directly from the Quran. Some Islamic scholars say that women should cover only their heads (i.e., their hair, not their faces) whereas others claim that only a woman's face and hands should be visible. Only the husband, male relatives, and young boys are allowed to see a woman without the veil.

In some Islamic countries (e.g., in Kuwait), these rules are not strictly observed. In Turkey they are hardly observed at all. In Saudi Arabia, however, women must veil even their faces. Few professions are open to Saudi women, and women may not leave the house by themselves, or drive, or travel alone. They cannot leave the country without written permission from their husbands. They may not compete in sports, swim, read uncensored fashion magazines, or try on clothes when shopping.[18] Also, in Saudi women may not see their prospective husbands before marriage. Saudi women *can* get an education, but the educational system is segregated. Although divorce is permitted for both sexes, it is more common for a man to divorce his wife (if she does not bear him children, for instance).

Many Middle Eastern countries also have strict rules about sexual conduct and promiscuity, which apply to men and women alike. For instance, sex before marriage and adultery are strictly prohibited. Unmarried offenders may receive one hundred lashes for premarital sex. In some countries, the punishment for adultery is house arrest for the rest of the offender's life; in others, it is stoning (using small stones to ensure a slow death). Nevertheless, stonings are rare. This is partly because four witnesses must testify that adultery has taken place—and it is often difficult to procure four witnesses to a sexual act. For those who are found guilty, however, there's often a difference in *how* men and women are stoned: men are buried to their waists in sand before stoning; women are buried to their heads (though the Quran doesn't make this distinction). According to Amnesty International, women are stoned more often than men.

THOUGHT QUESTIONS

1. What problems does this case raise for relativism?
2. Do you think that countries (and cultures) have a *moral* right to create laws and endorse practices that impose different behaviors and requirements on different sets of people? What difference, if any, does it make if those laws reflect that country's culture or religion?
3. Although women in Saudi Arabia certainly seem to enjoy fewer rights than men, the law is harsh for both—just consider the punishment for adultery. Can one society be morally justified in imposing more severe punishments than other societies do for the same offense?
4. Interfering with the laws or practices of a sovereign country can have both good and bad consequences. How serious must the injustice or the resulting harms be for outside intervention to be justified or even necessary? (For instance, the United Nations has occasionally sent forces into a country to halt genocide,

---

[18]"Eleven Things Women in Saudi Arabia Cannot Do," *The Week*, July 28, 2015, accessed August 31, 2016, http://www.theweek.co.uk/60339/eleven-things-women-in-saudi-arabia-cannot-do.

and much of the world joined together to impose severe economic sanctions on South Africa because of its policy of apartheid.)

5. Suppose relativism is false and that all persons have the same basic moral rights. What do you think these most basic moral rights are? To what degree should world powers act to ensure that all persons enjoy these same rights?

6. Your best friend has recently married, and the couple is planning to move back to an Islamic country. Up till now, your friend—a convert to Islam—has not worn the veil. Because of family and societal pressures, however, her husband is now asking her to wear the veil once they move. She has come to you for advice. What do you think she should do? How does your answer reflect on the issue of relativism?

CHAPTER THREE

Personal Autonomy and Moral Agency

I. INTRODUCTION

Throughout our lives, we make choices and then act on them. These choices range from the trivial (What should I wear today? What should I have for dinner?) to decisions that profoundly affect our lives (What career should I pursue? Whom should I marry?). In making our choices, we take it for granted that we, along with most others, are self-determining or **autonomous** individuals.

Autonomous persons are morally responsible for their choices and may be praised or blamed for what they do. People lacking autonomy, however, are not normally responsible for their choices. What is it, then, to be genuinely autonomous? Consider the following.

- An eight-year-old boy is rushed into the emergency room from a hit-and-run accident. He is badly injured, drifting in and out of consciousness. As the doctor surveys her patient, she ticks off the following observations: some bones are broken, the patient is bleeding badly and needs blood, and he is rapidly going into shock. Yet just as she starts barking orders, the boy feebly raises his hand as if to push her away, whispering "No, please don't." Shortly afterward, the hospital reaches the boy's parents, who likewise refuse all treatment for religious reasons. The hospital then contacts the authorities and within a few hours is ordered by the court to proceed with all necessary life-saving treatments.
- JoAnn, a working mother of two, is running behind this morning because of the kids and is going to be late for a meeting with her most important client. Traffic is moving slowly, and she's almost beside herself with impatience. Disturbing thoughts of losing the client and maybe even her job flit through her mind. She had texted the client just before leaving to say she'd be late. Crawling along now at 25 miles an hour, her cell phone chimes, and she sees a text from her client. Feeling that she needs to send some response immediately, she picks up her phone and starts thumbing a reply. She looks up just

a moment too late to avoid rear-ending the slowed car in front of her. Both cars are damaged, and the other driver has suffered a whiplash neck injury.

• An Alzheimer's patient at a nursing home is waiting in her room for lunch. Although the nurse has worked with this patient almost daily for the past nine months, the patient usually doesn't recognize him and is often disoriented. When he brings the patient's lunch into her room, she suddenly starts screaming and kicking, imagining she is being attacked by a stranger. One particularly well-aimed kick throws the nurse and lunch onto the floor so that his back is injured. He yells to two other nurses on the floor, who forcibly restrain the patient.

The boy, the mom, and the Alzheimer's patient all apparently made choices for themselves. Still, we must ask how much autonomy each actually exercised as these events unfolded. Since each choice had the potential to cause injury or even death, this question has considerable moral significance. Is the patient to be held responsible for injuring her nurse? What could justify the court ordering treatment against the boy's expressed wishes? How responsible is the driver for her accident? To answer these questions, we need to explore the nature of autonomy.

For Discussion
1. *Why doesn't the Alzheimer's patient have autonomy?*
2. *Why doesn't the boy have autonomy?*
3. *Does the mother have autonomy? Is she responsible for causing the accident? Why?*
4. *Imagine that the boy's parents are in an accident and refuse treatment for themselves, risking death. How does this differ from the boy's case? Explain.*

Summary
People constantly make choices, and many of these choices have important moral implications. We take it for granted that most people are autonomous. But not everyone is autonomous, and those lacking autonomy may not be morally responsible for their actions. If we are to respond appropriately to the choices others make, we need to understand what makes a person autonomous.

Key Terms
  • **Autonomous:** *able to make free choices as a self-determining individual.*

II. PERSONAL AUTONOMY

To be autonomous, one must satisfy several conditions. The most basic is this:

Independence condition: a person must have the capacity to make choices and not be under the control of any external constraint or inner compulsion.

An autonomous person must certainly be able to make choices. Infants and comatose adults lack this fundamental capacity—they can't make any choices at all. In addition, an autonomous person must be free from the control of other things. The key concept here is *control*. If you are being controlled by hypnosis or terrorized by threats, you lack autonomy. It isn't *you* who are in control; rather, these *external constraints* are making you act as you do. The same holds if you are controlled by an *inner compulsion*. Obsessive/compulsive behaviors, addictions, and even phobias can keep you from controlling your actions in certain situations. Similarly, overwhelming physical or emotional pain can drive someone to quit a job, leave a spouse, or even attempt suicide without appreciating what she is doing. She is *not herself*, we say—and so we shouldn't treat her choices as if they were her own. Whenever someone fails the independence condition, that person cannot be autonomous.

When my choice is *influenced* by certain considerations, however, that doesn't control me or remove my autonomy. If I've invited a friend to dinner who doesn't like spicy food, that may *influence* my choice of restaurants, but it doesn't *control* my choice. Not having much money can also influence my choice. But facts like these don't *control* my choice—they establish the nature and the parameters of my choice; they determine what my choice is actually *about*. Although every choice is affected by various influences, mere influences do not control us or take away our autonomy.

> **Competency condition:** a person must have the capacities necessary to deliberate rationally about her choices.

Satisfying the independence condition is not enough to make a person autonomous. You must also be able to deliberate appropriately. Specifically, you must have the capacities (a) to know and understand the applicable facts and (b) each choice's consequences, (c) to identify your relevant values, and (d) to draw rationally supported conclusions (i.e., reason appropriately) from the available information.

To illustrate the role of these capacities in making a choice, imagine that you (an autonomous person) are late for a morning appointment but want something to eat. You have two options—grab a cold bagel and apple from the fridge or stop at a fast-food place. To decide between these options, you must know that these *are* your options, which means you must (a) be capable of determining that there's a bagel and apple in the fridge and where there's a fast-food restaurant. Next, you need to understand the consequences of each option. Thus, you must (b) be able to grasp that even if the bagel and apple don't sound terribly appetizing, they'll meet your needs, and also that while the fast food sounds appealing, it will set back your healthy diet. You must then (c) be able to identify your relevant values—for example, your health is more important to you than the fleeting pleasures of a fast food fix. Finally, you must (d) be able to appropriately figure out which option's consequences best serves what you most value. Applying your capacities in these ways leads you to your choice: go with the bagel and apple.

Finally, an autonomous individual should satisfy the authenticity condition.

Authenticity condition: a person must have the capacity to discern and personally evaluate his own values, goals, and commitments.

The most important part of this condition is that, as an autonomous person, you must be able to *assess* your own values. This is something more than simply being able to *use* or *refer to* your values, as competency requires. Authenticity requires the capability of weighing or evaluating your relevant values themselves and even of altering the degree of importance you assign to each.

Notice that to be autonomous, you don't always have to be *exercising* either this or any of the other capacities described by the three conditions. An autonomous person simply should *have* all of these capacities and so *be able* to exercise them. Thus, normal adults are usually autonomous, since they commonly have all of these capacities.

In contrast, very young children may not even satisfy the independence condition. Most older children also lack autonomy, since their reasoning powers and lack of experience leave them unable to fully satisfy the competency condition. Until later adolescence, therefore, children are thought to lack autonomy. This is why children are treated differently than adults in a court of law.

Returning to the authenticity condition, a child's earliest values are simply "given" to him—by upbringing, culture, and genes. Having little exposure to anything beyond their immediate environment, even adolescents are usually not yet able to put their values under scrutiny or compare their values to other values. For most children (and some adults), their values decide their choices, but they cannot yet decide on their values. This, arguably, is not autonomy.[1] As we learn and grow, however, we are given more independence and our capacities increase. By accumulating experience, we steadily broaden to the point that we can begin to evaluate our own values. A friend, an event, or a major life change may then stimulate us to adjust our values. In this way, people gradually make their values more *authentically* their own.

Our discussion so far may suggest that being autonomous is an all-or-nothing affair: either you're autonomous or you're not. But there are several qualifications. First, even normally autonomous persons can temporarily lose autonomy. Severe pain or an illness can interfere with the capacities necessary for autonomy. It's also possible to lose autonomy on a more continuing basis. When a previously autonomous adult contracts Alzheimer's, she slowly becomes unable to weigh options and make choices until there's an irreversible loss of autonomy. Of course, children start out lacking autonomy, and this lack can continue for some into early adulthood. (Growing older doesn't automatically create autonomy!) People with serious mental and emotional disabilities may lack autonomy their whole lives. Any individual whose condition precludes autonomy on a continuing basis *lacks* **moral capacity**.

One can also be autonomous in certain *situations* but not others. If an intense fear of heights makes me incapable of climbing a ladder to retrieve a cat on my roof, I

---

[1]Since our values largely guide our choices, we have little control over our choices if we don't have some control over our values. Thus, a robust concept of autonomy requires a *capacity* to assess one's values. *Using* that capacity relates to agency (see §IV).

fail the independence condition *for that situation*. Yet I may still be able to choose between job offers or draw up a will with full autonomy. Powerful interpersonal forces can also take away autonomy for certain situations. For instance, people caught in abusive relationships can be too disempowered to break the relationship or even act to protect themselves. They may lack autonomy in most situations connected to their relationships. More generally, oppressive social structures can limit or remove autonomy from women, the poor, and members of certain ethnic and religious groups for a variety of social situations (e.g., for choosing certain jobs). Because autonomy depends on what capacities one has and is able to exercise in different situations, there will always be grey areas regarding who does and does not have autonomy.

For Discussion

1. *Do you have any fears or other inner compulsions that make it impossible for you to choose freely in certain situations?*
2. *Consider your choice of a college, a field of study, or a career or job. How did you deliberate over this choice, and what values guided you the most?*
3. *Have you made any adjustments to your values recently? Why?*
4. *At what time in your life did you start rethinking some of your values?*
5. *Have you ever lost autonomy for a time after previously having autonomy? What led to this?*
6. *What segments of our society are denied autonomy in certain situations by various social structures (e.g., laws or practices)?*

Summary

Although many factors can influence your decisions, this is true of most choices and does not undermine autonomy. What can limit or even remove autonomy is when a situation puts you under the control of some external constraint or inner compulsion. To be autonomous you must also be capable of appropriately making deliberate choices and assessing your values for yourself. Autonomy (having capacity) doesn't require that you always employ these capacities, but you must at least have them, as do most normal adults in most situations. People can gain or lose autonomy; people can also lack autonomy for just certain specific situations.

Key Terms

- **Independence condition:** *a person must have the capacity to make choices and not be under the control of an external constraint or inner compulsion.*

- **Competency condition:** *a person must have the capacities necessary to rationally deliberate about her choices.*

- **Authenticity condition:** *a person must have the capacity to discern and personally assess his own values.*

- **Moral capacity:** *fulfilling the three autonomy conditions; when one's state precludes autonomy for a period of time, one lacks capacity over that time.*

III. IMPLICATIONS OF AUTONOMY

Autonomy has great moral importance. For one thing, anyone having autonomy usually has some degree of **moral responsibility** for her actions. If an autonomous person acts in a selfish or criminal way, she will normally deserve blame or punishment. If another acts kindly and self-sacrificially, he likewise is morally responsible and so may deserve praise or some reward. Those lacking capacity are not usually responsible for their actions at the time. If I'm forced to carry out some dastardly deed under the threat of horrible torture, then the one threatening me is much more responsible for "my" deeds than I am. Persons driven by inner compulsions likewise have little or no moral responsibility, since "their" actions are not really *their own*. They may not even realize what they are doing! This is why we don't consider it right to *punish* the criminally insane, even when they have committed heinous crimes.

Having moral responsibility goes hand in hand with the right to be shown **moral deference**. Showing moral deference means respecting a person's choices without interfering. We almost always owe autonomous persons a fair degree of moral deference, even when we think they are being foolish. This doesn't mean that we may just look the other way as they are wronging or harming someone. But when there's no such danger, it's our moral duty to show deference toward other autonomous individuals.

People lacking capacity are not *necessarily* owed moral deference. Still, it's appropriate to show even these persons *some* deference whenever possible. If the Alzheimer patient wants carrots instead of peas for dinner, we should normally honor her request unless there's a good reason not to (e.g., she's allergic to carrots). Therefore, when we *are obliged* to interfere with another's choice—whether they have capacity or not—it's a serious matter. To justify such interference, there should normally be a great deal at stake, as when a person is likely to harm herself or another. In that case, we interfere for another's good. Interference is likewise justified when a child decides to try a drain-cleaner milkshake, or plays on the interstate, or (although the matter is more complex) refuses lifesaving treatment. Overruling people's choices for their own good is called **paternalism**.

For Discussion

1. *As an autonomous person, how important is it for you be accorded moral responsibility and deference? Why?*
2. *Think of some justified instances of paternalism, and some that are not.*
3. *It was once argued that the government was acting paternalistically by requiring motorcyclists to wear helmets. What do you think?*
4. *When and how often should parents allow their children to make their own choices? Why is this important?*
5. *How could you attempt to influence a friend who is making bad choices, while still showing them full moral deference?*
6. *If a person is suicidal, a great deal is at stake—would this justify our interfering with their attempting suicide?*

Summary

An autonomous person is usually morally responsible for her choices and is owed moral deference. People lacking moral capacity cannot be held morally responsible, nor are they owed deference to the degree autonomous persons are. Yet even with those lacking capacity, we are not usually justified in overruling their choices except when much is at stake. There can be times, however, when we may justifiably overrule another's choice for her own good.

Key Terms

- **Moral responsibility:** *being morally accountable to others for one's own choices (deserving blame or praise).*
- **Moral deference:** *respecting another person's choices without interfering.*
- **Paternalism:** *overruling people's choices and actions for their own good.*

IV. MORAL AGENTS

Let's now consider how autonomous persons actually exercise their capacities to make moral choices. An autonomous person making a specific moral choice acts as a **moral agent** by exercising her autonomy in a specific situation. One who lacks capacity—whether permanently or temporarily—cannot act as a moral agent while incapacitated. Likewise, someone whose capacities are undermined in specific kinds of situations (e.g., I have a compulsive fear of heights) cannot act as a moral agent in those situations (e.g., I can't climb very far up a ladder). Nor should such people be accorded moral responsibility or much deference (depending on what's at stake) in such situations.[2]

Yet even autonomous persons (i.e., those who *are able* to act as moral agents) don't always exercise their autonomy to the same degree. Since autonomy involves a person's *capacities* but not what they *do* with those capacities, people sometimes just "give in" to a feeling or don't bother to think through their choices. At other times, they may not consider a choice important enough to give it much thought, or they may deliberate with care but not to the point of assessing their values.

Thus, autonomous persons can act as moral agents at different levels, depending on how much they employ their capacities. Not surprisingly, these levels correlate with differing degrees of moral responsibility and deference. When someone acts as an agent at the highest level—employing the capacities of all three autonomy conditions—they ought to be accorded the highest degree of moral responsibility and deference. A person acting at a lower level, meanwhile, should normally be accorded less responsibility and deference.[3] Since responsibility and deference depend on the level at which a person acts as an agent, it's important for

---

[2]Of course, we often do so anyway, not realizing the person's actual condition.

[3]It's not always so simple. For instance, the harms I cause, or the opportunities I had to think more carefully before I acted, can also affect how responsible I am for my action.

us to understand the three levels of moral agency. These closely match the three conditions of autonomy.

> **Independent choice:** to make a particular independent choice, a moral agent must exercise his capacity to choose, while being under no constraint or compulsion.

A *merely* independent choice doesn't deliberate; nor does it make an authentic assessment of values. It comprises the lowest level of moral agency; it's also the level at which we make most of our day-to-day choices. We decide what cereal to eat or what clothes to wear without much thought, just following a whim or habit. This is not a bad thing. These sorts of choices tend to be pretty insignificant, and if we were to make all of our choices with the same deliberation and care we invest in more important decisions, we'd exhaust ourselves from the strain. Following good habits and even whims saves time and energy for more important decisions.

Still, even merely independent choices give us *some* responsibility. If I unthinkingly say something offensive to another, the offense remains my fault and my responsibility. After all, I still *had the ability* to avoid giving offense—I just should have been more careful. More seriously, people sometimes commit crimes because they "give in" to strong feelings they *could* have controlled. These people are usually less to blame than those who deliberately plan out a crime, but they still deserve moral censure. This difference is captured by the legal distinction between "crimes of passion" and "premeditated crimes."

With responsibility goes deference; thus, it isn't usually right to interfere with an autonomous person's independent choices. Yet interference *can* be justified and even become obligatory when the stakes are high enough. Imagine yourself standing at a corner next to a harried looking man, waiting for the light to change. The instant the light turns, the man steps into the street without even noticing the taxi headed directly at him. Suddenly comprehending the situation, you make a grab at him, throwing him sprawling back onto the sidewalk. This is a paternalistic act toward an autonomous man who originally acted on an independent choice. Yet your act is justified in view of the urgent need to avert great harm. More important, you had every reason to think that by pulling the man out of the car's path, you accomplished what the man *himself* would have wanted had he been aware of the danger. By *not acting* this way, in fact, you would have allowed a preventable harm and thus *failed to respect him* as an autonomous person of intrinsic worth.

> **Competent choice:** To make a particular competent choice, a moral agent must (a) make an independent choice and (b) exercise her capacities to engage in rational deliberation.

Competent choice takes moral agency to a much higher level than independent choice. Competent choices make essential use of our reason and our values (but still do not assess any values). We make most important decisions at this level. For instance, Joan (an autonomous person) decides to become a teacher because she values investing in the future and working with kids. If she is accurately assessing her abilities and her willingness to be with children, then she makes a good choice. Of course, we can make poor choices at this level as well. Jerry (also autonomous) has decided on a career in management because he values good earnings and the excitement of the business world. Unfortunately, Jerry doesn't realize what everyone else around him recognizes—how easily he caves in under pressure. His weakness will surely hurt his ability to succeed in management. Nevertheless, Jerry's mistake doesn't eliminate his autonomy, nor does it keep him from functioning as a moral agent at the level of competent choice. His deliberations about this are simply flawed. This is a normal part of life: autonomous persons make choices that may not always be best, and we all must learn from our mistakes.

We must contrast Jerry's poor deliberations, however, with situations in which a person has autonomy but is *not allowed* to draw on important, relevant facts. If I am deliberately deceived by another or denied access to crucial facts, I cannot make a competent choice. Although I still have the capacities to make such a choice, I'm being barred from making my choice appropriately by including relevant facts in my deliberations. As a result, I probably won't make the choice I would have made if these facts had been available to me. The choice I make, even though I am autonomous, isn't truly *my* mistake but one that has been forced upon me. For instance, a doctor might not inform his patient of an alternate treatment, society might convince a woman that she can never attain a certain high level job, or a salesperson may falsely convince a customer that no better prices can be found elsewhere. In such cases, the decision maker is led to choose poorly through no failure or lack of her own. For this reason, we should not consider her to be acting as a moral agent at the level of competent choice.

Competent choice employs our capacities much more than independent choice and so should be accorded much greater responsibility and deference. Except when a great deal is at stake, it is rarely justified to interfere with another person's competent choice.

> **Authentic Choice:** To make a particular authentic choice, a moral agent must make a choice that is both (a) independent and (b) competent; he must also (c) exercise his capacity to authentically assess his values.[4]

This is the highest level of moral agency and so should be accorded the greatest moral responsibility and deference. In making a competent choice, I only *apply* my existing values; in authentic choice, I *assess* or re-evaluate my values. This doesn't require that I actually *change* any part of my value system, but it does require that I thoughtfully assess my relevant values before I apply them in my deliberations. Since it includes my assessing my values, an authentic choice is most fully my own—I place more under my own control than with any other type of choice.

Suppose I've just previously made an authentic choice. Can the value assessments I made for that choice carry over to make my next choice authentic as well?

---

[4]Strictly, this is redundant, as making a competent choice already ensures it is an independent choice. It is stated this way to emphasize how each level includes all previous levels.

Not usually. The values my next choice brings into play may not be the same as the ones I assessed just previously. Also, I might have experienced something in the meantime that would alter my system of values. Since we are constantly evolving as persons, it probably holds that *each* authentic choice must *itself* be an occasion for assessing the currently held values that are most relevant to *that* choice.

As authentic choices demand additional effort, we don't make them as often as we do competent choices. Still, authentic choices are not particularly rare or difficult. Making an authentic choice might merely require you to reaffirm your current values—to run a quick "checkup" to make sure you remain committed to them. In other cases, the situation itself may give you reasons to assess your values. Experiencing a tragedy, undergoing religious conversion, or addressing some overwhelming challenge can demand much more of us as we choose our responses and so require larger scale value adjustments. Whether accomplished with ease or with much soul-searching, all of these sorts of assessments can satisfy the requirements of authentic choice.

Acting as moral agents is our right and privilege as persons. But as such actions can take place at different levels, it is often morally important that we discern at what level a person is acting as a moral agent. Only then can we know how much responsibility and deference we should accord to that person at that time. The moral implications of this become especially significant when much is at stake. For instance, we normally have no right to prevent someone from driving home when and how they wish. But that can drastically change if the driver is drunk or is the disoriented victim of an injury. Likewise, in deciding on an appropriate punishment, a judge needs to consider if the criminal's act was competent (and thus pre-meditated) or merely an independent choice (e.g., arising from a fit of passion). Yet again, suppose a patient refuses a critical medical treatment. If the patient is able to act as a moral agent (unlike the child) and the issue is a matter of grave consequence, then nothing less than a competent choice seems sufficient to earn our full deference to their choice. Although some might insist that such a refusal requires authentic choice, that probably asks too much.

For Discussion

1. *Describe some merely independent choices you often make. Contrast these with choices you've made at the level of competent choice.*
2. *How much do you exercise your capacities of autonomy when driving a very familiar route or in your morning routine? Is this a good thing?*
3. *What authentic choices have you made? What choices would you only make at this level?*
4. *Do you agree that in going from independent to competent to authentic choices, responsibility and deference should roughly increase as well? Why?*
5. *Can advertising effectively keep you from making a competent choice about the product? Give some examples.*

Summary

Even when a person is autonomous—and so can function as a moral agent—he doesn't always exercise moral agency at the same level. There are three levels of moral agency: independent choice, competent choice, and authentic choice. The highest level is authentic choice; though choices at this level are not common, neither are they particularly unusual. Agents acting at higher levels should usually be accorded greater moral deference and moral responsibility. This holds even when a person makes mistakes in his deliberations. However, a person who is deliberately misled into making a poor choice cannot function as a moral agent in that situation, which greatly reduces his responsibility and the deference owed to his choice.

Key Terms

- **Moral agent**: *a person who satisfies the conditions of autonomy and is able to appropriately apply these capacities to a specific choice.*

- **Independent Choice**: *a moral agent exercises his capacity to choose while being under no constraint or compulsion.*

- **Competent Choice**: *a moral agent (a) makes an independent choice and (b) exercises his capacities to engage in rational deliberation.*

- **Authentic Choice**: *a moral agent makes both (a) an independent choice and (b) a competent choice and (c) exercises his capacity to authentically assess his values.*

V. OTHER CONCEPTIONS OF AUTONOMY

A nearly universal problem for exercising our autonomy is that we don't always know which values are truly important to us. We sometimes even deceive ourselves about what we believe to be important. Further, we often hold conflicting values; for instance, suppose I place great value on family life, but I also want to be highly successful in a demanding career. I'm going to find it difficult to balance these values and their time commitments. It even seems that we can be just plain *wrong* about the importance of certain values. For example, people often pursue a large income, luxuries, and personal comfort though studies repeatedly show that centering one's life on self-gratification typically leads to depression, anxiety, and illness. In contrast, values such as strong relationships, purposeful work, and helping others create a sense of joy, good health, and deep personal satisfaction.

These considerations suggest that our analysis of autonomy may not yet be complete. So far, we have put a premium on *self*-determination, making the assumption that autonomy maximizes personal freedom and independence. Indeed, our culture's individualism implies that *ideal* autonomy places as few influences and limitations upon us as possible. But it's worth observing that this concept of **value-neutral autonomy** is purely negative.[5] In particular, it leaves our choice of

---

[5]The normative standard of rationality must at least apply even to value-neutral autonomy, but this places no restrictions on what one's goals or values may be.

value systems wide open by offering no guidance or boundaries for choosing our values. It thus can make no sense of any value being better or worse than any other. Taken to the extreme, this view makes each individual's autonomy the *only* non-negotiable value and the sole determinant of the good.[6]

Yet there's doubt that a purely value-neutral autonomy is even possible. As we've seen, authentic choice requires that we choose our values—but on *what basis* can we make these choices? We could simply aim at the values that most appeal to us. But this can change from moment to moment and can be strongly affected by a friend's comment, a recent experience, or even brainwashing. As a result, our choices can move rapidly beyond our own control and even become largely arbitrary—the very opposite of autonomous self-determination.

Should we instead choose values that strike us as most natural and important? But this puts our value systems largely under the control of our upbringing and culture. Nevertheless, suppose that I could somehow remove all such outside influences so that my choices arise solely from my innate personal nature. Unfortunately, this would take my choices even more out of my control, since my innate personality is determined by my genetic make-up and not by *anyone's* free choice. Thus, we cannot make *any* value choice purely by *ourselves*.

Furthermore, value-neutral autonomy is not the kind of autonomy that anyone should want. Genuine autonomy is not purely negative; it also requires that we realize our full potential and *expand* our range of opportunities. No one will get rich by simply reducing his expenses without increasing his earnings; likewise, no one will achieve her full powers by merely escaping constraints without investing in her overall personal development. Lacking valuable skills and knowledge, our options and opportunities will never be all that they could be. Genuine autonomy requires expanding our abilities and options, not just freeing ourselves from the influence, control, and authority of others.

It thus appears that our value choices could use some guidance, for while some choices will contribute to our potential, others will reduce our options and thus our actual freedom. What we need is to commit ourselves to the *right* sorts of values—those most consistent with human fulfillment and our own personal flourishing. According to many thinkers, these *right* values include foundational moral values, and genuine autonomy requires that we make morally right choices.[7] Such a value-based autonomy—as opposed to *value-neutral* autonomy—is called **substantive autonomy**.

There is much support for this. Most dramatically, a person who abandons himself to masochistic desires, self-directed violence, or thrill-seeking may simply get himself killed, which doesn't exactly promote autonomy. Thinking a bit more subtly, it doesn't seem that a decision to commit suicide or sell oneself into slavery

---

[6]Sartre is particularly known for holding this view. He maintains that our freedom is so radical that it transcends even the bounds of morality. Because our values are established solely by our own choices, we also have a radical responsibility for what we choose.

[7] This view is advocated, in one form or another, by Socrates, Plato, Confucius, Jesus, Kant, Rousseau, natural law theorists, care ethicists, many virtue theorists, and Dewey, among others.

could ever be reconciled with the notion of autonomy—no matter how "authentic" the choice may be. As one philosopher sees it, such choices effectively elevate other values over the intrinsic value of oneself as an autonomous being. Given this perspective, embracing faulty values actually undermines autonomy.[8]

We've mentioned the haunting worry that we don't always know what's best for ourselves or what can enlarge our human potential. Children mistakenly see school as denying their freedom rather than as supplying the resources they need to become free and empowered adults. Similarly, someone who avoids relationships out of fear of being "tied down" ultimately denies herself the many opportunities and satisfactions relationships make possible. Yet again, some dedicate their lives to seeking wealth, fame, or power, only to discover later that their pursuit of these values has kept them from activities and experiences they would have much preferred.

To maximize our freedom and the range of our choices and opportunities, we must therefore reject value-neutral autonomy and authentically embrace those values that best promote personal and human growth and fulfillment— moral values in particular. This is what substantive conceptions of autonomy maintain.

For Discussion

1. *Do you agree that some sort of substantive autonomy is better than value-neutral autonomy? Why or why not?*
2. *Suppose that autonomy is best understood as value-neutral. Can you think of any way a person could autonomously choose her values?*

Summary
People often think of autonomy in purely negative terms, as the absence of any controls or influences. However, there are doubts about both the possibility and the desirability of a value-neutral autonomy. In its place, we must consider substantive autonomy, which maintains that by basing our choices especially upon moral values, we increase autonomy by expanding our human potential and our range of choices.

Key Terms
- **Value-neutral autonomy:** *the view that maximum autonomy amounts to choosing our values without constraint and that any set of values can serve equally well as the basis for a person's choices.*
- **Substantive autonomy:** *the view that maximum autonomy requires that our basic values be consistent with human fulfillment and flourishing, including the foundational values of morality.*

---

[8]This is Kant's view, which we will explore further in Chapter Eight.

VI.** RELATIONAL AUTONOMY

A particularly important type of substantive autonomy is **relational autonomy.** Deriving particularly from care ethics (see Chapter Twelve), *relational autonomy* hotly rejects individualism and instead emphasizes our interdependence and connectedness. In this view, autonomous individuals don't create relationships; rather, relationships create autonomous individuals. This is undeniably true of young children, since a child's earliest relationships form much of his ability to function as a person. Yet even adults are defined to a large degree by the important relationships in their lives.

Relational autonomy has been analyzed in many different ways. Here are a few of the most compelling ideas that have emerged. First, one of the primary ways we learn about ourselves is through our interactions with others. Other people can tell us how they see and understand us; we can also learn much as we observe ourselves relating to them. Second, relationships are central to how our personalities and identities develop. We are immersed in interpersonal relationships throughout our lives, and these naturally affect what we become as well as how we conceive of ourselves. The latter especially influences our actions as moral agents, since our choices usually align with our beliefs about what we are capable of. Third, our values are strongly influenced by others and the values they consider to be important. Does this diminish our own authenticity? According to the relational perspective, the *only* way to develop our own authentically held values is through a constant give-and-take with others, who can bring us new perspectives, challenge our previously held values, and introduce us to new experiences. We learn about ourselves, establish our own identity, and develop our authentic values through relationships.[9]

One further idea from relational autonomy has to do with the degree to which a person develops self-trust, self-esteem, and self-respect. Having a healthy dose of each of these self-directed attitudes enables us to make choices with assurance and expect others to show us deference. People without these attitudes second-guess their decisions and find themselves paralyzed when they must make even the simplest choices. This drastically limits their various abilities to act. What does this have to do with relationships? The recognition and respect we receive from others, as well as the way our social environment treats us, directly affects our attitudes about ourselves. "Oppressive social conditions of various kinds threaten those abilities by removing one's sense of self-confidence required for effective

---

[9]Diana Meyers calls this "self-discovery, self-definition, and self-direction" in her article "Intersectional Identity and the Authentic Self: Opposites Attract!" *Relational Autonomy*, eds. Catriona Mackenzie and Natalie Stoljar, (New York: Oxford University Press, 2000), 174–175. Originally quoted in Virginia Held, *The Ethics of Care: Personal, Political, and Global* (New York: Oxford University Press, 2007), 48.

agency. Social recognition and/or support for this self-trusting status is required for the full enjoyment of … [autonomy]."[10]

As you'd expect, then, healthy relationships contribute constructively toward one's autonomy; oppressive, manipulative, degrading relationships diminish autonomy. Thus, the moral quality of our relationships, our immediate social environment (e.g., friends and family), and the larger social and cultural systems in which we live all affect our development of autonomy. But the normative aspects of relational autonomy are not limited to just the moral realm. Other aspects of our relationships—intellectual, aesthetic, and more—affect us as well. Clearly, then, relational autonomy cannot be value-neutral.

If the previous ideas are correct, then we have some strong reasons for accepting some version of relational over individualistic autonomy. There are other reasons as well. For instance, a strong individualistic concept of persons is absurdly unrealistic. Humans are hardly more independent of each other than are different fauna in a sealed aquarium. Such interdependence is especially pronounced in modern society, where each person's safety, health, and even survival are at the mercy of others within a complex social network. Because we are essentially social beings, most of our emotional and psychological needs likewise can be met only through relationships.

All of us, furthermore, live large parts of our lives in almost total dependence upon others—as children, when we become sick, destitute, or disabled, and often as we become elderly. As for the important relationships in our lives, we have very little autonomous control over most of these. No child has a choice of who she will depend upon for many years, nor can anyone cease to be their parents' child. Even adults seldom have the luxury of choosing their instructors, neighbors, supervisors, or co-workers. And the social and cultural systems in which we live very much controls who we can relate to, how we relate to each other, and our view of ourselves.

Developing and exercising autonomy is of great importance to each of us, being an essential part of what it is to be a human person. Due to its many implications, it's also of central importance morally. It's encouraging, then, that new insights and perspectives on autonomy continue to develop. Among these, the normative conception of relational autonomy is a particularly promising recent contribution, and is worthy of careful consideration.

For Discussion

1. *What is there about relational autonomy that you find appealing, and what do you not find very appealing?*
2. *How do you understand "individualism"? Describe ways that our culture emphasizes individualism.*
3. *Does it bother you that there seem to be several strong reasons favoring relational autonomy over value-neutral autonomy? Why?*

---

[10]Christman, John, "Autonomy in Moral and Political Philosophy" in *The Stanford Encyclopedia of Philosophy* (Spring 2015 Edition), ed. Edward N. Zalta, accessed August 31, 2016, http://plato.stanford.edu/archives/spr2015/entries/autonomy-moral/.

Summary

One version of substantive autonomy is relational autonomy. This rejects our culture's emphases on self-sufficiency and independence, maintaining instead that full autonomy can only be realized through healthy relationships.

Key Terms

- **Relational autonomy:** rejects individualism and emphasizes the role of human interdependencies in self-discovery, establishing identity, developing authentic values, and trusting oneself.

Chapter Assignment Questions

1. *Courts commonly order children to undergo life-saving treatments (e.g., blood transfusions), regardless of their own or their parents' wishes. Courts seldom order adults to be treated against their wishes. Applying the analysis of autonomy, explain why this is so.*

2. *What gives parents and other adults the right to order children around at home, school, etc.?*

3. *How well does a five year old fulfill the three conditions for autonomy?*

4. *How well does a seventeen year old fulfill the three conditions for autonomy?*

5. *How completely do you fulfill the three conditions for personal autonomy?*

6. *Describe and explain some situations in which a normally autonomous adult can temporarily lose autonomy.*

7. *Explain why someone who is being deliberately misled cannot make a competent choice.*

8. *Identify some competent choices people commonly make. Why do they make these choices at this level, and how do they typically proceed in their deliberation?*

9. *What sorts of decisions would most appropriately call for an authentic choice?*

10. *The United States has recently abolished the death penalty for those under the age of eighteen. Based on our discussion of autonomy, what reasons can be given to support this change? What could be said against it?*

11. *Explain the differences between value-neutral and substantive autonomy.*

Additional Resources

Christman, John. "Autonomy in Moral and Political Philosophy." In *The Stanford Encyclopedia of Philosophy* (Spring 2015 Edition), edited by Edward N. Zalta. Accessed September 2, 2016. http://plato.stanford.edu/archives/spr2015/entries/autonomy-moral/. This article provides an extensive philosophical exploration of autonomy.

Dworkin, Gerald. "Paternalism." In *The Stanford Encyclopedia of Philosophy* (Spring 2017 edition), edited by Edward N. Zalta. http://plato.stanford.edu/archives/spr2017/entries/paternalism/. This article provides a good philosophical discussion of paternalism.

Sartre, Jean-Paul. "Existentialism Is a Humanism: A Lecture Given in 1946." In *Existentialism from Dostoyevsky to Sartre*, edited by Walter Kaufman. New York: Meridian, 1989.

First published by Cleveland, OH: World Publishing Company, 1956. Html mark-up by Andy Blunden, 2005. Accessed September 2, 2016. http://www.marxists.org/reference/archive/sartre/works/exist/sartre.htm. This presents Sartre's atheistic existentialism and introduces his view of radical human freedom.

Case 1

The Drunk Driver

Oliver and Charlotte are having dinner at their favorite Mexican restaurant. "Did you see the guy at the bar?" Oliver asks Charlotte? "He's on his fifth drink, I've been counting." "Must be at least that," Charlotte replies. "He was wobbling when he went to the restroom."

As they leave the restaurant a few minutes later, they notice the same man has also left and is fumbling with his car keys. He seems unable to get his key into the lock. "You have got to be kidding me," Charlotte exclaims in shock. "He's gonna drive? He'll kill someone." "Maybe he lives nearby," Oliver says. "Anyway, this is really none of our business. We don't even know this guy." "Does that really matter?" Charlotte retorts angrily. "Someone needs to stop him." Although Oliver doesn't seem too keen about this, he says, "Well, go ahead then—tell him to get a cab. But I'm just going to wait right here and watch. I'd rather not get involved."

THOUGHT QUESTIONS

1. Should Charlotte or Oliver interfere in this case? Is there anything else either of them could do? What?
2. Do you think they have a moral duty to keep the man from driving? Or do they instead have a duty to respect his autonomous choices to first drive to a restaurant and then drink too much?
3. Does Charlotte's proposed act qualify as morally justified paternalism?
4. Is the drunk man autonomous? If not, what conditions does he fail to satisfy at this moment?

Case 2

Elizabeth Bouvia[11]

Elizabeth Bouvia was born a quadriplegic resulting from cerebral palsy. For the first few years of her life, both of her parents cared for her. When she was five, however, her parents separated, and Elizabeth went to live with her mother. Then, when Elizabeth was ten, her mother remarried, and Elizabeth was put in a home for disabled children. One thing young Elizabeth did not lack was determination. Despite her

Continued

---

[11]Mary Johnson, "Right to Life, Right to Die: The Elizabeth Bouvia Saga," "*BroadReach Counseling and Mediation* (from *The Ragged Edge*, January/February 1997), accessed September 4, 2016, http://www.broadreachtraining.com/advocacy/artbouvia.htm. The Bouvia case is a much-quoted case in medical ethics. Information about the case can also be found in the *National Review*, May 4, 1998; on November 8, 1998, the television show *60 Minutes* aired an episode about Bouvia.

Case 2 (Continued)

troubled start in life, Elizabeth eventually worked her way through college, earned a bachelor's degree (with support from the state), and married.

Unfortunately, events took a turn for the worse about the time she started working on her master's degree. First, Elizabeth suffered a miscarriage. Then, being unable to deal with her disability, her husband left her. Next, Elizabeth's mother became ill with cancer. In the midst of these traumatic experiences, Elizabeth's arthritis was putting her through nearly unbearable pain. Unable to cope any longer, she checked herself into a hospital, where she was put on a morphine drip to control the pain. Still unable to find relief, Elizabeth decided that she wanted to end her life. She refused to eat, so doctors inserted a feeding tube into her stomach. Elizabeth then petitioned the court of California to have the tube removed. When asked at a news conference whether she really wanted to die, Elizabeth explained that she felt that she no longer had any quality of life. The court initially denied Elizabeth's request; upon appeal, however, the courts reversed the earlier decision and allowed the feeding tube to be removed. Once this was done, Elizabeth again stopped eating but soon gave up on the attempt to starve herself to death. When another doctor offered Elizabeth an aggressive program of pain management, she accepted. Elizabeth Bouvia is still alive today.

Although it's certainly very difficult to judge Ms. Bouvia's attitudes and actions, they do raise several important concerns. Most obviously, of course, Elizabeth's trying to die amounted to an attempted suicide. Furthermore, a number of disability groups have been highly critical of Elizabeth's efforts to end her life. As they see it, Ms. Bouvia's actions demean persons with disabilities because they imply that life with a disability is not worth living. These people feel that a meaningful life is possible even for a person in Elizabeth's situation. If a disabled person were to desire to commit suicide, it would probably be because that person is not receiving proper care—a problem common within our society. Proper care certainly includes effective pain management but also much more. The state of California offers home support services, for instance, which allows a severely disabled person to live in her own home and receive all necessary care. In addition, there are work programs designed to help the disabled find suitable employment.

Was Elizabeth Bouvia familiar with these opportunities and open to them? She claimed that she knew all about these options but refused to take advantage of them. She did not like the idea of someone else taking care of her. Elizabeth also steadfastly refused any counseling or help. Anxious over her behavior, her ex-husband requested that she receive a psychiatric evaluation (which the court refused). Elizabeth's father was also upset by her actions. In response to her claim that she had received no love, her father maintained that she had refused his help. Was Elizabeth's attempt to end her life simply an act of despair resulting from an episode of deep depression, self-pity, and withdrawal?

Elizabeth insisted that it was not. In thinking about ending her life, she claimed to have reviewed her options and that her decision was based on careful reflection. She also strongly emphasized her right to autonomy. Elizabeth was only twenty-six years old at this time. In representing Elizabeth, her lawyer maintained that Ms. Bouvia had the right to make her own choice, regardless of what choice that was.

THOUGHT QUESTIONS

1. Do you think that Elizabeth's attempt to end her life amounted to an autonomous, carefully reasoned decision of a fully competent adult? What evidence, pro and con, is there to support your view? (What is necessary to make an autonomous decision?)
2. Do you think that Elizabeth ever seriously meant to end her life?
3. Was Elizabeth making a morally right choice? Why or why not?
4. Could it ever be morally justified for a person in a situation like Elizabeth's to choose to end her life? If so, what level of moral agency would be necessary for such a choice to be justified?

Case 3

Should the Drinking Age Be Eighteen?

In the majority of countries around the world, the legal drinking age is eighteen. Germany, Ethiopia, Brazil, and China, just to name a few, all allow both the purchase and the drinking of alcohol at that age. In the United States, however, the purchase and consumption of alcohol under the age of twenty-one is prohibited, even while the legal age for both smoking and voting is eighteen.[12]

The reasons for this are largely connected to drinking and driving. According to a November 2008 press release by the National Highway Traffic Safety Administration, a report showed that the strict drinking age laws saved 3,940 lives between 2003 and 2009.[13]

Younger drivers tend to be less safe. The high insurance premiums for drivers under twenty-five attest to that. One reason for this is surely that younger drivers are less experienced. Add alcohol to that, and the mix can be deadly. If it results in fewer alcohol-related traffic fatalities, then surely the idea of restricting the drinking age must be a good thing, right? Oddly, no one seems to consider the alternative of raising the driving age or strengthening driving requirements.

The idea that a higher drinking age lowers fatalities seems to imply that those under the age of twenty-one are not sufficiently competent to make reasonable decisions about drinking and driving. In short, they are not fully autonomous. Even if they understand the risks associated with drinking and driving, they may still not appreciate these risks sufficiently to make wise choices. Restricting those choices protects others (i.e., passengers, pedestrians) as well as the driver.

Still, one may wonder why the rest of the world does not restrict drinking in the same way. Of particular interest here may be the case of Germany. Because Germany does not have a speed limit on freeways and because it is densely populated, there are many traffic fatalities. Wouldn't the government want to prohibit drinking under the age of twenty-one? Here's one line of argument for why it

Continued

---

[12]There is no national law that sets the drinking age. But if a state sets a drinking age lower than twenty-one, it forfeits 10% of its federal highway funds. Consequently, all fifty states have set the drinking age at twenty-one.

[13]This report can be downloaded from the National Traffic Highway Safety Administration. "Lives Saved in 2009 by Restraint Use and Minimum-Drinking-Age Laws," *National Traffic Highway Safety Administration,* July 2010, accessed August 31, 2016, http://www-nrd.nhtsa.dot.gov/Pubs/811383.pdf.

Case 3 (*Continued*)

would not: autonomy is something that must be learned. If freedoms are gradually increased and if people are sufficiently educated (learning to drive in Germany requires up to forty driving lessons with a licensed professional and a rigorous course of study of traffic laws), then they can learn to make better choices earlier in life. In other words, the sooner you give people responsibility, the sooner they will learn to live up to it. It seems that the German government thinks eighteen-year-olds are old enough to accept and deal with certain issues, including drinking and driving.

A similar argument is made by a U.S. nonprofit group called *Choose Responsibility*, which tries to get the drinking age lowered to eighteen. The group says that if eighteen-year-olds "have the right to marry, adopt children, serve as legal guardians for minors and purchase firearms from authorized dealers, and are trusted with the vote and military responsibility," then they can and should also be trusted to drink responsibly.[14] The group suggests that the current drinking age "infantilizes adults." It advocates a program by which young adults are educated about alcohol and become licensed to use it, so that they can make more responsible choices about drinking.[15] Because illegal drinking in dorms has led to many deaths on campus (students hide their binge drinking, making it hard to identify and help a drinker in trouble), numerous college presidents have also come out in support of a lower drinking age.[16]

THOUGHT QUESTIONS

1. Other than drinking and driving, what reasons do you think the U.S. government has for prohibiting alcohol to those under the age of twenty-one?
2. What level of moral agency do you think is required to make well-reasoned choices about drinking and driving?
3. Discuss the role of reasoning in decisions about drinking and driving. Why do some people risk drinking and driving when others do not? Do they not fully appreciate the consequences of their choices or do they just not care?
4. What different values do German lawmakers seem to be using compared to U.S. lawmakers? Explain. Given Germany's dense population and fewer speed limits, are the German lawmakers taking unnecessary risks?
5. Are the U.S. drinking restrictions paternalistic? To what degree should we limit individual freedoms to keep people from harming themselves?
6. Do you think that the drinking age in the United States should be lowered to eighteen? Use the analyses of autonomy and agency to support your view.

---

[14]George F. Will, "Drinking Age Paradox," *Washington Post*, April 19, 2007, A27.

[15]Choose Responsibility, accessed August 31, 2016, http://www.chooseresponsibility.org.

[16]See the Amethyst Initiative Statement, accessed August 31, 2016, http://www.theamethystinitiative.org/statement/ and the Amethyst Initiative signatories, accessed August 31, 2016, http://www.theamethyst initiative.org/signatories/.

Case 4

The Living Will

Since the ordeal of Terri Schiavo—the woman in a permanent vegetative state who spent more than ten years on a feeding tube (partly because she had no living will)—the number of people preparing living wills has dramatically increased.

These documents are intended to extend the moral agency of an individual beyond the stage at which they are competent to make informed healthcare decisions. A living will allows individuals to state their medical preferences for times when they have a terminal condition (e.g., cancer), have deteriorated mentally (e.g., Alzheimer's disease), or are in a permanent vegetative state. In such circumstances, the will would specify the individual's choice regarding the continuation of life-sustaining treatment or regarding resuscitation.

Filling out a living will requires a great deal of preparation and thought. The document itself should be read very carefully. A doctor and lawyer should be consulted to discuss one's health concerns along with family and friends. It's also wise to establish a medical power of attorney for someone to be named as a proxy—someone who can enforce the patient's wishes as necessary. Once the will has been completed and signed, copies should be distributed to the individual's doctor, health care institution, and the medical proxy. Family should also be informed.

What does a living will look like? Here are excerpts from the New Jersey Instruction Directive.[17]

GENERAL INSTRUCTIONS: … Initial ONE of the following two statements with which you agree:

1. _____ I direct that all medically appropriate measures be provided to sustain my life, regardless of my physical or mental condition

2. _____ There are circumstances in which I would not want my life to be prolonged by further medical treatment. In these circumstances, life-sustaining measures should not be initiated and if they have been, they should be discontinued. I recognize that this is likely to hasten my death. In the following, I specify the circumstances in which I would choose to forego life-sustaining measures.

… SPECIFIC INSTRUCTIONS: …

Here you are asked to give specific instructions regarding two types of life-sustaining measures-artificially provided fluids and nutrition and cardiopulmonary resuscitation.

In the space provided, write in the bracketed phrase with which you agree:

1. … I also direct that artificially provided fluids and nutrition, such as by feeding tube or intravenous infusion, _____

[be withheld or withdrawn and that I be allowed to die]

[be provided to the extent medically appropriate]

Continued

---

[17]Directives can differ significantly, depending on the state and its laws. "Instruction Directive," *The New Jersey Commission on Legal and Ethical Problems in the Delivery of Health Care,* accessed September 1, 2016, http://www.nj.gov/health/advancedirective/documents/instruction_directive.pdf. For more on the New Jersey advanced directives, see "Advanced Directive," *State of New Jersey Department of Health,* accessed September 1, 2016, http://www.nj.gov/health/advancedirective/ad/forums-faqs/.

Case 4 (Continued)

2. ... If I should suffer a cardiac arrest, I also direct that cardiopulmonary resuscitation (CPR) _____

[not be provided and that I be allowed to die]

[be provided to preserve my life, unless medically inappropriate or futile]

3. If neither of the above statements adequately expresses your wishes concerning artificially provided fluids and nutrition or CPR, please explain your wishes below. _____...

The directive also contains clauses addressing cases in which the patient is severely mentally deteriorated or pregnant; additional requests can also be added as desired.

Living wills appear to provide a desirable means for extending a person's moral agency to situations in which that person still has important interests but cannot act on their own behalf. Because living wills address life-and-death issues, however, it's morally necessary that the person's will be made up of competent or even authentic choices; a lesser choice wouldn't provide sufficient moral justification for following a will's instructions.

As we've seen, a person lacking important knowledge relevant to making their decisions may still make a bad competent choice. But when it is a life-or-death matter, even one's competent choice may sometimes be justifiably ignored (paternalism). Consider this: could a person who has never given birth really understand what that experience is like? Could a person who has never fought correctly anticipate how they would act in a battle? If you've never experienced anything like *that* before, then can you accurately judge what will be most important to you when *that* comes your way later on? People often see a situation differently once they actually experience something like it. So imagine a healthy person, in life's prime and full of the pleasures and struggles of everyday life; can she adequately anticipate the values and concerns most important to her when she is dying of an incurable illness? Or experiencing severe, chronic pain? It's not clear that making a sufficiently knowledgeable choice about such things beforehand is even possible, though it appears to be a moral necessity (see also Chapter Fourteen, §II).

THOUGHT QUESTIONS

1. Do you understand all the terms used in the excerpts of New Jersey Instruction Directive? If not, what terms are not clear to you? How would you clarify these terms for yourself?
2. Is it morally okay for someone to sign such a document if the signer does not understand all of the terms in the document? Why or why not?
3. Pregnancy is singled out as a condition warranting special consideration. What moral issues are behind that?
4. What moral values come into play with the use of living wills?
5. What are the problems and advantages of setting up a living will for yourself while you are still in good health?
6. Do you think that, at present, you can adequately imagine what medical care you might want or not want in the kinds of situations addressed by a living

will? This is why people are now encouraged to establish medical proxies as well. What advantages does having a carefully chosen proxy add to having a living will?

Case 5

Buy Now, Pay Later: Student Credit Card Debt

You've seen it, right? Someone is sitting at a table outside the college cafeteria, wanting eagerly to offer *you* a special student credit card with no annual fee! To sweeten the deal, they may offer you a 0% interest rate for the first six months and immediate approval as well, even if you've never previously held any credit. Who could resist such a deal?

Apparently, many can't. The average college student has $500 in credit card debt according to NASDAQ.[18] Even more unsettling is the fact that 10% of educational debt is carried by credit cards—an extremely expensive way to attend college.[19]

Credit cards are valuable financial tools, but they require careful and knowledgeable use. People don't always realize, for instance, that they may be charged hefty fees for a late payment or if they run over their credit limit.

Many companies aggressively market their credit cards to people who are a high credit risk. Why? If they play their cards carefully enough, credit companies can make good money off of these sorts of borrowers. Suppose you build up a large card balance and then can't afford to pay much more than the minimum required monthly payment. This can easily leave you paying *nothing but interest* for years while never actually freeing yourself from the debt itself (the borrowed principal). That may be bad for you, but not for lenders who make most of their profits on interest and fees.

Some of the worst arrangements come from stores that issue their own credit cards. For one thing, having a particular store's card increases the likelihood the customer will make more purchases at that store. Second, store cards often have a higher interest rate than regular credit cards—even 20% or more. (Ordinary cards sometimes set their rates this high for new credit holders, such as students.) So, do the math: a $1,000 purchase stretched out over a year at 20% costs the cardholder $200 in interest, even without any other fees. Not paying can take the interest rate up as high as 30%—even at a time when the government is lending at almost no interest.

When a lender has a good thing going, would he want you to pay down your debt? Actually, companies call those who pay off their entire balance every month "deadbeats" (because they avoid paying the company any fees or interest charges). Really smart deadbeats may even earn "rewards" on their purchases so that they *make money* by using their card. Naturally, credit companies much prefer more naive borrowers who don't manage their money well, who spend beyond their means, and who don't understand all the ins and outs of credit. Students are high on their targeted list. Want to keep your card company happy about you? Just spend and borrow in ways that will make you the loser who pays loads of interest and maybe some fees every month.

---

[18]"Credit Card Debt Statistics," Nasdaq, September 23, 2014, accessed October 15, 2015, http://www.nasdaq.com/article/credit-card-debt-statistics-cm393820.

[19] Blake Ellis, "Class of 2013 Grads Average $35,200 in Total Debt," CNN Money, May 17, 2013, accessed September 1,2016, http://money.cnn.com/2013/05/17/pf/college/student-debt/.

THOUGHT QUESTIONS

1. Do you have your own credit card? Do you fully understand its terms and conditions or at least know how to find out? Should the government require credit companies to inform individuals about the risks of credit card debt?

2. How does the temptation to buy a new TV, iPhone, or new clothes affect a person's ability to make a responsible choice? Are older people likely to resist temptations better than teens and/or college students?

3. Do you think that lenders share some of the *moral* responsibility when a student gets into serious credit card debt?

4. American credit card debt is higher than anywhere else in the world. Why do so many Americans get themselves into trouble with credit? At what level do you think these people have acted as moral agents regarding their credit?

5. Other sorts of systems exist. For instance, a German "credit card" is more like a debit card. There's no interest and all charges are automatically deducted from a specified account monthly. To extend your debt longer than a month, you must overdraw your account at whatever interest the bank specifies. Most accounts allow automatic overdrafts, usually limited to about one month's pay. Is this system paternalistic? Is it morally preferable to the American system? Why?

6. Make a self-assessment: do you pay your credit card bill each month on time? Do you make only minimum payments? What is your favorite' card's interest rate? What do you buy with it—only special things or everyday items like pizza and groceries? Have you ever needed someone to bail you out with your monthly payment? What do your answers tell you about yourself as a moral agent regarding your use of credit cards? If there's a problem, what is it?

CHAPTER FOUR

Making Moral Judgments

I. INTRODUCTION

Although she was driving through torrential rains, Sandra Mendenez barely noticed the weather. The chaos of water washing down her windshield seemed like nothing compared with the turmoil swirling inside. Sandra, the director of an adult English as a second language (ESL) program, was returning home from teaching her regular Friday night ESL class. Her favorite student, José, had seemed particularly nervous and distracted, and Sandra had asked him after class if everything was okay. At that, José had broken down completely. Piecing his story together, Sandra learned that José was an illegal immigrant from Honduras and had lived 13 months in the United States. His troubles had started after he'd refused to join a street gang that controlled his Honduran hometown. From that time on, he had been repeatedly threatened, robbed, and beaten. After he some-how managed to get out and make his way to New York, José had met Edgar, a Guatemalan who had come to the United States two years ago from a similar background. They had become friends, pooled their resources, and begun work-ing to establish a better life for themselves in the United States. Just a few weeks ago, however, Edgar had been deported back to Guatemala. Then, last night, José had heard that Edgar had been murdered by a gang soon after his return. Grief stricken and terrified, José felt he had nowhere to turn.[1]

Beside the heart-wrenching emotions this was causing Sandra, it also began to dawn on her that she had a real dilemma on her hands. Because she received government aid for her ESL program, she occasionally had to fill out a report documenting her students. However, she could hardly imagine reporting José as an illegal. That could lead to José's deportation—which she found unthinkable. However, her program funding could be suspended if the government were to determine that she had harbored an illegal. Nor could she ask José to drop the

---

[1]This story is based on an Associated Press article by Jennifer Kay, "Fleeing the Gangs of Central America; U.S. Denies Asylum to Desperate Youths," *The Star Ledger*, May 25, 2006. Edgar Chocoy, a Guatemalan teen, was killed by gang members shortly after being deported back to his homeland.

program, for he now needed the friendship and support he found there more than ever. But how could she submit a false report about José to the government? That would also put her program at risk; worse, it would be lying. Despite her turmoil, Sandra felt sure about one thing: It was extremely important that she do the *right* thing. She just didn't know what that was.

*   *   *

Although Sandra's predicament includes legal matters, her professional responsibilities, and her own personal feelings, what Sandra ultimately seeks is a *moral* solution to the question: *What should she do about José?*

For Discussion

1. *What different sorts of normative claims (prudential, legal, moral, etc.) come into play in Sandra's situation?*
2. *What is the morally right thing for her to do? Why?*
3. *What moral dilemmas from ordinary life have you faced, and how have you responded?*

Summary
Moral dilemmas and problems can develop in very ordinary, day-to-day situations. Moral concerns can conflict with prudential, legal, and other normative concerns. They can even pit moral claims against other moral claims.

II. CONFLICTS

In discussing values (see Chapter One), we saw that there are several different normative realms, each with its own values and prescriptive claims. As Sandra's story shows, a single situation can bring several of these realms into conflict with each other. A number of considerations pull Sandra in the direction of truthfully reporting José: she has a *legal* duty to report him, a *prudential* motivation to not jeopardize her ESL program, and a *moral* responsibility to tell the truth. But other considerations push Sandra in the opposite direction: she also has prudential reasons for protecting her program by *not* reporting him, and she has moral duties to remain loyal to José, to support his need for friends, and to do what she can to protect his life—a genuine concern in this case. Whether we describe her situation in terms of conflicting normative realms, values, or prescriptions, life has clearly handed her a serious predicament. No wonder Sandra is torn about what to do!

One fact about normative realms can help Sandra a little. Although claims from any normative realm are important, *moral* values and prescriptions tend to **override** other normative claims. Let's explore this.

Surely, claims of etiquette should not take precedence over moral claims. But what about legal and prudential claims—don't these sometimes rival moral claims in importance? There is no tension when a claim from another realm *agrees* with an applicable moral claim—for instance, Sandra is legally and morally called upon to be honest. This sort of overlap is not unusual, since many laws derive from moral claims. Yet doesn't this imply a priority of the moral over law? There is also a long-standing precedent for deferring to moral values when a law violates those requirements. In opposing racially discriminatory laws, Martin Luther King Jr. appealed to the moral requirements of justice, as did those nations that boycotted South Africa's system of apartheid. Abolitionists likewise battled slavery on moral grounds.

As for the prudential, it must be admitted that people sometimes do put their own interests before the demands of morality. However, it's also notable that we usually judge such choices to be *wrong*. We condemn politicians who sacrifice their constituents' good to keep themselves in office; we admire people who lay aside their own interests for some greater good. For instance, we commemorate civil rights protesters who risked being attacked by dogs and clubbed by police as they fought for equality. We also commend those soldiers, doctors, and relief workers who risk their lives to combat genocide, rampaging diseases, and injustices around the world. These observations support the priority of moral values over other normative concerns.

Is it also possible for one *moral* value to override other *moral* values? Cases like Sandra's—where moral values also conflict with each other—suggest that this must be possible. Sandra's situation pits the moral value of truth telling against that of loyalty. Clearly, one of these values will have to take precedence over the other if Sandra is to resolve her dilemma.

For Discussion
1. *Do you think that moral claims always override other types of claims? Why or why not?*
2. *Identify several moral values and then discuss which seem most important.*

Summary
When moral claims conflict with other normative claims, moral claims tend to override other types of claims. It's fairly obvious that the moral overrides etiquette; it also seems to override both legal and prudential claims. It's also possible for one moral claim to take precedence over another moral claim.

Key Terms
- **Override:** *to take precedence or priority over other claims.*

III. CHARACTERIZING MORAL CLAIMS

By now, you should be fairly clear about what moral claims *are* and what they *are not*. But let's try to be more precise. It seems that any moral claim—whether value or prescriptive—must be:

1. *Normative:* Moral claims are not descriptive. Instead, they ultimately derive from some moral norm or standard. A moral prescriptive claim says something about what we should or should not do. A moral value claim usually asserts something about a person or a character trait like honesty or dishonesty, kindness or selfishness.

2. *Truth claim:* Moral claims are statements and so make assertions that are either true or false. This is important, because it places moral discussions within the range of rational consideration. Being true or false, moral claims can be supported or opposed by reasoned argument rather than, say, our mere feelings.[2] Truth claims contrast with questions ("Why did you arrive early?") and pure expressions of emotion ("Oh no!"), neither of which can be true or false.[3] Truth claims can also be contrasted with commands ("Don't lie"), which likewise cannot strictly be true or false. Nevertheless, commands are easily converted into prescriptive claims ("No one should lie"), which *are* either true or false. Allowing for this, we will treat moral commands as indirectly expressing their corresponding true or false prescriptive claims.[4]

3. *Universalizable:* Moral claims can commonly be generalized. It doesn't seem possible for one person to have a moral right, for instance, that others could not also have. Even when addressed to a single person, a moral claim can be extended to other persons in similar circumstances. Since every person belongs on the same moral footing, any moral claim should hold for everyone in the same way. Universalizability distinguishes moral claims from the claims of both law and etiquette, which vary depending on governments and social convention, respectively.

4. *Overriding:* Although non-moral normative claims are important for guiding our behavior, moral claims tend to override or take precedence over other kinds of normative claims. We saw this in Sandra's case as well as in the cases of many moral reformers who engaged in civil disobedience. Moral claims also override claims of etiquette and even prudential claims.

For Discussion

1. *Why is it important that moral claims be truth claims?*
2. *Would you remove or add anything to this characterization of moral claims?*

---

[2]An argument is a set of statements (the premises) intended to support the truth of another statement (the conclusion).

[3]Against this requirement, *emotivism* maintains that although moral claims *appear* to be truth claims, they actually express nothing more than one's emotional approval or disapproval.

[4]In our terminology (see Chapter One, §III), any objectively true claim *holds* for everyone, though it may not *apply* to everyone, depending on their particular circumstances.

3. *Emotivism maintains that moral claims express nothing other than our emotional approval or disapproval. (See footnote 3.) What do you think about this?*

Summary

Moral claims have certain defining characteristics. Like claims in the other normative realms, moral claims are normative and are truth claims. More distinctively, they also seem to be universalizable. Moral claims may be uniquely overriding.

Key Terms

- **Truth claim:** *asserts something true or false.*
- **Universalizable:** *can be generalized to all people, not just some.*

IV. MORAL REASONING

We have seen (see Chapter One) how one or more foundational values might serve as a basis for deriving and explaining *all* moral claims. Any instrumental value (or instrumental value claim) can ultimately be derived from more foundational values. In addition, any prescriptive claim can ultimately be derived from some value or values. But since moral claims can only be either prescriptive or value claims, all moral claims should ultimately be derivable from some set of foundational values—whether those values are moral or non-moral. This is what most ethical theories attempt to show.

To understand these derivations, we must understand *moral reasoning*. Although people engage in moral thinking all the time, it will help to explicitly lay out a reasoning pattern people follow when they do this. Understanding this pattern will then equip us to understand how moral theories work.

Let's return to Sandra and her moral dilemma concerning José. In struggling with this problem, Sandra's thought of several important moral values. She was particularly concerned about José's life and about being dishonest. Laying out each step of her reasoning with regard to the first might yield something like the following:

1. A human life is a great moral good. (principle)

My reporting José could later endanger his life. (descriptive claim)

_____

Thus, I shouldn't endanger José's life by reporting him. (judgment)

Similarly for dishonesty:

2. No one should lie or deceive others. (principle)

By not reporting José on the form, I would deceive others. (descriptive claim)

_____

Thus, I ought to report José. (judgment)

These examples include three distinct kinds of claims—a *principle*, a *descriptive claim*, and a *judgment*.[5] In the first example, Sandra appeals to a moral value claim about human life. This is a *moral principle* because it expresses a generalization: it holds for everyone and says nothing about any particular situation or person. However, the principle alone can't entail what *Sandra* should do *in her particular situation*; it says nothing about deportation, murderous gangs, Sandra, or José. So Sandra also needs to summarize the situation using a descriptive claim: reporting José could later endanger his life. Remember that descriptive claims are *not* normative: they say something about the world as it is and not as it should be. By itself, the descriptive claim doesn't tell Sandra what to do either. What it does do is relate José's life directly to the principle about human life. Taken together, these claims then support the *judgment* that Sandra should not report José. Unlike moral principles, a **moral judgment** makes a *limited* moral claim: it says something about *specific* persons and *specific* situations.

The same pattern is evidenced in the second example. Again, there's a moral principle, though this time the principle is *prescriptive*. Since principles are too general to say what Sandra should do, a descriptive claim is added to relate the principle to her situation. The combination of these (their order makes no difference) then leads her to the conclusion—a moral judgment—that she ought to report José.

The pattern of reasoning in both examples comes to the following.

Principle + Descriptive Claim(s) → Judgment

Again, *principles* hold for everyone; *judgments*, however, apply only to particular individuals and circumstances. Any *descriptive claims* (there may be more than one) link the principle to the judgment by describing the situation being addressed by that judgment.

We will call this standardized pattern of thinking **moral reasoning**. We often employ moral reasoning to make moral judgments, and it doesn't matter whether the principle happens to be a value or prescriptive claim. But Sandra now has conflicting judgments to deal with. Is there any way for her to resolve this conflict and so determine what she ought to do? There may be. Suppose that another moral principle asserts that protecting human life is more important than telling the truth. She might then reason as follows:

3. It is morally more important to protect someone's life from danger than to tell the truth. (principle)[6]

My situation forces me either to endanger José's life by telling the truth or to protect his life by lying. (descriptive claim)

———————

Thus, it is right in this situation to lie about José to protect his life. (judgment).

———————

[5] Descriptive, prescriptive, and value claims were introduced in Chapter One, Section II.
[6] We do not mean to suggest that we hold this or any of the principles used in these examples.

Even young children follow this pattern in their thinking (though people seldom do this explicitly):

4. I know that, when asked a question, people should tell the truth. (principle)

Mom just asked me if I ate the last cookie. (descriptive claim)

I did eat the last cookie. (descriptive claim)

_____

Thus, I should tell Mom that I was the one who ate the last cookie. (judgment)

All of these examples use the same reasoning pattern to arrive at a moral judgment. It turns out that a very similar pattern can be used to derive other principles from more fundamental moral principles. Let's go back to the moral principles Sandra might appeal to:

(a) Nobody should lie or deceive others.
(b) A human life has foundational moral worth.

Being principles, these two claims are already universal. However, Sandra might also have given thought to more fundamental principles like:

(c) One should always do what promotes the greatest amount of overall happiness.
(d) We should never treat persons as mere means to achieve our own ends.
(e) We should act toward others the same way we'd like them to act toward us.

Can you see that these five principles differ in their generality? Principle **(a)** talks about lying, but doesn't say anything about capital punishment, murder, or burglary. While **(b)** has implications for murder (and perhaps for capital punishment), it says nothing about breaking promises. In contrast, **(c)**, **(d)**, and **(e)** seem relevant to just about anything we might consider doing. Let's call these **foundational moral principles**—principles from which other moral claims (including other principles) can be derived. Because we don't want an endless string of derivations, we should add that foundational principles must also be truly basic: no foundational moral principle can be derived from any yet more foundational moral principle.

Foundational principles can support many other principles. For instance, **(c)** seems to support moral principles like "People shouldn't commit murder" and "No one should intentionally injure an innocent person," since violating these normally reduces overall happiness. Principle **(d)** supports principles against lying, holding slaves, and bribing politicians to change their votes. Principle **(e)** likewise seems to support a great many derived principles.

The pattern of reasoning for deriving principles is:

Foundational principle + Descriptive claim(s) → Derived principle

Here are some examples:
6. One should do what best promotes overall happiness. (foundational principle)

Taking others' things produces more pain than happiness. (descriptive claim)

No one should take what belongs to another. (derived principle)

7. Never treat people as mere means to achieve your ends. (foundational principle)

Lying treats another person as merely a means to get something we want. (descriptive claim)

We should not lie. (derived principle)

Each of these cites a more general principle, which is then brought "down to earth" a bit by some descriptive claim(s) to yield some less general principle. This suggests that any non-foundational moral principle (whether a prescriptive or a value claim) can ultimately be derived from one or more foundational principles. If the latter consist solely of value claims, then all moral claims can be derived, as suggested previously, from just one or a few foundational values. Much of ethics has tried to identify a set of truly foundational moral principles or values—what an ethical theory takes to be the basis of the moral realm.

For Discussion
1. *Come up with some moral principles. Use the pattern* **Principle + Descriptive Claim(s) → Judgment** *to infer judgments from each of these.*
2. *Come up with some moral judgments. In keeping with the pattern* **Principle + Descriptive Claim(s) → Judgment**, *suggest principles from which each of these judgments could be inferred.*
3. *Thoughtfully evaluate the moral principle: "It is wrong to do anything that could harm another." Is it true? Is it foundational?*
4. *Following the same pattern demonstrated with principles (c) and (d), show how principle (e) can also be used to derive other moral principles.*

Summary

Moral judgments may be inferred from moral principles using the pattern we are call-ing moral reasoning:

Principle + Descriptive claim(s) → Judgment

Moral principles are general moral claims (whether value or prescriptive) that are not specifically about any particular situation. In contrast, a judgment is limited and only applies to some specific set of cases. Though we are seldom explicitly aware of it, we often employ this pattern. Roughly the same pattern can also be used to derive more limited moral principles from more foundational principles:

Foundational principle + Descriptive claim(s) → Derived principle

A foundational moral principle supports all other moral principles and is also basic: it cannot itself be derived from any more foundational moral principle. A complete set of foundational moral principles can serve as a basis for deriving all other moral claims. Most ethical theories attempt to identify such a basis.

Key Terms

- **Moral principle:** *a moral generalization that holds for everyone in the same way. Principles are not limited to particular people or situations.*
- **Moral judgment:** *a moral claim limited to specific people or situations.*
- **Foundational moral principle:** *a moral principle that can serve as the basis for deriving other moral principles but that cannot be derived from any more foundational moral principle.*
- **Moral reasoning:** *the reasoning pattern above that yields a moral judgment.*

V. MORAL REFLECTION

The previous pattern has often been considered the only way to arrive at moral judgments. However, this view has come under fire by those who challenge the universalizability requirement for moral claims.[7] According to **moral particularism**, many moral judgments are not inferred from moral principles but can only be made case by case. In this view, it's particularly important that we reflect carefully upon the moral features and nuances of the setting before making any judgment. (See Chapters Eleven and Twelve for theories taking this approach.)

Your eight-year old child is dying of cancer, and is very afraid. She has asked whether or not she will survive. What should you tell her? The moral principle about always telling the truth furnishes a clear answer, but is it that simple? Perhaps there's a conflicting moral principle about not harming others, and you know she will fall into painful terror if told the truth. Given this conflict, is your problem now just a matter of determining which principle takes precedence? In fact, it seems that you need to reflect more deeply than this. Imagine, then, that you have previously seen your child demonstrate an inner resolve that has enabled her to reconcile herself to fears and disappointments. Furthermore, you know that she trusts you implicitly and would be deeply hurt if she ever thought that you might mislead her. You also know that she would want you close to encourage and support her attempts to understand and accept her dying. You expect that, in the end, she will arrive at a state of moral and emotional strength that she could not achieve any other way. You also know yourself, and that while you cringe at the thought of her initial terror, you want to "be there" for her as a trustworthy companion, and you want to share her struggle with sensitivity and care. Finally, you recognize that if you did not personally tell her, you would feel compromised and guilty for the rest of your life. In view of all these reasons, you decide that you should tell her.

---

[7]This is why we initially referred to the pattern as the "standardized" pattern, meaning to imply that it's not the only possible pattern for moral thinking.

It's hard to imagine arriving at this judgment without reflecting in this way upon all the situation's particulars. Although these reflections are clearly moral, it seems too difficult and even unnatural to insist that they all be reformulated into a set of inferences that all follow the pattern: *principle, description, judgment.*[8] Notice that these reflections focus especially upon (a) the nature and expectations of each person involved and (b) the nature of the relationship(s) between them. This is no accident, for as moral particularists often maintain, the moral problems of individuals and relationships involve too many unique but crucial details for any universal principle to capture. If this is true, then maybe there's another way to think through moral judgments. This alternate pattern—***moral reflection***—is still a kind of moral thinking but not one that infers judgments from principles. Although it does include descriptive claims, these no longer serve to relate principles to circumstances. Their role, instead, is to *"frame" the entire moral setting.* They indicate what the moral judgment needs to be about and which considerations are most relevant to arriving at this judgment. The pattern seems to be:

Descriptive claim(s) +

Moral considerations about the persons involved +

Moral considerations about the interpersonal relationships involved

→ *Moral judgment*

Here is how this might work out for the dying child story:

Your eight-year-old child is dying of cancer. (descriptive claim)

She is very afraid of dying. (descriptive claim)

She has asked you whether or not she will survive. (descriptive claim)

You and she have an ongoing and close relationship. (descriptive claim)

She has the strength to overcome her fear. (moral consideration: child)

The truth will develop her morally/emotionally. (moral consideration: child)

Not telling her would wound and compromise you. (moral consideration: you)

She trusts you and expects your honesty. (moral consideration - relationship)

She needs your support while dying. (moral consideration - relationship)

You want to caringly share her struggles. (moral consideration - relationship)

——— ———

You should tell her the truth that she is dying. (moral judgment)

---

[8]Of course, just because a thing is hard doesn't prove it can't be done. A *universalist* would reply that these considerations *could* be analyzed into several separate uses of *moral reasoning,* each having its own principle and each describing distinct facts about the situation.

We do seem to think through many of our moral judgments—particularly those that center on personal characteristics and relationships—in this way. Does this pattern genuinely differ from that of moral reasoning? Could it at least be strengthened by adding some relevant moral principles as well? These questions raise controversies. But in any case, moral reflection has a feel of familiarity and reality that sometimes seems lacking in the more analytic, principle-based pattern of moral reasoning.

For Discussion

1. *What is the morally right thing for the parent to do in this situation? Why?*
2. *Do you think that moral reflection and moral reasoning genuinely differ?*
3. *Could this example of moral reflection be reformulated into a series of distinct applications of moral reasoning that end with the same moral judgment?*
4. *Does your own moral thinking follow either or both of these patterns? Do you follow one more than the other?*

Summary

The standardized pattern of moral reasoning may accurately analyze much of our moral thinking. But moral particularism has challenged this by arguing that—especially when the case involves people and relationships—our moral thinking follows a different pattern. That pattern, called moral reflection, doesn't explicitly appeal to moral principles:

Descriptive Claim(s) +

Moral considerations about the persons involved +

Moral considerations about the interpersonal relationships involved

→ Moral judgment

Key Terms

- **Moral particularism:** *many moral judgments are not inferred from moral principles but can only be made case by case.*
- **Moral reflection:** *a pattern of moral thinking that doesn't infer judgments from explicit principles but instead emphasizes the individuals and relationships involved in a setting framed by a set of descriptive claims.*

Chapter Assignment Questions

1. *Consider the following moral judgments. What moral principles do these judgments derive from? For each judgment, lay out a complete pattern of reasoning:* **principle + descriptive claim(s) → judgment.**

   a. *I shouldn't shoplift a candy bar from this grocery display.*

    b. *I should accurately report my income on my federal tax form.*

    c. *I shouldn't copy test answers from my friend sitting next to me.*

    d. *I ought to pay my friend the $10 I owe him since he needs it right now.*

2. *Consider the following moral principles. What judgments could be inferred from these? For each, lay out the complete pattern of reasoning:*

    principle + descriptive claim(s) → judgment.

    a. *It is morally wrong to steal from others.*

    b. *A morally upright person is honest.*

    c. *Adults should respect the choices of other adults without interfering.*

    d. *One should aid others in the world by giving to international charities.*

3. *Fill out the following story further and then describe how you could reach a judgment regarding what to do using moral reflection:*

    A good friend has lost her job and has nowhere to go. She is nearly broke and cannot afford an apartment. She has no family. Should you offer her your home and share some of her expenses for a while?

4. *Tell another story that requires making a moral judgment and show specifically how it would be analyzed by the pattern of moral reflection.*

Additional Resources

"Cultural Relativism." Accessed September 2, 2016. https://www.youtube.com/watch?v=PmvtbnXBoCQ. This YouTube video is a fairly good introduction to objectivism, relativism, and subjectivism. Note: cultural or popular relativism is described as "intersubjective" in this video.

Timmons, Mark. "Introduction to Moral Theory: The Nature and Evaluation of Moral Theories." In *Conduct and Character, Readings in Moral Theory.* 5th ed. Edited by Mark Timmons. Belmont, CA: Wadsworth, 2006. This provides an excellent introduction to the nature of ethics and especially to ethical theories.

Case 1

Mr. Research

"Mr. Research" conducted his business at X University for at least ten years, starting in the mid-1980s. Mr. Research was not his real name, of course, but this is how most people referred to him. Mr. Research (himself an alumnus of X University) worked mostly out of the university library. Although he was not the only one providing such services, his work had a good reputation. For a fee of around $100, he would provide "research" on any topic to students with the full knowledge that the students would turn this research in as their own papers.[9]

    Were these activities legal? Mr. Research claimed that they were, because he was providing *research*, not papers. Whether students turned this research in as their own

Continued

---

[9]All of this case's material derives from an interview conducted by Yvonne Raley on April 22, 2007, with an individual who wishes to remain anonymous.

Case 1 (*Continued*)

was not his responsibility—or so he claimed. Mr. Research had consulted a lawyer, who assured him that he was protected legally. When faculty approached him about his "work," he would usually refuse to talk. Although his livelihood depended on these students, Mr. Research expressed great contempt for those who sought his services.

These days, most students can cheat from the privacy of their own homes. Typing "term papers" into Google results in a long list of Web sites that provide papers for a fee (sometimes they are even free). Some sites explicitly offer A-grade papers written by experts, which betrays the assumption that these papers will be handed in for a grade with the student's name on it. To protect against legal challenges, the Web sites usually also include a disclaimer saying that the services of the site are for purposes of assistance only and that proper referencing should be provided.[10] As a result, the only one who can be penalized is the student who turns in work that is not her own; whoever sponsors the Web site can't be touched.

Despite the obvious risks of punishment, downloading entire papers and plagiarizing parts of papers from Internet sources is becoming more and more widespread. Repeated large-scale studies conducted at Rutgers University have found that approximately half of undergraduate as well as graduate students admit to copying at least a few sentences from an Internet source without proper referencing. The numbers are even higher among high school students.

Many colleges and universities are aggressively fighting this trend. They have toughened their punishment for plagiarism, they have instituted honor codes, and they have taken out licenses with sites like *Turnitin*, which compare submitted papers against content on Web sites, research databases, and archived student papers. If a paper is plagiarized, it's usually not hard for instructors to find that out.

THOUGHT QUESTIONS

1. Do you think that Mr. Research's activities, or the activities of Web sites that supply term papers, can be defended morally? They apparently are legal.
2. What interests conflict in this case? Which of these should take precedence?
3. Does Mr. Research share any moral responsibility for his customers' cheating? Provide some arguments to support your view.
4. What is your moral evaluation of the students who use these services? Give your reasons. How might a Web site help students learn about a subject and write better papers but not encourage dishonesty?
5. What supportable universal moral claims provide reasons for or against Mr. Research's conduct?

Case 2

Who's Not Coming to Dinner?

Alice and Arlene had been going out for a while now, and things were getting serious between them. It had started when they met each other at a meeting

Continued

---

[10]See the disclaimer at "Welcome to Essay Town, *Essay Town*, accessed September 1, 2016, http://www.essaytown.com/.

Case 2 (Continued)

of the feminist club. Now here they were, a year later, applying to the same law school. There was one problem, though. Whenever Arlene pressed Alice to introduce her to her parents, she evaded. "They won't understand," was her attitude. "They don't discriminate, I swear, but they are overprotective. They'll see how much I love you, and they'll respect that and love you too. But, like all parents, they want me married to a boy, be taken care of, and all that. Also, they'll worry that others won't approve of our relationship, that I'll be marginalized professionally, and that any kids we adopt will be teased in school. So what can I do? I don't want to hurt them."

There's mixed news about same-sex relationships. The number of same-sex marriages has increased since they were declared a constitutional right by the Supreme Court in 2015 (though new census data are not yet in). Yet there's still a social stigma against same-sex relationships in many parts of the country and for many groups of people.

The media has often reinforced that stigma. How often have same-sex couples been depicted on TV or in movies? Things are changing rapidly, and there are a few notable exceptions (e.g., *Grey's Anatomy* and *Scandal*). Still, most TV shows and movies have stuck with portraying heterosexual relationships. In much of the rest of the world, any portrayal of same-sex relationships is even more taboo.

THOUGHT QUESTIONS

1. Do you think that Alice's concerns regarding her parents—that others will disapprove, that Alice could be professionally marginalized, and that their kids would be teased—are factually correct? Evaluate the social stigma attached to same-sex relationships today, particularly in your own family's social circles.

2. If they do come to know about Arlene, would Alice's parents be morally justified in cautioning Alice against such a marriage? Would they have a moral responsibility to caution Alice?

3. List some moral principles relevant to this case and use them to argue for your position regarding same-sex relationships. Apply the pattern of moral reasoning to support your concluding judgment.

4. Given your movie and TV experience, how do you think same-sex relationships should be portrayed? Should the media take a pioneering role in this area, should it instead portray things more as they used to be, or should it just try to match social trends and attitudes?

5. Does the media have a moral responsibility to include more portrayals of same-sex relationships than they have previously? If a TV network owner was morally uncomfortable with certain kinds of relationships, would she be morally wrong to avoid including such portrayals in her network's programming? Apply the pattern of moral reasoning to support your concluding judgment.

6. Alternately, answer the preceding question in terms of interracial relationships or relationships between ethnic or religious groups that presently tend to oppose each other. Apply the pattern of moral reasoning.

Case 3

Who's Responsible for Obesity?

The recipe for combating widespread obesity in America has added a newer ingredient: people have been suing major corporations because of the health risks associated with their foods. For example, Kraft was sued to stop marketing Oreo cookies because they contain high amounts of trans fats. When Kraft offered to change the recipe, the lawsuit was dropped.

One of the most interesting lawsuits was brought against McDonald's in 2003: two teens just under eighteen, Pelman and Bradley, filed a suit alleging that they had developed serious health problems—including obesity, high blood pressure, diabetes, heart disease, and high cholesterol—as a result of their consuming large amounts of McDonald's food (they ate there about ten times a week). They also argued that McDonald's advertising had misled the public by claiming that its foods were nutritious, while not acknowledging the health risks posed by many of its most popular products.[11]

The judge dismissed the lawsuit, maintaining that the plaintiffs hadn't adequately proven their case. First, as he explained in his court opinion, the McDonald's ads about its food being nutritious had been pulled from TV in the late 1980s, and the plaintiffs couldn't establish that they had seen them. Second, it's well known that much of McDonald's food contains "high levels of cholesterol, fat, salt and sugar, and that such attributes are bad for one." Any *reasonable* consumer, therefore, could determine that some McDonald's foods can adversely affect health. Lastly, the judge stated that the plaintiffs failed to prove that McDonald's food had caused their health problems. Proving this would make it necessary to "isolate the particular effect of McDonald's foods on their obesity." It would also require information about the plaintiffs' other dietary habits, exercise, and their families' relevant health history. That information had not been provided, nor was any expert medical testimony supplied to support the plaintiffs' claims.

The teens appealed, arguing that McDonald's was still responsible for false advertising. In 2005, the Appeals Court reversed the part of the case regarding deceptive advertising and allowed the case to be reopened. To win, however, the plaintiffs would *still* have to show a causal connection between McDonald's food and their health problems.

Since then, McDonald's has made several positive changes. Nutritional information is now fairly easily available, and the company has also stopped using trans fats. Perhaps because of the 2004 documentary film *Super Size Me*[12] (which explored the connection between obesity and widely available supersized portions), it has also dropped its supersized offerings.

Meanwhile, over twenty states now have "commonsense consumption" laws that prevent suing for damages related to obesity. These laws don't include damages for deceptive advertising, however. Meanwhile, 60% of Americans consider fast-food restaurants responsible for obesity in children; 86% also hold parents responsible.[13]

Continued

---

[11] The information for this case, including quotations, is taken from Pelman v McDonald's, Docket No. 03–0910, United States Court of Appeals (2004).

[12] Morgan Spurlock, dir., *Super Size Me* (New York: Hart Sharp Video, 2004).

[13] "Second Opinion in *Pelman v. McDonald's* Now Finally Dismissing Case with Prejudice," Banzhaf.net, accessed September 1, 2016, http://banzhaf.net/docs/mcop2.html. John Banzhaf represented Pelham and Bradley in their 2003 suit.

Case 3 (Continued)

From a moral perspective, any company that deliberately misleads the public about the risks of consuming their products is clearly doing wrong. In general, businesses have a responsibility to ensure that their products are safe and measure up to reasonable expectations. At the same time, many view lawsuits like the one against McDonald's to be frivolous. After all, any intelligent consumer knows that fast food and "junk" food aren't the healthiest things to eat. Also, isn't each person's choice of how they eat and exercise their own responsibility (or, for children, their parents' responsibility)?

THOUGHT QUESTIONS

1. A recent study indicated that people significantly underestimate the amount of calories contained in restaurant food. It stands to reason, therefore, that people also don't know how much cholesterol or sodium is contained in what they eat. They also probably don't know how much cholesterol or how much sodium they *should* consume in a day. How much, in your view, does a reasonable consumer need to know about such facts to be able to make a proper determination about what foods to eat?

2. Suppose you decide to follow a healthy diet. How difficult will it be to follow through on your decision? What factors—both internal and external—make proper eating more difficult? What sort of information do you need to achieve a healthy diet? Is this information readily available? If you later fail to keep to your diet, whose fault would that be?

3. The plaintiffs failed to establish their side. What sorts of facts *would have* more strongly supported their claims?

4. Consider the following statements (note: these may not all be true!):

    A. McDonald's has the right to sell whatever foods it likes.
    B. It is wrong to intentionally cause harm.
    C. If you don't want to gain weight, you must eat a healthy diet.
    D. Any company should make their food products' nutritional information available on the label.
    E. You shouldn't enter a fast-food restaurant without wearing shoes.
    F. Fast-food companies shouldn't sell any foods that are unhealthy.
    G. Greasy foods taste best.
    H. It's illegal for a company to engage in false advertising.
    I. Parents have a responsibility to provide a healthy diet to their children.
    J. Fast-food companies have an obligation to warn about the adverse effects of their foods in all their advertisements.
    K. All consumers are equally and fully responsible for their eating habits.
    L. People have a right to choose whatever they want to eat.
    M. If I go out to eat, I'll take a cheeseburger over a salad any day.
    N. Older children and adults are responsible for their own food choices and health habits.

    O. Parents and schools are responsible to educate children in good eating and good health habits.

First, categorize the preceding statements into the several categories introduced in Chapter One (i.e., moral, legal, prudential, etc.). Are there any additional moral principles and values that are not mentioned but that you think apply to this case? Do any principles from your complete list of moral principles (both mentioned and added) conflict? Are any false? Why? Which principles override the others?

5. If you think fast food restaurants share at least some responsibility for people's eating habits, what do you think they ought to do? Why? Apply the pattern of moral reasoning to support your judgments.

6. Does it make a difference that these teens were under eighteen (see Chapter Three)?

7. Compare the teen's lawsuit to those previously brought against tobacco companies regarding the health risks of cigarettes.

CHAPTER FIVE

Moral Psychology and Egoism

I. INTRODUCTION

Stanley Milgram, a Yale psychologist in the 1960s, wondered why so many ordinary Germans had participated in Nazi atrocities. Would most people have acted similarly? To find out, Milgram advertised for male volunteers aged twenty to fifty to participate in a "learning study."

From a volunteer's point of view, the study ran as follows. After the volunteer was randomly assigned a "teacher" role, another volunteer was randomly made a "learner." Strapped in a chair with electrodes attached, the learner was asked to memorize a set of word pairs. He would then be given a word and told to identify the correct paired word from four choices. Meanwhile, the teacher sat in a nearby room with a large control panel. Whenever the learner answered incorrectly, the teacher was told by an experimenter to give the learner an electric shock. The shock would increase with each mistake. The teacher selected the shock voltage from switches labeled in 15-volt increments from 15 volts (slight shock) to 450 (danger/severe shock). As the learner inevitably began making mistakes, the teacher would be told to keep raising the voltage. Soon, the learner would beg for the shocks to stop; later, the learner would shriek at each shock, screaming to be released. If the teacher objected to an increase, the experimenter would quietly say "please continue." Further objections were answered more and more firmly: continuing the experiment was "required," then "essential," and, finally, "there is no choice"—though nothing forced the teacher volunteer to stay.

In reality, everyone was an actor except the "teacher"—the experiment's actual subject. The shocks weren't real, and nothing was random. Nevertheless, the subjects *believed* that they were administering increasingly painful and dangerous shocks. The most shocking part of the experiment, however, was its results: *every one of forty subjects raised the voltage to at least 300 volts, and *two-thirds* of them raised it to *the full 450 volts*. In one variation, the subject had the shock procedure explained to him and was then asked to order another person to actually administer the shocks. In this version, *nearly every subject* had the shock voltage taken to maximum—apparently because the presence of a "middleman" made subjects feel less responsible for what they were doing.[1]

Despite the evidence, it's hard to accept Milgram's results and their implications. Apparently, most of us can be easily persuaded by authority to do terrible things to others. After all, Milgram's subjects could have simply refused to continue as a small number in fact did. It's especially disconcerting to think that even though we know it's wrong to inflict pain and put innocent persons at risk, most of us would do such things under little pressure. Is this because most of us lack moral character?

Since Milgram's experiments, thousands of psychological experiments relating to moral behavior and attitudes have taken place, creating the field of **moral psychology.** Primarily a combination of experimental psychology, biology, and philosophical ethics, moral psychology investigates the *psychological* side of morality. In its relatively short life, it has established some surprising results and intensified some ethical controversies. What it has *not* done—since empirical studies cannot usually solve philosophical problems—is decisively alter much of ethics itself. As it does speak to a number of ethical questions in significant ways, however, moral psychology can tell us more about ourselves as moral beings. That makes it worth looking at before we begin our study of ethical theories in earnest (Part II).

For Discussion

1. *How do you feel about the ethics of Milgram's experiments themselves?*
2. *What is your reaction to Milgram's results? How do you think you would have acted as a "teacher" in his experiment?*
3. *Suppose that our brains are completely programmed morally by age five, so that from then on our moral choices are fully determined and never actually free. How would this affect ethics?*

Summary
There is, naturally, a psychology of moral behavior, attitudes, and emotional responses. Like all psychology, moral psychology works through empirical observation and experiment. Its results can have interesting things to say to ethics. Milgram's experiments, for instance, raise some unsettling doubts about our moral character. We must understand, however, that such investigations cannot directly resolve most philosophical problems of ethics.

Key Terms
- **Moral psychology:** *a largely empirical field that particularly brings together ethical theory and human psychology to investigate moral phenomena.*

---

[1] S. A. McLeod, "The Milgram Experiment," Simply Psychology, 2007, accessed September 1, 2016, http://www.simplypsychology.org/milgram.html.

II. MORAL CHARACTER

Milgram's experiments lead us to wonder about people's moral character. But there are other factors that influence our actions. A wide range of experiments suggests that a problem's *decision frame* can also strongly affect us. A *decision frame* includes the entire setting of a problem as the agent sees it: (a) how a problem, along with its choices and consequences, are *presented* and (b) the problem's wider context.[2]

(a) *Presentation:* A particularly striking demonstration of framing comes from Tversky and Kahneman.[3] They presented two groups with differently framed problems, each problem offering a choice between two options:

- Problem 1: An imported disease threatens the nation. Experts expect six hundred people to die unless countermeasures are taken. Two different programs have been proposed. "If Program A is adopted, 200 people will be saved. ... If Program B is adopted, there is a 1/3 probability that 600 people will be saved and 2/3 probability that no people will be saved."
- Problem 1:

Program A	Program B
100% chance: 200 saved	33% chance: 600 saved
	67% chance: 0 saved

- Problem 2: Given the same disease story: "If Program C is adopted 400 people will die. If Program D is adopted there is 1/3 probability that nobody will die, and 2/3 probability that 600 people will die." (p. 453)
- Problem 2:

Program C	Program D
100% chance: 400 die	33% chance: 0 die
	67% chance: 600 die

Which program looks best to you for each problem?

Did you notice that the two problems are exactly the same? "The only difference is that the outcomes are described in problem 1 by the number of lives *saved* and in problem 2 by the number of lives *lost*."[4] For Problem 1, 72% of respondents wanted to make sure that at least some are saved (Program A) rather than risk losing

---

[2]A choice's frame refers "to the decision-maker's conception of the acts, outcomes, and contingencies associated with a particular choice." Amos Tversky and Daniel Kahneman, "The Framing of Decisions and the Psychology of Choice," *Science*, 211.30 (January 1981), 453, including social and cultural influences (see this chapter, §III). A decision frame relates closely to how descriptive claims frame a moral problem in moral reflection (see Chapter Four, §IV).

[3]Tversky and Kahneman, "The Framing of Decisions and the Psychology of Choice." This example is also presented in John Doris and Stephen Stich, "Moral Psychology: Empirical Approaches," in *The Stanford Encyclopedia of Philosophy* (Fall 2014 ed.), ed. Edward N. Zalta http://plato.stanford.edu/archives/fall2014/entries/moral-psych-emp/, accessed September 1, 2016.

[4]Tversky and Kahneman, "The Framing of Decisions and the Psychology of Choice."

all (Program B). For Problem 2, 78% found it more appealing to take a risk to save all (Program D), rather than accept the certain loss of four hundred people (Program C). People desired to avoid risks when considering positive outcomes (Problem 1) but willingly took risks when faced with negative outcomes (Problem 2). People react very differently depending on how a problem is presented.

(b) Context: Early experiments in social psychology also found the following:[5]

- *Emotional influences:* Subjects were "set up" to find a dime (in 1972; today, this would probably take at least a dollar!). They were then placed near a woman who dropped some papers. These subjects were *twenty-two times* more likely to help the woman than those who had not previously found any money.[6]

- *Noise and gender:* These also seem to affect people's *helping behavior*—their willingness to help someone in need. A 1975 study by Mathews and Canon[7] had subjects encounter an injured man who was having trouble picking up several dropped books. Subjects were over five times more likely to help the man when background noise was normal compared to when it was high (due to a lawnmower running nearby). Later studies indicate that noise and the subject's sex may interact in even more complex ways to affect helping behavior (in part, men help others, especially women, more often than women help others).[8]

These results have been given different interpretations, and there are also many conflicting studies. Nevertheless, a few things stand out. First, there seems to be significant support for **psychological situationism**: the view that various aspects of a person's situation (i.e., its *decision frame*) influence their behavior (particularly their willingness to help others) and even how they think. These include factors completely irrelevant to morality.

It may not be so surprising that social pressures and perceived authority can influence us (Milgram), but it certainly is surprising that such trivial framing differences can affect us so substantially. After all, we think of ourselves and others as remaining fairly consistent over time—as having enduring personal characters. We thus expect people to behave much as they have previously: honest and friendly people will stay that way, and selfish people will continue to act selfishly. We think that people have distinctive personalities and character traits that define them over time.

Yet this is where things get complicated. Studies of character traits (excluding mental capabilities) have failed to correlate traits with behavior. This lack of

---

[5]Much of what follows is based on Doris and Stich, "Moral Psychology."

[6]Ibid., section 4.

[7]Doris and Stich, "Moral Psychology", section 4.

[8]"The results of a field study on the streets of a major city supported the major hypothesis and revealed that sex of the participants involved was the major predictor of helping behavior." Daniel M. Geller and Gregory P. Malia, "The Effect of Noise on Helping Behavior Reconsidered," *Basic and Applied Social Psychology*, 2.1 (1981): 11–25.

correlation was underscored by Walter Mischel's 1968 bombshell, *Personality and Assessment*.[9] In fact, Mischel largely rejected the notion of personality itself, leading Lewis Goldberg later to sarcastically comment, "Once upon a time, we had no personalities."[10] Since Mischel, however, Goldberg and others have argued that the case against personality traits doesn't rule out *all* types of traits; rather, it mainly challenges our most *familiar* trait concepts. In place of the latter, the *Big Five* personality model correlates five psychologically oriented traits to behavior: extroversion/introversion, neuroticism (stability), agreeableness, conscientiousness, and openness (in attitude and perspective). Of these, agreeableness ties closely to moral behavior, as it includes moral inclinations like sympathy and empathy; it also includes **altruism**—a concern for the well-being of others independent of any self-interest.

Human psychology is complex. On one side, there's evidence that character traits and enduring personalities *do* exist, as common sense has long contended. This helps explain the *consistencies* we find in people's attitudes and actions over even long periods of time. On the other side, there remains much evidence in support of psychological situationism, which helps explain the *inconsistencies* we observe in people's behavior from time to time. It seems that personality and moral character *somewhat* influence our actions, though each problem's situation or decision frame can significantly influence how we think and behave as well.

Next, since situationism shows that personality and moral character are not as influential as previously assumed, this casts doubt upon any ethical theory (e.g., virtue theory) that assigns an important moral role to personal character (see Chapter Eleven). Some virtue theorists have replied by suggesting that moral character traits (e.g., honesty, courage, generosity) are often quite rare: "Virtue is not widely instantiated, but is expected to be found in only a few extraordinary individuals."[11] But if this is true, then virtue theory is largely irrelevant to most people's moral experience. Another response proposes that virtuous behavior depends more upon our social environment than upon what is within ourselves. If my society consistently rewards and approves of moral behaviors while it marginalizes those who fall short, then I am likely to act morally as long as I feel this social pressure to conform.[12] But this response likewise largely abandons the position that our actions reflect our *personal* character.

There may be a different way to respond to the challenge of situationism. Let's begin by noting that our society has long emphasized laws and general principles as essential tools for making people act rightly. Our moral thinking, therefore, tends to refer to moral principles. Moral character, on the other hand, has not received much attention for a century or more. As a result, parents and teachers hand kids "the rules"—usually along with a list of threatened punishments. But

---

[9]Walter Mischel, *Personality and Assessment* (New York: Wiley, 1968).

[10]Lewis R. Goldberg, "The Structure of Phenotypic Personality Traits," *American Psychologist*, 48.1 (January 1993): 26–34.

[11]Doris and Stich, "Moral Psychology," section 4.

[12]Ibid

neither seems to be aware of what Aristotle insisted upon long ago: that people can only achieve a "firm and unchangeable moral character" through years of practice. Moral character is established by repeatedly acting morally—by building moral habits—and not by the imposition of rules, threats, or rewards. But if Aristotle is right, then wouldn't our society's neglect of moral character make it likely that many people, including experimental subjects, have no very well-established character? Those with the least developed characters would be most strongly influenced by momentary circumstances, just as situationism has shown.[13]

This response essentially agrees with the suggestion that people with strong moral characters are rare but not because character is hard to achieve. Rather, it explains the rarity of strong moral character by the fact that our society does very little to nurture it. Perhaps a change in our methods of moral education would lead to more people having well-established moral characters and exhibiting greater consistency in moral behavior. This might result in fewer people succumbing so easily to the influence of situational factors (see Chapter Eleven, §III).

Finally, psychological situationism may tell us something about how people think through moral questions and problems. Especially in view of the Tversky and Kahneman findings about framing, it is doubtful that people follow the pattern of *moral reasoning* in their spontaneous decision-making. If they did, there would not be nearly as much influence from irrelevant external factors upon their moral judgments (see Chapter Four, §IV). The pattern of *moral reflection* with its consideration of framing, personal character, and relationships seems to fit more naturally with situationist findings. Nevertheless, we mustn't jump to any conclusions. For a start, even if most people's moral thinking *does* broadly match moral reflection, that doesn't show that moral reflection is better than moral reasoning. Both have their place. Nor does it follow that people *must* think this way. Situationist studies have typically tracked people's choices in highly spontaneous, unreflective moments. However, when people describe how they have deliberated at length over some choice, it often sounds as if they have followed the pattern of moral reasoning. With practice, furthermore, one can presumably learn to apply this pattern habitually.

For Discussion

1. *What situational influences can you think of that might affect whether people help others? Why would these influences make a difference?*
2. *Watch your own behavior for a few days. Does your sympathy toward others and your willingness to help vary over time? What influences these changes?*
3. *Describe your own moral personality or character as you see it.*
4. *Do you think most people have a (more or less) enduring moral character?*

---

[13]It's very difficult for a study of people's actions in a particular situation to "control" for the presence or absence of a well-established character, since the latter can only be confirmed indirectly and by long-term observation.

5. *How do you think through a moral problem? Do you approach sudden momentary problems differently than you do important long-term issues?*

Summary

Besides Milgram's studies on how social pressure influences moral behavior, other studies and experiments suggest that a problem's decision frame can also strongly influence us. This includes how the problem is presented and aspects of the problem's context, both of which can influence our moral attitudes and choices. First, these findings support psychological situationism. Second, situationism may weaken the notion that people's actions are primarily controlled by their enduring moral characters. However, there is also evidence that we do have enduring personality traits like agreeableness. Is this enough to support ethical theories that treat moral character as primary? It's hard to say at present, since many in our society may not have developed much of a moral character. Finally, psychological situationism may tell us something about how people think through moral problems.

Key Terms

- *Decision frame: includes how a problem is presented and the entire context of the problem as the actor sees it: the choices, their consequences, and all surrounding influences.*

- *Psychological situationism: maintains that various aspects of a person's situation (their decision frame) can strongly influence how a person behaves and, in particular, how willing they are to help others.*

- *Altruism: a concern for the well-being of others independent of any self-interest.*

III. SOCIAL AND CULTURAL INFLUENCES

In discussing relativism (see Chapter Two), we urged that moral social and cultural differences are not as great as they first appear. Often, different groups arrive at different moral judgments because they hold different beliefs or views of the world (e.g., about the afterlife) rather than because they hold opposing moral principles.[14] Still, genuine moral differences do exist. One outstanding moral disagreement involves polygamous versus monogamous marriages and the defining principles of marriage.

Studies in anthropology and social psychology have added to our collection of cultural moral differences. One early study, carried out by philosopher Richard Brandt, explored cultural differences in moral attitudes and values. Brandt found a well-defined difference between the attitudes of the Hopi people (living in northern Arizona) towards animal suffering and the more widely held American attitudes. Brandt reported that Hopi children would catch wild birds, which they

---

[14]These differing beliefs function as non-moral descriptive claims in moral reasoning (See Chapter Four, §IV).

then tethered by a string "to be taken out and 'played' with. This play is rough, and birds seldom survive long."[15] While perfectly acceptable to the Hopis, this practice would have bothered most Americans sixty years ago; it would be considered offensively cruel today. But Brandt could find no difference between Hopi and other Americans' non-moral beliefs (e.g., about whether the birds could experience suffering) to explain this difference in moral judgments. Rather, it simply appeared that there was a "basic difference of [moral] attitude" between the Hopis and the wider U.S. culture.[16]

A more recent set of studies explored the moral influence of a "culture of honor"—in which personal honor is a strong controlling value—by comparing northern and southern whites in the United States.[17] The latter evince a strong culture of honor even today. (Cultures of honor also appear in other social groups around the world. What is particularly interesting about this case is that northern and southern whites nevertheless share most other values from the wider "American" culture.) We could expect that those holding a culture of honor would be more likely to defend their honor and reputation than those not sharing this culture. Such a culture would also be more accepting of crimes committed in defense of one's honor (e.g., retaliatory killings). The studies bear out these expectations:

1. Surveys found that white southerners tended to feel fully justified in responding violently when their honor was challenged or not properly respected. Northern whites did not hold this feeling to the same degree.
2. One experiment sent letters to employers across the United States requesting that the sender be considered for a job. The letters described the sender as a young Michigan man, eager to work. They also explained that he was having trouble finding employment because he had been convicted of killing another man in a fight the other had started by insulting, taunting, and slandering the sender. In analyzing responses, the researchers found that southern employers were more tolerant and sympathetic toward the writer's plight than northern employers.

The moral differences between U.S. northern and southern whites, as evidenced by these findings, again have nothing to do with these groups holding different non-moral beliefs. Instead, the differences seem to depend on how strongly each group values personal honor and reputation, along with accompanying differences in attitudes, emotions, and moral judgments.

This agrees with our claim (Chapter One, §II) that people tend to hold the same values but can differ in how they prioritize these values. Without a doubt, northern whites—as do all human beings—have a sense of personal honor and reputation. But apparently this value doesn't occupy as important a place in their value system as it does for southern whites.

---

[15]Doris and Stich, "Moral Psychology," section 6.
[16]Ibid.
[17]Ibid.

Differences in value priorities may thus explain the difference between American northern and southern moral judgments about personal honor. Can it also explain the difference between the Hopi and the wider American attitudes toward animal cruelty? Consider the following account. The Hopis long sustained themselves through farming and hunting. They were thus accustomed to such agrarian realities as animal slaughter. But those realities were very far removed from the experiences of most 1950s American city-dwellers who got their meat at stores, kept family pets, and were rapidly becoming immersed in an artificial technological world. For today's Americans, experiences of animal suffering or death, inevitable in the natural world, have become even more unfamiliar. When people do have contact with animals, it is usually friendly and sympathetic. An interesting evidence of this is the fact that veterinary medicine served farm animals almost exclusively until after World War II, when this began to change significantly.[18] As Americans have befriended domesticated animals, they have become increasingly upset by animal pain; in contrast, the Hopis continued to encounter animal suffering and death as commonplace and so considered it of relatively little moral importance.

Even if this explanation is on track, it doesn't undermine Brandt's conclusion that he had found a cultural difference in moral attitudes. But this isn't surprising, for we've known all along that differences sometimes exist between cultures in their moral beliefs. It's also worth remembering that such differences don't imply anything against objectivism, which can be true even if there are substantial differences between different groups' moral beliefs and practices (See Chapter Two, §IV).[19]

The important conclusion to draw here is that each of us is very much the product of our culture. Our social environment can significantly influence our moral beliefs, attitudes, and values. This should give us pause, for just as other social groups have occasionally accepted grievous moral errors without question (e.g., slavery), we may be doing the same with our own moral errors. This disagreeable realization should encourage us to think more critically about own society's moral *status quo*. Ethics can help us with this, for ethical theories can be valuable tools for placing our culturally embedded morality under rational scrutiny. With any luck, our doing this may improve our moral thinking and help us make moral progress.

---

[18]"The change to small animals is often explained as due to increasing standards of living and people's desire for companion animals after World War II. A new report by Andrew Gardiner . . . shows the real reason is the rise of animal charities. . . ." Andrew Gardiner, "The Surprising History of Veterinary Medicine for Dogs and Cats," *Companion Animal Psychology*, October 8, 2014, accessed September 1, 2016, http://www.companionanimalpsychology.com/2014/10/the-surprising-history-of-veterinary.html.

[19]Differences in how groups prioritize certain moral values is also compatible with mild versions of relativism such as that of Wong -- see Chapter Two §VII. Yet that section also suggests how objectivism might handle such differences without having to allow for even a mild relativism.

For Discussion

1. *What moral changes have occurred in our society over the past fifty or so years?*
2. *How much do you think your social environment determines your moral values and beliefs?*
3. *What moral beliefs or practices have you largely accepted without question?*
4. *How do you feel about being (if the studies are correct) so much a product of your culture?*
5. *Are there any beliefs and practices in our society that you think may not be morally right? Do these call for moral reform?*

Summary

Studies show that some genuine differences in moral beliefs and attitudes exist between different societies. They also show that people are strongly influenced by their culture. These empirical conclusions don't prove that objectivism is mistaken. What they do establish is that our moral values and perspectives are not just our own but are also affected by social and cultural influences. This should cause us to critique some of the moral assumptions we've just blindly accepted. Ethical theories can help us do this.

IV. ETHICAL AND PSYCHOLOGICAL EGOISM

When confronted with a difficulty, one of our first questions is usually: "How is this going to affect *me?*" According to *ethical egoism,* this is the *only* question that really matters, morally speaking. In fact, this rather curious ethical theory maintains the following:

> **Ethical Egoism:** The morally right act, for any particular situation, is the act that will most greatly benefit oneself.

Ethical egoism maintains that our *moral* duty is to promote our own interests whenever we can—or at least to limit our losses. Although this may sound absurdly selfish, ethical egoism doesn't say that our actions must always be entirely self-centered. As long as an act benefits me, it's fine if it also happens to benefit others. Further, ethical egoism can *require* that we help others or serve their interests since it often is in *our* best interest to help others. If earning people's gratitude leads them to someday return the favor, then it's in my interest to earn their gratitude. Ethical egoism can also require us to sacrifice our *immediate* interests to come out better in the long run. This can include investing my present time and energy in, say, a friendship since making friends rather than enemies has great advantages. Building a friendship, in turn, can also require that I not lie or break my promises since losing another person's trust makes it nearly impossible to get anything out of them.

Naturally, ethical egoism doesn't always yield such agreeable results. First, it says that our sole motivation for making friends, telling the truth, and helping others should be for ourselves. The egoist's rule of thumb is: "Only do good to others so that they will do even more good for you"—not exactly what most would call a *moral* motivation. Further, a truly consistent egoist would often act in ways that are objectively wrong. If Gyges can benefit by cheating and get away with it, egoism says he *ought* to cheat: his *moral duty* is to cheat. The same holds for skimming money off financial funds or even committing murder. At least occasionally, therefore, ethical egoism goes against our deepest and clearest moral intuitions—a good reason for rejecting it.

Rachels provides an interesting argument against ethical egoism.[20] His argument appeals to *moral equality*—the notion that all persons have equal moral worth and deserve equal treatment. Rejecting equality, arguably, rejects morality itself. Still, egoism does reject equality. According to ethical egoism, others' interests don't count the same as one's own; in fact, they don't count at all. By making others' interests and needs morally irrelevant, egoism violates moral equality. Yet ethical egoism can offer no reason for treating others differently from oneself, despite all of us having the same sorts of interests, needs, and desires.

Ethical egoism also runs into a practical problem. It's undeniable that humans need love and friendship. Since having such relationships is in our best interest, egoists ought to pursue such relationships. Yet love and friendship require a commitment to value another person to the point of sacrificing our own interests for the other's welfare. When there is no such commitment, there can be no *genuine* love or friendship. But egoists *cannot* sacrificially commit themselves to the welfare of others since their sole duty is to promote their own interests. Worse, egoists can't *value* others at all since egoism denies that others have moral worth. As a result, ethical egoism cannot reconcile its principle of serving only oneself with the sincere "heart" commitments necessary for genuine love and friendship. Even as it demands that we have such relationships, it rules out our being able to do so.

Ethical egoism is too objectionable to keep as a working *ethical* theory. But why would anyone think it true in the first place? One reason is a psychological argument. According to **psychological egoism** (a theory about human psychology, not morality), we *must* always prefer our own interests since we are psychologically *incapable* of choosing anything besides what we think is best for ourselves. If this is the only way we can think or choose, we might as well view the self-serving demands of egoism to be *morally* acceptable.

Psychological egoism claims that *all human choices are purely self-serving.* Why? Since all of my choices are *my* choices guided by *my* values, it seems that they inevitably must be dictated by *my* interests. Even when I appear to choose against my interests—by telling the truth to my detriment or stepping into danger to save my friend—I cannot help making those choices for self-centered reasons. Perhaps I want to avoid feeling guilty for not acting, or I'm hoping for a heavenly reward, or I crave for others to think well of me.

---

[20]This discussion is based on an argument appearing in James Rachels and Stuart Rachels, *The Elements of Moral Philosophy,* 6th ed. (Boston: McGraw–Hill Higher Education, 2009), chapter 6.

Are even our most morally admirable choices equally self-serving? Although psychological egoism appears to show this, there are some problems. First, just because *I* necessarily make *my* choices, it doesn't follow that my choices must be self-serving. Next, even if my personal values inevitably guide my choices, those values don't all have to be self-serving. If my values include honesty and other people's happiness, my choices might sometimes be quite selfless. And even if my choices always seem best *to me*, that doesn't mean that I think they are best *for me*.

It certainly seems that we occasionally choose against our own interests with the intent of helping others or fulfilling some duty (e.g., visiting a sick friend in the hospital when we'd rather do something else). Don't we sometimes find these choices particularly hard precisely because we *do* feel that they go against our interests? People also seem to think they can recognize the difference between other-serving and self-serving intentions. Are these sorts of judgments accurate? It often seems so; for instance, people's apparent intentions—self-serving or not—often correlate with what they actually bring about by their actions.

From a common-sense point of view, then, there's evidence against psychological egoism. Further, it's difficult to imagine what other kinds of evidence could be used to show that people can make unselfish choices. This leads to one final criticism: the psychological egoist comes dangerously close to maintaining that *no matter what evidence there may be to the contrary*, all human choices are selfish. But once psychological egoists rule out the very *possibility* of anything counting against their remarkable theory, it becomes empty.

For Discussion

1. *Think of a few examples of acts that ethical egoism could require, depending on the situation.*
2. *If ethical egoism can require helping others, how can it also make others' interests and needs morally irrelevant?*
3. *Discuss: does genuine love or friendship require a commitment to value another person to the point of sacrificing one's own interests for the other?*
4. *Consult your own thoughts and intentions: do you ever act against your own interests for the sake of another or for some other reason?*
5. *Hold a debate: (a) Have one side think of situations in which people act in ways that seem beyond doubt to be other-serving. (b) Have the other side give a psychological egoist's evaluation of each of these.*
6. *Supposing psychological egoism is true, try to explain how we have managed to develop a distinction between selfish and unselfish acts.*

Summary

Ethical egoism requires that one always act to benefit oneself. This can actually require that we help others. Still, ethical egoism can also prescribe clearly selfish and immoral acts. It also both calls for and precludes relationships of love and friendship. Psychological egoism, which claims that we are only capable of making self-serving choices, has been offered in support of ethical egoism. However, philosophers have argued that psychological egoism is either false or empty.

Key Terms

- **Ethical egoism:** *the morally right act, for any particular situation, is the act that will most benefit oneself.*

- **Psychological egoism:** *a psychological theory maintaining that, as a matter of psychological necessity, we can only choose what we think is in our interest.*

V. EGOISM AND MORAL PSYCHOLOGY

So much for philosophical evaluations of ethical and psychological egoism. But moral psychology has also investigated egoism at length.

In the literature addressing this, psychological egoism is usually contrasted with *altruism*—a concern for others' well-being regardless of any self-interest (see the trait of agreeableness in §11). If it can be shown that people sometimes act for purely altruistic reasons, then those actions (by definition) are not entirely self-interested, which entails that psychological egoism is false. But this is not easy to show. First, we must find actual examples of altruistic actions. Now we certainly *seem* to have many such examples available to us; as philosophers have argued, people sometimes act at great personal sacrifice for the sake of others. Bolstering this, there is evidence of a psychological link between *empathy*— an emotional response that identifies with another's suffering—and helping behavior. Daniel Batson states, "There is indeed an empathy-helping relationship; feeling empathy for a person in need increases the likelihood of helping to relieve that need."[21] The more fully people can be brought to empathize with the suffering of another, the more likely it is that they will try to help (depending, of course, on a wide range of situational factors). Since it isn't particularly unusual for people to feel empathy, people are often moved to do what they can to help others. When such actions require personal inconvenience or self-sacrifice, they appear altruistic.

Unfortunately, this so far proves little. We must further establish that such apparent acts of altruism are actuated by pure altruism. The trouble is that there can be subtle self-interested motivations for acting in these ways. For instance, (a) an observer may be pained at seeing another suffer and so help the sufferer simply because he wants to escape his own emotional pain. Another possible motive for helping may be (b1) to earn the approval of others or, on the negative side, to avoid being blamed for not helping. A related reason may be because (b2) the helper wants to feel good about herself or because she doesn't want to feel guilty about not helping. All of these possible motivations would be self-interested or egoistic "internally," despite their looking altruistic on the "outside."

---

[21]Doris and Stich, "Moral Psychology," sections 5.3–5.5.

Many studies to test these various motivations have been headed by Batson. One set of experiments attempted to determine whether social pressures—positive or negative—motivated subjects to help another (b1). This was done by making subjects either believe or not believe that their actions could become known to others. One group of people thought that no one else would ever find out what they did; these clearly could *not* be motivated by any expected approval or disapproval from others. Another group, believing that others would find out how they had acted, *could* be motivated by social pressures. Upon comparison, Batson found no difference between the two groups' actions. He did find, however, that both groups were more likely to help the more they empathized with the person they could help. These results seem to dispose of the peer pressure motivation (b1). If the more internal motivation (b2) is stimulated primarily by the social environment, then Batson's results may dispose of that egoistic motivation as well.

Other experiments tested motivation (a), the desire to escape the personal discomfort of watching another person suffer. Subjects watched person X experience a set of mild electric shocks that seemed to distress X significantly (X merely acted distressed). Subjects were told that X was unusually sensitive to even small shocks—shocks that would barely be noticed by most people. In one set of situations, subjects were given the option of changing places with X, thereby relieving X's distress by undergoing the shocks themselves. In another set of situations, subjects could choose between taking X's place or simply leaving. The first situation allowed subjects to both help X and to escape their own emotional discomfort, the second allowed subjects to escape their discomfort by leaving. Both situations allowed subjects to escape their personal discomfort, but if they simply chose to leave, that would not require the self-sacrifice involved in taking X's place.

If people are *only* motivated to help by the egoistic desire (a) to escape their own discomfort, they would choose to leave whenever possible. When that option is not available, they would choose to take X's place as the only way to escape their discomfort. On the other hand, if people are motivated by genuine altruism, they would typically take X's place regardless of what other options they had.

Overwhelmingly, people chose to take X's place. This seems unexpected if they simply had egoistic motivations (a) and leaving remained an option. Taking Batson's results together, therefore, may we now dispense with psychological egoism? Unfortunately, even these ingenious experiments don't entirely settle the issue. As Doris and Stich note, Batson's experiments assume that once a subject leaves, he will no longer experience any discomfort over X's suffering; also, that the subject expects to experience no such lingering discomfort.[22] If these "out of sight, out of mind" assumptions are mistaken, however, then subjects would not experience relief by leaving. Their best choice for fully relieving their personal discomfort would then be to take X's place. Thus, taking X's place remains compatible with having the egoistic motivation (a) simply to escape one's own discomfort.

---

[22]Ibid., section 5.5.

Although Batson's and others' studies clearly raise doubts about the hypothesis of psychological egoism, it still remains a possibility.

*   *   *

People like to make the cynical observation that philosophy never solves any problems. But it's clear that empirical attempts to resolve questions about egoism, or to determine the nature of moral character, or to assess the influence of character likewise do not easily yield definitive answers. Furthermore, since moral psychology is *descriptive*, it cannot directly address the *normative* issues of ethics. Moral psychology will never replace philosophical ethics, therefore, or render it obsolete. This is not to say, however, that empirical findings cannot shed any light on morality; as we have seen, they already have.

Still, we must ask in what ways moral psychology should influence the overall field of ethics. A few points emerge. First, by giving us a better understanding of the psychological aspects of morality, moral psychology can indicate (to some degree) which ethical accounts are most likely to be viable. If it someday manages to show that certain human capabilities do *not* actually exist (e.g., that there is no such thing as moral character or that people cannot be purely altruistic), then that would undermine any account that assumes that such capabilities *do* exist. Thus, moral psychology could impose certain constraints upon the presuppositions of ethical theories. Next, findings about how we think through moral problems and what influences our moral choices can indicate which theoretical approaches are most psychologically realistic. Such information would be especially helpful as we attempt to improve moral education and social policy. Finally, moral psychology may have important things to say to *applied ethics*—the part of ethics that relates ethical theories to practical problems in specific fields like medicine, business, and environmental policy (see Chapter Fourteen). But this gets us way ahead of ourselves; before we can even consider such implications, we must first develop an understanding of several ethical theories. This is what we next turn to in Part II.

For Discussion

1. *Which of the three options in Batson's experiment do you think you'd choose? Would it change things if you personally knew the distressed person X? Why?*
2. *How altruistic are you? Describe one of your recent altruistic acts.*
3. *We often ask children: "How would you feel if someone else did that to you?" How does this encourage empathy?*
4. *People often want to help close family and friends more than others. How would you explain that?*
5. *We are constantly exposed to terrible human suffering via the news and even much entertainment. How might this affect our empathy toward others?*
6. *When you do, why do you help people you don't even know?*
7. *Describe a purely altruistic act. How would you defend that example against the claims of psychological egoism?*
8. *To what degree do you think moral psychology may ultimately be able to make important contributions to ethics?*

Summary

What does moral psychology tell us concerning psychological egoism? It's difficult to say at present. Even apparently altruistic acts may be motivated in subtle ways by self-interest. Batson attempted to disprove psychological egoism, but one of his most convincing studies makes a crucial assumption that can be challenged. Like this study, most empirical studies are open to challenge. Still, moral psychology has a few things to offer ethics. It can help us evaluate presuppositions incorporated into ethical theories. It can press us to take more psychologically realistic approaches to ethics. It also may help us as we carry ethical theories over to applied ethics.

Chapter Assignment Questions

1. *The Milgram experiments were afterwards denounced as unethical. They would presumably not be allowed in the United States today. Why? Summarize the experiment and what you think was unethical about it.*

2. *Compare Milgram's experiments with Batson's somewhat similar studies. Note that deception alone is not normally a reason to consider a psychological experiment unethical. What then is different between the two studies?*

3. *Summarize what makes up a* decision frame *and provide examples of how it can influence moral attitudes and choices. Suppose a person has developed a strong moral character; to what degree might that reduce the influences of a decision frame upon that person? Discuss.*

4. *Do you see any way to defend ethical egoism from the text's criticisms?*

5. *Explain the difference between psychological and ethical egoism. Could ethical egoism be false even if psychological egoism were true?*

6. *Why can't moral psychology directly resolve many of the problems in ethics? Discuss this in terms of descriptive versus normative claims.*

Additional Resources

"Big Five Personality Test." *Psychology Today.* Accessed September 2, 2016. http://psychology-today.tests.psychtests.com/take_test.php?idRegTest=1297.

Doris, John and Stephen Stich. "Moral Psychology: Empirical Approaches." In *The Stanford Encyclopedia of Philosophy* (Fall 2014 Edition), edited by Edward N. Zalta. Accessed September 2, 2016. http://plato.stanford.edu/archives/fall2014/entries/moral-psych-emp/. This is a detailed and lengthy article on moral psychology.

Eagly, Alice H. and Maureen Crowley. "Gender and Helping Behavior: A Meta-Analytic Review of the Social Psychological Literature." *Psychological Bulletin,* 100.3 (November 1986): 283–308.

"Experimenter Official Trailer (2015)." Accessed September 2, 2016, https://www.youtube.com/watch?v=O1VOZhwRvWo. The trailer and movie itself can be streamed or purchased from various sources.

Isen, Alice M. "The Influence of Positive Affect on Decision Making and Cognitive Organization." In *Advances in Consumer Research.* Vol. 11. Edited by Thomas C. Kinnear. Provo, UT: Association for Consumer Research, 1984, 534–537. Accessed September 2, 2016. http://www.acrwebsite.org/volumes/6302/volumes/v11/NA-11.

"Lewis R. Goldberg, Personality Research, Online Full-Text Archive." Accessed September 2, 2016. http://projects.ori.org/lrg/. This website is a large set of papers, largely addressing personality traits, written Lewis Goldberg and others published on Goldberg's personal webpage.

"Mike Wallace Interviews Ayn Rand." Accessed September 2, 2016. https://www.youtube.com/watch?v=HKd0ToQD00o. This is the famous Mike Wallace interview of Ayn Rand about her ethical egoism.

"Milgram Obedience Study." Accessed September 2, 2016. https://www.youtube.com/watch?v=fCVII-_4GZQ. This YouTube video presents Milgram's experiment, with a great deal of actual experimental footage.

Rachels, James and Stuart Rachels. "Ethical Egoism." In *The Elements of Moral Philosophy.* 6th ed. Boston: McGraw-Hill Higher Education, 2009.

Shpancer, Noam. "Framing: Your Most Important and Least Recognized Daily Ment." *Psychology Today.* December 22, 2010. Accessed September 2, 2016. https://www.psychologytoday.com/blog/insight-therapy/201012/framing-your-most-important-and-least-recognized-daily-ment. This article applies framing to everyday life.

Tversky, Amos and Daniel Kahneman. "The Framing of Decisions and the Psychology of Choice." *Science,* 211.30 (January 1981): 453–458.

Case 1

Declaring Wages

Jenna works at the local diner as a waitress, earning minimum wage. She doesn't have the education to get a better job; because she has a young child, further school right now is out of the question. The job is not bad though, since she's popular with the customers and does pretty well in tips. At the end of her first year on the job, she asks her friend Joe to help her with her taxes. Joe explains that Jenna needs to declare her tips as wages. Having already spent the money on diapers, Jenna is really upset. It's only her tip income, she says, that is keeping her and the baby off the streets.

THOUGHT QUESTIONS

1. Do you think Jenna should just keep her tips unreported? Discuss this both legally and morally. What moral conflict does Jenna face?

2. Would egoism tell Jenna to keep her tips? How so?

3. Imagine Jenna's real name was "Jivika; she's called "Jenna" by her American friends. For her culture, family always comes first because family is the ultimate unit of support; the government, meanwhile, cannot be trusted since it's usually corrupt. Assuming she holds these beliefs, what do you think Jivika would most likely do? Does this make any difference to what she morally should do?

4. Suppose that Jivika's culture is a strong culture of honor, and that by failing to take care of her family, she dishonors herself and her family. Her first thought, furthermore, is that she earned those tips by her own hard work, and being forced to give up a portion of them is insulting. How do these additional facts affect the case?

Case 2

The Scratched Bumper

Coming out of the supermarket from running errands, you see that two cars have parked on either side of you, leaving you pretty tightly wedged in. You can still get out, but it's going to be tricky. As you maneuver back and forth, you feel yourself bumping against the car behind you. You get out and see scratches on the other car's bumper. Looking further, you find that it has scratches in several different places too. You're not sure, but you might have added one of those scratches just now.

THOUGHT QUESTIONS

1. What would you do next?
2. What does the law require that you do? (Do you know?)
3. What would ethical egoism say you should do? What's the morally right thing for you to do? Are these different?
4. You could just drive away, or you could leave a note on the car's windshield with your phone number. How would psychological egoism explain either choice?
5. Think of situational (framing) differences that might make it (psychologically) more or less likely that you would leave a note on the car. For example, suppose (a) you just got a large raise at work or (b) that when you last parked in that lot, you found your car with a bad scrape on its side, but no one left you a note.

Case 3

Job Competition

The local ice cream shop, Milk and Sugar, is seeking applicants for a summer job. Two high school students, Joshua and Elias, are top in the running. As the manager, Emma, reviews the applications, she is faced with a dilemma. Both applicants seem to have the same grades, both go to the same high school even, both have worked for an ice cream shop the previous summer (the same one, incidentally), and both are highly recommended by the previous employer.

THOUGHT QUESTIONS

1. Emma's interest as a manager is to hire the person who will do the best job. How should she choose? Can egoism help her solve her dilemma?
2. Imagine Joshua and Elias are best friends. Joshua tells Emma that she should hire Elias, and Elias tells Emma she should hire Joshua. How does this dilemma reflect on some of the problems for egoism?
3. Imagine that the customers Emma serves are predominantly Jewish. Elias is pretty obviously Jewish, Joshua is definitely not. Should this affect Emma's choice? How would egoism respond to this question?

Case 4

Human Trafficking

The U.S. State Department defines human trafficking as the "recruitment, harboring, transportation, provision, or obtaining of a person for labor or services, through the use of force, fraud, or coercion for the purpose of subjection to involuntary servitude, peonage, debt bondage, or slavery."[23] According to United Nations, about 21 million people are currently victims of human trafficking or forced labor. Often, these victims are lured in by false promises of money and a better future

For an employer, human trafficking can be lucrative for business. It provides cheap labor and so allows goods and services to be produced at a lower price. For instance, it was recently uncovered that several shrimp processing companies in Thailand had kept men, women, and children like slaves. The Thai shrimp were exported to the United States at a substantial profit, where American consumers benefited from the resulting low prices. Human trafficking is also widespread on fishing industry boats, where it's easy to keep workers trapped. Most people know that many cocoa farms thrive on child slave labor. According to the Trafficking in Persons report, forced labor and human trafficking lead to profits of over $150 billion annually in private industry.

Most human trafficking takes place outside of U.S. borders. Still, among the 800,000 people smuggled around the world each year, a good portion end up in the United States. Because the United States presents the promise of better living conditions and better earnings for many people, it's easy to lure workers into the country. Given the cost of paying legal workers in the United States, using slaves can look very tempting to some business people. In a scheme called debt bondage, employers first charge workers ridiculously high fees for transportation into the United States. They then require the workers to pay off this debt to obtain release. When these employers only pay their workers very low wages or only pay them food and lodging, they can keep the workers from every being able to buy their freedom.

A 2007 ABC news series called "Slavery in America: Living in the Shadows" covered several stories of illegal immigrants that lived under slave-like conditions in the United States. One was José Martinez from Mexico, who was kept in a camp in Florida. During the day he worked in tomato fields in unbearable heat. At night, he was locked in a trailer with twenty-eight other people. The trailer had only one stove and one bathroom. José was paid $4.00 a day, with "rent" for the trailer deducted. But José was unusually lucky—he escaped after four and a half months with $250 in his pocket.[24]

THOUGHT QUESTIONS

1. What advantages could a business owner expect to realize by engaging in human trafficking?

---

[23]"Trafficking in Persons Report: July 2015," U.S. State Department, accessed September 1, 2016, http://www.state.gov/documents/organization/245365.pdf. Peonage forces a person into servitude to work off a debt.

[24]Pierre Thomas and Theresa Cook, "Sold for $350: A Slave's Story of Toil and Fear," ABC News.com, accessed September 1, 2016, http://abcnews.go.com/print?id=3201696.

2. With a view to both short- and long-range consequences, could ethical egoism justify a business owner using human trafficking victims? Suppose the owner acted more benevolently toward his workers than do other traffickers—would that make a difference?

3. According to ethical egoism, could a victim be morally justified in trying to escape? What means could he use? What means, on the other hand, could the trafficker use to keep the worker? What conflict does this create for egoism?

4. How do we, as consumers, benefit from widespread human trafficking? In what ways do we preserve or promote such exploitation?

5. Leaving egoism aside, do consumers have any moral obligation to work against human trafficking? How might we best go about doing so? Should we research products on the Internet, learn more about human trafficking, and find out where the products we buy come from? Discuss these questions first as a consumer and then imagine yourself as one of the slaves. Do these framing differences lead you to different conclusions?

PART II

Ethical Theories and Perspectives

INTRODUCTION: ASSESSING ETHICAL THEORIES

We have by now covered most of the preliminaries needed to consider actual ethical theories. What remains? There are two questions we can ask about the origins of moral claims. First, we can ask: "How do people form their beliefs about moral right and wrong?" Young children obtain most of their moral convictions from their parents—both from what they are told and from how their parents act. Religious teachings (e.g., from catechisms, the Quran, the Talmud, Jesus' Sermon on the Mount, etc.) can also have a formative influence. Conscience—that intuitive, inner prodding that guides us and makes us feel guilty when we do wrong—may contribute. For adolescents, the influence of teachers and other significant adults may enter into the mix. Sometimes people are even influenced by an ethics course!

A very different question is: "What *makes* something right or wrong?" Are moral principles just *given* to us—like the laws of nature? A major task of an ethical theory is to address this second question, which it attempts to do by fulfilling two related goals. First, it should *simplify* the vast realm of morality down to a few foundational principles or values. It should do this as *completely* as possible without neglecting any part of morality. Second, these principles or values ought to *explain* why certain things are good or bad, right or wrong. To some degree, the first goal serves the second: if we can distill the entire realm of morality down to just a few foundations, we will probably have located the essence of morality in those foundations.

To be fully adequate, an ethical theory should satisfy a couple other criteria as well. Adding these to our previous observations, we have four key criteria for assessing any moral theory:[1]

1. Completeness: Does the theory encompass and support the *entire* range of meaningful moral claims? If a theory neglects certain kinds of moral claims or if it can make no sense of a moral concept, then it leaves something out that ought to be included.

Hedonistic theories, which explain moral right as that which promotes the greatest pleasure/happiness, have been charged with not making adequate sense of justice. If this indeed is one of their weaknesses, then they are not sufficiently complete. Completeness is clearly a crucial goal for any ethical theory. Please note, however, that completeness has nothing to do with whether the theory's claims are *true*. If an ethical theory is complete, then it fully addresses its subject; whether its account is actually true is another matter entirely.

2. Explanatory power: A theory should provide a satisfying unifying and explanatory basis for the moral realm. It ought to supply us with genuine moral insights that powerfully contribute to our understanding of what *makes* things good or right. Ideally, it should capture the essence of morality. Hedonistic theories, for instance, explain morally right acts as those that promote happiness. To the degree this is true, we thus learn that morality and happiness are closely related—an instructive and useful discovery. Compare this to a computer program that can tell us whether *anything* is morally good or bad, right or wrong. It does this with perfect accuracy but can tell us nothing more. Such a program would clearly satisfy *completeness,* but it would lack explanatory power since it says nothing about what makes something good or right. Does fulfilling this criterion, meanwhile, make the theory any more likely to be true? Once again, no: explanatory power, like completeness, has nothing to do with an account's truth.

3. Practicability: Practicability measures how useful a theory can be to us in actual practice. It includes several components. First, a theory should generate clear and precise moral claims. If its prescriptions, say, tend to be *vague*, leaving us unsure about what it is telling us to do, then it isn't much help. For example, consider the principle: "Don't hurt people unless they deserve it." A little reflection quickly reveals that this prescription isn't very practicable; in fact, it raises more questions than it answers. How much hurt are we talking about? When does someone deserve to be hurt? Next, an ethical theory must furnish substantial moral guidance to *ordinary* people, taking into account human intellectual and physical limitations. Suppose a theory tells us that "No one should spend money on a lottery if they are not going to win." Since this requires godlike knowledge of the future to determine when it would be right to buy a ticket, it isn't much use to those of us who are not gods. Finally, a theory's values or prescriptions should not generate irresolvable conflicts. For instance, a practicable theory should not

---

[1]Other more technical criteria (e.g., consistency) are also important. The more practically oriented criteria provided here, however, should be sufficient to satisfy our purposes.

leave us unable to resolve Sandra's dilemma about whether lives or lies are more important.

Yet again, practicability has nothing to do with an account actually being correct. None of the preceding criteria, important as each is, can tell us much of anything about the truth of a theory or its claims. We thus need one more criterion:

4. Moral Confirmation: A theory is *morally confirmed* if we have good reasons for thinking it actually gives *correct* answers to our moral questions. But if we already know what is right, why do we need ethical theories? We do in fact have pretty good ideas about what is right for at least *some* parts of the moral realm. To start with, then, a moral theory's claims should agree with what we know about these parts. We have deep, clear, and widely shared moral intuitions about wrongs like torturing innocent children, cold-blooded murder, and widespread dishonesty. How do we know we are at least right about these things? Well, we have to start somewhere, and our strongest and clearest intuitions are the best place to start. While we *could* be mistaken even about *these*, it doesn't seem likely. After all, people throughout human history have agreed that such things are wrong or at least have gotten upset when such things have been done to them.

Doing ethics resembles doing science in certain respects. In science, we begin testing a theory's major claims by experiments and observations. If those claims completely fail, the theory should probably be abandoned. But if only some fail at only certain points, we seldom simply reject the theory. Instead, we make adjustments and additions to achieve a better match between theory and observation. The revised theory may then yield new implications that can be tested. More observations may confirm parts of the theory while suggesting needed changes for other parts. This give-and-take process—testing, adjusting, testing new things, adjusting again, and so on—usually continues for a long time. Yet even as the process goes on, our scientific understanding becomes increasingly more sophisticated and accurate.

The enterprise of ethics can be carried on in a roughly similar way. Although an ethical theory can't be tested by experiments, its claims *can* be "tested" by applying it to cases to see if its results match our best moral intuitions. If the theory prescribes wholesale murder, it should be abandoned! But if its results match most of our best intuitions—and if we can adjust it for an even better match—then we may consider it partly confirmed. Having made further adjustments and finding more confirmations, we may start applying our evolving theory to less clear cases. Further extensions, confirmations, and adjustments may gradually produce an account that seems sufficiently correct to guide our moral choices. As our trust in the theory grows, we might next start allowing it to replace our own less certain intuitions, and so the process continues. Along the way, our moral insights and understanding will become increasingly sophisticated and accurate.[2]

---

[2]This give-and-take process, involving a gradual evolution of both theory and our less clear moral intuitions roughly resembles the process John Rawls describes for achieving "reflective equilibrium." The process continues until our intuitions agree with each other and with a theory-based set of principles and values. The result, ideally, will be a satisfactory account of ethics. John Rawls, *A Theory of Justice* (Cambridge, MA: Harvard University Press, 1971)

e sciences, an objection or disconfirmation to an ethical theory
.omatically show that the theory must be abandoned. Objections and
.ns can instead be useful for showing us where a theory needs adjustment.
.er learning about important problems with most ethical theories, people fre-
quently conclude that ethics must be hopeless. But just as it would be foolish to
give up on science because of problems with its theories, it would be foolish to give
up on ethics because we find problems with ethical theories. We may never arrive
at perfection, but we can still make valuable progress along the way.

Summary

*Ethical theories address the question of what makes something right or wrong, not
how we come to our beliefs about right and wrong. A good ethical theory should satisfy at least four criteria. It must (a) be complete and (b) have significant explanatory
power; it must also (c) be practicable, and it should (d) be confirmed by our best moral
intuitions.*

Key Terms

- **Completeness:** *a theory should encompass and support the entire range of
  meaningful moral claims and concepts, not leaving anything out.*

- **Explanatory power:** *a theory should give us insight into what makes something moral or immoral.*

- **Practicability:** *a theory should be useful in actual practice:(a) being clear and
  precise, (b) furnishing understandable moral guidance,(c) not generating irresolvable conflicts.*

- **Moral confirmation:** *a theory should fit with our deepest, clearest, and most
  widely shared moral intuitions.*

For Reflection and Discussion

1. *Explain in your own words the criterion of completeness.*
2. *Why does the computer program described in the text lack explanatory power?*
3. *Explain in your own words the three parts of the criterion of practicability. Can
   you think of other moral claims that fail practicability?*
4. *How is ethical theorizing like developing and testing scientific theories? (Can you
   name some scientific theories?) How do you think it may differ?*

CHAPTER SIX

Consequentialist Ethics: Act Utilitarianism

I. INTRODUCTION

A small pharmaceutical company is nearing what Ed Flourens hopes will be his company's big break. After struggling for fifteen years, the company's stock soared last fall when Ed announced a new drug that effectively controls seizures. Better still, the drug works in small doses, which appears ideal for children. One night, as Ed pores over the first six month's report on 2,800 human trials, a number grabs his attention. He specifically remembers more cases, but the report only mentions two patients who developed serious gastrointestinal problems—stomach bleeding or perforations. Delving into the files, his anxiety grows as he finds records of eight … ten … and more patients showing the same symptoms. Slowly the terrible truth dawns on Ed: a total of twenty such patients was mistakenly reported as two—a simple decimal error. Yet this means that 0.7% of the subjects developed serious problems, rather than 0.07%. The difference is substantial; in fact, with the uproar about drug risks over the past decade, Ed realizes that this difference could block FDA approval of his product. His exasperation nearly moves him to tears. Will this be the fatal blow to his dreams? For one fleeting moment, he is tempted to disregard everything and just pretend that nothing is wrong.[1]

As reality sets in, Ed realizes that there's more at stake than his company's prospects. Trials with 2,800 patients—including children—are still ongoing. In view of the risks, shouldn't he call for their immediate halt? Clearly, the answer depends on the consequences of doing this compared to continuing the trials. What are some likely consequences? On the one hand, if the trials are halted, the rosy prospects for Ed's company will collapse for at least the near future. Several more years of research and testing may be required—if the drug's problems can be overcome at all. Those presently taking the drug will lose the benefit of their seizures being controlled. This loss becomes much greater for them if the best alternatives to Ed's drug are less effective or cost more, particularly for those with seriously debilitating

---

[1] A fictional case. For new seizure drugs, a rate of 0.02% for life-threatening side effects can be acceptable.

or dangerous seizures. On the other hand, continued trials would produce important additional information about the drug, contributing to better and safer drugs that can help more people in the future. It would also help Ed's company, although probably only in the short run. Meanwhile, most of those taking the drug would continue to benefit, though a few might suffer some of the drug's worst side effects.

All actions have consequences. Whether those consequences are wide ranging (as in Ed's story) or limited (as when I make a thoughtless comment to someone), consequences also have *moral* significance. The idea that consequences—and *only* consequences—make something morally right or wrong is the foundation of **consequentialism**, and the basis for a wide range of *consequentialist* moral theories.

For Discussion
1. *If you were Ed, what would you do?*
2. *The government would probably require that Ed's drug trials be halted. Would that be best morally?*
3. *Clinical trials compare two groups: those who receive the real drug and those who don't. If a new treatment proves very effective early on, the trial is usually stopped and all receive the treatment. Why?*

Summary
Everything we do has consequences. Consequentialist theories define what is morally right solely in terms of effects or consequences.

Key Terms
- **Consequentialism:** *a general approach to ethics that maintains that only consequences determine what is morally right or wrong.*

II. UTILITY AND CONSEQUENTIALISM

Consequentialism focuses on consequences or effects. But how should we evaluate consequences? Typically, this is done in terms of utility. In classical theories, **utility** measures the degree to which a consequence promotes the foundational hedonistic value of pleasure/happiness (see Chapter One, §5). Thus, utility is desirable; *disutility* is undesirable, being associated with pain and suffering. When the consequences of something happen to be mixed, the amount of disutility is subtracted from the utility; if the utility is greater, then the resulting utility is still positive.

It's undeniable that people pursue pleasure while they normally try to avoid pain. In view of this, hedonists have thought that it's only a small step from saying that people *pursue pleasure* to saying that they *ought to promote pleasure*. Nevertheless, it's fair to ask if promoting pleasure should be our sole moral goal—the thing we should base morality upon. After all, there are some questionable or even immoral pleasures (e.g., enjoying child pornography and acting sadistically). Further, aren't there things besides pleasure that have value? The hedonist replies that anything else (e.g., friendship or learning) is instrumental—valuable only as much as it leads to pleasure. But this seems wrong. Although learning can be hard work and friendship can be costly, we still pursue both as valuable in themselves. In fact, why should we view pleasure as a foundational good in the first place? We often *do* pursue pleasure, but is that reason to conclude that we *ought* to?

Logically, this is not a small step at all. Nor is it particularly compelling. People often do things they shouldn't. People act selfishly or eat too much, but just because they *do* these things hardly shows that they *ought to*. Although hedonists take it for granted that pleasure/happiness is the only foundational value, they owe us a fairly strong argument for assigning pleasure so much importance.

Actually, this loose talk of the value of pleasure/happiness is not very satisfactory, because pleasure and happiness are not the same. Pleasure can *contribute* to happiness, but it is also possible to enjoy a constant stream of pleasures without being happy, as some celebrities have demonstrated. The distinction seems to be that a pleasure is fairly immediate and short-lived—a kind of *feeling*—while happiness is more of an ongoing *state of mind*. Happiness also relates closely to personal fulfillment or achievement. Finally, happiness must somehow be grounded in reality since it's hard to imagine achieving genuine fulfillment through mere illusions.

Since pleasure and happiness are not the same, it would be a mistake to gloss over their differences. Further, our discussion suggests that mere pleasure (as distinguished from happiness) doesn't look very promising as a basis for morality. It's not surprising, therefore, that some consequentialists have tried to shift from pleasure to other concepts of utility, including that which better captures the special nature of human happiness.

For Discussion

1. *Would you be happy living out the rest of your life in a pleasure machine? It suppresses all discomforts and provides virtual experiences of any pleasure you choose; the hitch is that everything is illusory—nothing is real!*
2. *How do you conceive of happiness and pleasure? (Be careful about how these words are often used.)*
3. *Do you think that pleasures are good, bad, or neutral?*
4. *Should utility be pleasure or happiness? Why?*

Summary

Consequentialist theories often employ a concept of utility, describing desirable consequences as having utility and undesirable consequence as having disutility. Hedonists define utility as pleasure/happiness—their only foundational (non-moral) value—and disutility as pain. Still, we must distinguish between pleasure, a more short-lived feeling, and happiness, a state of mind related to personal fulfillment. Treating utility as mere pleasure creates some problems: there are morally bad pleasures, and other things appear as good as pleasure. Thus, it's tempting to try to define utility to include happiness rather than mere pleasure.

Key Terms

- **Utility:** *whatever makes consequences desirable; disutility, then, is undesirable.*

III.** UTILITY AND MILL'S ACCOUNT

For consequentialism to be practicable, we must be able to accurately assess how much utility something might produce. Hence, utility needs to be both predictable and measurable. Pleasures are fairly predictable; they arise in most people in roughly similar ways and may even be measurable in terms of electrical brain activity. Happiness, however, is much more elusive. Happiness doesn't just *happen;* it's more the product of how one lives. Nor is there any guarantee that you will be happy in the same situation in which another person is happy. And suppose someone is happy: exactly how do we tell?

Despite its abstract appeal, identifying utility with happiness thus has some problems. However, John Stuart Mill (1806–1873), an influential consequentialist, thought it possible to get around these difficulties. Being sympathetic with hedonism, Mill's view is that anything pleasurable or conducive to happiness should count as having utility. As an *empiricist*— believing that only observation and experience can provide a basis for human understanding—Mill also holds that utility must be observable and even measurable.

In addition, however, Mill wants us to recognize that there are different *kinds* or *qualities* of pleasure, where "pleasure" here includes experiences that relate to happiness as well as to "mere" pleasures. Although Mill grants that all pleasures are good, he observes that some pleasures are on a higher plane than others. The pleasures of artistic creation, of helping others, or of solving a challenging problem, for instance, are "higher" and thus preferable (in some sense) to, say, getting drunk or pigging out on junk food. Likewise, the satisfactions we experience from pursuing knowledge or cultivating a deep friendship—the kinds of things usually thought necessary for happiness—are ultimately more important to us than the pleasures of, say, a pleasant meal. Mill associates higher-quality pleasures with more intellectual and distinctively *human* experiences—ones particularly conducive to human happiness. The lower-quality pleasures, meanwhile, he associates more with bodily instincts and appetites.

Mill famously observes, "It is better to be a human dissatisfied than a pig satisfied."[2] In saying this, Mill means to say that we usually draw much more satisfaction from distinctively human experiences—associated with the higher pleasures—than from those body-pleasing pleasures that many animals can also experience—the lower-quality pleasures. This leads Mill to propose that

---

[2]John Stuart Mill, "What Utilitarianism Is," *Utilitarianism* (Public Domain, 1863), chapter 2.

we give greater weight to higher-quality experiences than to lower-quality ones and that we also incorporate this difference directly into our evaluation of consequences.

There still remains the problem of measuring *quality* in some sufficiently precise way. Mill answers that we should assign weights to different kinds of experiences based on what most people say they prefer. Mill remains confident that most would prefer the higher-quality pleasures when faced with a choice. Although Mill has no desire to denigrate *any* pleasures, he argues that no sensitive and experienced person could find satisfaction in a life that satiates only the body. By weighting quality according to people's preferences, Mill thus provides a consequentialist ethics that incorporates both pleasure and happiness in a measurable way.

Mill may be getting at something important here. Still, there are difficulties. Can we be sure that most would agree to Mill's ranking of higher- versus lower-quality experiences? Mill grants that not *all* people would agree, for although anyone can enjoy the lower pleasures, it requires training and experience to appreciate many of the higher pleasures. You can't appreciate the joys of reading until you learn to read and even then a good course in literature might increase your enjoyment. The drunk on the street probably can't tell any difference between cheap wine and the connoisseur's choice. The danger is that those lacking experience with the higher pleasures will mistakenly *think* that they prefer the lower pleasures, simply because they don't know any better. To arrive at a more accurate ranking of various experiences, therefore, Mill tells us to consult only those who are well-equipped to appreciate both higher- and lower-quality experiences.

Even if we limit our consultations to such "experts," can we be certain that the resulting rankings will turn out as Mill thought they *should*? Despite its appeal, the idea of assigning greater weight to some pleasures over others may be wrongheaded. After all, we value all kinds of experiences. While few would be happy living as pigs, a life without simple sensual pleasures would be monotonous and depressing as well. We need both "higher" and "lower" pleasures, for a life that lacks either would be greatly diminished. We might even say, "It's better still to be a human *fully* satisfied (experiencing both kinds of pleasure) than to be Mill dissatisfied (experiencing only the higher pleasures)." If every kind of morally legitimate experience has its place, it may not make sense to assign greater importance to some experiences over others.

Further, it's a mistake to assume that pleasures only differ in importance by being higher or lower pleasures. After all, even the higher pleasures can be abused or perverted, for example, by an artist who enjoys creating works that debase women or a businessman who enjoys applying his intellect to take advantage of others.

In view of these considerations, it may be best to simply abandon the hedonist tradition. However, this brings us back to the question of how utility should be defined. Consequentialists have suggested a number of alternatives.

Some suggest that we give up trying to include anything positive or desirable in utility and simply define it in terms of avoiding the undesirable. It's fairly uncontroversial, after all, that people usually find pain and suffering undesirable. Others propose that utility includes *whatever* those affected may desire at that time. Whatever way we define utility, that definition will yield its own particular version of consequentialism.

Although the question of defining utility is important, it's not something we can settle here. However, we can still explore other important features of consequentialism without taking a definitive stand on utility. Leaving the issue open, therefore, we will follow common practice and simply speak of desirable consequences as having *utility* and undesirable consequences as having *disutility*. With these terms in mind, we next turn to a consideration of *act utilitarianism*, a consequentialist theory that remains very influential today.

For Discussion

1. *List several kinds of pleasures. Which would Mill call "higher" and which would he call "lower"? Would you agree?*
2. *Mill said: "It's better to be a human dissatisfied than a pig satisfied." The text also suggests: "It's better still to be a human fully satisfied than to be Mill dissatisfied." What are your reactions to these slogans?*
3. *How would you define utility?*

Summary

For utility to encompass happiness while remaining measurable, Mill introduced different qualities of experience, proposing that greater moral weight belongs to higher-quality pleasures. To determine which experiences are higher, we ask those familiar with both higher- and lower-quality experiences. But there may not be any genuine moral difference between these. Other consequentialists have abandoned traditional hedonism and define utility in other ways.

Key Terms

- **Qualities:** *allow us to distinguish between higher and lower pleasures; Mill thought the lower-quality pleasures deserve less moral weight.*

IV. ACT UTILITARIANISM

Act utilitarianism treats all individuals impartially, counting every individual exactly the same. It also focuses on *specific situations*. The situation determines what choices of action there are, along with the likely effects of each choice. This means that act utilitarianism can only be applied to particular situations, as what *can* and *should* be done both depend on the situation's circumstances. Finally, utilitarianism considers the *right* act to be the one that produces the greatest *overall* utility:

Act Utilitarianism: The morally right act, for any particular situation, is that act that results in producing the greatest *overall* utility.[3]

It's important to understand, first, that act utilitarianism is intended to *explain* right and wrong, to answer the question: *what makes an act morally right?* Act utilitarianism's answer is that it is right to distribute the most utility we can (overall) to those individuals affected by an act. Achieving the greatest overall utility is what makes an act right. That act *being* the right act, furthermore, is an objective fact since it depends solely on what generates the most overall utility in that situation. Opinions, desires, and even ignorance make no difference to what is right. Furthermore, an act's "overall" utility depends on *all individuals* affected. This includes not only the actor herself (who is always affected by her actions) but also everyone else affected.

Those affected by a particular act fall within the *scope* of that act's effects. Scope is just one aspect of the *overall* effects. One early utilitarian, Jeremy Bentham (1748–1832), identified seven aspects of an act's overall effects. Setting things up a little differently, we will be able to adequately assess an act's overall effects by using just the following four aspects.

1. Scope: Which individuals will be affected? How many? The greater the number affected by an act, the greater the scope of its effects. The greater the scope, the more that act influences overall utility. Whether Ed continues or stops the trials, for instance, all 2,800 of the participating patients fall within the scope, some being affected positively and some negatively. In addition, each patient's family and friends will be affected by Ed's choice to the degree they care about the patient. Thus, they too are part of the scope, as are the owners, employees, and investors of Ed's company and even those of rival companies. Finally, the scope includes all who could benefit from the availability of a better drug.

2. Duration: How long will each effect last? Some effects are short-lived; others continue a very long time. The longer an effect lasts, the more it influences overall utility. For those whose seizures are being controlled by Ed's drug (and for their family and friends), the positive effects will last as long as they take the drug. The same holds for people who take the drug in the future. On the other hand, some will suffer the drug's side effects. The effects of suffering a permanent injury last for the rest of their lives, and a roughly similar time period applies to many of their family and friends. Anyone who dies from the drug's effects suffers up until death; their family and friends will suffer over that time and for an indefinite time afterward. Finally, various company owners, workers, and investors will benefit (or suffer) for as long as their financial gains (or losses) last.

3. Intensity: Experiences can differ in their degree of strength or force. Some desirable effects as well as some kinds of suffering can be intense; others are fairly mild. Effects can also vary in intensity from one person to another. Thus, suppose that some of those participating in Ed's drug trials no longer experience small

---

[3]As mentioned at the end of the preceding (optional) section, we will hereafter understand *utility* generically – as simply encompassing good or desirable consequences.

seizures. The effect for these people is mild relief—an effect of limited intensity. For others, the drug prevents debilitating or even fatal seizures, which is clearly a much more intense effect. Those who suffer severely or die from the drug's effects experience intense disutility (though maybe not for a very long time). Their family and friends likewise experience fairly intense disutility, depending on their closeness to the patient.

4. Probability: We don't know the future so we don't know for certain what effects any particular action will produce. The best an act utilitarian can do, therefore, is to estimate the chances of each possible effect. These estimates should then be used to assign weights to each effect (desirable or not). Ed's information indicates that less than one of every one hundred patients taking the drug will suffer dangerous side effects, leaving 99% to enjoy the drug's benefits. Because these positive effects are so much more likely, they should be assigned a much higher weight (0.99) than the negative side effects (0.01). In this case, the probabilities are known quite precisely. The likelihood of possible financial gains and losses depend on market conditions and so can only be roughly estimated.

Applying probability estimates as weights to *each possible effect* is the most reasonable way to take into account our uncertainties about the future. Unlikely effects shouldn't influence our choice of acts as much as more likely effects. Extremely unlikely effects are usually negligible and so can be dropped from consideration unless the low probabilities are counteracted by very large scopes, intensities, and durations.

The morally right act cannot be determined by considering any one of the four aspects by itself; *all* must be included. To do this, we first identify what choices are available (e.g., Ed's can either continue or halt the trials). Next, we calculate the overall utility (treating disutility as negative and utility as positive) of each choice's results. We do this for each choice by considering **(1)** the *scope* of its possible effects, **(2)** the *duration* of each effect upon every individual in the scope, **(3)** the *intensity* (desirable or undesirable) of each effect for every individual, and **(4)** the *probability* of each effect. Having determined the overall utility resulting from each choice, we finally compare these to identify the choice that will result in the largest overall utility (or the least overall disutility, if no choice can give rise to overall positive utility). That choice is the one act utilitarianism tells us we should make.

For Discussion

1. *Think of any simple choice you've made today. What individuals did it affect (scope)? What are the duration and intensity of its effects? Which effects are most likely; are any important but unlikely?*

2. *Given your responses to question 1, would act utilitarianism approve of your choice?*

3. *What do you find most appealing about act utilitarianism? Why?*

4. *Faced with a moral choice, you decide what to do by comparing the overall utilities of each choice's effects. How could this lead you to choose an act that your moral intuitions say is wrong? (If this bothers you, see §VI!)*

Summary

Act utilitarianism defines specific acts as morally right or wrong; the right act in a situation is the one that will produce the greatest overall utility. To determine which this is, we consider our possible choices and the overall utility produced by each, taking into account each effect's scope, duration, intensity, and probability. When an effect includes both utility and disutility, the disutility is subtracted from the utility. We then compare the overall utility resulting from each choice; the morally right choice is the one that will produce the most overall utility.

Key Terms

- **Act utilitarianism:** *defines the morally right act, for a particular situation, as that which produces the greatest overall utility.*

- **Scope:** *the individuals affected by an act; the greater the number affected, the greater the scope.*

- **Duration:** *the time period over which an effect lasts.*

- **Intensity:** *the degree of strength or force of an experience.*

- **Probability:** *the chance or likelihood of an effect actually taking place.*

V. ATTRACTIONS AND PROBLEMS

1. Act utilitarianism has several advantages.

- One of its main attractions is its *objectivity.*[4] Each particular situation involves a set of definite facts: what the choices are, what effects each choice would bring about, and what amount of utility/disutility each effect would produce. Based on these facts, the right choice—that which would produce the greatest utility (or the least overall disutility if no choice will produce positive overall utility)—is also an objective matter of fact.

  This objectivity is no accident, for act utilitarianism was meant to be a kind of scientific moral theory—a way of determining moral right and wrong based upon experience. Because cause-and-effect regularities exist in nature, our accumulated experiences (both individual and shared) enable us to predict the most likely effects of our actions. Experience can also tell us much about the utilities and disutilities we can expect for these effects. As our experience and knowledge grow, our knowledge of moral right and wrong becomes increasingly precise. Act utilitarianism thus promises to take the aura of mystery from ethics, placing it solidly on empirical grounds.

- Originally intended to help reform the British criminal justice system, act utilitarianism is also *impartial.* Since it only considers the *effects* of an act, it can't be influenced by who the actor is—whether high or low born, statesman or criminal, male or female. All individuals are counted within the scope as equals.

---

[4]Act utilitarianism is an objectivist and not a relativist theory. Only the circumstances of each situation determine the overall utilities, not opinions, beliefs, culture, or the like.

- Act utilitarianism is extremely *simple*: it explains all of morality by a single principle. This principle, furthermore, is highly intuitive in at least two ways. First, act utilitarianism is surely on the right track in treating an act's consequences as morally significant. Second, it resonates with human psychology since we all seek desirable experiences while we try to avoid experiences that we find undesirable.
- Act utilitarianism is very *flexible*. Although it defines right acts by a single principle, the utility for any act depends on each situation's particular circumstances. Since these can vary, there is considerable leeway in the moral judgments act utilitarianism makes. The results can be surprising. For instance, while act utilitarianism might require telling the truth in one situation, it might forbid it in another. This sensitivity to the circumstances is seen as a major advantage by many.
- Finally, many see utilitarianism as attractive because it so easily *extends* to include non-humans. Since many animals have both positive and negative conscious experiences, it seems unwarranted to neglect them in utilitarian considerations. Thus, the utilitarian evaluation of any situation involving animals usually includes them among the individuals within its scope.

2. Act utilitarianism also encounters some imposing problems.

- *Calculations:* You've already thought of this: how accurately can we determine the scope, intensity, and duration of several actions' consequences as well as accurately estimate the probabilities of each? Even for Ed's fairly simple case with drug trials, we must weigh the drug's benefits against its side effects, consider the survival of Ed's company and the larger financial picture, evaluate the duration and intensity of every possible effect upon a large number of people, and estimate the probabilities of each possible effect. Doing all of this adequately looks daunting. Unless this difficulty can be alleviated, it may be too troublesome to determine the objectively right choice for a particular situation. This is a problem with the theory's *practicability*.

    Utilitarians have a response. As they point out, people have been accumulating knowledge of cause-and-effect relationships for millennia. Thanks to this ever-increasing store of experience, we can predict the effects of most acts with considerable success. In fact, we each do this every day. It should not be hard, then, to formulate general **rules of thumb** to guide our choices. For instance, while lying may bring certain immediate advantages, it frequently entangles us in more complex troubles that ultimately affect everyone involved. As the ensuing unpleasantness usually outweighs the initial advantages, we learn that it's best to follow the rule: "Don't lie." By applying similar rules of thumb to everyday situations, we can forego most everyday utilitarian calculations. Such rules of thumb won't *always* lead us to the morally right choice, but they will with reasonable dependability.
- *Moral Saints:* A cluster of problems arises from the extensive moral demands act utilitarianism places upon us. First, the theory turns *everything* into a

moral issue. What clothes should I wear today? Can't I wear whatever I want? Not necessarily. From a utilitarian perspective, I must consider what effects my dress could have on everyone I encounter. For instance, if my clothes are too flashy, that might make others envious or unhappy. The point is that *whatever* I do affects others and so qualifies as a moral issue I ought to consider. But that doesn't seem right. Aren't most mundane choices morally neutral?

Next, utilitarianism tells us that for any situation, there is always some *best* choice. This entails that I *ought* to reject all alternatives in favor of that *best* choice; choosing anything less amounts to my failing to act morally. Suppose I give $2 to a homeless man who really needs it. Haven't I done a good thing? Maybe, but probably not the *best* thing. Wouldn't $4, $5, or a $100 do a lot more good? Sure, it may hurt me a bit to part with that kind of money, but if I'm not homeless, the disutility I experience won't compare to the benefits I bring to that man. A contemporary act utilitarian, Peter Singer, has argued along these very lines. His conclusion is that well-off Americans have a moral obligation to give a large portion of their income - potentially up to half or more--to alleviate suffering in the rest of the world.

Or, think about the many health providers who risked their lives to care for victims of the 2014 Ebola outbreaks or the Doctors without Borders who treat people in war zones. If their actions in these situations produce more utility than they would in their usual jobs, then act utilitarianism says that it's their moral *duty* to do such things. But we view such self-sacrificial acts as going way "beyond the call of duty." Act utilitarianism doesn't recognize the difference.

In these ways, act utilitarianism can make it our duty to act as moral *saints*. It says that when people act in "saintly" ways, they usually have just done what they should have, nothing more. This clashes with our intuitions regarding what count as actual moral duties--a problem with *moral confirmation*. It's hard to see, furthermore, how to avoid this problem without altering the very nature of act utilitarianism.

• *Promises, justice, and rights:* Act utilitarianism often supports our moral intuitions that lying, murder, breaking contracts, and cheating are wrong. Yet there can be situations where even these wrongs could produce the greatest utility, making them right instead. For instance, as executor of his estate, I promise a dying man to pay the $20,000 debt he incurred forty years ago. This debt is owed to one of the richest men on earth who has long since forgotten all about it. Should I pay the debt? The money would do much greater good invested in cancer research or given to the local soup kitchen. Also, the dead man can't be affected by what I do, and no one else witnessed my promise. Thus, my breaking this particular promise would likely produce more utility than my keeping it. But would that be right? Many people feel very uncomfortable with cases like this. "A promise is a promise," isn't it? Also, note the strangeness of the utilitarian position here: it's not merely *allowed* that I break my promise; rather, it's my *moral duty* to break it.

More generally, if act utilitarianism were true, then any sort of action could become one's moral duty *given the right sorts of circumstances*. This opens the door to all sorts of outrages. Among these are act utilitarianism's failures with justice and human rights, which many consider its most objectionable results. Imagine that you belong to a small group of people with a rare genetic profile; although your organs and blood are compatible with others in this group, none of you can receive organs or blood from anyone else. A devastating earthquake injures countless people in California. Because you weren't there, you remain in excellent health. It turns out that three of the injured belong to your genetic group—a mother of four, an important political leader, and a research scientist. You happen to visit California, and while you are there a doctor identifies you as the only compatible donor for these victims. Would it be morally right for the doctor to entice you into the hospital, put you to sleep, and then remove a kidney, a couple pints of blood, and maybe some other tissues to save these people? Wouldn't this involuntary organ "donation" grossly violate your rights? Or suppose a heinous crime has been committed, but the authorities can't find any clues. As public fear and outrage grow, the police realize that they need to find *someone* to punish or riots will ensue. Would it be *just* for them to take some innocent drifter, frame him with the crime, and punish him to head off a riot? It's not hard to see how utilitarianism could judge both acts to be morally "right." All that's needed is for them to create more utility than any other option.

The trouble is with act utilitarianism's aim of promoting *overall* utility. This must include *all* of those affected, making it possible for the majority's interests to "swamp" or outweigh the interests of the minority when these conflict. For act utilitarianism, "the good of the many outweighs the good of the few, or the one,"[5] and this can lead to injustices that utilitarianism must approve. In addition, act utilitarianism can make little sense of personal moral *rights*. Rights apply to individuals, but utilitarianism views an individual as only part of what in included in overall utility. Can a theory that has such difficulties with *moral confirmation*—requiring rights violations, injustices, and the like—be an acceptable ethical theory? The end (maximum overall utility) does *not* justify the means, critics say—especially when the means requires a travesty of justice or rights. For these reasons, many have concluded that act utilitarianism is morally bankrupt.

Similar problems, by the way, can appear when a situation pits human and animal interests against each other. Most utilitarians count humans and animals *equally* in determinations of scope. Does this mean that utilitarianism views humans as no different from animals? Utilitarians often temper this with the following argument. Human intelligence gives us a greater capacity to anticipate suffering compared to most other animals. Therefore,

---

[5]The last words of Mr. Spock in *Star Trek II: The Wrath of Khan*, directed by Nicholas Meyer, Paramount Pictures, 1982.

humans will often experience more suffering (disutility) than an animal in similar situations. For instance, while a hamster may dislike the prick of a needle, its suffering hardly compares with that of a child who experiences dread terror when the doctor pulls out a syringe. The child suffers more in both intensity and duration, and this makes the child's total disutility greater than that of his hamster counterpart. Yet even when an effect for a human has a greater impact on overall utility than for an animal, it's still *possible* for the interests of a few humans to be swamped by the interests of many animals.

For Discussion

1. *What do you view as act utilitarianism's greatest advantages? Why?*
2. *Suppose two or more options yield the same amount of expected overall utility—they tie. What would be right in that case?*
3. *Do you think that act utilitarianism should count animals?*
4. *How well do rules of thumb address act utilitarianism's problems regarding calculations?*
5. *Do you think that you have a moral duty to keep your promise to the dying man or should you use that money to help poor people instead? Why?*
6. *How much do you think animal and human mental capacities affect their capabilities of experiencing suffering?*
7. *A teen is charged with petty theft in a bad neighborhood. The judge decides to make an example of him to deter others in the neighborhood from committing more serious crimes, so he triples the teen's sentence. What do you think about this? What would act utilitarianism say?*
8. *The argument to drop atom bombs on Hiroshima and Nagasaki maintained that only something drastic could drive the Japanese to surrender. Otherwise, the war would continue much longer, causing huge losses on both sides. Does this look right from an act utilitarian perspective?*

Summary

Act utilitarianism has several advantages. It's objective, simple, very flexible, and it easily extends to include animals that can be aware of pleasures and pains. The theory also encounters several objections. It requires that we do calculations to determine what is right, and these can be unduly difficult. It also demands that we act as moral saints, and it encounters all kinds of problems with promises, justice, and rights. Of these, the calculation problem can be at least partly solved via rules of thumb, though this will sometimes lead us to make choices that are wrong according to act utilitarianism. The most serious set of problems go with promises, justice, and rights.

Key Terms

- **Rules of thumb:** *rules that tell us what we should do based on what usually promotes utility best in similar situations.*

VI.** BEYOND CLASSICAL UTILITARIANISM

We have mainly considered classical act utilitarianism, which clearly founders upon several objections. Since its earliest formulation, however, theorists have tried to improve upon classical utilitarianism—for example, Mill attempted to include each pleasure's quality when calculating utility. Although we cannot survey every other alternative, it's only fair to describe some of the more important variants that have emerged from the ongoing efforts to answer the previously noted objections.

1. Different concepts of utility: Besides Mill's redefinition of utility, we've mentioned a few other alternatives as well. Each distinct concept of utility yields a different version of utilitarianism. These different accounts, furthermore, can sometimes support different moral judgments. In any case, the important thing is to avoid defining utility by appealing to any foundational *moral* values—something Mill may be doing by so closely associating higher qualities with greater moral weight. After all, if we already know what is morally good, then there is no need for consequentialist explanations of morality in the first place.

2. Ideal and expected utility: Doing utilitarian calculations remains a problem, even when we use rules of thumb. First, no matter how carefully we formulate these rules, there's no guarantee that they will always lead us to do what act utilitarianism itself says is right. This is because of a theoretical limitation regarding rules: none can ever be specific enough to take into account every circumstance in the way that act utilitarianism does.

More seriously, there's a practical limitation: even our best probability estimates can't anticipate *actual* consequences with unfailing success. By applying probabilities as weights to each possible effect, we can only arrive at **expected utilities**—our best assessments given our human limitations. But act utilitarianism defines the right act *ideally*, in terms of what *actually will result*. Inevitably, then, even our assessing expected utilities as accurately as we can won't always lead us to the right act (as act utilitarianism defines it). Given classical utilitarianism's definition, there's nothing we can do about this except to base our estimates on as much information as possible.

An alternative is to replace *ideal* utilitarianism with an account that doesn't require a godlike knowledge of the future. Suppose we *define* morally right acts in terms of our best probability estimates and resulting expectations. Then *that which appears best to us at the time* literally becomes the *right* act—on the condition that we reason correctly using all we could reasonably be expected to know at the time. If it turns out that another choice would have produced more overall utility, then we can acknowledge that as the *ideal* choice while still maintaining that we made the morally right choice at the time. By softening utilitarianism in this way, we cut into the more serious aspect of utilitarian calculations.

3. Characterizing the right: Act utilitarianism's goal of maximizing overall utility has the serious disadvantage of letting majority interests swamp those of the few, leading to injustices and rights violations. But there are other possible ways to characterize right acts. For example, a right act could be described as that which achieves the greatest overall utility as long as no individual's harms or benefits differ by more than 25% from the average for all others. This would rule out an involuntary organ donation that costs the donor ten units of disutility when the three recipients' average utility is twenty:

Donor:	Recipient's average:	Difference:	25% of average:
-10	+20	30	5 = 25% of 20

In this case, the proposed characterization allows for a difference of up to five units of utility (25% of the recipients' average of twenty), but the actual difference is thirty. This is six times more than what the proposal allows, making this forced donation morally unacceptable. As this demonstrates, the proposed characterization works against swamping by requiring that consequences be distributed more evenly, leaving no individual harmed or benefited much more than anyone else.

There are countless other ways to characterize the right. These would likely yield different moral judgments even for the very same problem and circumstances. By choosing with care, utilitarians can avoid some of the most serious objections leveled against classical utilitarianism. Of course, the utilitarian should also provide very good reasons for using one characterization over others.

4. *Accommodating justice*: Some of the most intriguing defenses of act utilitarianism have been made in response to its weaknesses with justice and rights. Utilitarians point out that when justice and rights are regularly violated, people's lives become filled with fear and uncertainty over when they might be required to sacrifice *their* interests for the overall good. Turning the point around, it seems that a general respect for justice and rights could surely promote utility. Why then should we grant the criticism that act utilitarianism works against justice and rights?

The problem is this: to achieve the desired gains in utility, a set of principles must be established that uphold rights and justice *regardless of the circumstances*. Yet act utilitarianism *cannot* establish such principles. Since act utilitarianism deals only with particular acts, it cannot support general principles because there will always be situations in which such principles must be violated to attain the greatest utility. By its very nature, act utilitarianism can't attain the gains in utility that justice and rights could offer. But what if it were possible to establish principles based on the utility these principles themselves would produce? *Rule utilitarianism*, the theory explored in the next chapter, attempts to do this.

For Discussion

1. *Consider a rule of thumb like "Never lie." Can you think of situations for which act utilitarianism would require a lie?*

2. *What do you think of the proposal to maximize expected utility rather than actual utility? What are some advantages and disadvantages with each option?*

3. *Suppose morally right acts are defined as what will produce the greatest overall utility given our best probability estimates and knowledge at the time. Does this undermine act utilitarianism's objectivity?*

4. *Can you think of other ways to characterize the right besides maximizing overall utility and the text's suggestion? What improvement would your characterization introduce?*

5. *Why can't act utilitarianism support, say. the right to one's property? Explain.*

Summary

Given the many serious objections to classical act utilitarianism, we might consider altering it. The most direct way to do this would be to redefine utility. We also might try replacing the ideal goal of maximizing actual utility with the goal of maximizing expected utility. More significant changes would involve recharacterizing right acts to require a fairer distribution of utility than what we get by merely maximizing overall utility. In the next chapter, finally, we will consider an attempt to use utility to define right principles or rules instead of just right acts.

Key Terms

• **Expected utilities:** *our best assessments of the utilities likely to result from each choice's effects given our limitations and knowledge at the time.*

Chapter Assignment Questions

1. *How does act utilitarianism differ from ethical egoism (see Chapter Five, §IV)?*

2. *Discuss the pros and cons of treating pleasure/happiness as the only good value, as Hedonism maintains.*

3. *How well does the proposal to use rules of thumb solve the problem of making utilitarian calculations?*

4. *Can you think of any act utilitarian way to get around the problem of requiring everyone to act as moral saints?*

5. *Act utilitarians respond to people's moral intuitions against breaking promises as follows: although breaking a promise may feel wrong, what this really shows is that our moral intuitions are sometimes mistaken; they don't sufficiently take utility into account. How would you reply?*

6. *Explain how the act utilitarian emphasis on overall utility gives rise to the problems with justice and rights.*

7. *Evaluate act utilitarianism using the criteria for assessing theories (see the Introduction to Part II).*

8. *Changing the organ donation story a little, suppose that you, the potential donor, are told about the situation and then asked—not forced—to donate some organs. Would you have a moral obligation to comply?*

9. *What do you consider to be the strongest objection(s) to act utilitarianism?*

Additional Resources

Bentham, Jeremy. *An Introduction to the Principles of Morals and Legislation (1781)*. Amherst, NY: Prometheus Books 1988. This book is also available online. Accessed August 5, 2009. http://www.utilitarianism.com/jeremy-bentham/index.html. See especially chapter 4, "Value of a Lot of Pleasure or Pain, How to Be Measured," in which Bentham discusses his seven-part measure of utility.

Mill, John Stuart. *Utilitarianism*. Public Domain, 1863. The entire text may be found online. Accessed August 27, 2016. http://www.utilitarianism.com/mill1.htm. See chapter 5, "On the Connection between Justice and Utility," for Mill's analysis of the nature of justice and his defense of utilitarianism in reply to the objection regarding rights and justice.

Smart, J. J. C. and Bernard Williams. *Utilitarianism: For and Against*. New York: Cambridge University Press, 1973. A classic discussion of utilitarianism in which Smart defends his version of utilitarianism and Williams responds with his criticisms of the utilitarian approach.

Singer, Peter, ed. *A Companion to Ethics*. Oxford: Blackwell Publishers, 1993. See section 19, "Consequentialism," by Philip Pettit for an exploration of more contemporary approaches to utilitarianism, in contrast to classical utilitarianism.

Case 1

Charity vs. iPad

Josh has his eye on the latest iPad and has been saving up his earnings from the tutoring job he works at his college. Although he's been really looking forward to getting this new toy, he's now having second thoughts. Joe is an international studies major and also a member of the international student club. Just last week, his friend Samesh made a presentation to the club about Kenya students who can't afford to finish high school. In Kenya, attending school is mandatory, but since it costs money, many people cannot afford it. Samesh proposed that the club start collecting for a reputable charity that sponsors Kenyan high school students. Both Josh and most of the club felt they really wanted to help; still, Josh also would like that new iPad. He is torn, but realizes that by donating the iPad money to the charity, he could do a lot more good than by just spending it for himself.

THOUGHT QUESTIONS

1. What would you do if you were Josh? Provide reasons.
2. According to act utilitarianism, is Josh morally obligated to donate the money to the charity? What are the good and the bad effects of Josh donating the money instead of buying his new toy?
3. Who belongs to the scope of individuals affect by Josh's decision?
4. Suppose that since Josh doesn't really need an iPad—he'd just like it to play games, watch movies, and listen to music—he decides to donate the money now and keep saving to buy the iPad later. According to act utilitarianism, would Josh's donation today morally justify buying the iPad later?

Case 2

Sponsoring a Child

Kazi's father had died, and his mother was left to support him and his three siblings. Thanks to a child sponsorship Kazi started receiving soon afterwards, he was able to finish high school—something that otherwise would have been impossible. He did very well at school, which qualified him to get free tuition and books for any future schooling. Since his sponsorship also provided him with occasional career counseling, he has now decided to continue to college and become a medical doctor.[6]

Sponsoring a child is easy, relatively inexpensive, and tax deductible. Some charities offer sponsorships for just $22 a month; others run about $1 a day. Many also provide medical care and other types of support. Often, potential sponsors can choose the child they want to help by examining photos the charity displays on their website. The sites also usually include the personal stories of the children in need. Once sponsors have chosen their child, they can develop a personal relationship with the child by exchanging letters and photos. Because sponsorships offer this personal and holistic approach, many people opt for child sponsorship over contributing to a more general child relief fund. However, a child sponsorship can be less cost effective than simply donating to a fund since it involves more overhead costs. After all, someone has to oversee the money and care that go directly to a particular family.[7]

Another approach doesn't allow prospective sponsors to choose individual children. SOS, for instance, establishes children's villages instead. These villages provide homes for children who have lost their parents (a trained "surrogate mother" takes care of them and so replicates a sort of family life for the children). Sponsors contribute a certain amount monthly toward the village. However, after the sponsorship starts, sponsors start receiving personal information and pictures of "their" child, which still allows for the sponsor to develop a personal relationship with a particular child. SOS takes this approach because it doesn't consider it appropriate to make personal information about needy children available publicly.[8]

THOUGHT QUESTIONS

1. Many middle-class Americans don't feel that they can spare $22 a month to sponsor a child. Do you think this is true? What do you think they use the $22 for instead?
2. Do you think that many Americans ought to sponsor a child? What moral considerations do you see as relevant to this question?
3. What advantages and disadvantages does each of the described approaches have—choosing a child to sponsor, a village sponsorship, or donating to a general relief fund? Which approach would act utilitarianism prefer? Why?

---

[6]Children International, accessed August 27, 2016, http://www.children.org.

[7]Some organizations, like Compassion and Catholic Charities, keep these costs to a minimum by working in partnership with local churches.

[8] Information about SOS is available at SOS Kinderdorf International, accessed August 27, 2016, http://www.sos-childrensvillages.org/. A similar Christian village ministry is called Rafiki. Other individual child sponsorships are also run by Compassion, World Vision, and other organizations as well.

Case 3

Should Your Next Car Be a Hybrid?

Hybrid cars—cars powered by a small gas engine and a battery—are now considered a mainstream alternative to a regular car. Their current market share, according to various Internet sites, is about 3.5%. The main factor driving America's growing interest in hybrids is probably fluctuating gas prices, although it would be nice to think that we are also becoming more "green" conscious. Since hybrid cars use less fuel, they also release fewer pollutants into the air. Of course, pollutants are still created by the electric generating facilities used to charge hybrid batteries.

So, should you consider getting a hybrid? Act utilitarianism would answer this question by comparing the main advantages and disadvantages of owning a regular car to owning a hybrid. One nice benefit to the owner is that a hybrid saves money on fuel and so can soften the impact of future surges in gas prices. For example, the 2014 Toyota Prius has an average fuel economy of fifty-three highway miles per gallon, twice what most other cars can offer. In addition, many states offer tax advantages for buying a hybrid.

One disadvantage to hybrids is that they are more expensive than regular cars, even with the tax advantages. Also, because hybrid engines contain more electronics, repairs can cost more than for conventional cars. In addition, the price of replacing a hybrid battery is probably not cost effective (current estimates say the batteries should last up to 100,000 miles). Meanwhile, some environmentalists object that the production and disposal of lithium batteries is not environmentally friendly.

Still, there are several nonmonetary benefits to hybrid cars. Our using less gas could reduce or maybe even eliminate our dependence on foreign oil from some of the world's most unstable regions. It could also reduce air pollution. Gasoline exhaust causes respiratory problems, increases the risk of cancer and asthma, and can harm people's immune systems. Reducing air pollution would also help put the brakes on climate change, since carbon dioxide, the main component of automobile exhaust, is primarily responsible for greenhouse warming. Limiting pollution may become a major benefit, since there's growing evidence that climate change is already melting the earth's ice caps, warming the oceans, intensifying world weather patterns, allowing disease-carrying mosquitoes to spread northward, and destroying a large number of animal and plant species.

Electric cars are another emerging option; these promise many of the same desirable effects as hybrids. Electrics presently cost substantially more than hybrids, although that didn't stop Tesla buyers in 2016 from putting down deposits on new Tesla cars that wouldn't even be manufactured for another year or two. In any case, and given the many very negative effects being fueled by gasoline automobiles, our moving from conventional cars to either hybrids or electrics may soon not merely be an option, but a moral imperative.

THOUGHT QUESTIONS

1. List all the effects that your next car purchase will have, both positive and negative. Comparing a hybrid to a regular car purchase, identify the scope, duration, intensity, and probability of these effects. Given this analysis, should you, according to act utilitarianism, buy a hybrid car?

2. How difficult was it to make this calculation for question 1? What do you now think about the calculation problem? How serious is this problem for act utilitarianism?
3. Is it too much to expect of you (or anyone else) to include issues like climate change in your deliberations about what kind of car to buy? Why or why not? How does your answer relate to the problem of moral sainthood?
4. What main factors do you think are presently driving more people to consider buying hybrids or even electric cars? Are people thinking their decisions through? Do you think that environmental concerns are playing a greater role in people's thinking? Should they be playing a greater role?

Case 4

Factory Farming and Animal Suffering

"Factory farming" refers to the concentrated animal feeding operations (CAFOs) used to produce the foods most Americans like best: chicken, beef, and pork. The practice is widespread, because about 9 billion chickens and half a billion turkeys are raised for human consumption in the United States each year. Let's look at these farming practices in a little more detail.[9]

When raised on a CAFO, few chickens or turkeys ever catch a glimpse of the outside world in their lifetimes (which run about six weeks for chickens and a little longer for turkeys). To save space (and thus money), these poultry are raised in pens that provide about half a square foot for each chicken and less than three square feet for each turkey. When the birds are grown, they don't have enough room to even stretch their wings.

Perhaps because they're so close together or because they are bored stiff, these birds can get rather feisty. To prevent them from injuring each other, their beaks are cut off. For turkeys, the tips of their toes are clipped as well—without using anesthetic. To prevent infection (which can rapidly spread in such crowded conditions), the birds are given heavy doses of antibiotics. These antibiotics are also necessary because the pens normally remain quite unsanitary. As you can imagine, this also produces a pretty horrible stench, mainly from bird feces.

Both chickens and turkeys have been genetically altered to grow faster and bigger. A faster turnover in birds allows for faster profits, which helps keep the cost of meat lower for the consumer. Fatter birds also mean fatter profits. Unfortunately, some chickens grow so heavy that their legs collapse under their own weight. Turkeys grow breasts so large (Americans prefer breast meat!) that they can't reproduce normally; they must be artificially inseminated. Turkeys are also prone to falling down and may be injured by other turkeys stepping on them.

When the birds are brought to the slaughterhouse, they are dumped from their crates onto conveyer belts, and some fall off. Because of the speed at which workers process the birds, the fallen birds may not get picked up again; as a
Continued

---

[9]The information for this case has been gathered from the website of Farm Sanctuary, accessed August 27, 2016, http://www.factoryfarming.com, and from the book by Peter Singer and Jim Mason, *The Way We Eat: Why Our Food Choices Matter* (New York: Rodale, Inc., 2006); see specifically Part I, chapter 2, "The Hidden Cost of Cheap Chicken."

Case 4 (Continued)

result, they either die from exposure or from getting torn up in the machinery. Once on the conveyer belt, the birds are hung upside down by their feet and are first run though a bath of electrified water. This step adds a humane touch of stunning the birds; however, it's not legally mandated because chickens and turkeys don't fall under the Federal Humane Slaughter Act. In fact, the stunning is done primarily to expedite the slaughtering process. However, some birds emerge from this bath still conscious. Conscious or not, they then proceed toward a mechanical knife that cuts their throats. Because of the high processing speeds, some birds manage to survive even this step. Thus, some are still alive as they reach their last stop—a scalding tank that submerges the birds in boiling water.

As repulsive as some of these facts may be, there are points in favor of CAFO processing. First, although birds are obviously capable of suffering, it is unlikely that they have the sorts of experiences we may imagine as we think about the slaughterhouse. We tend to anthropomorphize—to think from a human point of view. For instance, we may picture a bird experiencing overwhelming terror as it proceeds along the conveyer belt. Yet birds are not likely to even remotely appreciate the fatal significance of the process. In addition, human beings benefit from factory farming in many ways. For one thing, chicken farmers don't earn much, and factory farming helps their businesses remain profitable. Cheaper methods also pass significant savings on to consumers. For a family living below the poverty line, this savings could make the difference between having meat at the dinner table or not.

THOUGHT QUESTIONS

1. Because utilitarianism is inclusive and as birds can clearly experience pain, most utilitarians include them in their calculations. Do you agree that animal experiences *ought to be* included in the moral evaluation of factory farming?
2. One of the objections to act utilitarianism is that it turns everything into a moral issue. Do you think that this objection applies here?
3. Do the important human benefits of factory farming outweigh the disutility of the animal suffering?
4. Birds don't anticipate much of their suffering or impending death. Nevertheless, any human parent can fully appreciate the significance of not being able to afford dinner for her child. How should such differences enter into our utilitarian considerations? Are there other relevant differences between humans and animals that need to be considered?
5. Are there any morally preferable alternatives to factory farming?
6. Walking down the meat isle of the grocery store, you are thinking of buying some chicken to grill for dinner. You can buy the store brand on sale for $0.89 a pound, or you can buy some humanely raised chicken for $3.49 a pound. Do you have an act utilitarian moral obligation to buy the free-range poultry rather than the store brand? How much does this depend on your particular situation?

Case 5

Torture Lite

What is "torture lite"? The term, coined by the popular media, refers to sophisti-cated interrogation techniques that do not cause visible physical harms, as do more traditional forms of torture. Examples of torture lite include sleep depriva-tion, isolation, standing in stress positions, noise bombardment, humiliation, mock executions, and subjecting the prisoner to heat and cold. One notorious technique is *water boarding*: the suspect's head is dunked into water or his head is wrapped in a wet towel to induce the sensation of drowning. In contrast to traditional forms of torture, which inflicts pain directly, torture lite causes suffering more indirectly. Indeed, many of these interrogation techniques do not require any physical con-tact between the interrogator and the victim.

Such "advanced" interrogation techniques have been employed by a number of democratic governments, including by the United States during the Bush ad-ministration as well as by France and the United Kingdom. These methods are mainly used for intelligence gathering. Since the Geneva Convention forbids more classic forms of torture, these are not used by democratic governments. Torture lite, as some argue, is thus the only legal alternative and is sometimes necessary to prevent even greater harm. For instance, lite techniques have been used in an attempt to prevent terrorist attacks. Since 9/11, the use of these techniques has become more common. Torture lite has become particularly notorious due to its use at Guantánamo Bay and Abu Ghraib.

The primary moral defense for using these techniques is utilitarian. Support-ers argue that by subjecting prisoners to these techniques, we can gain important information that may prevent great harm to society. The suffering of one (or a few) individuals is relatively minor, after all, compared to the potential suffering of a great many. This rationale follows what's called the "ticking bomb scenario": imag-ine that there's a bomb hidden somewhere that threatens to kill millions of people; the only way to find the bomb and prevent these deaths is to torture the individual who knows where the bomb is hidden. Isn't it obvious that we should torture the individual in such a situation?

Georgetown Law Professor David Luban has offered some interesting chal-lenges in reply. According to Luban, the scenario makes some assumptions that are seldom if ever met in reality. For instance, it assumes that we know *for sure* that the suspect has the information we want. But is that ever the case? Not knowing what useful information the suspect might be able to reveal, could we justifiably torture someone? How high must the odds be in our favor? Is a 50/50 chance of obtaining important information sufficient? Could just a 20% chance of success justify torture if enough is at stake? Should this be a game of odds in the first place? Also, how many individuals could we justifiably torture, for how long, and to what degree if we think we might gain some needed information?[10]

Philosopher Jessica Wolfendale, meanwhile, argues that the line between or-dinary torture and torture lite is not well defined, for even the latter can cause per-manent psychological and physical harm. Standing in stress positions can cause
Continued

---

[10]David Luban, "Liberalism, Torture, and the Ticking Bomb," *Virginia Law Review,* 91 (2005): 1425–1461.

Case 5 (Continued)

swollen ankles, blistering on the feet, and a raised heart rate. Carried far enough, it can lead to kidney failure and heart attack. Sleep deprivation can produce delusions that sometimes can remain even after deprivation has ceased. Torture lite can also cause post-traumatic stress disorder to such severity that the victim may never be able to function again as a normal member of society.[11]

THOUGHT QUESTIONS

1. Torture lite is less direct than traditional forms of torture. Do you think that this invites us to use it more often and for less compelling reasons? Is its use easier to rationalize?

2. Traditional torture has not typically produced very reliable information. Those in great physical pain will often "confess" to whatever the torturer asks of them. Is this likely to be true for torture lite as well? How is this relevant to act utilitarian arguments regarding torture lite?

3. According to act utilitarianism, using torture lite can only be justified if it would maximize utility in that particular case. Can you think of such a case?

4. Does the issue of torture lite add additional force to act utilitarianism's problems with rights and justice?

5. Suppose that in some particular case the use of torture lite would definitely produce greater overall utility than any alternative. Would you agree with act utilitarianism's approval of torture lite in that instance? Why or why not?

---

[11]Jessica Wolfendale, "The Myth of Torture Lite," *Carnegie Counsel for Ethics in International Affairs*, 23.1 (Spring 2009): 47–61.

CHAPTER SEVEN

Consequentialist Ethics: Rule Utilitarianism

I. INTRODUCTION

- On the campaign trail, candidates make all kinds of promises. Once elected, they usually fulfill some of those promises. Others they may try to fulfill but can't. Then there are usually several promises they don't even try to fulfill.
- You borrowed $40 from a friend last week and agreed to pay him back today. But you then forgot all about it. This afternoon your friend asked you for his money. You realized that you forgot; you also discovered that you didn't have enough on you to pay him. You asked if you could pay him back tomorrow instead, and he said yes.
- You just bought a car, and the salesperson said she'd have it ready for you the next day at noon. You arrived a little before noon and found the salesperson. She said that the car was all ready for you except that it was just then going through their complimentary car wash. She disappeared, and at five minutes after noon, she brought the car right to where you are standing and handed you the keys.
- James and Eileen were deeply in love. He proposed to her and nine months later they married. Both their vows and wedding dance song had the phrase, "Our love is forever / and after the end of time." Things started out pretty well, and both were very pleased when James landed a great new job. His immediate supervisor, Amber, who was also married, was strikingly beautiful, charming, and quite smart. After working closely together for a couple of years, James and Amber began an affair. James still cared for Eileen, and in fact their first child was just nine months old. But James was wildly infatuated with Amber. A few months later, James and Amber both filed for divorces, and six months after that, they got married. James left the child with Eileen.

How often do you make promises? Think about typical promises: "I'll be there." "I promise to get that done by noon." "I pledge allegiance. ..." "By signing this contract, I agree. ..." "I take this man to be my husband. ..." We make promises to others, and others make promises to us. Promises are so much a part of our lives that we seldom notice how much we depend on them. Of course, contracts still get broken, marriages fall apart, and commitments are not always kept. Yet we keep making promises, as the practice of promising remains fairly dependable. If more promises and commitments were kept, the world would be a much better place. But even as things stand, we all seem better off with promises than without them.

What would a world *without* promises be like? Business deals would be extremely difficult and uncertain. Financial exchanges would require immediate payment, treaties would not exist or could not be depended upon, and friendships and marriages would be crippled. Without the practice of promising, ours would be an unfriendly, untrusting, and unstable world.

Widespread social rules and practices like promising generate consequences just as individual acts generate consequences. In particular, promising generates much more utility for us than if it didn't exist. This and other social practices— like respecting individual rights and enforcing justice—all promote overall utility. These observations lead us to a different consequentialist theory, *rule utilitarianism*.

For Discussion

1. *Describe a world that has no practice of promising. How does this world have less overall utility than a world which includes this practice?*
2. *Employing the social practice of promising is mastered in childhood. What requirements and qualifications define this practice? For instance, under what conditions may you justifiably fail to fulfill a promise? Could some promises never be binding?*
3. *Choose one or two of the broken-promise stories that open this section and morally evaluate the situation and each person's actions.*

Summary
Act utilitarianism considers Individual acts and their consequences. But certain social rules and practices (e.g., promising) can also produce consequences and affect overall utility. Building upon this fact, rule utilitarianism offers an important alternative to act utilitarianism.

II. RULE UTILITARIANISM

Many give up on act utilitarianism because of its difficulties. However, it's possible to reject act utilitarianism without abandoning all that utilitarianism stands for. *Rule utilitarianism* gives us a way to do this.[1] Like act utilitarianism, rule utilitarianism

---

[1] Some consider J. S. Mill to be an early rule utilitarian but the theory developed primarily in the mid-twentieth century and was intended as a serious rival to Kantian ethics.

maintains that positive consequences—utility—determine what is morally right. However, it doesn't consider the utility resulting from *individual acts* but from generally followed *rules and practices*. **Rule utilitarianism** has two fundamental principles:

> **Principle of rules**: A morally right *rule* or *practice* is one that would promote significantly greater overall utility, if widely followed, than if it did not exist.

> **Principle of acts**: A morally right *act* is one that follows a morally right rule or practice. Rules identified as morally right by the *principle of rules* should be followed except when they come into direct conflict with each other.[2]

While act and rule utilitarianism agree that morality ought to promote overall utility, their crucial difference is that rule utilitarianism assesses the effects of *general* rules and practices, *not specific acts*. Put another way, rule utilitarianism tells us what *kinds* of actions (e.g., keeping one's promises) are morally right. Furthermore, it says that the morally right thing to do is (usually) to follow such rules regardless of the specific situation. This also contrasts with act utilitarianism, which says that right acts depend on the details of each particular situation.

These seemingly small changes lead to important differences in what act and rule utilitarianism judge to be morally right. For instance, act utilitarianism must *approve* of promise breaking when that would best promote overall utility. But suppose that the principle of rules supports the rule: *one should always keep one's promises.* By the principle of acts, then, I should *not* break a promise—even in situations when act utilitarianism says I *should.*

For Discussion
1. *Can you think of other situations for which rule and act utilitarianism prescribe different acts?*
2. *Which theory's prescriptions in such situations best match your strongest moral intuitions?*

Summary
Rule utilitarianism supports general moral rules and practices (such as the practice of promising) that would promote utility. This contrasts with act utilitarianism's focus on individual acts. The right act for act utilitarianism also depends on the particular situation; for rule utilitarian, rules hold in general. Given the rules generated by rule utilitarianism, morally right acts are then those acts that follow those rules.

Key Terms
- **Principle of rules:** *a morally right rule or practice would promote significantly greater overall utility than if it did not exist.*
- **Principle of acts:** *a morally right act follows a morally right rule or practice.*

---

[2]We will discuss how rule utilitarianism addresses such conflicts shortly.

III. RULE VS. ACT UTILITARIANISM

What advantages are there to rule utilitarianism? To start, it shares most of the attractions of act utilitarianism. Specifically, it also is objective since it bases right rules—just as act utilitarianism bases right acts— on objective, empirical consequences. Rule utilitarianism is impartial, counting all individuals equally. It maintains an impressive simplicity. For better or worse, rule utilitarianism also readily extends to include non-human animals. The one act utilitarian attraction not shared by rule utilitarianism is flexibility, an issue we will take up in a moment.

Rule utilitarianism also does better with the problems act utilitarianism struggles with. For instance, act utilitarianism often requires us to do difficult *calculations* to identify right acts. Its solution to this problem is to rely on "rules of thumb" in place of precise calculations. But no rule of thumb can take into account all aspects of the different cases that fall under it. In fact, following a rule of thumb would sometimes lead us to obtain *less* utility than by doing what *act utilitarianism itself defines as right*. In contrast, if rule utilitarianism gives us a rule against promise-breaking, then we will never violate *what rule utilitarianism defines as right* by following that rule. In sum, although both kinds of rules can save us from doing calculations, rules of thumb can lead us to violate act utilitarianism's own standard, whereas rule utilitarianism's rules *are* its standard.

Rule utilitarianism also makes progress with the problem of *moral saints*. It does this by taking into account *the effects of the rule or practice itself*. Consider a rule that requires those whose wants are being met to give, say, 40% of their income to people in greater need. Clearly, this rule would be of great help to the poor; indeed, their resulting gain in utility would outweigh the disutility suffered by those much better off. Thus, wouldn't rule utilitarianism require such a rule?

Not necessarily, for the rule has a greater impact than the gain just mentioned. Suppose that, in the actual world, you enjoy a high standard of living because you work well and hard and so earn a very good income. Now imagine another world where there's a rule requiring you to give 40% of your income to others in need. Would you exert yourself as much in this second world, knowing that you may only keep a little more than half of all you earn? Few people would. Such a world offers its people much less of a financial incentive to work than this world does (assuming that this world has no such rule). As a result, those in the second world would tend to achieve less and so would not produce as much overall utility as people do in this world.

Next, suppose that in this world you plan to invest several years of your life and a great deal of money to earn a medical degree. In the 40% rule world, your medical career wouldn't reap nearly the same benefits nearly as soon. Would you be just as willing to invest so much of yourself in that world? The second world offers less incentive to pursue *any* sort of long-term professional training and so would produce fewer doctors, lawyers, scientists, and others who are crucial to any society's well-being. As a result, everyone in that world would suffer from these shortages, and there would be less overall utility than in worlds where there are stronger incentives for long-term personal investment.

Finally, note that with less incentive to work, people in the second world would work less and so earn less, leaving less money to go to the poor. Thus, even the poor wouldn't gain as much utility as it first seemed. Putting all of these considerations together, it appears that the 40% rule world is likely to generate *less* overall utility than a world without this rule. If this is so, then rule utilitarianism would *not* support such a rule after all. As other "moral saint" rules would likely have similar results, most would probably not be supported by rule utilitarianism.

Rule utilitarianism also makes substantial headway against the cluster of problems involving *promises, justice,* and *rights.* These problems arise for act utilitarianism because it determines the moral right for each specific set of circumstances. It thus can end up allowing *anything* to count as a morally right act as long as that act in those circumstances brings about the greatest overall utility. Promise-breaking, assassination, torture, the mass killing of civilians—any of these can qualify as morally right under the "right" circumstances.

Rule utilitarianism significantly sidesteps these sorts of problems, again thanks to its focus on the effects of *general* rules and practices rather than the effects of a specific act in specific circumstances. Once the theory determines the moral rightness of a given rule, that rule remains untouched by the varying influences of most special cases. For instance, we have seen that fulfilling the rules of promising remains a moral duty even when greater overall utility might be gained by breaking a promise. Furthermore, rule utilitarianism creates rules against lying, murder, and torture which must likewise be followed regardless of the specific circumstances. Since the rules of rule utilitarianism do not apply case by case, the theory is able to "rein in" many of the cases in which act utilitarianism would tell us to do something clearly wrong.

How does rule utilitarianism handle some of act utilitarianism's worst problems with injustice and rights violations? Let's return to the involuntary organ donation example. Could rule utilitarianism support a rule that forces individuals to sacrifice their organs for the sake of meeting other persons' needs? Act utilitarianism can allow forced organ donations in cases where the benefits to the many outweigh the losses for the one. But things change when we consider the consequences of an involuntary donation *rule.* Such a rule makes everyone a potential organ donor. At any moment, therefore, your health or even your life might be demanded of you. What would living under such conditions be like? Arguably, everyone would live under a continual fear that this demand might suddenly be imposed upon them. This would also affect people's plans for their futures. A woman wants to have a child or prepare for some profession, but she then realizes that her plans could be seriously thwarted if she is made an organ donor. Indeed, why would any of us invest ourselves in any long-term commitments when such life-changing uncertainties are always looming over us? Given the disutility of widespread fear and the difficulty of pursuing any long-term goals, it's not at all clear that rule utilitarianism could approve of a forced organ donation rule.[3] Similar

---

[3]The point is not that rules imposing saintly or unjust requirements could *never* be supported by rule utilitarianism. It's only that rule utilitarianism tends to deal with these sorts of problems more successfully than act utilitarianism.

arguments can be brought to bear against practices that punish innocent persons to quell riots, to deter others, and so on.

Moreover, rule utilitarianism can support many principles of justice and personal rights. It's beyond doubt that the most basic principles of fairness, justice, and rights extended equally to all would generate a tremendous amount of overall utility. Although no one would be allowed special advantages, neither would anyone be placed at an unfair disadvantage compared with others. Since people could expect to be treated the same way and to enjoy the same opportunities regardless of their circumstances, they could plan their lives with much greater confidence and much less anxiety than under act utilitarianism.

For Discussion

1. *Suppose that rule utilitarianism supports a general rule against taking other people's property. Why can't this rule hold for act utilitarianism?*
2. *Rule utilitarianism must still do calculations to determine right rules, but calculating a rule's utility tends to be easier than calculating an act's utility. To see why, compare the effects of a rule about bribery with a single act of bribery. Or, compare a rule about truthfully reporting the news with a single news report.*
3. *Copyright and patent laws are designed to ensure that writers, artists, and inventors get a reasonable return from their work. In terms of incentives and overall utility, are these laws a good thing?*
4. *Copyrighted works may not be freely distributed or even used without permission. A work under "copyleft," meanwhile, may only be used and distributed freely; it must not be sold. Would rule utilitarianism require one, the other, or some balance of both of these?*

Summary

Rule utilitarianism can reduce the force of many of the objections brought against act utilitarianism. For instance, it largely avoids the calculation and moral saints problems; it also seems to make significant progress in dealing with promises, justice, and rights. These successes all result from rule utilitarianism's shift from individual acts to rules, which requires that we assess the overall consequences of an entire rule or practice.

IV. PROBLEMS WITH RULE UTILITARIANISM

Rule utilitarianism yields some encouraging results, but it also runs into some difficulties. We will look at several of these, though our discussion won't necessarily exhaust its problems. For instance, there is still the general problem of how to define utility (another set of problems is discussed in §V).

1. *Dilemmas:* One problem arises precisely because rule utilitarianism generates rules: if right kinds of acts are determined by rules, what should we do when circumstances bring rules into mutual conflict? It's inevitable that such moral

dilemmas will develop. Suppose my neighbor, heading off for vacation, places his favorite handgun in my care for the time he expects to be gone. I dutifully promise to return it to him as soon as he asks for it back. Later that evening, this same neighbor gets into a loud argument with his father-in-law and suddenly comes storming to my door, demanding his gun back. What should I do? I ought to return his gun because of the rule that I keep my promises. Yet rule utilitarianism presumably supports another rule to the effect that I should act to protect the lives of innocent persons when I can readily do so. Under this rule, I should refuse to return the gun for fear of a tragedy that may ensue given my neighbor's present state. Either way, I am forced to violate a moral rule. Rule utilitarianism has thus placed me in a moral predicament—something act utilitarianism can never do.

Although this problem may look pretty serious, most rule utilitarians believe that the theory can be easily patched up to handle it. The usual recommendation is that when rules come into direct conflict, we should revert to an act utilitarian procedure to determine what should be done. In the previous example, for instance, I should act so as to achieve the greatest overall utility (or to avoid the greatest disutility)—keeping the gun from my neighbor until he calms down. Making this "fix" requires adding a third principle to rule utilitarianism:

> **Dilemma principle**: When circumstances place two or more moral rules in conflict, the morally right act, for those circumstances, is that act which will produce the greatest overall utility.

The complete rule utilitarian account thus consists of three principles: (a) the principle of rules, (b) the principle of acts, and (c) the dilemma principle.

2. *Inconsistency:* Possibly the most interesting criticism of rule utilitarianism comes from act utilitarians. Their complaint centers on cases where the two theories render different judgments of what is right. In particular, although act utilitarianism may judge a specific act (e.g., breaking a promise) to be morally right in a situation where that act achieves the greatest utility, it may be judged morally wrong by rule utilitarianism (if it violates a rule). But this, they maintain, makes rule utilitarianism inconsistent with utilitarianism's foundational goal of promoting overall utility. If achieving the greatest utility were *really* our purpose, how could it ever be right to let some rule keep us from achieving that? We should maximize utility in everything we do. But because rule utilitarianism's rules can require that we fail to maximize utility in certain situations, rule utilitarianism has deserted the utilitarian concept of morality.

Rule utilitarians have two responses. First, they can argue that although we occasionally lose utility by following the rules, rules can also establish practices (such as promise making) that generate vastly more overall utility than could ever be achieved by act utilitarianism. As John Rawls (1921–2002) explains, it is *part of the very concept* of promising that when I make a promise, I bind myself to doing what I have promised. For this practice even to exist, therefore, there must be a *general* moral rule that binds promise makers to their promises.[4] Rule utilitarianism supplies rules of just this sort; in contrast, the right act for act utilitarianism can vary depending on the circumstances. Although act utilitarianism might produce the greatest utility in particular circumstances, it can never achieve the gains in utility made possible by rules and practices. Since these gains compensate many times over for the losses that occasionally occur if we follow the rules, rule utilitarianism generates more utility than act utilitarianism. If our goal is truly to maximize utility, then rule utilitarianism wins, hands down.

Second, the rule utilitarian might point out that rules don't always have to be such coarse and simplistic generalizations as "Never kill" or "Never torture." Nothing in rule utilitarianism keeps us from **fine-tuning** such rules. Instead of "Never kill," for instance, rule utilitarianism would probably prefer the rule "Do not kill except when forced to in self-defense." Similarly, instead of "Never torture," rule utilitarianism might add qualifications that yield the rule: "Do not torture a person unless that's the only way to extract information needed to save a great many people." By adopting more finely tuned rules, rule utilitarianism can often achieve even more utility while reducing the number of cases in which following the rules would diminish utility. The strategy of fine-tuning—even if it never manages to address every case that bothers the act utilitarian—thus helps to answer the complaint that rule utilitarianism is inconsistent with the foundational goal of utilitarianism.

3. *The collapse of rule utilitarianism:* However, suppose we keep fine-tuning rules by adding more qualifications, exceptions, and adjustments to every rule. Each rule will then become increasingly specific and more limited in its application (e.g., "Don't kill a terrorist unless you kill him just before he attempts to set off a bomb that is likely to harm at least several people and there is no other way of stopping him without endangering others. . . ."). As we continue toward increasingly specific rules, many additional rules become necessary to handle those cases no longer covered by the more finely tuned rules. Ultimately, we will have a distinct rule for each distinct situation— each rule being formulated to ensure maximal utility for that situation. But this, in essence, is equivalent to act utilitarianism, which likewise seeks to insure the maximum utility in each distinct situation. In short, the strategy of fine-tuning could ultimately collapse rule utilitarianism into act utilitarianism. But if this is where rule utilitarianism ultimately takes us, why bother with it at all?

The last two objections clearly go together, and they drive the rule utilitarian into an uncomfortable dilemma. On one hand, the rule utilitarian could indefinitely fine-tune the rules, but this would just turn rule into act utilitarianism, making rule utilitarianism pointless. Alternately, rule utilitarianism could avoid doing any fine-tuning. This would avoid the danger of collapsing into act

---

[4]Bear in mind that our practice of promise-making includes special conditions that can excuse one from fulfilling a promise (e.g., when the other person "let's us off" or when we are prevented from fulfilling a promise due to reasons beyond our control).

utilitarianism but would still mean that, in some situations, our obeying a rule would produce less utility than if we followed act utilitarianism.

This dilemma, and the collapse objection in particular, has been viewed by many as fatal to rule utilitarianism. But there's an interesting response. Rule utilitarianism is concerned with the utility produced by its rules; but having to deal with a large number of very complex fine-tuned rules does *not* promote utility. It follows, then, that there will be greater utility when there aren't too many moral rules and when these rules are kept fairly simple and straightforward. This gives rule utilitarianism a natural stopping point for fine-tuning. Once fine-tuning starts to generate too many complex rules, they become impracticable; from that point on, further fine-tuning would create more disutility than utility and so should cease. This allows rule utilitarianism to avoid collapsing into act utilitarianism, which in turn allows it to sidestep this dilemma.

For Discussion

1. *Do you agree that I should not return my neighbor's gun at the time?*
2. *Would the following be rule utilitarian rules? (a) We should act to protect the lives of innocent persons when we can readily do so. (b) People should work at their own growth and development. (c) We should not take others' property.*
3. *Act utilitarians complain that rule utilitarianism has us sometimes producing less utility by following a rule. How serious do you think this problem really is?*
4. *To a reasonable degree, fine-tune some simple rules such as Never get angry, Never hurt another, and Don't take anything that isn't yours.*
5. *Which seems to you to be the better ethical theory—act or rule utilitarianism? Why? Apply the criteria for theory assessment from the Part II Introduction.*

Summary

Rule utilitarianism fares better than act utilitarianism with several utilitarian problems. Still, it has some problems of its own. Its difficulty with dilemmas appears to be met easily by the dilemma principle. The act utilitarian's charge of inconsistency is at least partly met by the argument that rule utilitarianism achieves greater overall utility than act utilitarianism ever could; the strategy of fine-tuning may also help. However, when taken too far, fine-tuning makes rule utilitarianism collapse into act utilitarianism. A rule utilitarian argument for keeping its rules practicable (not to complicated) may provide a way to avoid this collapse.

Key Terms

- **Dilemma principle:** *when rule utilitarianism encounters a moral dilemma, the morally right act for those particular circumstances is that which produces the greatest overall utility.*

- **Fine-tuning:** *introducing qualifications to a rule or practice, allowing it to generate more utility over a more limited set of situations.*

V.** JUSTICE AND RIGHTS AGAIN

Let's return yet again to involuntary organ donations. As we've seen, rule utilitarianism makes important progress with this problem since a general rule requiring such organ donations would arguably lose utility for society. However, the argument for this addressed just one particular organ donation rule. Suppose we replace that rule with the more finely tuned rule: "Healthy persons with no family or friends and who offer little promise of contributing to society should have their organs harvested when that can save several other persons." Adopting *this* rule might not create much disutility; it might even promote a fair amount of utility. After all, this rule restricts potential organ donors to a much smaller group than the entire populace, thus relieving most people from any fear of undergoing a forced organ donation. Still, it makes replacement organs available to more of those who need them. Thus, this more limited rule may be supported by rule utilitarianism, though it's clearly as unjust as its predecessor. Does rule utilitarianism remain open, then, to allowing serious violations of justice?

The rule utilitarian could argue that even if this rule were supported by utilitarian considerations, it would inevitably come into conflict with certain other rules. In particular, it would conflict with the principles of equality, justice, and rights that rule utilitarianism also supports. After all, a rule granting all people the same basic rights— regardless of their circumstances—would generate greater utility than if there were no such rule. Likewise, a society whose institutions are in keeping with our usual conception of justice would probably enjoy greater overall utility than a society that allowed unfair practices. Given such principles of justice and rights, the rule utilitarian might want to propose an **alternate dilemma principle** that gives priority to such principles. This principle could require that when rules conflict, the *rule* that generates the greatest utility must take precedence over the others. The right *act* would then be to follow that rule. Assuming that principles of justice and rights would generate greater utility than most other rules, rule utilitarians could thereby block even a fine-tuned version of involuntary organ donation and give much greater respect to the requirements of justice and rights.

Unfortunately, the issue is more complex than this. For one thing, act utilitarians will complain that the alternate dilemma principle takes rule utilitarianism even further from the ideal of maximizing utility in each situation, thereby strengthening the inconsistency objection. Further, there remains some doubt that rule utilitarianism can support our *full* conception of justice and rights. Being a consequentialist theory, rule utilitarianism must still define justice and rights in terms of resulting utility. But just as the utility produced by any act depends on the act's circumstances, utility produced by any rule will depend, to some degree, on the circumstances of the society in which that rule is implemented. In different social environments, the same rule might create different effects. The validity of any rule utilitarian rule thus appears to depend on a particular social setting. This works against our view that justice and rights hold for all in the same ways, regardless of any circumstances. The view that justice and rights hold universally, independent of circumstances, is taken by most *deontological theories*, which we will begin examining in the next chapter.

For Discussion

1. *Carefully consider the fine-tuned involuntary organ donation rule. How does it contribute to greater overall utility?*
2. *How do general principles of equality, justice, and rights contribute to greater overall utility?*
3. *Which do you prefer—the original dilemma principle or the alternate dilemma principle? Why?*

Summary

Although rule utilitarianism makes progress with justice and rights, it's unclear that it can fully support these. Rule utilitarianism certainly supports important principles of both and can even apply the alternate dilemma rule to give these principles priority. Still, rule utilitarianism inevitably depends upon a rule's consequences, which can vary across social settings. This means that rule utilitarianism's principles of justice and rights fall short of applying universally, and that seems at odds with a fully adequate conception of either.

Key Terms

- **Alternate dilemma principle:** *requires that when rule utilitarianism rules conflict, the rule that creates the greatest overall utility takes precedence and is the rule that should be followed.*

Chapter Assignment Questions

1. *What utility do institutions like governments, police forces, courts, and other social policies and practices bring into the world?*
2. *How does rule utilitarianism differ from act utilitarianism? What decides the moral rightness of an act in each theory?*
3. *What do you think is the most important advantage of rule utilitarianism over act utilitarianism? Explain.*
4. *How does rule utilitarianism create moral dilemmas, and why can't dilemmas arise with act utilitarianism?*
5. *Explain rule utilitarianism's response to the act utilitarian complaint about not consistently maximizing utility.*
6. *Why can't act utilitarianism make sense of the practice of promising?*
7. *Could rule utilitarianism support a fine-tuned rule requiring the death penalty?*
8. *Give a couple examples of some other fine-tuned rules that would allow injustices and rights violations. Explain each.*

Additional Resources

Brandt, Richard. *A Theory of the Good and the Right.* Amherst, NY: Prometheus Books. 1998.

Hooker, Brad. "Rule Consequentialism." In *The Stanford Encyclopedia of Philosophy* (Winter 2016 Edition), edited by Edward N. Zalta. Accessed February 26 2017. http://plato. stanford.edu/archives/win2016/entries/consequentialism-rule/. This article provides a good overview of the rule utilitarian approach.

Mill, John Stuart. *Utilitarianism.* Public Domain, 1863. The entire text may be found online. Accessed August 27, 2016. http://www.utilitarianism.com/mill1.htm. Mill's theory is considered by many to anticipate and include elements of rule utilitarianism.

Rawls, John. "Two Concepts of Rules." *The Philosophical Review,* 64 (1955): 3–32. Also reprinted in Mark Timmons, ed. *Conduct and Character,* 4th ed. Toronto: Wadsworth, 2003, 125–135. In this paper Rawls distinguishes between acts and practices and discusses the practice of promising in particular.

Case 1

Transgender Students at College

According to a 2013 article in *Inside Higher Ed*, about 150 colleges around the country now offer housing designated only for transgender students. Some student insurance policies also cover gender reassignment surgery and hormone therapy.[5]

Transgender individuals, which includes individuals dressing as or living as the opposite biological sex, drag kings or drag queens, gender queers (who identify with both sexes), and any others whose behavior crosses gender lines, are only recently getting attention as a distinct set of people in our society. This increased attention has prompted new measures at colleges, among other places.

Should special allowances be made for transgender individuals, and for their unique needs and concerns? If so, what sorts of things ought to be provided? There are a host of issues. Most bathrooms, for instance, are designated for males and females only. Locker rooms, housing, and medical services are likewise either designated for either males or females. Sports and teams likewise offer no third option. In an initial attempt to address these problems, some colleges now include "self-identity: ____" as a third gender option for students to mark for college administrative documents.

This gesture hardly solves the numerous dilemmas that transgender students face. Many experience tremendous anxiety from having to use either "male" or "female" bathrooms or locker rooms. Some have been harassed or bullied in classes, on teams, and in dorms; not surprisingly, many more are fearful of these things happening to them. For those struggling with such anxieties and fears, colleges may first and foremost need to provide counseling by trained staff.

On the other hand, could a college's making various accommodations for transgender students cause the rights of other students to be violated? There has been considerable controversy over "bathroom laws;" going one way on these is hard on transgender people; going the other way can make ordinary gender

Continued

[5]Allie Grasgreen, "Broadening the Transgender Agenda," *Inside Higher Ed,* accessed August 27, 2016, https://www.insidehighered.com/news/2013/09/18/colleges-adopt-new-policies-accommodate-transgender-students.

Case 1 (*Continued*)

people very uncomfortable. Some colleges, meanwhile, have started allowing transgender students to choose between being on men's or women's sports
teams. But non-transgender students don't have this choice; female athletes can't
join the male team, and male athletes can't join the women's team. Arguably, then,
transgender students are being offered more choices— possibly to their athletic
advantage—than non-transgender individuals.

THOUGHT QUESTIONS

1. Should a biological male who wants to live as a female be allowed to attend an
   all-women's college?
2. Do you think that all colleges and universities ought to make allowances for
   transgender students and their particular needs? How far should such accommodations be taken? What about private schools with a religious affiliation that
   forbids them from knowingly admitting transgender students?
3. In your view, should transgender individuals be allowed to choose their sports
   teams? Would it be unfair to allow this but not allow non-transgender students
   to make similar choices?
4. Apply rule utilitarianism to these issues: does it support a rule that requires
   public schools, for instance, to provide special accommodations for their transgender students? Could such a rule nevertheless be unjust?
5. Do you think that student insurance should pay for gender reassignment surgery? (Remember that this would force all policyholders to contribute toward
   such surgeries by paying higher premiums.) If so, would this rule call for some
   fine-tuning?
6. Would rule utilitarianism produce a rule that goes against act utilitarianism
   judgments about accommodating particular transgender students at college?

Case 2

Curbing Grade Inflation

When you get an A grade on a paper or an exam, what does that grade really
mean? According to many college catalogues, an A indicates an "excellent" or "outstanding" performance, which suggests that an A should be reserved for achievements above the norm, that is, above what most other people get. In contrast,
many colleges define a C as "average" or simply "satisfactory."

Nevertheless, these definitions don't reflect the reality of recent trends in
grading, especially at private colleges and universities. According to Professor
Stuart Rojstaczer from Duke University, the C grade represented about 25% of all
grades in 1969, whereas a mere 10% of all grades are Cs nowadays. This in effect
affirms that only 10% of all students do *average* work—everyone else does better!
This makes no sense. Indeed, Rojstaczer calls the C grade an "endangered species."[6]

Continued

---

[6]Stuart Rojstaczer, "Where All Grades Are Above Average," *Washington Post*, February 28, 2003.

Case 2 (Continued)

Do the higher grades mean that students have improved over the past couple decades? In the early 1990s, Princeton University used to give out As about 35% of the time. By 2003, that number had increased to 46%. Did Princeton students get that much better? Although the rising grades seem to say so, research shows that college students aren't really any better now than they used to be.[7]

To address its grade inflation problem, Princeton took a drastic step: in April of 2004, the faculty voted to restrict As to just 35% of the grades assigned by a department to its undergraduate students. This would bring the number of As back down to early 1990s levels. This ceiling was not to be applied class by class, but *only by department*. Otherwise, there could not be more than three As given to a class of, say, nine students, even if more of the students in that class did genuinely A-level work. In a 2005 news release, Princeton reported that its number of As had dropped 5% in the first year of the new policy.[8]

Was Princeton's solution a good one? One concern with this policy is that students who entered the university under the old system could suffer a decline in their GPA. This would send a misleading message to future employers and graduate schools. Also, some students reported that they felt even more pressure to earn a good grade at Princeton. Another concern was that peer institutions had not adopted similar policies, making grade comparisons between schools more difficult.

Thanks to its reputation, Princeton's students with high GPAs already had a better chance with their job and graduate school applications. Yet the new policy allowed their best students to stand out even when compared to other Princeton students. This improved these students' job and placement prospects even further. And why shouldn't they be given preference? Hadn't they earned it? After all, when most students are given honors, there's no longer anything special about honors. Further, when the achievements of the majority are overvalued, the achievements of the highest-quality minority are effectively undervalued. That's unfair to those students who are truly gifted and work the hardest. Arguably, then, the new policy simply gave outstanding students their due.

Many schools now pressure their professors to give out fewer As, and other schools have implemented their own grade inflation controls. Notably, Princeton gave up its policy after ten years. Still, the problem of grade inflation in higher education hasn't gone away.

THOUGHT QUESTIONS

1. What are some consequences of grade inflation? Discuss these for students, the college, and employers and graduate institutions.
2. As an undergraduate at Princeton, would you have supported this policy? Given that grade inflation can hurt nearly everyone, what would you suggest?
3. Are there other ways to deal with grade inflation besides Princeton's strategy?

[7]Stuart Rojstaczer, "National Trends in Grade Inflation," accessed August 27, 2016, http://gradeinflation.com.

[8]Faculty Committee on Grading, "Committee Issues Message on Grading Results for 2004–05," Princeton University, accessed August 27, 2016, http://www.princeton.edu/main/news/archive/S12/71/58E12/index.xml?section=newsreleases.

4. Should trends in grade inflation be slowed or even reversed by establishing a policy like Princeton's? Apply rule utilitarianism in your argument.

Case 3

Universal Healthcare

After several days of a strep throat infection, Dana suddenly developed a high fever and went to the emergency room. After waiting several hours, she was finally examined and given antibiotics. Twenty-four hours later, Dana had sunk into a coma—the bacteria had entered her bloodstream. Luckily, Dana survived. After about two weeks, she regained consciousness, was removed from life support, and was able to begin eating on her own. But since she only had student insurance, she was sent home from the hospital just twenty-four hours after leaving intensive care. She received little aftercare.

Fanny, also on student insurance, needed an emergency operation on her spleen. The cost for the operation exceeded what her insurance company was willing to pay. It took Fanny several years to pay back the $10,000 she owed the hospital.

Dennis, a disabled Medicaid recipient, must take thyroid medication indefinitely. Unfortunately, Medicaid won't pay for the name-brand product, though the generic product is less consistent. This means that Dennis must go to the doctor regularly to have his medications levels checked and adjusted. Dennis is always the last to be seen by the doctor since he's not covered by regular insurance.[9]

According to Physicians for a National Health Program, the United States has been the only industrialized nation that doesn't guarantee its citizens universal access to healthcare. Ironically, the United States also spends more per person on healthcare than most other countries, yet it has a lower life expectancy than other nations which offer universal healthcare.[10] According to philosopher Norm Daniels, this lower U.S. life expectancy is because access to healthcare closely depends on income. Under privatized healthcare, people with more money can afford better care and thus tend to live healthier and longer lives. Healthcare inequities thus match economic inequities; both, furthermore, correlate with educational inequities. Better educated people are usually healthier people. More generally, nations with poorer educational systems tend to have fewer healthy people as well. This inequity may be because less educated citizens tend to participate less in politics, which reduces their political impact and makes their local or national governments less responsive to their needs.[11]

While health tends to reflect economic and educational inequities, the reverse also seems to hold. The unequal distribution of healthcare leads to inequalities of education and opportunity. In short, healthcare, economic, and educational inequities feed each other in a perpetual circle.

From a utilitarian point of view, universal healthcare would seem able to add a great deal of utility to any society. Improving people's health would support more

Continued

---

[9]All of this case's material derives from personal interviews, conducted by Yvonne Raley on June 15 and 22, 2009, of individuals who wish to remain anonymous.

[10]Physicians for a National Health Program, accessed August 27, 2016, http://www.pnhp.org.

[11]Daniels, Norm, "Justice, Health, and Health Care," *American Journal of Bioethics*, 1.2 (2001): 3–15.

Case 2 (Continued)

productive work and thus improve the economy for all. People would be happier when they feel better. Dependable healthcare could also create more opportunities for everyone by breaking the cycle of economic inequality. For instance, the Affordable Care Act, signed into effect in 2010, made health insurance available to anyone, regardless of pre-existing conditions or sex. It particularly helped those under the poverty line since it enabled many of these people to obtain health insurance at rates they could afford.

Universal healthcare also risks producing disutility. For one thing, the cost of a universal healthcare system can be much higher than the cost of ensuring all citizens a fair share of food, shelter, and education. This can place burdens upon society as a whole. Further, higher costs may in turn impose new limitations on the availability of certain medical services, since the country's medical resources may not be able to meet increasing demands as more people qualify for such services.

A related concern with universal healthcare is that it might increase taxes. Those with higher incomes would effectively pay some for the healthcare of the poor along with paying for their own care. In addition, healthy people would effectively shoulder part of the health costs incurred by those who smoke, drink, and live an unhealthy lifestyle. These are not really new problems, since they already arise for any system that is designed to distribute goods to meet widespread needs, including all insurance programs.

One special worry about universal healthcare is that it could introduce rationed healthcare based on age. The argument is that the elderly have already enjoyed a long lifetime and will not live much longer, so more expensive treatments should only be made available to those who can most benefit from them. Utilitarianism presumably supports this argument; on the other hand, it can also be argued that denying some types of healthcare to the elderly is unjust and violates their rights. This is another instance of utilitarianism's problems with justice.

THOUGHT QUESTIONS

1. What are the important positive and negative effects of universal healthcare?
2. From a rule utilitarian perspective, do you think it is *morally* right for the United States to establish some sort of Affordable Care Act?
3. Do you think it is unjust that some people in our society still have no healthcare? Would it be more unjust (in terms of taxes, rationing, etc.) to address this problem by establishing a truly universal healthcare?
4. Does rule utilitarianism conflict with principles of justice in this case?
5. What do you think of the idea that healthcare should be rationed based on age? Would that better promote utility? Would that be morally just?

CHAPTER EIGHT

Deontological Ethics

I. INTRODUCTION

As "Honest Al" slouched contentedly back in his chair, he glanced out the office window at his large and profitable used car lot. It had been a great day. Four sales just this afternoon—that should be enough to cover his kid's college expenses for the whole next month! And it had sure been satisfying to chew out Fred, one of his salesmen, for losing the Atlas account. That should keep Fred humble for a while, and with Fred lying low, there'll be no need to put up with his incessant pleas for a raise until the end of summer at least. Al chuckled to himself—he had wanted to dump Atlas anyway, so Fred's mistake really worked out just the way Al wanted it. Best of all, though, was the sale Al managed to pull off to Mrs. Satzoner that morning. The blue SUV with the transmission leak—yes, Al was certainly glad to get rid of that. It had been a real pain moving it each morning so customers wouldn't notice the oil that collected underneath. "I wonder what was wrong with it?" Al mused. "Oh well, I'll find out soon enough." The great thing about the sale was that Satzoner had also taken Al up on his "great deal" to fix any problems that might show up over the next six months at a discount. "With the jewelry she wears, she can sure afford that repair more than I can; this way, I even make a profit while she thinks I'm doing her a favor." He shifted comfortably down in his chair. Al knew his business. He had a right to be satisfied . . .

Did Al do anything wrong? If we apply act utilitarianism to Al's actions, it isn't at all clear that Al brought more disutility into the world than would otherwise be there. Fred won't get a raise right away, but he may work harder over the next few months, and what Fred doesn't get, Al will keep so it more or less balances out anyway. As for Mrs. Satzoner, it's too bad that she will soon need to repair the car she just bought. But if this helps Al pay for his kid's college education—a worthy cause—then isn't that better than Mrs. Satzoner wasting more money on her gaudy jewelry? Further, none of this is likely to threaten Al's business—in fact, Mrs. Satzoner will probably rave to others about her super deals.

On the other hand, if we evaluate Al from the perspective of various deontological theories, then his behavior is morally unacceptable. In contrast to consequentialist theories, **deontological theories** reject consequences as the basis of morality. Typically, deontological theories focus on particular moral duties, calling something right or wrong depending on the *kind of act* committed. What kinds of things has Al done? He deceived others. Specifically, he tricked Fred into thinking that losing the Atlas contract was a bad thing, he hid the SUV's leak from his customers, and he led Mrs. Satzoner to believe that she had just bought a dependable vehicle and got a great backup deal on top of that. Deontological theories call such deceptive practices wrong. Because the kind of act is usually related to one's intentions (Al intended to deceive both Fred and Mrs. Satzoner), deontological theories also commonly consider the actor's motives and intentions. Al doesn't rate very highly in this respect either: he deliberately deceived others out of purely self-centered motives.

Deontological ethics determine right and wrong by identifying right kinds of acts and moral duties, not by considering the consequences.[1] In the next section, we will look at the theory of the twentieth-century moral philosopher, Sir William David Ross (1877–1971), which has important deontological aspects. Although it's not strictly true that Ross's theory is purely deontological,[2] it's close enough to give us a good feel for what a deontological theory can be like. Ross's theory is also simple and yet interesting in its own right.

For Discussion

1. *Do a rough act utilitarian calculation to confirm that Al's deceptions would probably be acceptable for act utilitarianism.*
2. *How important do you think intentions are to morality?*

Summary
Whereas consequentialist theories base moral right and wrong solely upon effects, deontological theories reject consequences as the basis of right and wrong and focus instead on our duty to practice or avoid certain kinds of actions. Deontological theories also often consider our motives and intentions.

Key Terms

- **Deontological theories:** *reject consequences as a basis for morality and instead focus upon duties (characterized by principles regarding specific kinds of acts) and, often, intentions.*

---

[1]Rule utilitarianism resembles a deontological theory in that its rules also identify kinds of acts or duties (e g., promise-keeping) that ought not to be violated regardless of the consequences. Rule utilitarianism would condemn Al's dishonesty. Still, rule utilitarianism remains essentially consequentialist in how it determines right and wrong.

[2]Ross's theory doesn't assign any real role to intentions; also, it doesn't appear to rule out a consideration of potential consequences when duties conflict (see §II).

II.** ROSS'S ETHICS

Ross offers us a very straightforward moral theory.[3] According to Ross, there are at least seven foundational moral duties:

- *Fidelity*: the duty to be truthful, pay back debts, and keep agreements.
- *Reparation*: the duty to set right any wrongs we have previously done to another (e.g., to apologize, pay for damages, etc.).
- *Gratitude*: the duty to make some return for favors and services others have done for us (e.g., expressing thanks, acting similarly as needed, etc.).
- *Justice*: the duty to ensure the fair distribution of goods according to merit.
- *Beneficence*: the duty to improve the condition of others.
- *Self-improvement*: the duty to improve oneself.
- *Non-maleficence*: the duty not to harm or injure others.

According to Ross, each of these constitutes a binding moral duty, and each is an essential part of any adequate moral standard. He does not claim that this list is complete; there may be other foundational moral duties. Are some of these duties more important than others? Ross emphasizes that these duties are listed in no particular order. Nevertheless, not all moral duties are equal. To the contrary, Ross observes that the duty of non-maleficence is usually "more stringent" than that of beneficence. Fulfilling a promise is likewise more important, in most cases, than showing gratitude. We also need to realize that each of Ross's duties is meant to encompass a wide range of activities; the duty of fidelity, for instance, encompasses *implicit* (unstated) commitments as well as formally made promises. Thus, fidelity also includes commitments we make simply by keeping quiet or by acting in a way that entails other commitments (registering for a course commits one to pay for it, to attend its classes, to do its assignments, etc.)

What's deontological about Ross's theory? For one thing, each of Ross's duties specifies a certain *way* we should act—justly, for instance, or with gratitude. Each duty thus functions as a general principle that prescribes certain *kinds* of acts. If I have a choice between either speaking the truth or deliberately deceiving someone, I have a moral duty to tell the truth. If I don't, I violate my duty and commit a wrong. Doing right amounts to acting in ways that fulfill these general moral duties.

More importantly, Ross doesn't base his duties on their likely consequences. Although fulfilling Ross's duties would probably promote utility in most cases, Ross doesn't think that moral duties depend on what happens *after* we act. It is more correct to think of each duty as resting upon something that already holds true *before* we act. For instance, my duties of fidelity or reparation rest on my having previously made a promise or having wronged someone, respectively. The same holds true for the duties of beneficence, self-improvement, and non-maleficence. Although these duties do aim at achieving (or avoiding) certain results, they do

---

[3] W. D. Ross, *The Right and the Good* (New York: Oxford University Press, 1930).

not *depend* on any consequence. Rather, these duties arise from the fact that there already exist those whose condition can be made better or worse by our actions. In keeping with the deontological perspective, then, Ross views moral duties in terms of what we already *owe,* not in terms of what we might *produce.*

Suppose, however, that I encounter a situation where two duties conflict with each other—a moral dilemma. For instance, I've promised to keep an appointment with someone, but along the way, I come upon an accident where my help is urgently needed. Fidelity calls upon me to keep my promise and my appointment. Yet if I do this and ignore the accident, I fail beneficence. Either way, I fail to fulfill one of my duties. What should I do? Ross's answer is that all moral duties initially hold as merely *prima facie* duties. A ***prima facie duty*** is one that I ought to fulfill *as long as* no more important moral duty overrides it. Yet when moral duties conflict, one usually turns out to be more important than the others. The most important duty then becomes my **actual moral duty**. In the example, I should probably help at the accident because I can make alternate arrangements with my friend later. On the other hand, suppose I'm a doctor rushing to the hospital to treat a heart-attack victim. Along the way, I pass someone who needs help changing a tire. Clearly I should continue on my way to the hospital, hoping, perhaps, that someone else might stop to help change the tire. Beneficence and promise keeping are both important, but the particular *circumstances* determine which duty becomes my *actual* duty in any particular situation.

In distinguishing between *prima facie* and *actual* duties, Ross makes an important contribution. However, you may be wondering *how* we determine which duty is most important in a given situation. You may also be wondering, for that matter, what supports Ross's moral duties in the first place. Ross answers that we know what is right by *intuition.* Just as mature and thoughtful persons can just *see* that two and two make four, sincere and thoughtful people can see that we ought to keep our promises, help others and not hurt them, and so on. We simply must carefully and honestly consult our inner selves. We don't discover moral duties by observing consequences or by reasoning; we just *know* of them intuitively. Similarly, we can know which duty is the most important in a given situation.

This makes Ross's theory **intuitionist**. This doesn't make it *subjectivist;* since each moral duty holds for everyone, his theory is an instance of *objectivism* (see Chapter Two, §II). If someone claims that she doesn't see herself having a duty of beneficence—or, perhaps, of self-improvement—Ross would just say she is wrong; perhaps she is not being sincere, or perhaps her moral intuitions have not fully matured.

Intuitionism is somewhat unsatisfying. For one thing, even if Ross's intuitionism is correct regarding how we come to *know* moral truths, it tells us nothing about what *makes* things morally right or wrong: it lacks *explanatory power.*[4] It also raises worries with *practicability* since there's always going to be some

---

[4]The intuitionist's would reply that there's no lack of explanatory power because there's nothing more to explain. Foundational moral duties don't derive from anything; they hold true in themselves.

disagreement between each other's moral intuitions. In fact, we aren't always sure even about our *own* intuitions. For instance, when people consult their intuitions about Robert Latimer, who killed his quadriplegic twelve-year-old daughter Tracy to spare her from the severe pain of her cerebral palsy, they often feel *both* that it was wrong to kill her *and* that it would be wrong to let her continue suffering.[5] Which of these conflicting intuitions is right? Further, even our most sincerely held moral intuitions are vulnerable to social influences. For instance, many good people have practiced polygamy, although the moral intuitions of most Americans condemn the practice. Intuition doesn't seem to be a very firm basis for discerning moral truth.

For Discussion

1. *Do you agree with Ross that his seven duties all describe genuine moral duties? Would you remove or add any?*
2. *How would you list Ross's duties in order of importance? Why?*
3. *Think of a situation in which two of Ross's duties conflict. Which would be the actual duty in that situation?*
4. *Do you think that normal people have moral consciences? Are these innate? Does the idea of conscience support intuitionism?*
5. *What would Ross's account say about the morality of Latimer killing his daughter? Do you feel the conflict of intuitions that many others do?*

Summary
W. D. Ross offers an intuitionist theory that includes seven foundational moral duties. It resembles a deontological theory in that these duties prescribe general kinds of acts and does not rest on consequences. Ross views these as prima facie *duties; when duties conflict, one of them overrides the others and so becomes the* actual duty *in that situation. Ross's theory is an instance of objectivism, not subjectivism. Its main weakness is its intuitionism, which refuses to explain these duties and can't help us when our sincerely considered intuitions differ.*

Key Terms

- **Prima facie moral duty:** *a moral duty that I ought to fulfill as long as no more important moral duty overrides it.*

- **Actual moral duty:** *the one prima facie duty that is more important than the others and so is the duty that ought to be fulfilled in a particular situation.*

- **Intuitionism:** *maintains that we simply know, by intuition, what our general moral duties are, with no further explanation.*

---

[5]"'Compassionate Homicide': The Law and Robert Latimer," CBC News, March 17, 2008, accessed August 27, 2016, http:// www.cbc.ca/news/background/latimer.

III. KANT'S GOOD WILL

We now turn to the most influential of all deontological theories, that of the eighteenth-century philosopher Immanuel Kant (1724–1804). Kant maintains that moral principles are based on reason. He therefore rejects any suggestion that moral truth can be discovered through intuition. As a deontologist, he also rejects any suggestion that morality could depend on consequences. For Kant, moral principles are both discovered and established through reason.

Kant particularly objects to the notion that morality could somehow depend on consequences. To embrace any consequentialist theory, we must first decide what values we should promote. This is not an easy matter even for consequentialists. Hedonists think pleasure should be promoted; other utilitarians also include other values (e.g., knowledge or creativity). The crucial question, however, is whether *any* of these values has foundational worth.

According to Kant, none do. While people may seek such things, none of these values are good in and of themselves. A foundational good, in contrast, has its goodness intrinsically and so will always augment the goodness of any situation to which it is added. But none of the preceding *always* increases goodness. Take pleasure, for instance. Although increasing pleasure often adds to the good, in some cases it decidedly does not. The enjoyment Al derived from "chewing out" Fred was mean-spirited; it certainly did not make that situation *better*. Or imagine an interrogator who enjoys "breaking" his subject through pain and fear. In both cases, the added sadistic pleasure only makes things worse, morally speaking, than if that pleasure were not there. Similar considerations go against other values as well. Knowledge and creativity, for instance, increase good when put to good uses. But suppose they are used to devise a more deadly terrorist attack or to pull off a more perfect murder. How can they be viewed as good in those circumstances?

From Kant's perspective, the problem with all these values is that they can either increase or decrease a situation's goodness, depending on the actor's motives. The same holds for *anything* we might try to promote among an act's *consequences*. None, therefore, can count as foundational values. To find something of genuine moral worth, we must give up on consequences and look in the other direction—at the motives and intentions of the agent. Here we will find, according to Kant, the only thing of foundational *moral* worth—the *Good Will*. Exercising the **Good Will** amounts to choosing to do something precisely because it is one's moral duty – because it is morally right. The Good Will is motivated *solely* by moral duty. It doesn't do something for the sake of gaining pleasure, knowledge, satisfaction, or any other such value. Its only motivation is the rightness of an act.

To make this clearer, imagine three Boy Scouts, who each help a little old lady across the street at different times of the day. Why do they do this? Well, each has his reasons:

- *Larry* helps her because he likes her, enjoys her company, and feels good about helping her out. Larry's just a nice guy and wants to help people.

- *Curly* helps her because that's the right thing to do. He helps because she needs help, and he can help her. He sees helping as his moral duty.
- *Mo* helps her because she's rich, and he hopes she might take a liking to him and either give him things or maybe write him into her will. She won't live much longer anyway.

One very important thing about this story is that the *consequences* of each scout helping the lady are exactly the same. In each case, she gets safely across the street; each scout may even inherit the same amount from her fortune! Despite the identical consequences, however, there certainly are moral differences among the three boys. Kant thus seems right—at least for this case—in claiming that consequences may not make much moral difference after all. What do make a difference are their respective motives or intentions. Mo clearly doesn't have Kant's Good Will; he helps only out of selfishness. What about Larry? While he has better intentions than Mo, when you really think about it, Larry also acts to fulfill his own personal desires. He helps because it makes him feel good. Would he continue to help if he no longer experienced these good feelings? In any case, Kant doesn't think Larry has the Good Will since what gets Larry out on the street really comes down to what he wants and feels, not duty. Only Curly has the Good Will. Curly, regardless of his feelings one way or the other, acts out of a commitment to do right. He may enjoy helping or he may dislike it, but that's all beside the point; Curly acts purely out of a sense of moral duty.[6] This, Kant thinks, is truly praiseworthy: the Good Will is the only genuine moral good.

This leads to an obvious question: if Curly's Good Will consists in his freely doing his moral duty precisely because it *is* his moral duty, then what determines his moral duty? After all, morality can't consist simply in having good intentions and then doing whatever we please! If Curly believed it his duty to rob the Savings and Loan to provide for his destitute grandmother, that wouldn't make his robbing the bank okay. Kant's reply is that the Good Will is dictated by reason because moral duties are determined by reason. But we again need to be careful here. Just as the Good Will doesn't consist solely of good intentions, the use of reason doesn't just consist of thinking carefully about what we might do. It would be even worse to interpret Kant as somehow inviting us to "rationalize" our doing something wrong. Rather, Kant makes reason the foundation of all moral duty, and because reason is the same for all, the duties of the Good Will are the same for all.

In sum, the Good Will—what might better be called the *rational* Good Will—has two essential aspects. First, it freely chooses to do its duty precisely because that *is* its duty; its choice is motivated solely by moral duty. Second, that duty is determined by reason. The Good Will is thus essentially rational: moral duty depends entirely on what reason demands.

---

[6]Kant has no objection to Curly enjoying his doing his duty; indeed, Kant thinks it morally desirable for people to enjoy fulfilling moral duties. Still, *duty* must be one's sole motivation.

For Discussion

1. *Why does Kant say that friendship, talents, and good health do not have foundational moral worth?*

2. *Assuming that you are not impressed by Mo, who do you feel is more morally admirable, Larry or Curly? Why? Can you see the appeal of each?*

Summary

Kant's deontological theory depends on reason. Kant argues that no consequence can have foundational or intrinsic moral worth; the only thing that is morally good in and of itself is the Good Will. The Good Will freely chooses to do its moral duty. That duty, in turn, is dictated by reason. The Good Will is thus motivated purely by reason.

Key Terms

- **The Good Will:** the only thing of foundational moral worth, the Good Will chooses to do something because it is one's moral duty.

IV. KANT'S PRINCIPLE OF ENDS

According to Kant, the Good Will freely chooses to fulfill its duty, and moral duties are determined by reason (the Good Will is closely associated with autonomy; see the following discussion and Chapter Three). Reason demands that every moral act satisfy one all-encompassing principle, which Kant calls the *categorical imperative*. This principle holds for all rational agents without exception.

An *imperative* is a command, something that tells us what we should do: "Shut the door" or "Pay your taxes." Imperatives can be either hypothetical or categorical.

- A **hypothetical imperative** tells us what we must do to achieve some goal: "*If* you want to become a doctor, you must attend several years of medical school." Those who don't want to be doctors don't have to attend med school. Hypothetical imperatives are conditional: whether the imperative (you must attend med school) applies to you depends on whether you fulfill the condition (you want to become a doctor). The condition in question is described by the "if" clause; the imperative makes up the rest of the statement.

- A **categorical imperative** does not depend upon any conditions: it holds *unconditionally* for everyone and every situation. A categorical imperative tells us what we must do or not do, regardless of our goals or purposes (e.g., "Tell the truth"; "Don't commit murder"). There is no "if" in the categorical imperative.

Although there are many instances of categorical imperatives, Kant provides us with just one fundamental categorical imperative—what is almost universally referred to as *the* categorical imperative. Although there's only one such categorical imperative for Kant, he does think that it can be expressed in several equivalent versions. The easiest version to understand is the *principle of ends:*

Principle of ends: Act so as to treat every person affected by your action (including yourself) as an end and never as a means only.

This principle tells us, roughly, that we should never simply "use" people for our own purposes; instead, we should treat everyone as having worth in themselves. That is, we should always act in ways that fully respect persons—something Mo does *not* do as he attempts to get his hands on the old lady's fortune. Why is there a duty to treat persons in this way? Remember that the Good Will has foundational moral worth. Since the Good Will requires the use of both reason and free will, the Good Will can only exist in rational moral agents (i.e., autonomous persons). Being the only sorts of things capable of exercising the Good Will, therefore, persons likewise have value and so deserve respect. Furthermore, since every person is capable of exercising the Good Will, each person has the same moral worth and so deserves the same degree of respect.[7] Since it would be irrational to value one person more than another, we have a moral duty to respect all persons, including ourselves. Reason thus requires that we obey the principle of ends (i.e., the categorical imperative).

Kant's principle offers us a profound moral insight. However, to appreciate its full significance, we need to understand precisely what Kant intends in describing people as *means* or *ends*.

Suppose you need to buy a shovel. Does it make sense to ask you what you are buying it for? Of course. People buy shovels, for instance, to dig holes for fence posts. Shovels are tools—*means*—for doing things like digging holes. A means is used to attain an *end* or goal: in this case, nice deep holes for fence posts. But clearly the shovel is not an end in itself. It is not something we value for its own sake. People don't usually collect shovels just to *have* (has anyone ever invited you to see their shovel collection?).[8] People value shovels because they are useful for attaining other ends—ends that they value more than shovels.

What does Kant have in mind when he talks of treating persons as means *and* ends? He is saying, first, that we have a moral duty to treat all persons as having intrinsic value or worth in themselves, not as mere tools. Treating someone as nothing more than a means or tool amounts to using or manipulating that person to obtain something else that we value more, much like the way we treat a shovel or like Mo treats the old lady.

Still, it is *not wrong* to treat persons as means *as long as we also treat them as ends at the same time*. In fact, we treat others as means all the time. When you

---

[7]From a Kantian perspective, a person is a rational free agent. However, persons need not be limited to humans—God, angels, and extraterrestrial intelligences like E.T. also qualify as persons. It's doubtful, however, that other animals qualify as Kantian persons.

[8]At a local school board meeting, one of us saw a shiny silver shovel carefully mounted in a glass display case. The superintendent explained that the shovel symbolizes the board's building projects. Apparently people sometimes *do* collect shovels!

attend a class, you use the instructor as a means to gaining knowledge and earning a grade. As long as you respect that instructor, however—having a genuine interest, say, in the instructor's own views—you treat her as an end as well. Similarly, the instructor uses her students as a means to earning a paycheck. But as long as the instructor genuinely cares about the students' learning (and doesn't contemptuously view students as necessary evils to be put up with), this is all morally acceptable. There *would be* something wrong with either the instructor or the student treating the other *solely* as a means without relating to the other as a person having intrinsic value. Classic examples of such wrongs include a master's treatment of a slave (a slave is often little more than a particularly versatile shovel) or a man's treatment of a prostitute. Neither slaves nor prostitutes are valued for their own sakes; rather, they are valued for what they can provide. Another example would be the businessman who climbs the corporate ladder on the backs of his co-workers.

Kant's categorical imperative requires that we always treat persons with respect, as valuable in themselves. But, to press further, what exactly does this come to? Since Kant's Good Will requires that persons be thought of as rational free agents, this suggests that respect for persons involves respecting a person's freedom together with that person's rationality—what Kant calls a person's *autonomy*.[9] Therefore, an act that diminishes or sidesteps a person's autonomy fails to respect that person; an act that acknowledges or even augments a person's autonomy respects that person.

Let's return to Al's treatment of Mrs. Satzoner. To encourage her purchase, Al tells her that the SUV is in tip-top condition. How does he treat her immorally by lying? It's easy to see that Al is using her as a means: she is his means to dumping the SUV, avoiding additional expenses, and making a tidy profit. But is Al treating her as a means *only*? Is he failing to respect her as a person—as something valuable in itself? In lying to her, Al gets her to think and act as if his falsehoods are actually true. This causes her to think and act in keeping with these falsehoods, which denies her the opportunity to act as she would if she knew the truth. This defeats her efforts at rational decision-making and thus her exercise of autonomy (see Chapter Three, §IV), which fails to respect her as a person. Al treats her as a means only, which the categorical imperative calls morally wrong.

For Discussion

1. *Give some examples of hypothetical imperatives. (Compare these to prudential claims (see Chapter One §III.)*
2. *How do we treat our friends as means? Do we treat them as means only?*
3. *How does stealing from someone treat them as a means only?*
4. *Describe other ways people treat people (and themselves) as means only.*

---

[9]Kant uses "autonomy" in a more technical sense than the way we used it in Chapter Three. This will be discussed further in §VI.

5. *Does the principle of ends seem to you to be a valuable and useful way to evaluate the morality of how we act toward others?*

6. *Suppose a person is so depressed and miserable that he contemplates suicide to escape his pain. How does this violate the principle of ends?*

Summary

According to Kant, the overarching principle of all morality is the categorical impera-tive. *A categorical imperative holds without exception, unlike hypothetical impera-tives, which apply only to those who fulfill some condition. One formulation of the categorical imperative—the principle of ends—requires that we treat persons as ends (having worth in themselves) but never simply as a means (for obtaining something we value more). It is morally okay to treat a person as both a means and an end. But using a person solely to accomplish our own purposes is morally wrong.*

Key Terms

- **Hypothetical imperative:** *a conditional principle that tells us what we should do if we satisfy some condition or hope to achieve some goal.*

- **Categorical imperative:** *a binding principle that holds unconditionally for everyone and every situation. One of its formulations is the* principle of ends.

- **Principle of ends:** *act so as to treat every person affected by your action (in-cluding yourself) as an end and never as a means only.*

V. KANT'S PRINCIPLE OF UNIVERSAL LAW

The preceding version of Kant's categorical imperative maintains that each person has the same moral worth. It follows that each person deserves the same degree of respect—for instance, being told the truth. It would be irrational to think we have a moral duty to tell the truth to one set of persons but not to others. Gener-alizing on this, any moral right or duty that holds for one person must extend to all persons, without exception. This powerful idea—that reason requires moral rights and duties to hold universally—comprises another key component in Kant's theory.

Kant did not invent the requirement that moral duties be universalizable; a related idea is found in the *golden rule:* "Do to others as you would have them do to you." This tells us to consider an act from the point of view of others and not just that of ourselves. For instance, lying to his customer no doubt looks like a good idea to Al. But suppose the situation were reversed. Let Al imagine his custom-ers and employees regularly lying to him. Would *that* look like a good idea to Al? Surely not, but if Al wouldn't like it when the tables are turned, then Al shouldn't act that way toward others either.

The crucial idea behind the golden rule is that of *universalizability*—the idea that something can be carried over from one person to others (see Chapter Four,

§III). Kant's theory also appeals to universalizability, but his principle is *not* the golden rule. For one thing, Kant doesn't just imagine some people lying to Al. Rather, Kant wants us to consider a truly *universal* practice of lying—in which *everyone* lies to *everyone*. Second, Kant wants to show that moral principles depend on reason. Kant's focus, therefore, is not with how Al would *feel* about being lied to but with whether the universalized practice of lying *could even make sense*. If it could not—if it would create inconsistency—then universalized lying is irrational, and thus immoral.

To see how an immoral act can create inconsistency, let's consider a different example. Having been too long under Al's influence, Al's co-worker, Fred, has started "picking up" valuables that he "finds" here and there. When Mrs. Satzoner left her computer tablet in the office, Fred quietly took it for himself, conveniently neglecting to inform Mrs. Satzoner. This is stealing—the act of taking another's *personal property*. In effect, Fred is following the *maxim*—a rule of conduct or behavior: "To get something I want for myself, I'll steal it from someone else." Now, suppose that Fred's maxim were universalized, so that all of us likewise followed this same rule of action. In such a world, would the notion of "stealing" continue to be meaningful? It seems not; where all property is equally available to anyone for the taking, it no longer makes sense to talk of taking someone's *personal* property. Personal property is *personal*—not available to just anyone. Nor does it make sense to "get something ... for myself" since I can't make it *mine* any more than anyone else can. But why else would I steal? Once the practice of stealing is universalized, the very intention people have for stealing (to make something their own) becomes impossible to achieve. Since a world of universal theft conflicts in this way with the intent of stealing, we get inconsistency, which shows that Fred's stealing is morally wrong.

Kant's strategy is to let the morality of an act depend on whether rational sense can be made of that act being made into a universal practice. He captures this idea in the most important version of the categorical imperative:

> **Principle of universal law**: Act only in accordance with a maxim that you can at the same time (rationally) will to be a universal law or principle.

Again, a *maxim* is just any rule of conduct or behavior such as Fred's personal rule about stealing. If one of my maxims is to always wash before I eat for the sake of my health, then I act in accordance with that maxim whenever I wash my hands before dinner. If I filled my car's gas tank yesterday to prepare for today's trip, I acted in accordance with the maxim that I should always have a full gas tank when I'm planning to take a long trip.

Let's work through Kant's ideas again, using Kant's principle of universal law to analyze Al lying to Mrs. Satzoner:

Al decides to lie because he thinks he can turn this lie to his own advantage.

1. What *maxim* does Al's act fall under? (*"I may tell a lie with the intent of promoting my own advantage."*)

2. What results from *universalizing* this maxim? ("*Anyone may lie with the intent of promoting their own advantage.*")
3. Would the practice of this universalized maxim be *consistent* or *inconsistent*?

   • If *consistent*, then the proposed act violates no moral principle.
   • If *inconsistent*, then the proposed act violates a moral principle.

There are two particularly crucial parts to this analysis. First, in formulating the initial maxim, we need to describe *both* the proposed *act* and the *intent* one would have in acting that way. This is because the inconsistencies arising after universalization usually involve some inconsistency with the act's intent, as will be seen in a moment.[10] The other crucial part involves step three: determining whether our obeying this universalized maxim would be consistent. In Al's case, our question is whether a universalized practice of lying would make rational sense. Note first that a lie can only succeed when the person lied to does not realize that he's being deceived. Next, suppose that the universalized maxim—that anyone may lie with the intent of promoting his own advantage—really does hold. Thus, everyone lies to each other. But then everyone also expects to be lied to; this makes it nearly impossible to deceive anyone by lying, which, in turn, makes it impossible to gain any personal advantage by lying. Therefore, the universalized maxim "*Anyone may lie with the intent of promoting their own advantage*" conflicts with its *intent* of gaining personal advantage by lying.

Here's another way to think of this: suppose that I act in a way that *cannot* be consistently universalized (i.e., it's morally wrong). Under what conditions could my act—stealing or lying, for instance—"succeed" in achieving my intended purpose? Most often, it can only succeed as long as most others *do not* act in similar ways. I can't successfully steal something for myself if everyone continually takes things from each other, including from me. I can't hope to succeed at lying if everyone lies and expects to be lied to. To personally benefit by committing a wrong, I must remain in the minority, with most people *not* acting the same way. Whichever way you look at it, one cannot *rationally* will that stealing or lying be made universal. Acts of lying fail Kant's categorical imperative, and this shows lying to be immoral.

Again, Kant's categorical imperative is *not* simply a restatement of the golden rule, which tells us that lying is wrong because we ourselves wouldn't want to be lied to. Nor does Kant's theory have anything to do with the disutility that widespread lying might bring into the world. Instead, Kant's point is that lying is fundamentally irrational: by willing to universalize the practice of lying, we set up a conflict with the very purpose of lying, which is to deceive. The dictates of reason—not how we feel or any consequences—are what determine moral right and wrong.

We've just determined if a couple *acts* are morally right using Kant's categorical imperative. But the categorical imperative can also be used to evaluate *kinds* of acts,

---

[10]Kant's own examples usually focus on inconsistencies with the *intent* of a proposed act (e.g., lying to benefit oneself). In keeping with this, we interpret a fully stated Kantian maxim as describing the intent of the act as well as the act itself. This interpretation is drawn from Eric Watkins, "Kant's Categorical Imperative," in *Metaethics, Normative Ethics and Applied Ethics*, ed. James Fieser (Belmont, CA: Wadsworth, 2000), 268–276.

thus allowing us to generate moral principles such as "No one should steal another's property" and "Everyone ought to always be truthful." These principles, Kant insists, hold without exception. But suppose that circumstances place two such principles into conflict, presenting us with a moral dilemma. How should we handle such dilemmas?

Unfortunately, Kant's reply is not entirely clear. On one side, Kant holds that since they derive from reason, most moral duties or principles should not conflict with one another, just as principles of mathematics and logic cannot conflict. Kant calls these **perfect duties**—obligations that cannot be obeyed by degrees. For example, you either steal or you don't; you don't "sort of" steal. Furthermore, Kant's principles reflect the absolute moral worth of persons. Thus, morality should never force us to respect one person's moral worth over another's or make exceptions regarding persons' moral worth. It can never be morally right to treat any person—even a liar, murderer, or terrorist—with less than the full respect due to autonomous persons.

On the other side, Kant does recognize that practical situations can seemingly pose moral dilemmas. Although perfect duties can't conflict with each other, a situation may produce a conflict with Kant's grounds of moral obligation. For instance, a counselor has two unscheduled patients wanting to meet with her at the same time. One has some questions to discuss; the other is suicidal. Although the counselor can't see both patients simultaneously, there are moral grounds—namely, the absolute moral worth of both persons—for her helping each as much as she can. Refusing to help either would be to act contrary to these grounds. Since the duty to help *can* be fulfilled to varying degrees (making it an **imperfect duty**), the counselor presumably should first help where she can help the most—the suicidal patient.[11]

We can draw a few reasonable conclusions. First, when a situation brings two imperfect duties into conflict, the one that can be best fulfilled usually deserves priority. Second, when a perfect and imperfect duty conflict, the perfect duty should presumably be given priority. As for conflicts between perfect duties, once again, Kant does not believe that these are possible, although not everyone agrees.[12]

For Discussion

1. *What behavioral maxims (not necessarily of a moral nature) do you regularly follow? (e.g., you take the same route to work to save time; you check your phone for messages every half hour because…, etc.)*
2. *Formulate maxims for each of the following acts, describing both act and intent: hitting someone, plagiarizing something, holding a door for someone, cutting off someone in traffic, and giving a small gift.*
3. *A gang leader murders a rival gang's leader. How does this violate Kant's principle? (Hint: his intent is to widen his gang's turf.)*

---

[11]As no promise or scheduled appointment was made and as the situation determines both who and how much to help, there is no perfect duty to help in this case.

[12]The issue of moral dilemmas in Kant is very complex. The present interpretation draws from Jens Timmermann, *Kantian Dilemmas? Moral Conflict in Kant's Ethical Theory*, accessed August 27, 2016, https://research-repository.st-andrews.ac.uk/bitstream/10023/5454/1/Timmermann_2013_AGP_Kantian.pdf.

4. *Business B1 spies on competing business B2's marketing plans. How does this violate Kant's principle? (Hint: B1's intent is to increase its profits by gaining some of B2's market share.)*

5. *You just observed someone place a suspicious package under a stairway and then hurry away. Worried, you immediately head off to report this but run into a friend who stops you to talk. How would Kant resolve this conflict?*

6. *Having now seen an alternative to utilitarian theories, how does that affect your attitudes toward act or rule utilitarianism?*

Summary

Universalizability is the key to Kant's principle of universal law—another version of the categorical imperative. This principle states that an act is morally wrong if it cannot be consistently universalized. Kant does not appeal to people's wants or to consequences. To determine if an act is morally right, we (a) formulate the maxim which that act falls under, (b) universalize that maxim, and (c) determine whether the universalized maxim generates inconsistency. If there's no inconsistency, the universalized maxim violates no moral principle; if there is inconsistency, then the act is morally wrong.

Key Terms

- **Maxim:** any *rule of conduct or behavior that one can act in accordance with.*

- **Principle of universal law:** *act only in accordance with a maxim that you can at the same time (rationally) will to be a universal law or principle.*

- **Perfect duty:** *an absolute obligation that cannot be obeyed by degrees; a perfect duty contrasts with an* **imperfect duty**, *which can be fulfilled to varying degrees.*

VI.** THE PRINCIPLE OF AUTONOMY

Autonomy lies at the core of Kant's ethical theory. According to our usual understanding, autonomy requires that persons both be able to choose freely and to employ reason in making their choices (see Chapter Three, §2). But Kantian autonomy is a much richer concept than ordinary autonomy.

Again, Kant views morality as essentially rational, as dictated by reason. In effect, reason itself determines or "makes" the moral law. Kant draws several results from this. First, the truly autonomous individual must act in accordance with the moral law, for acting immorally is irrational, and acting irrationally undermines genuine autonomy. Kantian autonomy always acts rationally and thus morally. Second, every person (by definition) has the capacity to reason. Since the moral law is "made" by reason, the moral law is fully available to every person. Each person, in short, is fully capable of *discovering* the moral law through her reason.[13]

---

[13]The moral law is discovered by reason, not by consulting one's conscience.

But reason has no existence in and of itself; it exists *only* in persons. Only persons, then, can "make" the moral law, by employing the reasoning capacity that resides in them. This means that persons don't merely *discover* the moral law for themselves—each actually *"makes"* the moral law for herself. In effect, each person is a lawmaker or "legislator" of the moral law. This result is so fundamental that Kant considers it another version of the categorical imperative:

> **Principle of autonomy:** *Every person is equally a creator of the universal moral law; that is, each person makes the moral law for herself.*

Since the moral law is autonomously made by each person, it is not imposed upon anyone by any other authority. It is imposed solely by each autonomous person upon himself, who then rationally "wills" or chooses to follow that self-imposed law. This has two important implications. First, as makers of the moral law, persons have *maximal moral worth*, since the makers of morality must be of greater worth than what they make. Second, autonomous persons enjoy *complete moral freedom*: although we are obligated to follow the moral law, that law is of our own making, freely willed and imposed by ourselves upon ourselves.

We mustn't misinterpret Kant here. Kant is *not* saying is that each person can just make up their own moral standard or that my morality could differ from yours. Kant's account is not subjectivism; in fact, it's the exact opposite. Kant insists that reason can only give rise to one set of moral principles, and, being universal, the same moral law is created or made by every person. The same moral standard thus holds for all.

For Discussion

1. *What do you think of Kant's fundamental position that immoral acts are irrational?*
2. *The Good Will and Kantian autonomy can belong only to* persons. *According to Kant, then, what does a* person *amount to?*
3. *How does Kant's theory explain moral freedom? What do you think of this concept of moral freedom?*

Summary
Kantian autonomy has a special meaning. The autonomous person not only exercises free will and employs reason; she is also able to "make" or legislate the moral law for herself. The autonomous person is thus not under the authority of any external moral authority but is under the authority of her own reason alone. Rationally, that person should then follow the moral law. Someone who violates the moral law acts irrationally and so cannot be acting autonomously.

Key Terms

- **Principle of autonomy:** *every person is equally a creator of the universal moral law; that is, each person makes the moral law for herself.*

VII. ATTRACTIONS AND PROBLEMS

1. Kant's ethics has many attractions—particularly in the very areas that utilitarianism tends to be weakest. It has no difficulty ruling out involuntary organ donations, attempts to avoid riots by framing innocent persons, or cases in which people break promises. It lends strong support to justice since every version of the categorical imperative maintains the equality of persons. And since it establishes general moral principles (e.g., "Do not kill innocent persons"), it makes it easy to derive moral rights (e.g., "Innocent persons have a right to life"). Its commitment to the foundational value of persons has considerable intuitive appeal. And, practically speaking, Kant's principle of ends is helpful for thinking through many everyday moral problems.

2. Naturally, Kant's theory also runs into some important problems.

   - *Consequences:* Consequentialists immediately object to Kant's deontological viewpoint that consequences have no moral relevance. Suppose that an acquaintance of yours who you just have learned has become radicalized quietly tells you of her plans to set off a bomb in a subway station and asks you when the station is most likely to be filled with people. Kantian ethics says you should answer her truthfully (e.g., "The station becomes most crowded at 6 PM") even if that enables her to cause hundreds of innocent deaths. But surely this can't be right. Don't such consequences have *some* moral relevance, at least, to how you answer her? Kant's reply is "not at all." His argument is as follows: no matter what the situation, we can never fully control or anticipate the future course of events. Your answering truthfully *could* lead to hundreds of deaths, but, then again, circumstances might work out so that it saves hundreds instead (e.g., because the electricity goes out at 5 PM, an evacuation is ordered, and the subway is completely empty by 6 PM when the bomb explodes). Further, we normally have little control over what others do. The terrorist might follow through on her plans, or she might undergo a change of heart and expose her organization. Because we have no real control over circumstances or over what others choose or do, we cannot be morally responsible for what ultimately takes place. What we *can* control—and what we *are* morally responsible for—is how *we* choose to act. Whatever else may happen, we ought to fulfill *our* own moral duties, at least, while leaving others to fulfill their moral duties as they should.

     Although Kant certainly has a point, this is surely an overstatement. As the consequentialist would observe, we often have *some* influence on others and their choices. We can try to persuade them to choose differently, or, if all else fails, we can try to interfere with their actions. Further, we usually have considerable control over what is about to take place. We thus do not seem as generally powerless as this suggests. And even when we have only a little influence over events, we still have responsibility to the degree we can exercise that influence. Since Kant seems to deny all of this, his theory has a problem with moral confirmation.

- *Many formulations:* Another difficulty arises whenever we apply the principle of universal law to determine the moral acceptability of an act. Imagine that Al is once again contemplating an act of lying. To evaluate the morality of his act, we must formulate a maxim characterizing the act Al contemplates. This is a critical step since this maxim characterizes the *kind* of act that is then to be universalized. If it can't be consistently universalized, then it will count as morally wrong. Everything thus hinges on how we formulate the maxim. But now the problem: *the very same act* can often be characterized by *different* maxims; even worse, some of these may consistently universalize while others may not.

  For instance, Al's contemplated lie can be characterized as an instance of (a) *telling a lie with the intent of promoting Al's own advantage.* But suppose that Al also intends to lie to Fred only when Fred suspects nothing. Does this make it a case of (b) *lying to Fred only when Fred suspects nothing and with the intent of promoting Al's own advantage?* Or what if Al tells a lie that, for once, is not for his own advantage but is instead (c) *lying with the intent of sparing someone from painful news?* Each of these characterizations is different, but each *could* characterize the very same act. Which, then, should be used to formulate the maxim?

  We have already seen that lying with the intent of promoting one's own advantage is *not* universalizable. On the other hand, it's difficult to decide about universalizing the maxim of lying to spare someone's feelings. This would be self-defeating (and thus inconsistent) if people could typically recognize bad news situations in which they should expect to be lied to. But if people can't usually recognize such situations, the maxim might be consistently universalizable. What about Al lying to Fred when he doesn't suspect anything? This maxim *cannot* create the usual inconsistency upon universalization, since it cannot even be universalized: it is limited to situations in which Al lies to Fred. Further, it is limited to just those times when Fred suspects nothing. As long as Fred remains unsuspecting, attempts to deceive him will typically succeed, and no inconsistency appears to arise.

  Although maxim formulation poses a genuine problem, a Kantian could respond by trying to clarify how appropriate maxims are to be obtained. For instance, the Kantian could argue that a maxim concerned solely with Al lying to Fred doesn't qualify as a genuine maxim because it is not sufficiently general. A maxim shouldn't refer to specific persons, times, locations, or situations. There's also something "fishy" about the ploy to avoid inconsistency by requiring that Fred suspect nothing.

  The Kantian could also argue that if the categorical imperative judges lying in general to be immoral (as Kant held), then no more qualified versions of lying (e.g., for the sake of sparing someone's feelings) should be allowed. Kantian moral laws cannot be fine-tuned. By making responses like these, it may be possible to address the many-formulations problem.

- *Rational agents:* Kantian ethics emphasizes the personal worth of individual persons, which impressively contrasts with utilitarianism's tendency to neglect justice and rights. However, it's important to note that Kantian ethics only requires the just and respectful treatment of *persons*—of autonomous (free and rational) moral agents. Kant thereby imposes no duties *directly* upon us to care for animals. Nor does he bestow animals with any moral *rights*. This will bother some. Still, Kant *does* claim that we have **indirect duties** toward animals—duties that arise from our moral duties toward other persons. Kant worries that if I act cruelly toward animals, I might act similarly toward humans since people's feelings toward animals and humans often resemble each other. I shouldn't harm animals because of my duties not to demean myself or harm the rest of humanity. Nevertheless, Kant's approach will not satisfy proponents of animal rights.

Similarly, Kant's theory does not seem to support any *direct* moral duties toward human infants, young children, or those lacking autonomy (e.g., patients with advanced Alzheimer's). We could reply that we still have important *indirect* duties toward such individuals, but this still doesn't respect such people (any more than animals) as having genuine moral worth. Another reply might be that infants and children, at least, have a unique *capability* to become autonomous, which makes them different from other animals. Perhaps creatures capable of future autonomy (or that have had autonomy in the past) are owed certain rights and have greater moral value than those which can never have this capability (e.g., animals).

For Discussion

1. *Which strengths of Kantian ethics do you consider most important?*
2. *Which problems for Kant appear to you to be most serious? Why?*
3. *For Kant, how would your duty to take your dog to the vet compare to taking your sister to the hospital when both involve emergencies?*
4. *How would you try to solve the problem with moral duties toward, say, infants or young children?*

Summary

Kant's deontological theory has considerable attraction, especially in how it emphasizes justice and rights. However, it neglects consequences, which seem to have some moral relevance even when we can't entirely control them. Further, the same act can be characterized by different maxims. Since some of these might be universalizable while others are not, an act being right or wrong may depend on how we formulate its maxim. Finally, since Kantian persons are rational free agents, his theory may not adequately respect human infants, children, and others.

Key Terms

- **Indirect duties:** *duties not owed directly to an individual itself (e.g., an animal) but arise from our moral duty to respect human beings as persons.*

Chapter Assignment Questions

1. *How do the consequentialist and deontological approaches differ?*
2. ** *Explain each of Ross's seven moral duties.*
3. ** *Explain how Ross resolves moral dilemmas using his distinction between prima facie and actual duties. Do you find this distinction helpful?*
4. *Explain the Good Will.*
5. *In your own words, explain Kant's principle of ends. Do you think this provides helpful moral guidance for everyday life?*
6. *How does Kant's principle of universal law differ from the golden rule?*
7. *In your own words, explain how the principle of universal law works with regard to lying or stealing.*
8. ** *Explain Kant's principle of autonomy. What do you think of Kant's belief that each person is a maker of the moral law? Why isn't this subjectivism?*
9. *Explain the problem of many formulations. How serious is this for Kant's theory? Provide an illustration of the problem.*
10. *Explain the difference between direct and indirect moral duties.*

Additional Resources

Ross, W. D. *The Right and the Good.* Indianapolis, IN: Hackett Publishing, 1988. First published in 1930. Presents Ross's theory, which includes several important distinctions that have been influential in twentieth-century ethics.

Kant, Immanuel. *Grounding for the Metaphysics of Morals.* 3d ed. Translated by James W. Ellington. Indianapolis, IN. Hackett Publishing, 1993. See especially sections 1 and 2.

Kant, Immanuel, "Groundwork for the Metaphysic of Morals." Accessed August 27, 2016. http://www.earlymoderntexts.com/assets/pdfs/kant1785.pdf. See especially sections 1 and 2.

Watkins, Eric. "Kant's Categorical Imperative." In *Metaethics, Normative Ethics and Applied Ethics: Historical and Contemporary Readings,* edited by James Fieser. Belmont, CA: Wadsworth, 2000, 268–276.

Johnson, Robert and Cureton, Adam, "Kant's Moral Philosophy." In *The Stanford Encyclopedia of Philosophy* (Fall 2016 Edition), edited by Edward N. Zalta. Accessed August 27, 2016. http://plato.stanford.edu/archives/fall2016/entries/kant-moral/.

Case 1

A Demanding Honor Code

After what seemed like an eternity, the exam was over. Fourteen students slowly made their way to the front desk, turned in their papers, and filed out of the room. As the group broke up, a few friends headed off together for lunch.

"That was unbelievable," Sue said, looking slightly dazed.

"Yeah. . . ." Matt said, trailing off.

Cory added, "I studied all night and thought I was ready, but . . ."

"At least Dr. B. is pretty fair about grading, so I should be okay," Sue interrupted.

Cory glared at her: "I don't know why I wasted my time. Maybe I should have pulled what those two did in the back."

Continued

Case 1 (Continued)

"What are you talking about?" asked Sue.

Cory paused. "You know, the two who are always talking? Johnson and Eberhart—they cheated by texting each other the answers."

"That doesn't surprise me," Sue observed. "Do you think Dr. B. saw anything?"

"Not a chance," Cory replied. "You know, I've heard them talking and they are both carrying like a 3.7 GPA, and one has some scholarship. What a joke! I'm killing myself going to work and studying, and they're cheating and getting handed scholarships! You know, this isn't the first time they've done this—they've got it down to a science. I'm so tempted to go back and tell Dr. B."

"You don't have to." A voice came from behind them. "I did a minute ago." Jinelle was just catching up to them. "I've had my eye on those two for a while. They pulled the same thing on the last test. When I saw them doing it again today, I waited for everyone to leave and told Dr. B."

"No way! What did he say? What's he gonna do?" Sue asked.

"Nothing," Jinelle said, slowly. "He thanked me, but said he couldn't do anything about it because he didn't see them himself—unless I wanted to file a written report to the honor council."

"I knew it!" Cory exclaimed. "They'll get away with it."

"Are you gonna file something?" Sue asked.

"No way!" Jinelle said, looking upset. "Would you? I told him I'd think about it. But no way am I getting into something that big."

Suddenly Matt spoke. "You know, you *are* supposed to, like the prof said." He continued, matter-of-factly, "The honor code says that anyone who knows about a student cheating has to report it to faculty."[14] Looking at Jinelle, he added, "And I think *report* doesn't just mean telling the teacher—you have to file a formal complaint."

"So *you* write up a complaint," Jinelle snapped back.

"I can't," Matt grinned. "I didn't see anything. I guess it's up to just you or Cor."

Later that afternoon, Dr. B. summarized Jinelle's charge to the dean. He was careful not to mention Jinelle's name. "Those two again," the Dean grumbled. "I've heard the same story before about Johnson, and Eberhart actually did get caught plagiarizing a paper last semester. One more documented charge, and she's on probation. But you know, I've also had my fill of students charging others with cheating, naming names, but not being willing to back it up. So we can't do anything about it. Don't they realize that by making an accusation like that and then refusing to stand by it, they are violating the code themselves? They just don't see that the code isn't about *us* enforcing honesty—it's supposed to be a *community* standard, something we are committed to together. But how can it work if the honest students don't carry out their duty to report the infractions they encounter? I wish these students recognized that every unfairly gained grade hurts all of us. When an employer discovers that one of our graduates hasn't learned what they are supposed to have learned, the college reputation suffers, our grads find it harder to get good jobs, and each one of those diplomas we applaud at graduation becomes worth a little bit less."

---

[14]The Vanderbilt University Honor Code identifies the "failure to report a known or suspected violation of the Code" as itself a violation of the code. Vanderbilt University Student Handbook, "Chapter 2: The Honor System," Vanderbilt University, accessed August 27, 2016, http://www.vanderbilt.edu/student_handbook.

THOUGHT QUESTIONS

1. Did the two offending students, Johnson and Eberhart, deserve to be reported and prosecuted by the Honors Council? Was Jinelle right in reporting these students to Dr. B? Why wouldn't she file a written complaint as well? Would you?

2. How does it hurt everyone when cheating takes place at a college? What are the pros and cons of a student like Jinelle or Cory taking the full responsibilities of the Honors Code upon themselves and making a formal charge against the two cheaters?

3. Which of Ross's duties apply to each of the students involved here?

4. If you were Cory, what do you think you should do in this case? Provide a Kantian analysis of this case using both versions of the categorical imperative.

5. Compare the Kantian moral judgment for this case with a rule utilitarian analysis of the honor code being a set of rules that hold for all.

Case 2

The Ayala Case

When she was only sixteen, Anissa Ayala, the daughter of Abe and Mary Ayala, was diagnosed with chronic myelogenous leukemia and was given three to five years to live. Only a bone marrow transplant could save her. Unfortunately, neither Abe nor Mary, nor their son, Aaron, had compatible bone marrow. A search conducted by the National Marrow Donor Program did not reveal a suitable candidate, and neither did several other bone marrow drives. So Abe and Mary decided to conceive another child in the hope that it would have compatible bone marrow that could be used to save Anissa.

Their chance of success was very small. Abe was forty and had had a vasectomy that would need to be reversed, leaving him with only a 50% chance of fathering a child. At forty-two, Mary's chances of getting pregnant were also low. In addition, there was only a 25% chance that their offspring would have compatible bone marrow. This reduced the odds of having a child that could save Anissa's life to 6.4%.

Nonetheless, Mary Ayala became pregnant and gave birth to a girl in April 1990. She was named Marissa-Eve. Miraculously, Marissa-Eve turned out to be a suitable donor for Anissa. When Marissa-Eve was just fourteen months old, her bone marrow was used in a transplant to save Anissa's life. The transplant was successful, and both sisters are alive and healthy.[15] The sisters reportedly share a close bond even today, and Anissa Ayala is now the assistant director of donor recruitment for the National Marrow Donor Program in Southern California.

---

[15]For an interesting discussion of the Ayalas's story as it relates to Kantian ethics, see Nancy Jecker, "Conceiving a Child to Save a Child: Reproductive and Filial Ethics," *The Journal of Clinical Ethics*, 1. 2 (1990): 99–103.

THOUGHT QUESTIONS

1. Because Abe had a vasectomy, we know that he and Mary had decided that they did not want another child. Apparently, it was Anissa's illness that changed their minds. Was Marissa-Eve conceived solely to save her sister? If so, could this have harmed Marissa-Eve's future relationships with her family? In what ways?

2. Kant says that we should never treat any person simply as a means and not also as an end. Was Marissa-Eve treated as a mere means in this case? Why or why not?

3. Clearly, Marissa-Eve had no input as to whether her bone marrow should be used to save her sister. Although a bone marrow transplant poses little health risk to the donor, it also offers no benefit to the donor and can be quite painful. Do you think that her parents had a right to decide to use her bone marrow? Why?

4. If it is permissible for parents to create and use one child to save another, what else could be permissible? Where should the line be drawn? Would it be right for parents to decide to use one child's kidney to save another?

5. Do you think that Abe and Mary should have conceived Marissa-Eve to save Anissa's life? Why or why not?

Case 3

Internet Bride—Straight from Asia

Men, just visit ThaiLoveLinks.com, blossoms.com, or LoveMeet.com, and your very own Asian wife might be just a few clicks away. These websites promise romance, dating, and marriage to lonely men. Sometimes they even provide legal services to help men import their "blossom" to their new home country. Of course, such Web sites can charge thousands of dollars for their services (lawyer fees are extra and can run in the tens of thousands). No wonder, then, that most of their clients are older, well-off men from America and other affluent countries.

Why get a wife from Asia and not from your own country? The following billboard, seen in South Korea, suggests one answer: "Vietnamese—They Don't Run Away—International Marriage Specialist!"[16] In many of the more affluent Asian countries (e.g., South Korea or Japan), advertisements for brides from less developed Asian countries (such as Vietnam or Cambodia) are standard fare. Obviously, there's an imbalance in power between someone from an affluent country and someone from a less affluent country. This will have an impact on the dynamics of the marriage. Second, if the women are smuggled into their new country illegally, they can't run away. Without proper paperwork, they won't be able to find a job and might end up getting deported. So brides from poorer countries usually stay with their new husbands.

In the United States and other Western countries, we don't find billboards as obviously prejudiced as the one just noted. But a certain attitude nevertheless

Continued

---

[16]Office to Monitor and Combat Trafficking in Persons, "Trafficking in Persons Report 2007," U.S. State Department, accessed August 27, 2016, http://www.state.gov/g/tip/rls/tiprpt/2007/index.htm.

Case 3 *(Continued)*

prevails. According to an article on ThingsAsian.com, John, a forty-three-year-old British man, found love with a thirty-two-year-old woman from Thailand. John sees Thai women as "more loyal" than British women. "They are not just 'take take take.' Also they have old-fashioned family values, which we used to have in this country." An American named Sullivan complained that American women "lack a certain femininity." By contrast, he found Thai women "less self-centered and more family centered." Sullivan started dating and ultimately married a young Thai woman, Yoshita. Yoshita seems happy. In her view, "Mr. Sullivan is a gift from God" and every day she thanks Buddha "for giving me Mr. Sullivan."[17] Yoshita doesn't refer to her future husband by his first name.

What happens if the marriage doesn't go so smoothly? After all, even though these men and women do meet in person before getting hitched, they don't usually know each other—or even each other's language—very well. It isn't surprising, therefore, that some of these marriages don't work out. Still, divorce or separation presents a challenge for even the legally "imported" Internet bride. A young Vietnamese or Thai woman may not know English well and may not have an education or the necessary skills to find a job and make it on her own in her new country. In the United States, if the couple divorces within the first five years of marriage, the woman loses her green card privileges. For these reasons, the man can usually expect that his new bride will go to great lengths to please him.

For a young import from Vietnam or Thailand, America may promise escape from poverty and a brighter future. But this, in turn, has given rise to the complaint that some Asian women are con-women. A short browse on the Internet reveals anecdotes of women who lured their prospective husbands in under false pretenses, only to turn out to be a devil in disguise once married and safely placed into the household of her American victim.

This raises several interesting questions. Who is using whom in these contexts? Are Western men looking for young woman who will be subservient to them? Are the young women just trying to get out of a poorer country? Also, is happiness possible with so many unknown factors? And do either the men or women fully appreciate what they are getting themselves into?

THOUGHT QUESTIONS

1. What do you think of the attitudes these Western men have toward Asian women? What do these attitudes tell you about what a Western man might expect from marrying a young Thai woman, for example?
2. Do you think that some of these men may be treating the women only as means to an end? If so, what does Kant's principle say about the morality of their actions?
3. Do you think that some Asian women may only be treating these men as mere means to an end? If so, what does Kant's principle say about the morality of their actions?

---

[17]Shino Yuasa, "Disillusioned Western Men Seek to Thai the Knot," Things Asian, accessed August 27, 2016, http://thingsasian.com/story/disillusioned-western-men-seek-thai-knot.

4. An American man and a Thai woman agree to a five-year marriage. The woman promises to be a loyal wife for this time, and the man promises to get her a green card. They agree that after the five years, they will split up if either wants out by then. Does this arrangement violate Kant's principle of ends? Why or why not?

5. Do you think it's morally wrong for a man to obtain an Asian bride along the lines described here? What particular circumstances, if any, make it wrong?

Case 4

A Personal Decision[18]

Alexis was getting angry, and she didn't mind showing it. "We've been here almost two hours now," she said to her friend Janet, "just to get my driver's license renewed."

"Typical bureaucratic efficiency!" Janet said under her breath. She was also tired of waiting, but she hoped that Alexis wouldn't make a scene. At least they were next in line.

"Next," said the woman behind the desk. "I need a photo ID, your social security card, and a check for $24; and please read this card and return it to me if you choose to sign." Her voice sounded bored.

"Wow, the fee has really gone up!" Alexis muttered while she wrote out the check. She then glanced down at the card the woman had given her. It read: "Organ Donation: Upon my death I am willing to donate the following." There were then a set of boxes labeled "eyes," "liver," "heart," "kidney," "any organ," and "none," together with a place for her signature. It also notified her that for $100, she could purchase a personalized organ donation license plate with a rose adorning it.

Feeling that she was expected to sign the card, but not sure she wanted to, Alexis avoided the woman's eyes, mumbled "Okay, thanks," and left. On the way out, Janet suddenly said, "I didn't want to say anything inside, but no way would I sign that card. If you get in an accident and they see that you have agreed to organ donation, they won't even try to save you. There's a real organ shortage, and the doctors want to grab whatever they can get. My mom says those organ donation cards are like signing your death warrant."

Later that evening, Alexis was still thinking about whether she should agree to organ donation. She didn't want to admit it, but she was a bit flustered by Janet's comment, although she only half believed it. She decided to discuss it with her boyfriend.

In typical fashion, Steve exploded when she told him what Janet said. "I just don't get why you're always hanging around that airhead. She's sweet, but she's got the intelligence of a goldfish. She's right about one thing, though—there's a serious organ shortage. I just read that in the United States, over 120,000 people are waiting for an organ transplant right now—and some will never make it.[19] Too many people won't let their organs be used. They are afraid like Janet, I suppose— or maybe they worry they won't look nice in the funeral home with their liver

Continued

---

[18]Our thanks to Stephen Thompson for helpful suggestions in writing this case study.

[19]For information on the current organ shortage, see the official government website on organ donation. OrganDonor.gov, U.S. Department of Health and Human Services, accessed August 27, 2016, http://organdonor.gov.

Case 4 (Continued)

missing. Not that the doctors do it so anyone could even tell. They even patch up a donated eye socket so only an expert could notice. And I know I'm not going to be wanting any of my organs once I'm dead."

"Oh," Alexis gulped. "That's repulsive."

"I suppose," Steve said airily. "But seriously, you ought to give it more thought. I'm not telling you what to do. But you could really help somebody, someday. To tell the truth, it doesn't appeal much to me either. But I sort of feel it's my duty, like, to my fellow human beings. Don't you agree that we ought to help others when we can —especially when it can't even cost us anything? As I said, the dead person sure won't care what they take out of him."

THOUGHT QUESTIONS

1. From a utilitarian perspective, should Alexis agree to donate her organs?
2. From a Kantian perspective, would refusing to donate one's organs violate a moral duty? Evaluate this using both versions of the categorical imperative.
3. Organ donation is a very personal decision that some people find difficult to make. Morally speaking, what level of moral agency is probably needed for a person to sign over their organs upon their death? What level of moral agency do you think most people actually exercise when they make this decision at the DMV counter? Why?
4. Do you think that people ought to donate their organs (morally speaking, not as a legal requirement)? Why or why not? Take the Kantian perspective into account as you think through your answer.

Case 5

Beefy Burgers and a Lean Future[20]

According to current estimates, our planet is inhabited not only by 7.3 billion people but also by almost 1.4 billion cows (using up 25% of space). Where is all this beef going? Mostly into American mouths. The average American eats about two hundred pounds of red meat, poultry, and fish each year, which, by the way, represents a twenty-three-pound increase compared with 1970 levels.[21] In many other nations, people are going hungry; many developing nations consume only a fraction of the meat we eat. Ironically, as these people starve, we Americans struggle with obesity and other health problems related to our overconsumption of red meat.

In effect, we are slowly eating away at the well-being of those who have the misfortune of not being affluent. In addition, the damage caused by our beef excesses may threaten the future of our own children and grandchildren.

Continued

---

[20]Anup Shah, "Beef," *Global Issues*, accessed August 27, 2016, http://www.globalissues.org/article/240/beef.

[21]Peter Singer and Jim Mason, *The Way We Eat: Why Our Food Choices Matter* (New York: Holtzbrinck Publishers, 2006), 42.

Case 5 (Continued)

These things are true because our appetite for beef significantly affects the resources of the planet. For example: to create cattle pasture, a large portion of Central America's rainforest has been cut down in just the past forty years. Deforestation not only destroys many plant and animal species but also accelerates atmospheric warming since trees are essential for removing carbon dioxide from the air. Burning the fuel required to transport all the beef further contributes to the problem.

Cattle are also drinking about half of the world's supply of fresh water, depleting supplies that will be needed to quench the thirst of future generations. This is especially serious because climate change is already causing major droughts. Looking at the matter from the other end, there's also concern over the amount of waste these cows produce. This especially poses a problem when many cows are kept together in feedlots since the resulting high concentration of waste pollutes ground water and surrounding rivers. They also produce a great deal of methane, a powerful greenhouse gas.

Last, cows have to eat too—and it's almost as if they are eating right off the plates of the hungry. Currently, most cows, in the United States at least, are grain fed. They consume about 70% of the grain produced in the United States and about 40% of the grain produced worldwide. That grain could feed a lot of hungry people.

Because it takes seven pounds of grain to create one pound of weight in a cow, the quarter-pound burger you may eat today or tomorrow represents several pounds of grain—grain that could have kept someone else from starving. That "someone else" may be a hungry person living elsewhere on the planet. But it could also be your own grandchild.

THOUGHT QUESTIONS

1. According to Ross's account, do we have a responsibility to cut down on eating beef for the sake of those going hungry in other countries? Do we have a similar responsibility to future generations? Which of Ross's duties might this involve?
2. From a Kantian point of view, do we have a responsibility to cut down on eating beef for the sake of those who currently go hungry in other countries? Do we have a similar responsibility to future generations? Why?
3. Which of *our* current interests would be put at risk if we cut back our present appetite for meat? Whose future interests are being put at risk thanks to our present appetites? Whose interests should have greater priority than the other, and why?
4. What, if anything, do Ross's and Kant's theories have to say about the environmental harms caused by our beef-eating practices? Should we change our behavior for the sake of the environment?
5. Alternative methods of raising cattle can somewhat reduce the environmental "hoofprint." Keeping cows on pasture requires much less fossil fuel than does a factory farm (which must be lit, heated, and cleaned). It also reduces the amount of grain needed to feed the cows—leaving more to feed the hungry. When cattle

are rotated from one pasture to another, the pastures are protected from over-grazing and are fertilized by the animal waste they absorb, which can spurt grass growth. Outdoor grazing also helps reduce water and other pollution. In view of these advantages, could we adequately fulfill our moral obligations by simply switching to pasture grown beef, or should we stop eating beef altogether?

6. Explain your view as to whether we each have some degree of moral responsibility to change our beef-eating habits. Include the facts mentioned in this case (including the health risks of eating too much red meat), and apply both Ross's and Kant's theories in your discussion.

Case 6

Suicide

In one particularly interesting application of his principle of universal law, Kant asks if I can consistently commit suicide as an act of self-love—that is, with the intent of improving my own welfare. He concludes that this is not possible, making suicide morally wrong. Why? Suicide amounts to treating oneself only as a means to attaining relief from suffering. It also violates the principle of universal law:

> Now we see at once that a system of nature of which it should be a law to destroy life by means of the very feeling whose special nature it is to impel to the improvement of life would contradict itself…; hence that maxim cannot possibly exist as a universal law of nature and, consequently, would be wholly inconsistent with the supreme principle of all duty.[22]

Kant's view is that one cannot consistently will to improve one's life via suicide because suicide destroys life. Interestingly, Kant's thinking seems more or less psychologically accurate: people often imagine themselves being free from their suffering as a result of suicide.

THOUGHT QUESTIONS

1. What's my mistake in imagining that suicide can free me from my suffering?
2. In your own words, fill out the Kantian test of suicide using the principle of universal law. What is the maxim and intent? What inconsistency arises? (Note that the inconsistency arises immediately; it doesn't depend on suicide being universalized.)
3. How does suicide violate the principle of ends? Who is the means and what is the end?
4. Can the maxim regarding suicide be reformulated so that suicide no longer creates an inconsistency?
5. What is your view of the morality of suicide? If it could ever be morally legitimate, what conditions would make it legitimate? Why? Apply other theories to see what positions they take on suicide as well.

---

[22]Immanuel Kant, *Fundamental Principles of the Metaphysic of Morals*, trans. T. K. Abbott (public domain, 1797), accessed August 27, 2016, http://www.constitution.org/kant/metamora.txt.

CHAPTER NINE

Natural Law Theory

I. INTRODUCTION

A pregnant mother is found to have uterine cancer. The doctors tell her that her uterus needs to be completely removed before the cancer metastasizes (spreads to other parts of the body). As the cancer is aggressive, this has to be done soon to save the mother's life. She is a little over six and a half months pregnant, so the fetus is quite developed, but they can't wait until the baby is born. Having a hysterectomy (an operation that removes the uterus) very soon will almost certainly kill the fetus but has about a 75% chance of saving the mother. If the mother were to wait just another five weeks longer, her chances of survival drop to 25%; the baby would have a 75% chance of surviving.

We have looked at both deontological and consequentialist approaches—and seen important advantages and difficulties with each. Can these help decide what to do in this case? Using Kantian ethics doesn't look very promising since this case presents the moral dilemma of choosing between two lives, and Kantianism isn't well-equipped to resolve this sort of dilemma.[1] Consequences also seem important to this case but are ignored by Kant. Rule utilitarianism would require a great deal of fine-tuning to sufficiently address this situation; more general rules would again land us in a difficult moral dilemma. Act utilitarianism can always be applied, but the probabilities in this case make the two choices roughly equal in expected overall utility. No theory thus provides much help. It's tempting to think, however, that if we could somehow combine the best of both the consequentialist and deontological approaches, we might be able to obtain a more helpful result.

Another tact might be to try a different approach entirely. If we could come at morality by some new angle, we might do better than either the deontological or consequentialist approaches can. Taking a new angle might also enable us to pick up on aspects of morality that we have not yet recognized through either of these approaches.

---

[1]Assuming that a six and a half month fetus counts as one of the lives at stake.

Natural law theory embodies a little of both tacts. It approaches morality differently than any of our previous theories. Natural law, for instance, aims toward certain goods, though not in the same way as utilitarianism. Further, it gives us principles that hold universally, but it allows for particular situations to be taken into consideration as well. It also offers an important procedure that combines both deontological and consequentialist considerations to resolve moral dilemmas.

For Discussion
1. *What should be done in the mother's case? Why?*
2. *What do you think are the greatest strengths of the utilitarian and deontological approaches? Do you think these could be combined into a new theory?*

Summary
Neither Kantian ethics nor utilitarian accounts seem ideal for addressing the hysterectomy case. Given these theories' strong opposition to each other, it is also tempting to wonder if some combination of deontology and consequentialism could offer a desirable alternative. Natural law theory offers one alternative.

II. NATURAL LAW THEORY

Natural law theory identifies several values upon which to base moral principles. This may give natural law an edge over approaches that center on just one value (e.g., hedonism). After all, using just one value raises the obvious question: why should we think that there is only *one* foundational good to the exclusion of all other goods? Isn't knowledge, or love, for instance, at least as valuable as pleasure? Natural law theory largely avoids this question by including all the values we naturally seek and treat as goods.

Traditional natural law theory[2] starts with the idea that everything has a *natural function* that serves to achieve some desirable end or goal. For instance, the heart circulates blood, the sun feeds energy into the earth's ecosystem, our minds equip us to gain knowledge, our sexuality makes procreation possible, and our deep need for human companionship creates society. Each of these functions reflects part of the fundamental design or structure of the world. Although things do not always function properly (e.g., hearts sometimes fibrillate, people reason mistakenly, and criminals act antisocially), such malfunctions are clearly undesirable, while the ends toward which nature aims are normally desirable and so have **natural value**.[3]

---

[2]Natural law theory has roots in Aristotle and the Stoics but was most fully developed by the medieval philosopher/theologian Thomas Aquinas.

[3]Many today dismiss traditional natural law theory as outdated because evolutionary theory denies that any natural thing has a function or purpose. Natural law ethics is still often referred to in medical practice and in theories of war, however.

Given such natural values, the theory then adds a fundamental *moral* principle: *we should maintain and promote those natural values toward which nature aims.* This creates moral obligations for us to act in support of these natural values. For instance, living organisms have a variety of biological mechanisms and instinctive behaviors that preserve life. Since part of the very nature of living things is to preserve life, life has natural value, and we ought to cooperate with nature in maintaining this good. Specifically, we have a moral obligation to care for the well-being of ourselves and others but are prohibited from acting in ways that could harm innocent persons. We also have an obligation to uphold life more generally—by protecting the environment and not destroying other species. Similarly, since procreation is a natural value, we have a moral responsibility to ensure the preservation of our species. Anything that opposes procreation (e.g., sterilization or anything that undermines the health or stability of a family) is morally wrong.[4]

The values of life, health, and procreation are shared with all living things; other values are more characteristically human. As social beings, for instance, we should value that which supports social interaction (e.g., trust and respect for others), which in turn implies the moral obligations to keep promises and speak the truth. On a more personal level, we ought to nurture relationships such as marriage and friendship. Since they help establish and maintain social stability, the state and its institutions are also good. It is thus morally right for us to participate in government and even wage defensive wars to preserve the state; it is wrong to incite a riot or commit treason. On yet another level, Catholic theorists observe that human beings exhibit a nearly universal inclination to seek meaning in life. While such spiritual sensitivity is good, its suppression via greedy materialism should thus be avoided.

Finally, natural law views our reasoning abilities as distinguishing us from other animals. Being rational by nature, we should apply and develop our reason. Education and scientific investigations are thus good; we should also work to sharpen our reasoning skills and extend our knowledge in all facets of life.

Natural law theory assigns particular importance to reason because it views the cosmic or natural order as *rational.* For this reason, the natural order and its laws can be discovered and understood by human reason (an assumption shared by science). Since natural law is rational, furthermore, it is only reasonable for us as rational beings to conform ourselves to it. By obeying natural laws, we harmonize ourselves with nature and allow our complete fulfillment as human beings.

Natural law ethics is not, in itself, a religious ethics. The Stoic conception of natural law theory, for instance, was compatible with atheism. Some contemporary biologists also propose a kind of natural law theory, understanding morality as resulting from naturally selected behaviors that have helped preserve our species. Nevertheless, natural law theory has been favored by Catholic thinkers since Thomas Aquinas placed his natural law ethics squarely upon a religious

---

[4]More controversially, Roman Catholic natural law theorists also view birth control and homosexual acts as morally wrong.

foundation. According to Aquinas, the rationality and goodness of the natural order are explained as the work of a rational and good God. As Creator, God assigned a function to each thing and ordered things to coexist in harmony. God also endowed us with reason so that we can discover these functions and understand the natural order. Since God is good, this explains the goodness of creation as a whole as well as the goodness of those particular ends (the natural values) which each thing attempts to bring about.

For Discussion

1. *What do you think of the idea that everything has a natural function?*
2. *Is it possible to still hold that there are natural goods (thereby allowing us to develop natural law theory) even if we reject the notion that everything has its own natural function?*
3. *Do you agree that human beings are distinctive primarily because of our reason? Are there any other unique things about humans?*

Summary

Natural law theory identifies natural values as things that human beings innately desire and need; more generally, they reflect whatever conforms to the cosmic order. It then maintains that since these natural values are good, we have a moral obligation to promote them. Human reason is a particularly important good and should guide all we do. Aquinas added that the entire cosmos is the creation of a good and rational God. This was to explain the inherent goodness of natural values as well as our ability to discover the structure of the natural world and its laws.

Key Terms

- **Natural value**: *some desirable end or goal toward which nature aims.*

III. FORFEITURE

Natural law theory identifies several foundational values that we ought to promote and pronounces anything we might do against these to be wrong. These foundational goods have most widely been thought to include life and health, procreation, knowledge and the use of reason, and social interaction. By applying its fundamental principle that we should maintain and promote these natural goods, natural law derives additional moral values and principles. Given that we should seek to maintain and promote life and health, for instance, we can deduce principles such as "You should not kill another person" and "Do not act in ways that might unnecessarily injure or harm yourself or others." From the values of reason and social interaction, we arrive at principles such as "Always tell the truth" and "Do not break your promises." Natural law theory thus generates all the commonly held moral principles.

Although we should maintain and promote natural values, natural law theory doesn't follow consequentialism by simply trying to maximize natural goods. It is more concerned with our preserving these goods and our acting in keeping with them. Still, when an act's consequences undermine these goods, the theory often judges that act to be wrong. Because it entails general moral principles, natural law also takes on a deontological character. This extends to its concerns with our intentions. Natural law theory thus incorporates both consequentialist and deontological elements. This becomes even clearer in the ways it addresses dilemmas.

Natural law *does* allow for exceptions under certain conditions. While killing another is normally wrong, for instance, it *could* be justified if one is forced to kill an attacker, say, in self-defense. This sort of exception is justified by the following principle:

> **Principle of forfeiture**: By deliberately attacking or threatening an innocent, an individual (or nation) forfeits its own moral claim to live (or to exist).

An **innocent** is a person or nation that has *not* attacked or threatened another. By attempting to harm another, an attacker ceases to be an *innocent*; that is, the attacker forfeits or loses his moral right not to be threatened by others. The idea seems to be that you can't claim a moral right that you deny to another. Thus, if the victim kills or harms the attacker in self-defense, that victim commits no moral wrong. Similarly, an innocent nation may justifiably defend itself against an invading nation. This principle can perhaps be extended even to justify capital punishment of murderers (who have forfeited their right to live). Note, however, that the principle does not *require* us to kill attackers and murderers; it only justifies our doing so. If an attacker can be thwarted without being killed, that would be preferable.

For Discussion

1. *Does the principle of forfeiture support capital punishment of murderers? Would there be exceptions?*
2. *It was once the law that, by breaking into your home, an intruder loses innocence, giving you a legal right to kill him. Since you can't know his intentions—which might be to kill you—your act is in self-defense. Discuss.*

Summary

Natural law theory presents an alternative to both deontology and consequentialism. It also attempts to combine their strengths. Consequences, intentions, and principles all have roles in this theory. To deal with one sort of special case, it adds the principle of forfeiture, which gives an innocent victim the right to self-defense. This extends to states as well as individuals.

Key Terms

- An **innocent**: *a person or nation that has a moral right not to be threatened by others because he (it) has not attacked or threatened another.*

IV. DOUBLE EFFECT

Another set of special cases is acknowledged by natural law theory. Inevitably, there are situations in which an act produces both good and bad effects. These situations pose a dilemma in which a natural value can only be supported at the expense of another natural value (or, sometimes, that same value in some other way). To determine what should be done in such situations, natural law theorists have developed the *Doctrine of Double Effect* or *DDE* for short.

Although DDE is mainly used by natural law theorists, it can in fact be used with *any* theory—Kantian ethics, rule utilitarianism, Ross's ethics—that generates moral principles. DDE decides cases by considering general moral principles, the act's consequences, how an act and its consequences relate, and the actor's motives or intentions. Intentions play a very significant role in DDE. For instance, DDE says that we should never intend to cause some bad effect, even if we also intend to bring about something good. The end never justifies the means! Nevertheless, DDE *does* permit certain acts for the sake of some good even though that act also results in something bad.

There are many situations in which an act produces both good and bad effects. Returning to our opening story, the doctors propose removing the mother's uterus (the act) to save the mother's life. The bad effect would be a loss of life (the fetus), and the good effect would be that the mother is saved. Or imagine a trolley heading toward several people walking on the track just a short distance ahead. Although the driver can't stop the trolley in time to save these people, he could steer onto another track, where there's only one person. By doing so, he would achieve the good of saving several lives, although he would kill the one person. These cases obviously present us with tough moral choices; DDE is designed to help guide us through such choices.

> **Doctrine of Double Effect (DDE):** When an act will lead to both a good and a bad effect, it is permissible to perform that action *only* if *all four* of the following conditions are satisfied:

1. **Moral principle condition**: The act cannot itself be of a kind that violates a moral principle, for that would make the act wrong. Examples of acts prohibited by this condition would include purposely killing an innocent life (even if that killing could save others), lying, and breaking promises. Violating a moral principle is *always* wrong since it works against natural values (e.g., life and truth). Acts that satisfy this condition would include administering a medicine or carrying out an operation to remove a cancerous uterus.
2. **Means–end condition**: The bad effect cannot itself be the means for achieving the good effect. We will discuss examples shortly.
3. **Right intention condition**: One must intend *only* the good effect, not the bad effect. Even if the bad effect is foreseen and expected, it must not be intended. For instance, a doctor must not intend to kill the fetus, for any intention to kill innocent life is wrong. Yet if the doctor intends to remove the uterus while foreseeing that this will kill the fetus, that satisfies this condition.

4. **The proportionality condition**: The good effect must be *at least* as great as the bad effect. For example, if the good effect is that a life is saved and the bad effect is that a life is lost, then the good and the bad effect are equal, and this condition is satisfied. If the good effect is to obtain a million dollars, while the bad effect is that ten people will die, then the good effect is not as great as the bad effect.

We must clearly distinguish between the *act* itself—what someone does—the *intention*, and the *two effects*. Condition 1 applies only to the act; Condition 3 to the intention, and Conditions 2 and 4 to the effects of that act.

Applying the means–end condition can be difficult because the effects can relate to each other in different ways. Sometimes an act simply produces two **independent effects:** Aladdin's stealing a loaf of bread may cause the baker financial loss and feed Aladdin's friends. But feeding the friends doesn't *require* that the baker suffer financial loss – they still get fed even if a sympathetic bystander reimburses the baker. Nor does the baker's financial loss cause Aladdin's friends to be fed (Aladdin might accidently drop the bread, depriving both the baker and his friends of the bread). Neither of these effects depends upon the other; what they *both* depend upon is Aladdin's initial theft of the bread.

On the other hand, some effects can only be achieved through another effect, one depending on the other. This makes them **dependent effects.** Suppose a terrorist desires media attention for some reform (an effect—let's even imagine it to be a good one). He thus plots the deaths of twenty people at a bus station (another effect) by blowing up a bomb (the act). Here, the media attention *cannot* be achieved unless the deaths occur because it is the deaths that draw the attention. Thus, the good effect depends upon the bad effect – the one relationship between effects that violates the means-end condition. Finally, it is possible for a bad effect to depend upon the good. Imagine that a drowning person is pulled into an already full lifeboat. This has the good effect of saving that person's life at the time, but the additional passenger's weight might then cause the bad effect of sinking the overloaded boat in a storm.

We cannot apply the means–end condition without first determining how the effects relate to each other. The three possible relationships are illustrated as follows (A stands for the act, G for the good effect, and B for the bad effect):

Independent effects	Dependent effects	Dependent effects
Effects depend on the act, not each other	Good depends on bad	Bad depends on good
(*acceptable*)	(*unacceptable*)	(*acceptable*)
$A \nearrow^{G}_{\searrow B}$	$A \to B \to G$	$A \to G \to B$

Let's now analyze some examples using all the DDE conditions. Again, we must first identify the act along with its good and bad effects; only then can we apply the conditions.

Example 1: The opening story of the pregnant mother with cancer. The act is doing the hysterectomy, removing the uterus. The good effect is that the mother lives, the bad effect is that the fetus dies. Is the act permitted?

Condition 1 is met because the act of removing a diseased uterus violates no moral principle and so is not bad in itself.

Condition 2 is met because the bad effect (the death of the fetus) is not the means used to achieve the good effect (the mother survives). The death of the fetus does not save the life of the mother. Rather, her life is saved by removal of the uterus, which has the death of the fetus as a side effect. In this case, the effects are *independent*.

Condition 3 is met as long as the doctor's only intention is to save the mother's life, not to abort the fetus.

Condition 4 is met because the good effect is at least as great as the bad effect—while it costs one life, it saves another.

Therefore, the act *is* morally permissible according to DDE.

Example 2: An innocent person must be tortured to get a terrorist to reveal details about his terrorist activities. Let's work off a scenario played out on the show *24*.[5] A terrorist has hidden a nuclear bomb in Los Angeles. He is captured but refuses to reveal where the bomb is hidden and will die rather than reveal this information. The interrogator therefore threatens to kill the terrorist's family. On the show, the agent set up a video feed to the terrorist's room so the terrorist could watch; the agent then had the terrorist's son shot. This led the terrorist to confess to spare the rest of his family; the bomb was then disarmed and millions were saved. It was later revealed that the child's murder was faked.

Let's change the scenario. The agent has not yet had the child killed, but wonders whether doing this—by a real shooting this time, not faking it—is morally permissible. The act in question is shooting the child; the bad effect is the child's death, and the good effect is finding the bomb and saving millions of innocent lives.

Condition 1 is *not* met because the act being contemplated violates the principle that prohibits killing an innocent person, which is morally wrong.

Condition 2 is *not* met because the child's death is the very means used to obtain the desired information from the terrorist. If the child isn't killed, the terrorist won't give the information—the latter depends upon the former.

Condition 3 is *not* met because the agent *intends* the child's death. He also intends to save innocent millions, of course, but he intends *both* of these things. Another way to put this is to say that the agent doesn't kill the child accidentally. The child dies as a result of the agent's deliberate choice, and a deliberate choice is always intended.

---

[5]This scenario appeared in the FOX television series *24*, Season 2, 2002, directed by Jon Cassar.

Condition 4 *is* satisfied, because the good effect (saving many lives) is much greater than the bad effect (the death of one child).

Although Condition 4 is overwhelmingly met, the act is not morally permissible since *all four* conditions must be satisfied for an act to be permissible.

For Discussion

1. *For the terrorist story (Example 2), what would act utilitarianism say instead?*
2. *Should the terrorist's innocent child be killed if that's the only way to save millions? Why or why not? (It might help to apply both utilitarian theories as well as Kant's ethics to see how these theories answer this.)*
3. *DDE includes much more than resulting utility, though it does include that too (Condition 4). How important are its other conditions?*
4. *Can we have more than one motivation at a single time? If so, can we separate these in ourselves and determine which is directing our response in a given situation?*
5. *It's not hard to think of cases in which an act causes two independently related effects. It's harder to find cases in which the good effect depends on the bad; it's quite difficult to find cases in which the bad effect depends on the good. Try to come up with an illustration of each.*

Summary

DDE addresses cases where an act both promotes and works against natural values (by its good and bad effects, respectively). To apply DDE, we must identify the act and its intent, the good effect, the bad effect, and the relationship between these effects. To be morally acceptable, a situation must then fulfill all four of the DDE conditions: (a) it violates no moral principles; (b) the good effect doesn't depend on the bad; (c) only the good effect is intended; and (d) the good effect is at least as great as the bad effect.

Key Terms

- **Independent effects**: *occur when neither of the effects depends upon or causes the other.*
- **Dependent effect:** *an effect that does depend upon or causes the other.*

V. PROBLEMS FOR NATURAL LAW THEORY

Natural law theory has important attractions. By encompassing several natural values, it seems more balanced than approaches based on a single value. It also provides some motivation for being moral. Since the theory maintains that things work best when everything is fulfilling its natural function (just as products usually work best when we follow the manufacturer's directions), we may expect the greatest personal satisfaction and fulfillment from following natural laws. The theory also has appeal in the way it balances consequentialist and deontological elements. Yet while natural law theory was well received until the advent of utilitarianism, many contemporary theorists now view it as seriously deficient.

Foundations: Probably the most serious theoretical problem with natural law theory is its first principle: *We should maintain and promote as good those values toward which nature aims.* The principle attempts to establish *natural* goods as the basis for the *morally* right. Now it's certainly true that we desire these natural goods—life, health, knowledge, social interaction—and that seeking them is probably also rational and prudent. But why should we think there is a *moral* obligation to seek such ends? Even if the world does aim toward certain ends, that does not entail that these ends *ought* to be maintained or promoted. Why think that the natural status quo is *good*?[6] For instance, a primary end of human sexuality is the propagation of our species. That's fine up to a point, but as the population soars, is it still good to be increasing our numbers indefinitely? It's also hard to deny that death is the natural end to life, although few people view death as a good.

In response, natural law theorists need to show that natural goods do support moral claims. This is particularly hard for nontheistic natural law theorists because their view doesn't leave much room for more basic supporting facts or principles. Aquinas's theistic account maintains that the natural order was created by a rational and good God. Since it reflects this good God's purposes, we may suppose that whatever is important to the natural order must also be good. This in turn supports the idea that we ought to promote natural goods.

Unfortunately, Aquinas's solution also runs into difficulties. There is, of course, the question of God's existence. But even if we grant that a good Creator God exists, we must also admit that most religions—including Aquinas's Christianity—view the present world as corrupted. The biblical book of Genesis portrays all things, including nature, as infected by mankind's moral fall. But this raises additional difficulties for natural law's first principle. If *anything* could be tainted by evil, then we cannot justifiably treat *all* natural processes and things as purely good. In view of this, we need to find some means for distinguishing natural goods that remain as God intended them from those that have taken on this general corruption. But doing this requires that we discern God's original intentions out of what we can presently observe—a nearly impossible task. Even Aquinas thus seems unable to satisfactorily support the first principle of natural law theory.[7]

Vagueness: Another obvious problem is determining exactly what "natural" means. The concept is inherently vague. For instance, we might think that pure nature is natural, while human technologies are unnatural. Yet it *is* natural for human beings to think, create, build, and improve their condition and so natural law theorists do not oppose technology. But at what point does technology cross the line from the *natural* to the *unnatural* or *extraordinary*? The sex organs

---

[6]The same sort of objection can be brought against hedonism: pleasure is not a moral good just because we all desire it. What *ought* to be the case doesn't follow from what simply *is* the case. According to a long-standing slogan, *you cannot derive an "ought" from an "is."*

[7]The Catholic tradition turns to revelation to make these distinctions.

clearly aim at reproduction; is it unnatural then to extend our control over their function by using birth control technologies to regulate family size? At what point do complex medical interventions qualify as unnatural? And if procreation is a natural good, are artificial insemination and cloning bad (as natural law theorists usually say) just because they require highly advanced technologies? These questions present natural law theory with important challenges, especially as technology continues to multiply our options enormously.

The natural law theorist replies that these questions are founded on a mistake: *natural* relates to the *ends* that things serve, not their *origins*. It doesn't matter that a technology is created by humans; it is acceptable as long as it serves some natural end. Yet even this raises questions. On one hand, why do many natural law theorists condemn efforts by a married couple to facilitate procreation (a natural good) by artificial insemination? On the other hand, human aggression—like competition between non-human animals—weeds out the less fit in favor of the stronger and more adaptable. Further, humans "naturally" incline toward conflict, as it shows up in all human cultures and first appears at an early age. Yet we don't exactly consider all aggression and conflict to be good. Natural law theorists have carefully developed replies to all these questions, but, as that suggests, there is no simple or straightforward account of *the natural*.

DDE: Despite its ingenuity, DDE has a problem with the criterion of moral confirmation. Although DDE often yields intuitively correct guidance, it can also yield intuitively implausible results. Consider, for instance, a mother who cannot give vaginal birth to a severely hydrocephalic infant because both would die.[8] Suppose, in addition, that neither would survive a cesarean section. The only alternative would be to save the mother by performing a craniotomy, which crushes the infant's skull so its pieces along with the remaining body parts can be removed vaginally. Carrying out a craniotomy probably violates three of the DDE conditions. It directly kills the infant, violating the moral principle condition. Because the infant's destruction is the only means to saving the mother, furthermore, the good effect is achieved by means of the bad effect. And since the intent is to destroy the infant's skull, even the right intention condition may be violated. DDE thus prohibits a craniotomy in such a situation. Yet as horrific as a craniotomy is, DDE's rejection of it doesn't look right, for how could it be wrong to save one person when the only alternative is for both to die?[9]

Another problem for DDE is that the *very same act* can appear right or wrong depending on how it is described. Consider our pregnant mother with cancer again. In our analysis, we described the act as removing a diseased uterus, which appears acceptable to the moral principle condition. But this is also an act that destroys the developing fetus's only means of life. On

---

[8] A hydrocephalic infant has a badly swollen skull due to fluid in the brain, which develops so abnormally that the infant can't survive on its own.

[9] The problem is raised on by C. E. Harris Jr., *Applying Moral Theories*, 3d ed. (Belmont, CA: Wadsworth, Inc., 1997), 84–85. This selection is reprinted in Mark Timmons, *Conduct and Character*, 4th ed. (Toronto: Wadsworth, 2003), 76–92. It is here given a somewhat different analysis.

that description, the act seems to amount to a killing. Can we turn a right action into a wrong one merely by changing how we describe it (compare this to the many-formulations problem with Kant)? This could make it very difficult to determine right from wrong in many cases —a problem with DDE's *practicability.*

Evolution: One of the main reasons natural law theory has fallen into disfavor is the acceptance of evolutionary theory with its denial of natural aims and functions (see footnote 3). If we could make sense of natural goods while rejecting the notion of natural functions, then perhaps some form of natural law theory could survive the evolutionary objection. But as this and other responses to this objection raise a host of additional issues, any evaluation of this objection lies beyond the scope of our discussion.[10]

For Discussion

1. *How do you understand the concept of something being "natural?"*
2. *What is natural and what is unnatural about (a) artificial insemination or (b) attempting some drastic medical intervention to save a life?*
3. *Can the act of switching tracks in the trolley story (see §IV) be described so that it fails DDE?*

Summary

Natural law theory has some important objections to it. First, there is the problem with its very foundation: why think that the natural is good (a weakness in explanatory power). Then there is vagueness in the concept of "natural" (a practicability problem). There are also problems with DDE. One is with DDE yielding intuitively wrong results (moral confirmation); another has to do with it leading to different judgments depending on how we describe the exact same act (practicability). Finally, evolution undermines the notion of natural ends.

Chapter Assignment Questions

1. *Derive some moral principles that you think follow from foundational natural values like life or reason.*
2. *Do you think that Aquinas's theistic basis to natural law theory is necessary or helpful? Why or why not?*
3. *How well are we able to identify natural goods from studying nature and people?*
4. *Is it really possible for a person to forfeit and thus lose his most basic moral rights?*
5. *What sorts of problems is DDE intended to address?*

---

[10]Most simply, the natural law theorist could redefine natural goods as whatever has been favored by natural selection, though this makes the *foundations* objection even more pressing.

6. *In DDE's Condition 1, the very same act might count as right or wrong depending on how we describe it. Compare "removing a uterus that supports a developing fetus," to "removing a woman's diseased uterus" or compare "shooting a missile at a target" with "killing an enemy and his family with a missile." How might the natural law theorist reply to this problem?*

7. *Explain in your own words DDE's means–end condition. Is there anything about this condition that you don't feel you understand?*

8. *How could someone expect a certain effect to take place but not intend it to take place? Can you give an example from your own experience?*

9. *What do you think of combining both deontological and consequentialist elements together as is done in DDE?*

10. *How serious is natural law's foundations problem—the question of why natural things ought to be seen as good?*

Additional Resources

Harris, C. E., Jr. "The Ethics of Natural Law." In *Conduct and Character.* 5th ed. Edited by Mark Timmons, 65–79. Belmont, CA: Wadsworth, 2006. From C. E. Harris Jr. *Applying Moral Theories.* 3rd ed. Belmont, CA: Wadsworth, 1997. This reading provides a good general discussion of natural law theory, the principle of forfeiture and double effect, and a number of illustrative applications.

Locke, John. *The Second Treatise of Civil Government.* Public Domain, 1690. This can be found online, Accessed August 27, 2016. http://www.constitution.org/jl/2ndtreat.htm. This is one of Locke's most important works; see especially chapter 5, section 27.

Murphy, Mark, "The Natural Law Tradition in Ethics." In *The Stanford Encyclopedia of Philosophy* (Winter 2011 Edition), edited by Edward N. Zalta. http://plato.stanford.edu/archives/win2011/entries/natural-law-ethics/. This article provides a more advanced introduction to natural law theory.

McIntyre, Alison, "Doctrine of Double Effect." In *The Stanford Encyclopedia of Philosophy* (Winter 2014 Edition), edited by Edward N. Zalta. http://plato.stanford.edu/archives/win2014/entries/double-effect/. This article provides a more detailed discussion of double effect, including its applications and some criticisms.

Case 1

Relieving Pain in a Dying Patient[11]

For some time now, Nicolas has had stomach pains. They usually appear when he's under stress, but lately he's had them almost constantly. Finally, he decides to go to the doctor to have them checked out. It turns out that Nicolas has stomach cancer and that he must be operated on immediately. After waking up from the operation, Nicolas receives more devastating news. The cancer has spread so far through his system that it is considered inoperable. There is nothing more the doctors can do.

Nicolas is eighty years old, and cancer grows more slowly in the elderly. He is thus sent home to spend his last months with his family. When the time comes,

Continued

---

[11]This case reports a true story.

Case 1 (*Continued*)

Nicolas will be able to die at home. A visiting nurse service will provide help to the family.

In the meantime, Nicolas will often be in pain. This pain will only worsen as he gets nearer to the end. He is therefore put on pain medication. As the months go by, the pain grows worse, until Nicolas is mostly confined to his bed. He requests that his doctor give him something stronger to control the pain.

The doctors tell him that a stronger pain medication will have its price. The pain reliever given most often in these cases is morphine. This can have significant side effects. For one, morphine is highly addictive so once he begins to use it, there will be no turning back. In addition, the morphine will often make him too drowsy to experience his surroundings lucidly. Most important, the morphine could hasten Nicolas's death. Morphine is a very strong drug and is mostly prescribed in cases that are medically futile, since it suppresses respiration. Nicolas is such a case, and he urgently needs pain relief. But as the amount of morphine is raised, it will increase the chances of his dying sooner as well.[12]

THOUGHT QUESTIONS

1. What are the likely effects of taking the morphine and of not taking it? How morally important are these effects?
2. Do you think Nicolas or his doctors actually intend to hasten his death? Why does this matter?
3. Are the bad effects a means to the good effects?
4. Under what conditions would the good effects outweigh the bad effects?
5. Would DDE permit Nicolas to take the morphine? What do you think would be morally right in this kind of situation?

Case 2

Birth Control[13]

A controversial example of the implications of natural law theory appears in former Pope John Paul II's arguments against the use of birth control. Peter Simpson, in his book about the Pope's philosophy, explains: "Sex is not something a couple may use as they wish. On the contrary they may only use it according to what it naturally is."[14] Simpson is saying that when sex is used in a way that violates its essential nature or function, that works against nature and so is morally wrong. But what is the nature or function of human sexuality? The sexual act is an act of creation that brings with it the possibility of new life. The use of birth control deliberately

Continued

---

[12]The use of morphine used to be considered quite risky; it now appears that carefully regulated use of morphine can be administered fairly safely, although high doses still have risks.

[13]Peter Simpson, *On Karol Wojtyla* (Belmont, CA: Wadsworth/Thompson Learning Inc., 2001).

[14]Ibid., 65. (Emphasis added.) All quotations that follow are taken from the same text.

Case 2 *(Continued)*

obstructs this natural function. As Simpson colorfully puts it, to use birth control is effectively "to de-sex sex," to change the sexual act into an *unnatural* act. This holds true for all *artificial* methods of birth control, including the use of condoms, intrauterine devices (IUDs), spermicides, and "the pill."

An important exception is natural family planning, sometimes called the "rhythm method" (a little misleadingly). The idea is to abstain from sexual intercourse during the woman's periods of fertility. If done properly (which requires instruction by a doctor), natural family planning is held to be more than 90% effective and thus compares very favorably with artificial methods. Unlike the pill and IUDs in particular, natural family planning also poses no risks of undesirable medical side effects.[15]

Why is natural family planning acceptable for natural law theory when artificial methods are not? The answer is that natural family planning doesn't interfere with the sex act per se. First, Simpson explains that "[t]o use nature's order is very different from breaking nature's order." Here, the distinction is on working *with* nature, rather than *against* it. After all, a woman's fertility cycles are part of how nature functions, so it's perfectly permissible for rational agents to make use of these cycles to achieve other natural purposes such as placing manageable time intervals between births. By contrast, birth control pills directly interfere with this natural cycle. Condoms, meanwhile, work against the very design of the sexual organs by blocking the union of sperm to the egg. Thus, neither method can be considered "using nature's order"; rather, both directly oppose natural processes. Simpson also observes, "It would be absurdly strict, even unnatural, to demand that every sexual act be actually procreative, or to say that intercourse is only permissible if the couple hope to have a child as a result of it." If it must always be used exclusively to conceive a child, then sex would have to be restricted to just those few days each month when the woman is fertile. Such a stringent limitation on sexual activity doesn't seem to be in accordance with nature. Indeed, it is worth emphasizing that the sexual act need not always be intended solely for procreation (i.e., it need not be reserved solely to "make babies"); its pleasurable aspects are legitimate and natural as well. Nevertheless, *never* intending to have children does conflict with a primary natural function of sexuality. Thus, it cannot be right for a married couple to intend never to have children. Rather, the purpose of natural family planning should be to space out births and even control the number of births - which can both reflect a couple's financial concerns as well. Again, this all follows from the fact that the sexual act is, by nature, an act of creation – a component that should never be separated from it entirely.[16]

THOUGHT QUESTIONS

1. Do you agree that the artificial birth control methods interfere with the design and natural functions of human sexuality?

---

[15]The "pill" is associated with increased blood clots, and IUDs is associated with bleeding and potentially permanent damage to the reproductive system.

[16]It should also be understood that natural law can support *medical* uses of artificial methods like the pill, say, to control an extremely uneven menstrual cycle or severe menstrual pain.

2. If artificial methods *do* interfere with natural functions, do you think this makes the use of these methods morally wrong? Why or why not?

3. What do you think about natural family planning? Is it correct to characterize it as a method that applies nature's order rather than opposing it?

4. Evaluate the Pope's natural law arguments regarding the moral permissibility of artificial birth control methods.

5. Would natural law allow condoms to be used to prevent the spread of HIV and other sexually transmitted diseases? Suppose a couple is already married when they discover that one partner is HIV positive. How might DDE answer this question?

Case 3

Just War Theory and the Killing of Noncombatants

After the September 11 2001 attacks and multiple military interventions, there has been a renewed interest in what qualifies as a *just war*. In the United States, the debate mostly refers to principles of "just war theory," which originated in the natural law writings of St. Augustine and St. Thomas Aquinas.

Just war theory deals with *when*—under what *conditions*—war is justified (*Jus ad Bellum*) as well as *how* a war may justly be fought (*Jus in Bello*). Naturally, there are disagreements about the details of what constitutes just wars and just ways of waging war. Nevertheless, most discussants agree on several general principles. Let's first examine *when* a war is justified. Such a war must, first, be fought for *just cause*. One has just cause, for instance, when there is an imminent threat, when one is protecting basic human rights, or when one is protecting the innocent.[17] A just war must also be declared by the *right authority* such as a recognized government and not just by some small group. It must be fought with the *right intention*, namely, the intention of obtaining the goal that *just cause* provides (e.g., eliminating the imminent threat). One must enter a war only as a *last resort*, once all other options have been exhausted. There must be a sufficient *probability of success*. Finally, the outcome must be *proportionate*; that is, the good of the intended goal must exceed the amount of damage that the war is expected to cause.

Once it has been determined that a given war is just, we must consider *how* the war may be fought. The two basic principles to be considered here are the principles of *discrimination* and of *proportionality*. The first principle requires that war be waged only against *combatants*—for example, against enemy soldiers and not against *noncombatants* or innocent civilians. The principle of *proportionality* tells us *how much force* is justified in a war. One is allowed to apply only as much force as is necessary to meet the goal of the war, which, again, is determined by the principle of *just cause*. To illustrate how these conditions work, most philosophers agree that the dropping of atomic bombs on Hiroshima and Nagasaki during World War II was *not* justified: combatants and noncombatants were killed indiscriminately, and the deaths and injuries of millions of people appear out of proportion to the war's outlined goal.

Continued

---

[17]The principle of forfeiture relates to determining just cause (see §III).

Case 3 (*Continued*)

Nevertheless, the killing of innocent civilians can at times be unavoidable. During World War II, for instance, it was difficult to hit a military target with precision. As a result, deaths occurred that were not intended. Also, many bombs destroyed a much larger area than just the target itself. Of course, today's missiles and drones can hit targets much more precisely. However, an enemy can exploit the presence of innocent civilians by hiding military personnel and equipment in hospitals, churches, schools, and mosques. This makes it virtually impossible to attack such targets without killing the innocent. Saddam Hussein, for instance, employed "human shields," as have many other regimes and armies since. Muddying things further, it is increasingly difficult to determine who is in fact a combatant. Soldiers may pose as civilians, and civilians may aid in fighting the war.

How can we decide whether, or when, the unintended killing of innocents is justified (the military calls this *collateral damage*). The first requirement, again, is that the war is being waged on just grounds; otherwise, no killing can be justified. Once this is settled, DDE can be used to distinguish military actions that are permissible from those that are not.

First, the act must be defined as destroying a military target, for instance, and not as the killing of innocent civilians. Otherwise, the act violates a moral principle and so is simply wrong. Second, innocent deaths cannot be the means to achieve one's goal (e.g., destroying the target); rather, their deaths may only be a secondary effect. Third, one must not *intend* to kill any innocent civilians. Finally, the good effect—destroying the target—must outweigh the bad effect—the deaths of innocents.

With this background, we can now consider some actual situations.

1. During the 1990 Gulf War against Iraq and Saddam Hussein, the Amiriya Shelter was destroyed by the United States using two "smart bomb" missiles. Many in the U.S. military believed the building was a military command center, basing their assessment on satellite reconnaissance and the detection of radio signals. It also appeared that it might be being used as a military personnel bunker. If the latter, then it could be assumed to have family members present but not a large number of civilians. At the same time, there was also some evidence that the building was being used as a major civil-defense shelter; it had previously been used this way in the Iraq–Iran war. The bombing killed up to 408 people, mainly women and children.[18]

2. During the initial phases of the 2003 invasion of Iraq, the United States went after Saddam Hussein and his regime. After Saddam was deposed, the political situation changed. In the subsequent chaos, various terrorist organizations and religious factions emerged. The terrorists want to rid Iraq of U.S. armed forces. They and the several factions also fight each other in their attempts to take political power in Iraq. To these various ends, public places have often been bombed, killing Iraqi and American civilians indiscriminately.

3. According to the CIA website, Saddam held as many as eight hundred foreign civilians involuntarily for use as human shields. These civilians were arrested by

Continued

---

[18]One report of these events may be found at "Amiriyah Shelter Massacre," Wikipedia, accessed August 27, 2016, http://en.wikipedia.org/wiki/Amiriyah_shelter. Reports as to what happened and what information the U.S. military actually had varied depending on which sources are consulted.

Case 3 (*Continued*)

Iraqi military and then kept at strategic locations in groups of eight to ten. Although the civilians were treated humanely, they suffered severe psychological stress. Saddam also placed Iraqi military facilities near mosques, schools, hospitals, and other places frequented by civilians.[19] More recently, 2015 news reports show Syrian rebels using captives locked in cages as human shields against air strikes; ISIS, meanwhile, is notorious for using human shields and killing innocents.

4. Casualty estimates say that between 2003 and 2013, several hundred thousand to over a million Iraqis were killed—mostly civilians—in the Iraq conflicts. In Afghanistan, hostilities caused more than 200,000 civilian deaths by 2015, and the number continues to grow. Over 7,000 American troops have also died so far in these two related conflicts. In both regions, furthermore, widespread destruction has caused nearly a complete breakdown of food and medical supply chains. This has led to many civilian deaths, especially among children, due to malnutrition. Neither of these conflicts has yet come to an end.

THOUGHT QUESTIONS

1. Would DDE justify the Amiriya shelter bombing? What moral problems are raised by this bombing?
2. Since the Geneva Convention forbids the use of human shields, Saddam Hussein's actions were clear violations of international law. Could this justify U.S. attacks upon military facilities that he had surrounded by civilians?
3. In any war, the number of *indirect* civilian casualties is both hard to predict and to later assess. What problem does this raise for our attempting to evaluate an action via DDE?
4. Does the inevitability of *indirect* civilian casualties pose a problem for just war theory in general?
5. In the United States, the GI Bill helps fund college educations. In light of the world's political unrest along with the preceding information, would you consider it ethical to join the military as a way to fund your college education? Apply just war theory and DDE to arrive at your answer.

Case 4

Permanent Vegetative State: The Case of Terri Schiavo[20]

In 1990, at the age of twenty-six, Terri Schiavo suffered a heart attack and permanently lost consciousness. After three years in a coma, she was diagnosed as being in a permanent vegetative state (PVS). A patient is considered in a PVS when one

Continued

---

[19]"Putting Noncombatants at Risk: Saddam's Use of 'Human Shields,'" Central Intelligence Agency, accessed August 27, 2016, https://www.cia.gov/library/reports/general-reports-1/iraq_human_shields.

[20]This case, as well as the discussion of the diagnosis of PVS, is based on the article by Yvonne Raley, "Wie Tot ist Tot?" *Gehirn und Geist* (December 2006): 30–35.

Case 4 (*Continued*)

or both of the cerebral hemispheres are irreversibly damaged and the patient is completely unaware of her surroundings. There is no hope for recovery.

It can take up to a couple of years to conclusively determine that a patient is in a PVS. The diagnosis rests on an electroencephalogram as well as long-term observation of the patient. PVS must be distinguished from brain death, in which the patient's entire brain including the brain stem has lost function. (A brain-dead patient is considered medically and legally dead in most of the world.) PVS must also be distinguished from a minimally conscious state, in which the patient is still minimally aware of his or her surroundings.

In Terri Schiavo's case, several physicians made the determination that Terri would not wake up. In 1998, her husband, Michael, requested permission from the courts to disconnect her feeding tube. Although Terry no longer swallowed automatically, she was still breathing on her own. This is common with PVS patients because the brain stem, which controls respiration, is still intact. In contrast, whole brain death requires life support to keep respiratory function going (which may be done, for instance, so the patient's organs can be donated).

Although Terri Schiavo did not have a living will stating whether she would want to be kept alive as a PVS patient, her husband testified that he was certain Terri would not want to be kept alive in those circumstances.

Terri's parents opposed Michael's request. They thought that they had seen Terri react to certain external stimuli (e.g., she would periodically open her eyes and her pupils would contract in light). She would also occasionally moan or cry. Behaviors like these are not uncommon in PVS patients, although the current medical consensus is that PVS patients are not aware of anything. Since some degree of consciousness is necessary to experience pain, PVS patients presumably cannot feel pain either.

In court, Terri's parents denied Michael's claim that Terri would not want to be kept alive. As a Roman Catholic, they said, Terri would consider it unethical to have a feeding tube disconnected. In fact, the Catholic Church had no official position on the matter of feeding tubes for PVS patients until 2004, when Pope John Paul II released a statement saying that providing basic nutrition to a PVS patient is a moral obligation. Here's an excerpt from what he wrote:

> The sick person in a vegetative state … still has the right to basic health care (nutrition, hydration, cleanliness, warmth, etc.), and to the prevention of complications related to his confinement to bed. … I should like particularly to underline how the administration of water and food, even when provided by artificial means, always represents a *natural means* of preserving life, not a *medical act*. Its use, furthermore, should be considered, in principle, *ordinary* and *proportionate*, and as such morally obligatory, insofar as and until it is seen to have attained its proper finality, which in the present case consists in providing nourishment to the patient and alleviation of his suffering.[21]

As the pope acknowledges, feeding tubes are an artificial means of providing a patient with nutrition. But natural law theory implies that receiving food and water is a natural part of keeping a person alive. Keeping someone breathing by using a

Continued

---

[21] Available at the Vatican Website, Caritas in Veritate, accessed August 27, 2016, http://w2.vatican.va/content/john-paul-ii/en/speeches/2004/march/documents/hf_jp-ii_spe_20040320_congress-fi-amc.html. Emphases are in the original.

Case 4 *(Continued)*

mechanical ventilator, on the other hand, is not a natural means of preserving life. There is no moral obligation to keep a PVS patient alive by non-natural or *"extraordinary"* means.

The fight over Terri Schiavo's life lasted over seven years. During this time, Terri's feeding tube was disconnected three times and twice reconnected by court order. The third time it was permanently removed because Terry's parents lost their battle in court. Terri Schiavo died on March 3, 2005, at the age of forty-one. An autopsy confirmed the diagnosis of PVS.

THOUGHT QUESTIONS

1. What caused Terri Schiavo's death? Can there be a moral difference between actively killing someone and letting them die? Which occurred in this case?

2. Is there any way, in a case like this, to reasonably determine what the patient would want for themselves? What level of agency ought to be reflected in determining the patient's wants?

3. If a PVS patient's living will requests continuing life support (including feeding), does she have a right to that support? Does she have a right to all support being suspended if her living will requests that? Does she have *any* moral rights? What moral duties do we have toward PVS patients?

4. What moral difference (if any) is there between other life-sustaining medical support and support by a feeding tube?

5. Why did the pope view artificially administered food and water as a natural means of preserving life? Does this reflect the "vagueness" of natural law theory?

6. Some doctors maintain that PVS can't be distinguished with certainty from a minimally conscious state (which has the possibility of recovery) except by doing an autopsy afterwards. How should this uncertainty affect any decision to disconnect a feeding tube?

7. Some think of PVS patients like Terri Schiavo as cases in which the person has already been lost (i.e., in effect, she has already "died"). There is no moral problem with removing a dead person's feeding tube. However, this view redefines death as the loss of a person rather than as a bodily loss of life. What do you think? What position would natural law take on this?

8. How would DDE analyze the act of disconnecting Terri's feeding tube?

CHAPTER TEN

Social Contracts and Rights

I. INTRODUCTION

Police officers, the IRS, and other authorities make and enforce rules the rest of us must submit to. Where did they get their power? They started out no different from the rest of us, so what made them the rulers and us the ruled? These questions are addressed by *social contract theory*, which maintains that those under authority give that authority by agreement to their rulers. Here's an example.

Your boss has assigned an important project to you and several colleagues, Jan, Tom, and Alison. You must create a proposal for a new line of products. This will require research on the market demand and on how readily your manufacturing processes can be retooled. It will also require choices about product design, quality and costs. The boss wants a carefully crafted draft in two months. If done well, this will raise your standing with him. But you suspect that he's also using this project to determine if any of you should be laid off, given the recent topside pressure to cut expenses.

You and your team meet right away. You first need to elect a project coordinator to make sure the project stays on schedule and to keep the boss in the loop. You also need a secretary to record meeting notes and relevant information gathered along the way. The team makes you coordinator; Tom volunteers as secretary, Jan and Alison agree to research the market, and you and Tom will start getting input from the people in manufacturing. Together, you also set up a timeline. You close the meeting with a little pep talk and are pleased that everyone appears on board.

You and your team have created a *social contract*: a pact or agreement established by people to organize themselves and share responsibilities for their mutual benefit. Beside project teams, social contracts can also establish a formal civil system (i.e., a government, laws, etc.). An important example of this is the Mayflower Compact, written by the Pilgrims to keep order and establish their new American colony. A portion reads:

> [B]y these presents solemnly and mutually, in the presence of God, and one of another, [we] covenant and combine our selves together into a civil body politic, for our better ordering and preservation ... and by virtue hereof to enact,

constitute, and frame such just and equal laws, ordinances, acts, constitutions and offices, from time to time, as shall be thought most meet and convenient for the general good of the Colony, unto which we promise all due submission and obedience. ... [1]

Key ingredients to both examples are that (a) the contract is voluntarily estab lished by those it will govern, (b) it's intended to be fair and good for all, (c) each contract negotiator promises every other to fulfill their own part of the agreement, and (d) the contract makes rules, grants authority, and places each under obliga-tion to fulfill their assigned roles. These obligations also confer rights. Since Jan and Alison have committed to doing the market research, you and Tom have a right to expect their findings on the appointed due date. Similarly, the Mayflower Compact set the stage for establishing *equal* laws, ordinances, and so on, which in turn gave each person certain equal rights.

Social contracts can also be used in political and ethical *theories*, though theo-retical contracts are *hypothetical*, not *actual*. Still, these theoretical contracts in-clude (at least to an approximation) all the ingredients just mentioned. Whether actual or theoretical, a social contract can attempt to justify an entire social system along with a moral standard. There are two methods for doing this. One appeals to some small set of *foundational moral values* (see Chapter One, §V) that guide the creation of the contract. Such contracts are *morally based*. Additional rights, principles, and authorities are then to be developed out of the contract.

Alternately, a social contract might *itself* serve as the basis from which a social and moral system is created. This *non-morally based* method does *not* draw upon any *moral* values. Since it must nevertheless be based on something, it appeals to *foundational non-moral values* (see Chapter One, §V). We will look at instances of each, beginning with Locke's highly influential morally based account.

For Discussion

1. *Why can't morally justified authority be based upon having the most power?*
2. *Can you think of any other explanation of authority besides its being bestowed by those to be governed?*
3. *What everyday social contracts have you entered into? These can be implicit— for example, how you drive around town, how players work together on a sports team, or how neighbors interact.*

Summary
One way to explain some people's authority over others is by a social contract—actual or theoretical. Theoretical social contracts have been used to justify entire moral and social systems. A social contract should be voluntary, it should be fair and for the ben-efit of all, and everyone should consent (explicitly or implicitly) to it. It also establishes

[1]The entire document is available at several online sites, including, accessed August 27, 2016, http://avalon.law.yale.edu/17th_century/mayflower.asp.

rules, obligations, authorities, and rights. Social contracts may be morally based *or* non-morally based.

Key Terms

- **Social contract:** *an agreement established by a set of people (in actuality or theoretically) to set up a social system that fairly benefits all.*

II. LOCKE

The English philosopher John Locke (1632–1704) developed a morally based contract theory that greatly influenced Thomas Jefferson's Declaration of Independence as well as the design of the U.S. government. Locke's account is also famous for its concept of a *natural right,* which Locke bases on natural law theory (see Chapter Ten). A **right** confers upon its holder a kind of privilege to protect, utilize, or exercise control over something. It allows one person to validly make some claim upon another. That claim in turn puts the latter under obligation to the rights-holder. While many familiar rights are *legal* rights protected by law, our interest here is with *natural* rights—moral rights that people have automatically. Natural rights include the most basic moral rights and correspond to certain basic moral obligations.

Locke starts off by imagining humanity existing in a **state of nature**—a moral and social condition without any government or formal civil society. This is *not* a moral anarchy, for the moral "law of nature"—natural law—still holds. Locke doesn't say a great deal about the natural law. Nevertheless, it's clear that even in the state of nature, there are foundational moral values (values from natural law) that place everyone under certain moral responsibilities.

However, it's not possible to be responsible for an action unless you have control over that action. If an electrode in your brain makes you hit and injure another person, you can't be morally responsible for that. Moral responsibility requires that there be areas in your life over which you reign supreme—where you can act as a moral agent, free from anyone else's authority, interference or control. You must have a *right* to exercise complete and unhindered control over these areas—areas that together make up what we might call (not Locke's term!) your own *personal domain*. Others are morally obligated to respect your rights in these areas.

Within the state of nature, everyone has the *same* moral rights and obligations and so are *moral equals*. Since no distinctions yet exist, every person's personal domain includes all the same things: each must be free to act without hindrance to his life, health, liberty, and property. These are Locke's four basic natural rights.

The right to *life* is obvious, for no one can do anything without being alive. Each person has an equal right to life—specifically, to his own life—but not to the life of any other. Protection from injuries or harms done by others—the right to *health*— is crucial for its contribution to ongoing life. Since impaired health limits choices, health is also necessary to ensure liberty. The right to *liberty* gives each person full control over their own personal domains, free from any control by others. Thus, all must enjoy *equal* liberty. Again, each holds these same rights equally, which also gives each the same responsibility to respect these rights in others.

The right of *property* is especially important in Locke's theory. Your property or possessions include everything you can exercise control over within your domain. Property includes whatever is properly yours, including yourself, your health, and your liberty—things over which you have exclusive rights. While these are clearly your own, how can something *in the external world* become your property? Locke explains that, in the state of nature, all external things are initially held in common. However, they don't necessarily stay that way. Since anything I do is *my* doing, my labor is mine. Once I expend effort to obtain or improve something, therefore, that thing ceases to be common property and instead becomes my property. As Locke puts it, common property becomes one's own as soon as he "has mixed his labor with" that thing.[2] By picking a wild strawberry, I make that berry mine; by cultivating and planting, I make the resulting crop mine; by mixing words or paints, I create my own writing or painting—things over which I then have a right of property.

Natural rights ensure that people can fully control things that are their *own*—life, health, liberty, and whatever they add their labor to. Since a right is a claim upon others, these rights obligate others to allow us full control over all that is ours. Thus, a moral right supports several moral prescriptive principles. The right to life, for instance, supports the principle: "No one should kill an innocent person" as well as principles that forbid placing lives at unnecessary risk. A right can likewise support *derived* rights, which expand the basic rights. For instance, the right to liberty supports a derived right to freedom from enslavement. Additional principles and rights can be derived from more basic moral rights.

We've so far considered Locke's account in the state of nature—before a social contract and so without government and law. But remaining in the state of nature doesn't adequately serve people's interests and needs. As more people lay claim to property, legal controls become necessary to protect that property and to resolve conflicting property claims. In living together, people also come to need military protection, a stable economy, and community essentials such as roads and bridges. They thus negotiate a social contract for themselves, thereby establishing a more formal civil system or *state*. By placing themselves under the rule of a state, their purpose is to improve their condition and to protect their natural rights.[3]

Locke insisted that a state itself remain morally bound by natural law. Still, it's necessary for the people to give over to the state certain rights and liberties if they are to enjoy the advantages the state can offer. By giving these over to the state, people leave the state of nature and so become unequal in certain ways. For instance, Locke assigns authority to the state to collect taxes, to require military

---

[2]John Locke, *The Second Treatise of Civil Government* (Public Domain, 1690), chapter 5, section 27, accessed August 27, 2016, http://www.constitution.org/jl/2ndtreat.htm.

[3]In this chapter (and most of the book), "state" refers to a formal civil system along with its laws and authorities. This differs from a "state of nature." Further, although Ohio can count as a state, we will normally use the term to refer to the highest level of government its citizens are under (e.g., the United States).

service, and to imprison and even execute offenders so as to protect and serve the general good. The state thus diminishes everyone's rights to some degree (i.e., taxes take property, military service risks injury and death, imprisonment denies liberty) and also adds certain obligations to what natural law already imposed.

For Discussion

1. *Do you think that any group has ever lived (or presently live) in a state of nature?*
2. *What falls within your personal domain? Do Locke's rights protect all of these things?*
3. *Is there anything that you think should remain common property no matter what?*
4. *Are there any private properties that, at some point, ought to turn into common property?*
5. *What specific rights must people give over for any state to adequately function?*
6. *What rights ought never to be given over to any state? Do any actual states nevertheless infringe on some of these?*
7. *Suppose that your society is supported by a social contract. When and how have you voluntarily joined yourself to this contract?*

Summary

According to Locke, everyone has moral responsibilities even in the state of nature under the natural moral law. To have responsibilities, a person must have control over her personal domain. The natural rights of life (and with that, health) together with liberty help ensure this control. Another natural right is that of property, which includes everything within one's domain as well as everything that we make our own by adding our labor. Everyone holds these rights equally in the state of nature. People leave that and place themselves under the authority of a formal system by establishing a social contract. The state protects and adds to our rights; it also requires our partly giving over certain rights to the state.

Key Terms

- **Right:** *confers upon its holder a moral privilege to protect, utilize, or exercise control over something; it is a claim one person may validly make upon another.*

- **State of nature:** *for Locke, a moral and social condition for people in which no government or formal civil society exists.*

III. HOBBES

Locke's theory describes a morally based social contract. But Thomas Hobbes (1588–1679), another English philosopher who just preceded Locke, developed a social contract account that attempts to be non-morally based.[4] It thus aims to

---

[4]Presented in Thomas Hobbes's, *Leviathan* (1651), accessed August 27, 2016, http://socserv2. socsci.mcmaster.ca/econ/ugcm/3ll3/hobbes/Leviathan.pdf. This book preceded Locke's account by about forty years.

provide a complete ethical theory in itself, and the rights it initially establishes are foundational for the rest of the theory.[5]

Hobbes likewise starts with a state of nature, though Hobbes's picture of this, notoriously, is much more pessimistic than that of other social contract theorists. First, there are *no* moral values or obligations; moral right and justice simply do not yet exist. If two need or desire the same thing, that puts them in conflict with each other—a common situation. This hostile competition between people makes Hobbes's state of nature an ongoing "time of war." With no moral standard, people have only their reason to direct them. Within this framework, therefore, the only rational way for people to act is to beat down the competition. Yet even this can gain no lasting advantage over others, since people have roughly similar physical strength and mental abilities. Further, no one can be trusted for, by trusting me, you simply signal your vulnerability, making it easier for me to get what I want from you. With no real social stability or personal security, people have little motivation to pursue knowledge, to build things, or to attempt any creative achievement (unless they can gain an advantage over others by doing so). To live in this state is to live in violence and continual fear; as Hobbes famously put it, such a life is "solitary, poor, nasty brutish, and short."[6]

Not a good situation! Hobbes's solution is to negotiate a social contract and establish a formal state that *forces* people to keep agreements, leave others alone, and act justly. Hobbes's contract does not share Locke's goal of protecting people's natural rights (there aren't any). Rather, its purpose is to allow each person to survive, which is only possible under the rule of a powerful state that can enforce its laws with a heavy hand.[7]

Hobbes's social contract provides a good that benefits all equally: escape from the ongoing state of war. But can people voluntarily consent to this contract? This is an important question for every social contract theory. Hobbes's initially suggests that at times there might actually be people in the state of nature who could explicitly consent to a contract. But his real basis for consent is theoretical: rational self-interest. That is, people in the state of nature would understand that a lasting social peace—one that allows them to meet their needs while being protected from injury or death—is very much in their interest. Since a contract is the only means for achieving such peace, consent to the contract becomes a rational necessity. No reasonable person could refuse a contract that offers this in place of living in a war. On this basis, Hobbes assumes the hypothetical consent of all rational persons.

By now it's clear that rationality and self-interest are the foundations of Hobbes's account. The demands of reason are non-moral. Hobbes's value of "liberty"—the

---

[5]Hobbes's basic views initially seem clear, but there is a much disagreement in the details. An important alternative to the interpretation presented here takes Hobbes as building upon at least one foundational *moral* right—liberty. We take this as a non-moral *rational* value rather than as a *moral* value.

[6]Ibid., 78.

[7]There is a kind of egoism in Hobbes, who argues largely on the basis of rationally promoting one's own interests. This is the primary purpose of everyone in the state of nature. See Chapter Five, §IV.

right to do whatever a person chooses out of self-interest—seems best understood as a non-moral, innate value of human nature (i.e., self-preservation). This value is discovered by reason and can be considered a component of rationality itself. In any case, the rational thing is for people to attain peace by establishing a state. It's at this point that a moral standard surfaces, for justice and rights are defined only through the contract and enforced by the state.

In making a social contract, people give over to the state much of their initial liberty, even as they gain justice and rights. It's rational to do this as long as the overall loss is less than the benefits gained by peace. But what if the state itself turns out to be oppressive? After all, since only a very powerful civil system can enforce peace, Hobbes requires that the monarchy or government have *great* power—"absolute" authority. This makes the risk of oppression very real.

Balanced against this risk is a set of rights.[8] Most controversially, Hobbes maintains that citizens have a right to disobey and even to defend themselves against the state when it threatens their lives. Hobbes also seems to provide for rights to equal treatment, to impartial judgments, and to property. Although these rights may seem at odds with the state having absolute power, they are quite consistent with Hobbes's overall standpoint. It wouldn't be rational for those in the state of nature (and thus of war) to exchange their existing risks for an equally bad set of state-created risks, particularly when the state also greatly reduces their liberty. However, if they can obtain peace, the right to protect themselves, and certain additional rights, then they can come out ahead. Thus, Hobbes's contract can remain the rational choice even if it legitimizes some degree of oppression by the state.

For Discussion

1. *Do you agree with Hobbes that the state of nature would be a state of war—solitary, poor, nasty brutish, and short?" Why or why not?*
2. *If a state is strong enough to ensure peace, how much personal liberty could there still be?*
3. *Do you think that a Hobbesian state of nature has ever actually existed? Do you think that people living in that situation would use a social contract to establish a state?*
4. *Locke, Thomas Jefferson, and Hobbes agree that citizens can be morally justified in rebelling against the state (though for different reasons). What do you think?*
5. *The text interprets Hobbes's account as based on non-moral values. Do you agree?*
6. *Do you think that a Hobbesian contract would support moral rights? Which rights?*

---

[8]These rights are somewhat implicit except for the right of liberty that exists even in the state of nature. But additional rights can exist even within a state. Indeed, Robert P. Kraynak credits Hobbes with "inaugurating the natural rights principles of modern liberalism." *Thomas Hobbes: From Classical Natural Law to Modern Natural Rights.* (2011). A *We the People* project of the National Endowment for the Humanities 2016 The Witherspoon Institute, accessed August 27, 2016, http://www.nlnrac.org/earlymodern/hobbes.

Summary

Hobbes essentially offers a non-morally based social contract that can be treated as both a social/political and ethical theory. It starts with people in a state of nature or "time of war"—a violent, ongoing battle for survival. There is no morality or justice in this condition. The only rational escape from this is through a social contract that establishes a powerful state, one that can enforce peace and so benefit all. This requires people to give up a fair amount of their liberty, but they are compensated for this by their enjoying peace along with certain additional rights. Once the contract establishes the state, justice, duties, and certain moral rights come into existence as well.

IV. RAWLS

Much more recently, the twentieth-century philosopher John Rawls provided an ingenious version of contract theory in his *Theory of Justice*.[9] Rawls invites us into an imaginary situation—**the original position**—where completely free and rationally self-interested persons negotiate a social contract. Each contract negotiator will want to protect her own interests so she can live a good life. Rawls then adds a special feature: these negotiations all take place under a **veil of ignorance**. No one knows anything about their actual lives—nothing about their family, economic class, or the circumstances they will be born into. Nor does anyone know anything about their gender, race, religion, personal attributes, career, or relationships. They don't even know about most of their own personal values and beliefs—moral or non-moral. What they *do* know about is the general structure necessary for any society; they also share certain essential moral commitments about fairness and equality.[10]

These shared commitments make Rawls's account morally based. This is further established by the veil of ignorance putting everyone on an equal footing, thereby ensuring fair contract negotiations. Rawls also gives the negotiators the non-moral value of rational self-interest. With no knowledge of their actual lives, these rational and self-interested negotiators won't risk favoring any particular aspects of life (e.g., career, race, talent, gender, etc.) over any others. Rawls argues that, under these conditions, the resulting contract will assign everyone the same basic liberties, rights and duties equally, thereby defining an ideally just society along with its accompanying moral system. He calls this *justice as fairness*.

The only limitations are those necessary to allow others to enjoy the same liberties and rights to the same degree. For instance, you and I both have a right to use a national park. We may freely use it as we wish, except neither of us may use it in ways that interfere with the other's free use. All of these liberties, rights and duties fall under Rawls's **equality principle**.

---

[9]Rawls, *A Theory of Justice.*
[10]Rawls intends these to be limited and uncontroversial. Of course, some object even to these.

This principle might also seem to require that everyone be given equal social privileges and receive compensations for their work at the same rate. But these kinds of equality would actually lead to unfairness since we are not all equal in non-moral ways. We have different degrees of intelligence, strength, and health as well as different personalities, talents, and abilities. Those with greater natural endowments can make better use of opportunities than others. Each of us also needs the services of those having capabilities we lack. To protect the less capable and maintain true fairness, any system must take these differences into account. Rawls handles this by his *difference principle,* which adds certain inequities to the contracted system (e.g., more pay for certain jobs and more power for certain positions of authority).

Two qualifications must be immediately emphasized. First, the difference principle always remains secondary to the equality principle. Equality in basic rights, opportunities, and general duties and liberties may never be suspended. This keeps minority interests from being sacrificed to promote the overall economic and social good (a sacrifice that utilitarianism willingly makes). Second, any inequality must still benefit all. The difference principle *can* bestow benefits to certain individuals that it denies to others but only as long as this substantially adds to everyone's good, especially that of the disadvantaged.

The difference principle is included to create as fair a society as possible. For instance, any civil system must establish a hierarchy of leaders and authority, leaving most of its other members with less power. But if the leaders use their power to settle disputes, direct constructive projects, enforce duties, and ensure social stability, then these inequalities in power will benefit all. For these inequities to be completely fair, however, Rawls also insists that every person have an equal opportunity to attain any of these leadership positions.

Economic inequities can also be justified. A fair and rational system would pay medical physicians more than, say, school janitors. Why? Physicians must invest more time and expense in preparing for their profession. In practice, they also incur greater health risks than most other professionals. Although these facts may discourage many from becoming physicians, society still needs them. To motivate people to pursue this and other demanding professions (e.g., as nurses, teachers, police, etc.), therefore, society must promise them greater compensations. Still, everyone should have the same *opportunity* to take up any of these professions. As long as a system *with* such economic inequities makes everyone better off than one *without* them, these inequities are morally legitimate.

Social contracts also support rights. But Rawls's account of rights extends further than that of most social contract theories. To keep things simple, we will discuss just two sets of Rawlsian rights. One is people's most *basic rights*. Since these are among the first things agreed to by the contract negotiators, they fall under the equality principle and so are equally held by all. These include basic *moral* rights such as a right to free thought and expression, to equal treatment, to personal liberty, and the like. Rawls's basic rights also include various *political* rights, such as a right to vote and to run for and hold public office. These basic rights must not merely be confirmed by law. They must also be proactively supported by state policies and actions so that everyone fully enjoys these rights in their everyday lives. As with everything under the equality principle, these rights can never be suspended or reduced for the sake of achieving other social goods.

Rawls calls his other main set of rights *human rights*. These rights don't merely hold within a state but for all members of the international community. Every state made up of "decent" people should guarantee these rights to their citizens. These include rights to property, security, and basic life necessities; they also guarantee protections from enslavement and genocide. These rights are essential for persons to function and participate in any civil society.

Human rights are so important that they have a special priority and urgency. According to Rawls, any association of decent nations (e.g., the United Nations) has a moral responsibility to ensure that all peoples have these critical rights. In fact, one country's egregious violation of these rights can justify intervention by other countries to end such violations even by military force.[11]

Where do human rights come from? Rawls employs the same approach to generate rights across nations as he does for individual states. First, there is a global original position, whose negotiators each represent the interests of various free and equal nations. These contract negotiators are also under a veil of ignorance: none knows anything about their own nations' resources, populations, global influence, and so. Under this veil, negotiators will work out fair principles that give no particular kind of state any advantage or disadvantage since they won't want to risk hurting their own nation's actual interests. Thus, the needs and responsibilities of every kind of society will be addressed equally and fairly—the global version of his equality principle. In essence, these imaginary negotiators work out a contract between nations like his earlier contract was worked out between individuals. Once established, this contract requires each nation to follow the same principles and to uphold the same human rights.

For Discussion

1. *Hobbes's contract negotiators know about and so can favor their own particular interests while negotiating a contract. Instead, Rawls makes everyone equal by the veil of ignorance. Which approach do you think is best? Why?*

2. *How does Rawls's equality principle reflect Kant's principles of ends and of universal law?*

3. *Have several groups imagine themselves in the original position and under the veil of ignorance, negotiating a contract for a state. What social and moral principles emerge?*

---

[11]Excellent presentations of Rawls's human rights and the global contract can be found in §5 of Leif Wenar, "John Rawls," in *The Stanford Encyclopedia of Philosophy* (Winter 2013 Edition), ed. Edward N. Zalta, accessed August 27, 2016, http://plato.stanford.edu/archives/win2013/entries/rawls/, and in §8 of Samuel Freeman, "Original Position," in *The Stanford Encyclopedia of Philosophy* (Fall 2014 Edition), ed. Edward N. Zalta, accessed August 27, 2016, http://plato.stanford.edu/archives/fall2014/entries/original-position/, accessed.

4. *Our society accepts a kind of economic "survival of the fittest" principle. It thus has no qualms about small businesses, for example, being overwhelmed or taken over by those more powerful. Is this good for society?*
5. *What social differences should be recognized by the difference principle, and how should it treat each difference?*
6. *In seeking to benefit all society by encouraging further education, our system has offered college students a temporary exemption to a military draft. This (utilitarian type) exemption violates Rawls's equality principle, which would instead allow no exceptions to the draft. Which position do you take?*
7. *What principles do you think would be set out by a global social contract for enforcing human rights and correcting rights violations by particular nations?*

Summary

Rawls offers an important theoretical and morally based social contract account. He imagines his contract negotiators originally starting out in perfect equality as free and rationally self-interested agents. Since these are under a veil of ignorance—*knowing nothing about their places in actual society—they will negotiate for equal duties and rights under the* equality principle. *These very basic rights, which are the same for all, include both moral and political rights. To then provide for different leadership positions and differences in ability, Rawls's* difference principle *allows for inequalities in power and financial compensation. Inequalities are justified only as long as they serve the good of all, especially the disadvantaged. Rawls later extended his account to contracts between nations, which create (among other things) what he calls human rights.*

Key Terms

- **Original position:** *imagines free and rational persons as contract negotiators.*
- **Veil of ignorance:** *those in the original position are under this veil, made equal by their lacking any knowledge about their actual lives, beliefs, advantages, and so on.*
- **Equality principle:** *gives equal liberties, rights, and duties to all by the initial contract.*
- **Difference Principle:** *adds certain social and economic inequities for the benefit of all but never so as to suspend the equality principle.*

V. ASSESSING SOCIAL CONTRACT THEORY

A number of points favor social contract theory, including those theories meant to serve as ethical accounts:

Moral objectivism. At first glance, it might seem that an *actual* social contract would be an instance of relativism (see Chapter Two, §II). The resemblance appears even greater if we imagine two neighboring societies that are based on distinct contracts and that therefore have different laws and duties. But *actual* social contracts (when they exist at all) are normally morally based and so assume a background moral standard (Locke assumes natural law, the Puritans assumed Christian morals). In presupposing a moral standard, furthermore, these actual contracts only establish a state's laws and social structures, not moral claims. Thus, this opens no doors to *moral* relativism. As for theoretical social contracts, these *can* serve as bases for a moral standard, but when they do, the results are meant to hold universally—for any society and any group of people.[12] This makes them objective, not relative. Objectivity gives social contract accounts important advantages, as argued in Chapter Two (see §V and §VI). Since an objective moral standard supports objective rights, the resulting objectivity of these rights is also in keeping with today's widely held view that all people, regardless of race, ethnicity, religion, and other differences, have the same moral rights.

Incentives. Whether the primary purpose is to escape from war (Hobbes), ensure natural rights (Locke), or achieve equality and fairness (Rawls), contracts are meant to serve the interests of all and provide for the general good. As Hobbes emphasizes, to reject the social contract is to act irrationally, to act against each person's own best interests. Broadly, then, there are strong incentives for people to agree to a contract. In addition, social contracts don't impose their requirements upon people externally; at least in the ideal, all who rationally consider a well-designed contract will consent to it for the sake of protecting and promoting their own interests. Contract theory thus includes its own motivation for people to keep it.

Authority. Social contract theory tends to blend moral claims with legal requirements and duties. This gives some degree of moral status to the formal civil system—its laws, rights, and authorities. Contract theory thus answers the question we began with: what gives some people authority over others? It explains this authority as being created via the consent (even if only hypothetical) of those under authority.

These are important advantages, and there are others as well. But social contract theories also encounter certain fairly general difficulties. We have touched on some of these in our previous discussion, but a few deserve further elaboration.

Contract negotiators. Who should be included among a contract's negotiators? The Mayflower Compact was written and signed only by the Puritan men, excluding women and most of the others also on the voyage. Hobbes may have intended that women be among the negotiators, but he doesn't emphasize that in his presentation. The United States initially excluded women, slaves, and those without property from voting; this suggests that, if we envision the United States as a social

---

[12]A theoretical social contract would not, strictly *have* to yield a universal moral standard, but there would be little point to it otherwise.

contract, it would exclude these people from its contract negotiations as well. In contrast, Rawls includes *all* persons (that is, autonomous human beings) as contract negotiators, at least hypothetically. Rawls's morally based account *cannot* exclude any particular group of persons since it is explicitly designed to ensure moral equality along with other values of a liberal society. But for social contracts based on different values—and especially for non-morally based accounts—there's no guarantee that particular groups could not be excluded. The problem is that nothing requires a social contract to either include or exclude any particular group from its negotiations. Failing to include certain people might cause some difficulty with moral confirmation, but this is the only consideration that seems able to affect a particular theory's choice of negotiators. We shall return to this issue shortly.

Consent. A related but broader issue has to do with consent. Rawls's account *guarantees* consent by all persons. Since Locke presumes natural moral law, his negotiators at least share their fundamental moral values, which should help bring them to mutual consent. On the other hand, if we adopt Hobbes's approach and imagine individuals negotiating a contract with their own interests in mind, can we really expect them to all consent to any final contract? At best, any resulting contract will be less than satisfactory to some negotiators. At worst, it might not be possible for the negotiators to resolve all their disagreements and reach general consent.

Next, suppose that a contract has already been established. What then places later generations under that contract? Not having participated in any negotiations, why should any previously agreed-upon contract hold for them? Can they consent to or reject such a contract? Most social contract theorists answer that, since the contract greatly benefits all, everyone has strong rational and self-interested reasons to consent to a contract—whether actual or hypothetical. We may thus assume everyone's consent.

Another way of approaching this problem is through **tacit consent**. First, this admits that being born into a contractually based civil system gives people no say about its defining contract or its control over their lives. Thus, they still ought to be able to decide for themselves whether they want to live under that contract. This choice should be made once they become autonomous adults, either by their staying in that society or by their leaving it for some other system they prefer. Suppose they stay and participate in their society by voting, paying taxes, and accepting governmental benefits (e.g., education). Then they have *tacitly consented* to that civil system's contract. Without making any formal declarations, they imply by their behavior that they accept the burdens and benefits of being part of that society. In this way, they become bound to obey and submit to its authorities and requirements.

The vulnerable. Our discussion has probably given the impression that social contract accounts, and that of Rawls in particular, must promote the interests of *everyone* who will live under the contract. Yet even Rawls's highly egalitarian account limits contract negotiators to persons who are rationally self-interested and thus autonomous. This same limitation appears necessary to any social contract if the resulting moral and social system is to be rational and beneficial to those who negotiate it. But where does that leave non-autonomous people like children, those suffering from dementia, the cognitively impaired, and other especially vulnerable people? Lacking autonomy, they can neither negotiate nor meaningfully consent to anything. Will their interests be adequately addressed by a contract they could have no part in? Nothing seems to require autonomous negotiators to look after the interests of the non-autonomous. Worse, it seems unlikely that self-interested negotiators will want to spend much of their society's resources on protections that do not benefit them. But this is exactly what they must do if they are to establish a contract that upholds the interests of the non-autonomous.

Social contract theories thus may not provide much for the most vulnerable members of society. This problem poses the greatest threat for *actual* social contracts (since it's so easy for the autonomous negotiators to marginalize others) and for *non-morally* based contracts (since these include no moral constraints that might impose some degree of protection for the vulnerable). How about an account like that of Rawls? Suppose that the original position assumes the *moral equality* of *all* human beings, *autonomous or not*. This would give autonomous negotiators a *moral* incentive to protect the non-autonomous but no obvious *self-interested* incentive (they are not among the non-autonomous). How far negotiators would go to protect the vulnerable - at no apparent benefit to themselves – thus remains uncertain. Could Rawls add that some negotiators might themselves turn out to be non-autonomous once the veil of ignorance is lifted? If this were possible, then the negotiators *would* have self-interested reasons to protect *all* people and not just the autonomous. This might work, but there's still the worry that autonomous negotiators might not be able to empathize sufficiently with those who lack autonomy so they can adequately champion their interests (see Chapter Fourteen, §2).[13]

For Discussion

1. *Can you think of any way a social contract could turn out to be an instance of moral relativism?*
2. *Can social contract theory adequately explain the state's authority to punish those violating the law?*
3. *Have you consented to live under your ruling state? How?*
4. *How much consent did Rosa Parks, say, tacitly give to the laws and authorities that discriminated against her?*
5. *Should we consider the possibility that consent can be given to different degrees ranging from full to partial to no consent?*
6. *Given social contract theory, could civil disobedience ever be morally acceptable? If so, under what conditions?*
7. *What actual interests could someone have with advanced Alzheimer's, with serious lifetime cognitive impairments, or who is in a permanent vegetative state?*

---

[13]There also may be non-autonomous humans so deficient in capacity that they have no interests that can be represented (e.g., someone in a permanently vegetative state; see Case 4 of Chapter Nine.

Summary
Social contract accounts have important advantages. Although contracts that generate a moral standard may appear to be morally relative, they normally generate an objective moral standard. Since social contracts are drawn up and agreed to by the governed for their own welfare, they also provide incentives for obeying their requirements. Furthermore, contract theory addresses the question: "What explains the authority some people have over others?" But like any theoretical approach, social contract theories also run into difficulties: They can exclude particular groups from contract negotiations. There's also the question of whether everyone would consent to a particular contract and how those born later can give their consent. A particularly important worry is whether social contracts can provide sufficient protections to the non-autonomous and their interests.

Key Terms

- **Tacit consent:** *the idea that people born into an existing contract effectively consent to that contract by participating as adults in the state and accepting its benefits.*

VI. ASSESSING RIGHTS

Rights and social contracts are often linked together. But rights can come out of any ethical account. If I have an obligation to keep my promise to you, you have a right or claim upon me to keep it. Since there's a general duty to respect another's property and life, there's a right to property and a right to life. Many moral obligations give rise to rights, and moral rights place obligations upon others.

The most important feature of moral rights is their universality. People have these rights simply because they are human and have equal moral value. This makes rights particularly useful for defending the marginalized and victimized. The mere mention of rights can carry the day in a moral argument, much like a "trump" takes all in card games.[14] Appeals to rights have been effective in combating discrimination, improving attitudes toward women, and even justifying military interventions against genocide. Another important advantage with rights, many maintain, is that they take the perspective of the oppressed rather than that of the oppressor.[15] Still, there can be too much of a good thing:

Overextending rights. Although rights have a clear place in moral discourse, some rights appeals have stretched beyond what can reasonably be justified. In popular thinking, having a "right" has become almost indistinguishable from having a personal interest: "I have a right to what I want." When we accord rights too much

---

[14]A high card in a trump suit beats all other cards in play. This striking analogy was first made by the contemporary American philosopher Ronald Dworkin.

[15]Brenda Almond, "Rights," in *A Companion to Ethics, Blackwell Companions to Philosophy*, ed. Peter Singer (Oxford: Blackwell Publishers, 1993), section 22.

prominence, we also foster a "victim mentality"—a self-centered moral perspective that only thinks of others in terms of what they owe us. According to care theorists (see Chapter Twelve), an overemphasis of rights feeds an exaggerated individualism that discounts the moral significance of human interrelatedness.

The antidote is not to abandon rights but to better balance rights with moral responsibilities. This isn't hard. First, every right is linked to a responsibility others have toward the rights-bearer. But any general moral right that one rights-bearer can claim can likewise be claimed by others. It follows that every rights-bearer is subject to the same kinds of responsibilities that others have toward her. Whether we speak of rights or responsibilities, the difference is largely one of perspective. In general, every rights claim can be re-expressed in terms of responsibilities. The value of doing so would be to draw greater attention to the moral responsibilities we all have toward each other.

Rights-Holders. The universality of rights helps underscore the moral equality of human beings. But paralleling the social contract problem of vulnerable populations (Kantian ethics has a similar problem with *rational agents;* see Chapter Eight, §7) is the difficulty over *who* (and even *what*) moral rights may be ascribed to.

The problem directly ties to the basis upon which we build the concept of rights. In Locke's account, natural rights are ascribed to all who can have moral responsibilities and obligations. This means that rights-holders must be autonomous individuals. In other contract accounts, those deserving rights must be capable of rational self-interest, which again requires being autonomous. But there are several important implications to rights being limited to autonomous persons.

For one thing, there can be no natural rights for non-human animals since they lack autonomy. Of course, this result may be just what we should expect since animals can never be held responsible for their actions either. For the same reason, however, there seem to be no natural rights for "defective" human beings such as the cognitively impaired or those suspended in a permanent vegetative state (PVS). For the latter especially, it's unsettling that they now lack rights that they previously had. Still more problematic is the result that younger children can have no natural rights. While not defective, young children still lack autonomy. Could we accord natural rights to members of these various groups by arguing that they either did or will have autonomy? Perhaps, but it's hard to see how someone's having autonomy at *another* time could justify ascribing rights to them at a time when they actually lack autonomy.

These problems are worrisome because those least able to defend themselves are the ones who most need the protections that rights afford. If rights do not protect these people—and historically, it has been children, the "defective," and the "subhuman" who have been most mistreated—then what good are rights? One alternative might be to consider basing rights upon something other than autonomy. Those with a utilitarian bent identify rights-holders with *sentient* creatures—creatures that can experience pain and suffering. This allows natural rights to include, in varying degrees, nonhuman animals as well as children, infants, and fetuses after the first trimester (although it still denies rights to PVS patients). Still, it's not at all clear why the ability to experience pain justifies an ascription of rights.

Perhaps the best alternative would simply be to abandon talk of rights for such cases and appeal instead to some moral theory that *can* ensure the needed moral protections. For example, Locke would presumably appeal to natural law theory, which probably already requires that we protect the fetus, the PVS patient, and the profoundly impaired because they are instances of human *life*. Since life is an end toward which other creatures also strive, there is arguably a moral obligation to protect some other animals as well.[16] Other ethical theories might likewise ensure some degree of protections for these sorts of cases—particularly if those theories shift their moral emphasis to something other than autonomy. The next two chapters introduce theories that make such a shift in emphasis.

For Discussion

1. *Do you sometimes appeal to rights to make your own arguments more convincing? Does a rights appeal make other people's arguments and positions more convincing to you?*
2. *Discuss cases in which appeals to rights have helped accomplish important social goods.*
3. *Describe cases where rights are overemphasized. What harms has this led to?*
4. *Does a four-year-old child have rights? Explain the basis of your answer.*
5. *Thomas has been autonomous most of his life, but the mild dementia he now has will only increase. Does this mean that his rights will diminish and ultimately be lost entirely?*
6. *What advantages and disadvantages are there to ascribing rights to all sentient creatures?*
7. *What is the best way to protect the interests of society's most vulnerable members?*
8. *The text suggests that a non-autonomous person could now be ascribed rights on the basis of their having autonomy at another time (before or after). How could this be supported?*

Summary

While appeals to rights can "trump" other moral arguments, many object that rights are overemphasized. Rights appeals at least need to be balanced by appeals to responsibilities. There's also a problem with who (and what) rights may be ascribed to: are rights-holders just those people who can have moral responsibilities and so are autonomous? That leaves out the people who may most need the protection of rights.

---

[16]Of course, natural law theory would also temper our responsibilities toward other animals and plants in view of the roles other living things play (e.g., as sources of food) in the overall natural order.

VII.** KINDS OF RIGHTS

We have talked mainly about legal and moral rights. But there are several other ways to differentiate rights. One way, familiar from the opening of Jefferson's Declaration of Independence, is to distinguish *alienable* from *inalienable* rights. An **inalienable right,** such as a right to life or the right to liberty, cannot *morally* be given up or taken away.[17] But I can easily transfer my *alienable right* to my property. By selling it or giving it away, for instance, I lose control over that property; someone else now holds that right. I can also let someone out of a promise, giving up whatever claim I had upon that person. These are alienable rights.

Rights can also be divided into *positive* and *negative* rights. **Positive rights** involve things people ought *to do or provide.* If I am injured and lying on the side of a busy road, I presumably have a right to expect help from others, especially from police officers or others specifically equipped to meet my need. Other positive rights might include a right to be provided food and shelter when destitute. Roughly, positive rights are claims we have on what others *should do for us*; negative rights are claims we have on what others *should not do to us.* My right of property, for instance, requires that others *not* trespass on my land or use my things without permission. My rights to life and liberty likewise require others to not take my life and to not interfere with my personal freedom. Negative rights are clearer and less controversial that positive rights. Locke's four natural rights are all negative rights.

Another important rights concept is **human rights,** a phrase Rawls uses to refer to a special category of rights from his theory (see §IV). In the 1948 United Nations' Universal Declaration of Human Rights, the phrase is used more widely, encompassing several different kinds of rights.

Since the UN Declaration attempts to identify important rights that all persons should hold equally, it's not surprising that it includes natural rights and rights that follow directly from these. For instance, Article 3 states, "Everyone has the right to life, liberty and the security of person" (closely resembling Locke's first three rights); Article 17 mentions the right to property.[18] The Declaration also includes rights derived from Locke's four rights (e.g., freedom from enslavement, the right to marry, and the right of religious freedom).

In addition to natural rights, the UN Declaration elaborates several *civil rights.* These are claims a citizen may make upon other citizens as well as upon the government. For instance, there's a right to equal protection from discrimination within the social and legal system, a right against arbitrary arrest, and a right to due process of law. Many of these match Rawls's *political* rights (see §IV).

---

[17]There's controversy over whether an inalienable right can be voluntarily transferred over to another.

[18]The Universal Declaration of Human Rights, adopted by the United Nations General Assembly in 1948, can be found at "The Universal Declaration of Human Rights," United Nations, accessed August 27, 2016, http://www.un.org/Overview/rights.html.

However, the UN's collection of human rights extends even further than this. For instance, the Declaration maintains that "everyone has the right to education" which also ought to be free.[19] In addition, it declares that "everyone has the right to rest and leisure, including . . . periodic holidays with pay" as well as "to a standard of living adequate for the health and well-being of himself and of his family, including food, clothing, housing, and medical care."[20] These statements highlight what philosopher Joel Feinberg calls **manifesto rights**—"rights" that are intended to emphasize the moral importance of certain pressing human needs.

Feinberg questions whether manifesto rights are genuine rights. First, it doesn't make clear sense to talk of a right or claim to something when it's not possible for that claim to ever be fulfilled. If I'm injured in a remote region where no medicines or facilities are available, I can't really claim a right to receive the level of treatment I'd get in a modern city. Similarly, the resources needed to support universal health care, paid holidays, and free education are not universally available, particularly in economically deprived parts of the world. Second, *who* has the responsibility to fulfill such rights claims? When a third-world government can't provide for the basic needs of its street children, is it the duty of some of its well-off citizens to each adopt a child to make sure each child's needs are met? If so, *which* well-off citizens? As Feinberg comments, a claim cannot reflect a valid moral right when there is no definite set of individuals to meet its demands. Manifesto rights may be useful for declaring important ideals, but treating them as genuine rights in any normal sense probably goes too far.

For Discussion

1. *If the right to liberty cannot morally be given up or taken away, how can a social contract legitimately give the state a right to imprison criminals who have harmed others?*
2. *What would be some additional positive rights?*
3. *Do you think that a right to paid work holidays is a genuine moral right? Why or why not?*
4. *Is a right to adequate medical care a genuine moral right? Why or why not?*
5. *See the UN Declaration (a web link is included in this Chapter's Resources). Find all the manifesto rights that appear there. What do you think of these manifesto rights?*

Summary
Rights can be described as alienable *or* inalienable; *inalienable rights cannot morally be given up or taken away. Rights can also be* positive *or* negative; *positive rights are claims about what people should do,* negative rights *are about what they* should not *do. The UN Declaration of Human Rights (which goes beyond Rawls's human rights) includes natural rights, derived natural rights, civil or political rights, and even some so-called manifesto rights. We should probably not view manifesto rights as genuine rights.*

---

[19]Ibid., Article 26.
[20]Ibid., Articles 24 and 25.

Key Terms

- **Inalienable right:** a right that cannot morally be given up or taken away (e.g., life, liberty); an alienable right can be (e.g., property).
- **Positive rights:** allow us to make claims on what others should do for us; negative rights allow us to make claims on what others should not do to us
- **Human rights:** the UN's list of human rights includes natural rights, civil rights, and manifesto rights. The UN's human rights extend beyond Rawls's set of human rights.
- **Manifesto rights:** "rights" intended to emphasize the moral importance of pressing human needs and concerns.

Chapter Assignment Questions

1. *Is there a reality show that portrays the establishment of a social contract? Describe the show's setting and how a contract arises from that.*
2. *Summarize the similarities and differences between Locke's and Hobbes's state of nature.*
3. *Which is the more realistic state of nature: that of Locke or Hobbes? Support your view.*
4. *Carefully explain how common resources are turned into personal property according to Locke. Why should there be a right of property?*
5. *Consider the authorities, laws, taxes, and protections provided to you by the state. Would you agree to all of this if you were negotiating its social contract now?*
6. *Carefully summarize all that holds for Rawls's initial position under the veil of ignorance.*
7. *How does Rawls's equality and difference principles block morally questionable utilitarian type strategies?*
8. *Is Rawls's account a complete ethical theory in itself? Why or why not?*
9. *Given social contract theory, could civil disobedience ever be morally acceptable? Under what conditions?*
10. *Do you think the notion of rights has been abused? Where should the line be drawn between rights and other desirable goods?*
11. *Summarize the problems involved in determining who can have rights.*
12. *** Explain the difference between alienable and inalienable rights and between positive and negative rights. Give examples.*
13. *** Compare and contrast natural rights with UN human rights.*

Additional Resources

Altman, Andrew. "Civil Rights." In *The Stanford Encyclopedia of Philosophy* (Summer 2013 Edition), edited by Edward N. Zalta. Accessed August 27, 2016, http://plato.stanford.edu/archives/sum2013/entries/civil-rights/.

Feinberg, Joel. "Nature and Value of Rights." *Journal of Value Inquiry*, 4 (1970): 245–257. Reprinted in James Fieser, *Metaethics, Normative Ethics, and Applied Ethics: Historical and Contemporary Readings*. Belmont, CA: Wadsworth, 2000, 237–247. A more advanced discussion of rights, this article includes Feinberg's evaluation of "manifesto rights."

"*The Giver*, Trailer 2." Directed by Phillip Noyce (2014). Accessed August 27, 2016, https://www.youtube.com/watch?v=xvp6FnYWRZU

Hobbes, Thomas. *Leviathan* (1651). Accessed August 27, 2016. http://socserv2.socsci.mc-master.ca/econ/ugcm/3ll3/hobbes/Leviathan.pdf.

Lloyd, Sharon A. and Sreedhar, Susanne, "Hobbes's Moral and Political Philosophy." In *The Stanford Encyclopedia of Philosophy* (Spring 2014 Edition), edited by Edward N. Zalta. Accessed August 27, 2016. http://plato.stanford.edu/archives/spr2014/entries/hobbes-moral/. A comprehensive presentation of Hobbes's work.

Lowry, Lois. *The Giver.* Boston, MA: Houghton Mifflin Harcourt Publishing, 1993. *The Giver* is one of a long line of dystopian novels that involve acts of disobedience to overthrow an unjust system.

Richey, Tom. "Thomas Hobbes and John Locke: Two Philosophers Compared." Accessed August 27, 2016, https://www.youtube.com/watch?v=N2LVcu01QEU. This YouTube video compares the social contract theories of Hobbes and Locke.

Shafer-Landau, Russ. *The Fundamentals of Ethics.* New York: Oxford University Press, 2010. See especially chapters 13 and 14 on the social contract tradition.

United Nations. Universal Declaration of Human Rights. Accessed August 27, 2016. http://www.un.org/en/universal-declaration-human-rights/index.html

Case 1

Socrates's Imprisonment

The ancient Greek philosopher Socrates was well known for his critical evaluation of highly regarded people in his society. As he publicly engaged with these people in discourse, he would expose their intellectual and moral weaknesses. Socrates did this to teach Athens's youth to always seek truth and never to blindly accept the claims made by such authority figures. The state of Athens came to regard Socrates as a threat to its stability. He was arrested, put on trial for "corrupting the youth," and sentenced to death. After being imprisoned, Socrates's friends encouraged him to escape. They had bribed the guards and arranged for him to flee to another city. Socrates, however, refused. He argued that he was obligated to obey the legal judgment against him because he had been raised, educated, and protected by the state. Although he could have previously left Athens, he had chosen to stay, effectively confirming his social contract with the state (by tacit consent). Thus, he should not now disobey the state. Although his treatment at the hands of the state was unjust, Socrates argued that this didn't make the laws themselves unjust, nor did that annul his contract with the state. Dissent should not be expressed by breaking laws but by working to change the system within, using the legal resources the system itself provides such as his trial itself (Athens was a democracy at the time).

THOUGHT QUESTIONS

1. Is Socrates's argument consistent with social contract theory? Why or why not?
2. Do you agree that Socrates was obligated to obey the judgment against him?

3. What do you think of Socrates's insistence that disobedience to the state is wrong, and that changes only may be made by working within the system?

4. Socrates arguments entail that acts of civil disobedience (e.g., those of Martin Luther King Jr. and the civil rights movement) are morally prohibited. What do you think and why?

5. Socrates's imprisonment and death sentence were unjust. By acting unjustly against Socrates, it appears that the state violated its side of the social contract. Could this fact justify Socrates violating the law in return by escaping?

6. If we view most states today as based on social contracts, the reality is that states usually fulfill parts of their contract but fail to fulfill others. What implications does this more complex reality have for civil disobedience?

Case 2

Lord of the Flies

In William Golding's *Lord of the Flies*, a group of children is stranded on a desert island without adults. To survive, they establish an agreement with one another. They choose a boy named Ralph as the chief and decide on three rules: to have fun, to survive, and to keep a smoke signal so that a passing ship can stop and rescue them. Over time, however, some members of the group get lazy and stop helping the others in supplying food and shelter.

One part of the group, led by a kid named Jack, did not agree to Ralph becoming the leader and slowly separates from the main group. At some point, they forget to keep up the smoke signal, and a passing ship fails to notice them. Jack and his group eventually challenge Ralph's leadership and tensions rise even further when a child named Simon is mistaken for a threat and killed. A struggle also arises with a boy named Piggy, whose glasses are their only means of starting a fire. Piggy is killed, and Ralph runs for his life. Finally, he and the other children are saved by soldiers that have stopped their ship because they saw the smoke on the island. Ironically, the world is at war at this time.

THOUGHT QUESTIONS

1. In this story a social contract goes awry. Did this happen because the protagonists were not adults? Would their social contract be binding given their preadolescence?

2. Do you think Jack and his followers were obligated to follow Ralph since he was elected by the majority? Should they first have agreed that their choice must be unanimous? If the latter, how could this rule have been established before any contract had been established?

3. Were the boys in a state of nature before they agreed to elect Ralph and establish rules? What version of a state of nature applied?

4. To what extent and by what means, if any, should the contract have allowed for the enforcement of its rules and Ralph's authority?

5. Suppose the boys had selected Jack instead of Ralph and then come to realize that Jack was a bad ruler. What would justify deposing Jack for Ralph?

6. The social contract was explicitly established by the boys, but it was not unanimously supported. How does this problem, discussed in the text, affect the contract's authority?

7. What values was the boys' social contract based upon? Were these moral values, non-moral values, or both?

Case 3

Locke and Load: Lockean Rights and Gun Control[21]

Locke maintains that in their original *state of nature*, everyone has four basic natural rights, life, health, liberty, and property; further, he implies that a person may defend himself against others when his rights are being violated. This fifth right is a "right of self-defense," which involves three "powers." In contemporary terms, these are *the right of proximate self-defense*, the *right of deterrence*, and the *right of retributive punishment*. The right of proximate self-defense gives us the authority to use force to defend our rights against nearby rights-violators. Deterrence allows us to wield and display force to discourage others from attempting to violate our rights. The right of retributive punishment gives us the authority to punish those who violate rights. Even though these rights pertain to people in the state of nature, Locke emphasizes that they should always be exercised with restraint.

We move from the state of nature by placing ourselves within a civil society; this relieves us from having to guard our rights individually. Another advantage with this move is that a neutral third party (i.e., a police force, together with the criminal courts) can be more impartial and restrained in dealing with rights-violators than victims will usually be. We thus consent to give over the powers of deterrence and punishment to the government to use on our behalf. Yet since it's not possible for government representatives to be present at all times and places where a rights violation might take place, we still retain the right of proximate self-defense as individuals.

Does the right of proximate self-defense imply a right to acquire and use *firearms*? The question remains extremely controversial.

On one hand, it seems that we ought to have such a right, at least in a country where criminals are likely to possess firearms themselves. If I have a right of self-defense and I encounter a dangerous criminal in a dark and abandoned place, I can't depend on police assistance for protection—there just isn't enough time. Thus, I need to take matters into my own hands, and having a firearm could be indispensable. Although social scientists disagree about the numbers, between 1.3 million and 2.5 million Americans defend themselves with firearms each year.[22] Here's a typical case: "A woman shot and killed an armed man she says was trying to carjack her van and her one-year-old daughter inside. ... She fired after the man pointed a revolver at her and ordered her to 'move over,' she told police." Apparently, the woman "offered to take her daughter and give up the van, but the man

Continued

  [21]This case is based on a talk presented by Dr. Irfan Khawaja, who has kindly given us permission to use his material here. Irfan Khawaja, "Locke and Load: Lockean Rights and Gun Control," presentation at Felician College, April 29, 2009.

  [22]Figures cited in James B. Jacobs, *Can Gun Control Work?* (New York: Oxford University Press, 2002), 14.

Case 3 (Continued)

refused." The woman "told the police she bought the .44-caliber handgun in September after her home was burglarized, and said she fired several shots from the gun, which she kept concealed in a canvas bag beside her car seat."[23]

Given the right of proximate self-defense together with the strong Lockean right to own property—presumably including firearms—then the case for citizens having their own firearms seems strong.

However, others have argued that there is no such right. For one thing, the right to own property surely cannot be completely *unregulated* because that would lead to absurdities. Do I have a right to carry a rocket-propelled grenade launcher in my car on the grounds that the grenades, launcher, and car are all my property? Can I store VX nerve gas in my basement? How about an atom bomb? These examples suggest that when certain kinds of property impose risks to other people, the government should regulate or perhaps even claim a monopoly over such items.[24] These could include firearms. Indeed, the contemporary philosopher Robert Nozick has argued that a legitimate Lockean government would have a monopoly on all uses of force within its territory such that "only it may decide who may use force and under what conditions; it reserves to itself the sole right to pass on the legitimacy and permissibility of any use of force within its boundaries; furthermore, it claims the right to punish all those who violate its claimed monopoly."[25] A government that *lacks* such a monopoly could not genuinely govern those under its jurisdiction since there is a great risk of anarchy and civil war. A vivid example of this is the case of northwestern Pakistan, where decades of unregulated weapons ownership have led to continuing large-scale violence and dislocation.

If a government has a monopoly on the use of force, how can it allow citizens to decide for *themselves* how and when to use force, in keeping with a right of proximate self-defense? This right seems incompatible with a governmental monopoly on force. Many prominent critics of gun ownership suggest that it would be most sensible to ban private ownership of all weapons and restrict ownership of weapons to the police, as is done in many Western European countries.[26] One way of doing this would be to ban the domestic manufacture and trade of firearms for private use and then ban imports of firearms from foreign countries. Although some weapons would still remain in private hands even after such a ban, the total number of guns would eventually decline, along with the rate of violent crime and violent death (which is much higher in the United States than in any other Western democracy). As the older guns break down or wear out, we would ultimately become a gun-free society, where the self-defensive use of firearms would be unnecessary because gun violence would have become unheard of.

If firearms were banned, that might help put an end not only to "ordinary" gun violence but also to spectacular killing sprees such as the Columbine High

Continued

---

[23]Cited in John R. Lott Jr., *More Guns, Less Crime: Understanding Crime and Gun Control Laws*, 2d ed. (Chicago: University of Chicago Press, 2000), 3.

[24]For an argument of this sort, see Hugh LaFollette, "Gun Control," *Ethics* 110 (January 2000): 268–272.

[25]Robert Nozick, *Anarchy, State, and Utopia* (New York: Basic Books, 1974), 23.

[26]Amitai Etzioni and Steven Hellend, "The Case for Domestic Disarmament· The Responsive Communitarian Platform, November 18, 1991," The Institute for Communitarian Policy Studies, accessed August 27, 2016, http://www.gwu.edu/~ccps/pop_disarm.html.

Case 3 (Continued)

School massacre in April 1999 (fifteen killed), the Virginia Tech massacre in April 2007 (thirty-two killed), the massacre at Newtown, Connecticut, in 2012 (twenty-eight killed), and many others even more recently. Arguably, all these massacres were linked to weaknesses in America's gun laws: three of the four firearms used in the Columbine massacre were purchased for the teenage killers at a Denver gun show.[27] Meanwhile, Cho Seung-Hui, the perpetrator of the Virginia Tech massacre, bought firearms from a gun shop in February 2007 even "after a Virginia court declared him to be a danger to himself in late 2005 and sent him for psychiatric treatment."[28] In the Connecticut shootings, Adam Lanza, the shooter, killed his mother and removed her guns (four!) from her house.

THOUGHT QUESTIONS

1. Do you think that individuals have a moral right to buy, sell, and use firearms? If so, should this right be regulated by the government? If so, how? Or should private ownership of firearms be abolished altogether?
2. If the right to firearms is a matter of self-defense, then what sorts of firearms are necessary for self-defense?
3. Is there a right to possess firearms for purely recreational purposes? If so, what sorts of firearms?
4. Locke says that in the state of nature, it is "lawful for a man to kill a thief, who has not in the least hurt him, nor declared any design upon his life" because there is "no reason to suppose that he, who would take away my liberty, would not when he had me in his power, take away everything else."[29] Is Locke right about this for those living in the state of nature? What about once we *leave* the state of nature?
5. Most legal systems allow for a right of self-defense but also impose a duty to retreat. The duty to retreat requires that one use force against an attacker only as a last resort. But opinions differ about the nature of this duty. One view holds that a victim must try to escape from any threatening situation, using only as much force as is necessary to escape. An opposing view holds that a victim, when confronted with a situation that might require force, may hold his ground and use as much force as is necessary to incapacitate a criminal. Do you agree that there is a duty to retreat? How should it be understood?

---

[27]Jacobs, *Can Gun Control Work,* 129.

[28]Michael Luo, "U.S. Rules Made Killer Ineligible to Purchase Gun," *New York Times,* April 21, 2007.

[29]John Locke, *Second Treatise of Government* (1690, public domain), chapter 3, paragraph 18. The spelling and punctuation of this quotation have been modified.

CHAPTER ELEVEN

Virtue Ethics

I. INTRODUCTION

Moodily staring at her food, Ashley was sitting alone in the company lunchroom. Lost in thought, she nearly jumped from her chair as someone shouted, "Hey Ashley!" right behind her. She turned just as Lauren, one of those teddy bear-type people you can't help liking, banged her plate down on Ashley's right. Lauren's big grin turned into a frown as she caught sight of Ashley's face. "What's up?" Lauren asked. "Oh, nothing," Ashley replied. "That's a lie, lady," Lauren shot back. "You look sadder than the hash browns on my plate." Ashley gave a little laugh. "Well," she said, "I just got that promotion I applied for, which means I can head up the office in Durham." "Fantastic!" Lauren boomed as she gave Ashley a hug. "You've been after that for ages, and it'll be awesome doing purchasing through you instead of old Joe down there. The Carolinas have nice weather, too." Lauren gave Ashley another glance. "So what's the problem?" she asked. "Oh, I don't think I can take the job." Ashley's words suddenly poured out. "Mike's mom isn't doing well, and neither of us feels comfortable leaving her alone up here, and there's no way she could handle a move." "No other family nearby?" Lauren asked. "No, we're all she has," Ashley answered, "and though she insists that we go, it would be really hard on her. If we leave the area, I think she would shrivel up and die." "Yeah," Lauren said, "but isn't your career important too?" "Sure," Ashley replied, "but still, it's just a job." "What does Mike say?" Lauren asked. "Oh, he says it's up to me, although I think he wants to stay near his mom. In fact, I think I've made up my mind to stay. I just *couldn't* let Mike's mom down." Lauren looked at her thoughtfully. "You know what?" Lauren asked after a long pause, "I *really* respect you. Not everyone would do what you're doing."

Is Ashley's decision a *moral* decision? What moral principles apply in this case?[1] While it doesn't seem that Ashley would be doing wrong either way, the choice she does make earns Lauren's respect—and this respect includes a strong moral element. Yet could Ashley's choice be universalized into a moral law

---

[1]When speaking of principles in this chapter, we have only *prescriptive* principles in mind.

following Kant's categorical imperative? That seems unlikely, although the alternative can't be either. Will Ashley's choice increase utility? That's not clear; but even if it decreased utility, it seems to deserve respect. Or better, Ashley *herself* deserves respect, as Lauren says. To use an outmoded sounding term, Ashley appears to be *virtuous*.

For Discussion

1. *What makes Ashley's decision a moral one?*
2. *Do you think she made the right choice? How does she appear virtuous?*
3. *Have you made choices that look like this, where no principles apply?*

Summary
Some moral problems don't seem to involve any moral principles; to arrive at a moral judgment, then, we must think through such problems using the pattern of moral reflection (see Chapter Four, §V). There may not even be a single definite right answer. A way to understand such cases is offered by virtue theory.

II. THE HEART OF VIRTUE ETHICS

Isn't "virtue" just an old-fashioned way to describe people who do the right things? Doesn't doing what moral principles say make one virtuous?

"Virtue" can actually be understood from two different perspectives. As just described—and in keeping with the approach taken by so-called principle-based theories—we might call people virtuous, simply meaning that they do what prescriptive moral principles tell them to do. In this view, prescriptive principles are more basic, and virtue becomes just this derived concept about keeping principles.[2] The virtue theorists' alternative perspective reverses this entirely. In their view, *personal character*—**virtue**—is primary. Moral theory begins by describing the *kind of person one should be,* not by saying what one should do. First and foremost, morality calls us to become virtuous persons—developing the attitudes and skills needed to live morally. Right actions—what we should *do*—are then derived from virtue; they describe what a virtuous person would do or what springs from a virtuous character. Virtue-based theories take a very different approach to ethics from that of principle-based theories. This reversal is virtue theory's most distinctive feature:

Primacy of character. Virtue theory maintains that our essential moral responsibility is to develop a virtuous personal character, a character full of virtues.

---

[2]Kant's theory is principle based, but he spends a great deal of time extolling moral virtue. Principle-based theories thus can talk of virtue, but that's not their starting point.

Right actions are then the things a virtuous person would typically do.[3] (See also Chapter Five, §II on moral character.)

In addition, most virtue theories affirm the following.

2. *Character motivation.* Virtue theory attributes a person's motivation for acting morally directly to his character, not to any duty or principle.

Ashley's question of what she should do is not a question of what duties are imposed from *outside*, but of what her loyalty and compassion call forth from *within*. She consults no external principle, but arrives at her decision once her mind, will, and emotions all fall into unity. Her sympathies and desires drew her to her decision, her deliberations aligned with those desires, and her will almost effortlessly agreed. In virtue theory, virtuous actions arise from the person herself. Once someone has established a virtuous character, it becomes relatively "easy" for her to act virtuously. Unfortunately, this can work the other way as well: if someone has formed a *vicious* character (from the word "vice," a bad character trait), then it will be easy to act badly but hard to do well. As experience teaches us, people tend to do what comes most naturally to them. We quickly notice when someone is acting "out of character"—as when the vicious person acts well or the virtuous person acts badly. By locating moral motivation in the character of the whole person, virtue theory largely avoids the problem of how to muster the "will power" to do right.

These two features come closest to defining virtue theory, though some share certain additional implications. Here's one of particular interest:

3. *Several right choices:* Virtue theory can allow for different choices to count as equally right in the same situation because different virtuous people might choose differently.

If moral principles alone cannot provide a complete ethics, then in some situations no *principles* will determine what *the* right thing to do is. Our moral thinking will then resemble *moral reflection* rather than *moral reasoning.* You may have already noticed the similarities between Ashley's story and the child dying of cancer discussed in Chapter Four (see §V). Virtue theory is usually considered an instance of *moral particularism,* which sees moral judgments as depending heavily on each particular situation—especially the moral characters of those involved—rather than on moral principles (see also Chapter Four, §V, and Chapter Twelve, §III).

Of course, this doesn't entail that there is *no* right act at all. In keeping with virtue theory's *primacy of character,* the right thing to do is what a virtuous person would do. But since different virtuous persons might act differently in, say, Ashley's position, virtue theory can allow for more than one morally right option for the very same situation.

---

[3]Aristotle doesn't follow most contemporary virtue theorists in this. For Aristotle, the right is a kind of moral ideal that accords with reason and that can be intuitively known via reason (particularly by the gentleman class). See Peter Simpson, "Contemporary Virtue Ethics and Aristotle," in *Virtue Ethics: A Critical Reader,* ed. Daniel Statman (Washington, DC: Georgetown University Press, 1997), 245–259.

This doesn't turn virtue theory into a type of moral subjectivism. Although it allows for a range of right actions, it doesn't allow *anything at all* to be morally acceptable. While several options might be right, all others can still be wrong. Thus, it's appropriate to treat virtue theory as an objectivist theory. Nevertheless, there's no denying that its "several right choices" feature distinguishes virtue theory from principle-based theories in an intriguing way.

For Discussion

1. *Name some virtues and some vices.*
2. *What virtues do you have or have seen in others? Can you think of anyone you would call virtuous?*
3. *What do you think about making personal moral character primary?*
4. *Have you ever found it too hard to do the right thing? Why was it so hard?*
5. *Should our motivations to act morally always be moral motivations? What amoral (not immoral!) motivations impel you to act?*

Summary

We may call someone "virtuous" because they obey moral principles. This makes principles primary. Virtue theory reverses this and maintains that our primary moral obligation is to become a virtuous person, which makes it natural for us to do what is right. This is the primacy of character—the idea that virtuous character, not moral principles, is the basis of morality. Virtue theories also see an established personal character as the source of moral motivation. While objectivist, virtue theory can even allow for there being several different right choices in the same situation.

Key Terms

- **Virtues:** *specific character traits, like honesty and courage, that are morally good values; a virtuous person has many virtues.*
- **Vices**: *specific character traits, like dishonesty and selfishness, that are the opposite of virtues and thus morally bad. A vicious person has many vices.*

III. ARISTOTLE'S VIRTUE ETHICS

It can be helpful to lay out the details of a particular virtue theory at some length. Since no real consensus exists among contemporary virtue theorists, we turn to the most famous and influential of all virtue theories, the theory of Aristotle.

According to Aristotle, human beings seek happiness—*eudaimonia*. Everything we do, say, and think is ultimately aimed at attaining happiness. What is happiness? It's not mere pleasure. In Aristotle's sense, **eudaimonia** relates to our "flourishing" or fulfillment as human beings. We can find fulfillment only when we achieve the purpose or "function"—the good—of human existence.

What is our purpose or function? Whatever it is, it must be uniquely human, as it must set human nature apart from everything else. Aristotle concludes that our unique function is our ability to order and direct our lives by reason—to live in accordance with reason. From this we can infer that to attain happiness or fulfillment, we must live by reason. Of course, some obviously do this better than others. Those who do it best achieve the highest degree of human excellence or *virtue*. Virtuous persons are those most skilled at ordering all facets of life in accordance with reason.

While a complete virtuous character includes *all* of the virtues, Aristotle distinguishes two different kinds. *Intellectual virtue* is developed through *teaching*. Acquiring *moral virtue*, meanwhile, requires *practice*. To develop any particular moral virtue, we must practice the very sorts of acts that the virtue typically produces. To become courageous, for instance, we must practice acting courageously; to become generous, we must practice generosity. I can *act virtuously* without yet *being virtuous*. Developing virtue is somewhat analogous to developing skill at playing a sport or a musical instrument. To become good at tennis, you must spend countless hours practicing forehand and backhand swings, serves, lobs, and so on. Pianists must practice finger positions, sight reading, scales, and countless other aspects of their art to become excellent pianists— *virtuosos*. No matter how much natural ability you may have, you cannot attain expertise without also practicing. Practice makes the necessary skills habitual, or, as we sometimes say, *second nature*. As this phrase suggests, the desired skill becomes part of one's very *nature*. Yet, because developed skills aren't inborn or innate, they count as *second* nature, as having been *added* to one's essential character.

Unfortunately, it is also possible to practice bad habits. By practicing a tennis serve incorrectly, one becomes worse at serving; by repeatedly using the wrong fingering, one becomes a poor pianist. As coaches and musicians know, avoiding such mistakes requires the learner to have a right knowledge of how things are to be done. In fact, one must fulfill several conditions to count as having attained excellence:

1. One must *know* what the right thing is.
2. One must *intend* to do the right thing because it *is* the right thing.
3. One's right actions must be the products of one's own "firm and unchangeable character"—one's behavioral patterns must be habitual or second nature.

To *have* the virtue of courage, therefore, I cannot simply have acted courageously once or twice. I must also (a) know what courage is and (b) must intend to act courageously because I hold courage to be a good. Finally, courage must be one of my enduring character traits as evidenced by the fact that I typically act courageously. I cannot properly be considered courageous unless I fulfill all these conditions.

No one becomes virtuous except by years of practice; there's no short cut. Further, no one is born virtuous. Aristotle's proof of this is simply that people's characters can change in the direction of either virtue or vice. Such changes are possible only if virtue and vice can be acquired; what belongs to our innate nature, after all, cannot normally be changed. Still, the *potential* for developing virtue is innate to normal human nature because virtue is living in accordance with reason, and the ability to reason uniquely characterizes human nature.[4]

What exactly *is* virtue? Aristotle's famous doctrine is that each virtue lies at the *golden **mean*** between some *excess* and *deficiency*. This balance involves how a person feels as well as how a person acts. One can face a threat, for instance, in a variety of ways: reckless adventurers who take foolish risks are at the excess while the cowardly fall on the side of deficiency. The courageous, however, achieve the **mean** or proper balance between these extremes. This is not to say that the mean always lies exactly halfway between extremes; true courage, for instance, probably falls closer to the excess than the deficiency. In any case, virtue achieves balance, while the extremes represent vices:

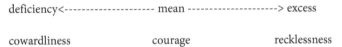

deficiency<-------------------- mean ---------------------> excess

cowardliness   courage   recklessness

For another example, consider generosity. Like courage, generosity probably lies more on the side of excess than deficiency because a generous person's giving is ready and free, far removed from the stingy actions of the world's Scrooges. Still, the virtue of generosity does not give excessively, which harms both the giver and the recipient. Finally, consider good temper, the virtue related to anger. Those who fly into a rage at the slightest provocation clearly fall on the side of excess. Apathetic and imperturbable individuals who remain unmoved even when they ought to get stirred up belong on the side of deficiency. The good-tempered person finds the proper balance between these. In *this* case, however, the virtue is located closer to the deficiency than the excess.

In sum, virtue achieves the mean in how one *acts* (e.g., courage and generosity) and in how one *feels* (temper) in accordance with reason. Yet virtue isn't merely a balance of *degree*. Aristotle describes a generous person as one who knows not only *how much* to give but who also knows how to give to the *right person*, at the *right time,* in the *right way*, and with a *right purpose*. Virtues involve more than a single skill; rather, they require a multi-dimensioned "skill set" that achieves the right balance with respect to degree, selection and timing, manner and purpose.

Aristotle cautions that the right balance won't be exactly the same for everyone. Just as the quantity of food needed by an athlete in training is very different from what a sedentary sixty-year-old with a desk job requires, the amount that a generous rich person should give will differ from what a generous poor man ought to give. Every individual's character and circumstances are unique, so it's possible for different persons in the same situation to respond differently, although both respond with equal virtue. This is how Aristotle's account allows for there to be several right choices (see §II).

---

[4]Notoriously, Aristotle made one exception to this for *"natural"* slaves, who he thought were innately inferior. Such people, allegedly, are incapable of developing their own virtue.

Aristotle's theory has a few practical implications. First, Aristotle warns us that simply thinking and talking about virtue won't make anyone virtuous. It's only by practicing virtuous behavior—and avoiding vicious behavior—that we develop virtue. Becoming virtuous requires a *transformation of character*, which needs to begin at an early age.

His theory also has things to say to us as a society, a society that may place too much emphasis on rules and rights and not enough on individual character and responsibility. On the one hand, Aristotle emphasizes that we will inevitably become what our repeated choices and actions make us. We are each the product of our accumulated past choices and practices. If I lie and deceive for most of my life, I will become a liar, even finding it difficult to be honest or sincere. Thus, we are not merely responsible for what we do but also for what we have made of ourselves.

Yet responsibility never falls entirely upon each person alone. The social environment also exerts a powerful influence upon the development of individual virtue and vice. A healthy society should promote virtue by creating a limited number of good laws under virtuous leadership. Bad laws, too many laws, and poor leadership, on the other hand, make virtue harder for anyone to develop. As Aristotle sees it, developing virtue is both an individual and social responsibility.[5]

For Discussion

1. *Do you seek personal happiness? What does that mean to you?*
2. *Do you think it's legitimate to talk about a unique human function—something necessary to our fulfillment as human beings?*
3. *How important do you think leaders and laws are for people to develop virtuous characters (e.g., in a home, classroom, our society)?*
4. *Identify and describe a few virtues and then explain the corresponding vices as excess and deficiency.*

Summary

According to Aristotle, we all seek to flourish as human beings, a state Aristotle calls eudaimonia. Happiness or flourishing requires that we fulfill our distinctive human function, which is to live virtuously—in accordance with reason. While intellectual virtues are learned from teaching, moral virtues must be developed by practice. Although everyone has the potential to develop both vices and virtues, neither virtue nor vice is innate. Several conditions must be fulfilled to count as having a virtue whether that virtue relates to our feelings or our actions. A virtuous response in any situation is balanced, falling at the "golden mean" between excess and deficiency.

[5]Aristotle lived in a *direct* democracy; in contrast, ours is a *representative* democracy (we elect people to represent our interests). In a direct democracy, citizens are directly involved in making decisions about laws, either by vote or referendum. Arguably, this requires them to be better informed than in representative democracies. Given their active political role, Aristotle strongly felt that citizens needed to have both intellectual and moral virtues.

Key Terms

- **Eudaimonia**: *Aristotle's concept of human flourishing (happiness) that is achieved only as we fulfill our human function of living by reason.*
- **Mean**: *a virtuous act or feeling that achieves the proper balance ("golden mean") between both excess and deficiency.*

IV. **CRITIQUING PRINCIPLE-BASED ETHICS

Virtue theory has ancient roots but has enjoyed an extraordinary resurgence in recent decades. This is partly because contemporary virtue theorists have forcefully criticized *principle-based* theories, particularly utilitarianism and Kantian ethics.[6] Here are some of the points they have made.

Principle-based ethics are incomplete. Theories in which moral principles are primary (e.g., utilitarianism, Ross's theory, Kantian ethics, etc.) have little to say about situations like Ashley's. No moral principle obligates her to stay,[7] nor would Ashley morally wrong her mother-in-law by leaving. Nevertheless, Ashley's situation brings important moral considerations into play. Her choice evidences compassion and loyalty, and these give her choice moral value. They imply, in fact, that Ashley may be making the morally *right* choice.

How can there be a morally right choice with no moral principle? *Moral particularism* maintains that this is a common occurrence. For virtue theorists, the answer primarily has to do with *the kind of person* Ashley is. Her choice to stay is right because it is what a compassionate and loyal person would do. In saying that she "just *couldn't* let Mike's mom down," Ashley makes an observation about *herself*. She finds that she cannot abandon her mother-in-law since any other choice would go against her very nature.

Ashley's virtues of loyalty and compassion, not principles, explain why her choice is right. Since this is an aspect of morality that principle-based ethics doesn't explain, principle-based theories cannot be complete. Morality consists of more than merely following principles and fulfilling duties.

Principle-based ethics overemphasize **impartiality**. In general, principle-based ethics ask us to "detach" ourselves from our feelings and to evaluate what is right without partiality. Kant's categorical imperative bypasses *personal* interests by requiring that morally right acts make sense as *universal* practices. Thanks to utilitarianism's focus on effects, it likewise can assign only limited importance to personal interests. While utilitarianism does include these interests in its calculation of

---

[6]Virtue theorists tend to categorize consequentialist, deontological, and rights theories as principle-based theories (even if their principles are supported by foundational value[s]).

[7]The principle most relevant to Ashley's case might require people to help with family needs, but the needs in this situation don't seem strong enough to create an actual obligation.

overall utility, they usually don't make much difference once all those affected are also taken into account.

Yet Ashley makes her choice largely because she is *not* impartial regarding the situation and people involved. Because of her love and sympathy, she wants to please and help Mike's mother. Out of family loyalty, she feels a special interest in her mother-in-law. She also recognizes that she would feel terrible about leaving her mother-in-law. Her inclinations, interests, and feelings all affect her choice. Despite her lack of impartiality, Ashley's choice appears morally laudable. By excluding personal feelings in the name of impartiality, therefore, principle-based ethics can't do justice to moral judgments for which feelings and inclinations are primary.

Principle-based ethics distort our picture of human nature. In her influential essay, "Moral Saints,"[8] Susan Wolf argues that we don't arrive at a very appealing picture when we imagine someone who perfectly embodies Kantian or utilitarian moral ideals—a **moral saint**. What, for instance, would someone who perfectly satisfies Kantian ethics look like? Going back to the Boy Scouts from our discussion of Kant, remember that both Mo and Larry were motivated to help the old lady by personal interests; thus neither could be said to have the Good Will. Curly, on the other hand, was motivated purely by duty. From the Kantian perspective, only Curly was morally praiseworthy.

Let's take Curly, then, as a Kantian "saint." What else could we expect of him? On the positive side, Curly could always be relied upon to tell the truth, to keep his promises, and to treat everyone with strict fairness. Yet in his helping the old lady, Saint Curly is motivated by moral duty, not by affection or concern for the lady herself. As similar motives must characterize his dealings with others as well, Curly would strike us as aloof and unsympathetic. Curly might also go too far in his unerring obedience to the moral law. His duty to truth could lead him to callously tell a co-worker that he is incompetent or a friend that she is getting fat. If Curly were a citizen of Nazi Germany, he would truthfully tell the Nazis everything they ask about his Jewish neighbors. Finally, Curly would probably seem extraordinarily naive in the way he takes no responsibility for any of the results of what he says or does.

Turning next to the *act utilitarian* saint, we encounter another unappealing picture. As an impartial maximizer of utility, Hughie the utilitarian could never afford to "waste" time relaxing with friends or pursuing a hobby if he could "better" apply his energies to helping the poor or alleviating someone's suffering. Throughout his life, he would remain morally bound to choose only those courses of action that offer the greatest opportunities for reducing the world's miseries. As a result, Hughie would probably eat too quickly, sleep only as necessary, and never take a vacation. His one-track mindedness would make him a conversational bore.

---

[8] Susan Wolf, "Moral Saints," in *Virtue Ethics*, ed. Robert Crisp and Michael Slote (New York: Oxford University Press, 1998), 79–98.

Besides all this, he would not make a particularly trustworthy friend—for as a utilitarian, he would probably not bat an eyelash over lying to you, or breaking a promise, or even betraying you completely if greater utility could be gained.

As Wolf compellingly argues, the moral ideals of these principle-based theories all seem "strangely barren."[9] They prescribe a way of life that no real person would want to live. Nor would any of us want *others* to treat us as they prescribe. How would the mother-in-law feel if Ashley decided to stay because that maximizes overall utility? Or how would the old lady feel if Curly told her that he helped her because it's his duty? Just as people normally do good for others because they care for those others, we want others doing good for us because they care for and value us.

Principle-based ethics don't motivate. Doing the right thing can be hard. It can be particularly hard when it isn't in our interests, or worse, when it goes against our interests. All of us can think of times we knew what we *should* do but still couldn't get ourselves to do it. Clearly, we all stand in need of motivators or incentives to stir us to doing right. But where can we find this? What reservoir can we draw from when the moral going gets tough?

Most ethical theories offer little in response. The utilitarian ideal is to promote overall utility—isn't more utility something everyone wants? But increasing *overall* utility doesn't guarantee that we will derive any *personal* benefit. Yet it's when there's no personal benefit that we most need moral strength. Kantian ethics calls upon the person to be motivated by duty. Yet duty only tells us *what* we should do—it doesn't equip us to actually do it. Is the call of duty a sufficient inspiration for moral living? Will duty be enough to get Curly out of bed every morning?

The trouble is that prescriptive moral principles impose their requirements upon us from "outside," so to speak. These principles exist independently of us and remain separate from us. What we really need is to be motivated by something driving us from "inside," born in our very selves. The more fully a motivation resonates in the whole person, the more likely it is that the person will act. This is what happens in the virtue account of Ashley's choice—it came out of her entire self, a necessary expression of who she is.

For Discussion

1. *Think about moral impartiality or objectivity. Isn't this something a parent or judge ought to have? Mustn't we sometimes evaluate ourselves impartially?*
2. *Come up with some situations where impartiality is very important, and where it seems inappropriate.*
3. *Consider the text's descriptions of the Kantian or utilitarian saints. Are these fair descriptions?*
4. *What would a* virtuous *saint look like? Is this saint more human and appealing than the others?*
5. *What most effectively motivates you to do right, especially in hard situations?*

---

[9]Ibid.

Summary

Virtue theorists advance a number of criticisms of principle-based ethics: (a) principle-based ethics are incomplete, saying little about moral choices like Ashley's; (b) they place too much emphasis on impartiality, although personal feelings and inclinations play an important role in our moral decision-making; (c) they present a distorted picture of human nature because their moral ideals appear unrealistic and inhuman; and (d) they fail to motivate because they impose requirements upon us from "outside" rather than arising out of the inclinations of the whole person.

Key Terms

- **Moral saint**: *drawn from Wolf's essay, a moral saint is one who perfectly fulfills the requirements of a given moral theory.*

- **Impartiality**: *the objective moral perspective prized by most principle-based theories; it requires us to detach ourselves from our personal feelings and bypass our personal interests.*

V. CLASSIFYING THE VIRTUES

The virtuous person has fully integrated all the virtues into an undivided and mature character and lives by that character. While we can focus attention on specific virtues, these are not really separate parts of the virtuous person. In a sense, virtuous people simply *have* virtue, and the appearance of any particular virtue simply manifests part of their overall virtue. This is because other virtues must always come into play when any one virtue is exercised. For instance, we may need courage to act with great generosity or to be friendly toward strangers. Similarly, a proper sense of honor is inevitably linked to one's sense of honesty and justice. This interlocking of the virtues includes the intellectual virtues as well, which have to do with skills such as making judgments, discerning truth, and exercising practical wisdom. To exercise the moral virtue of honesty, for instance, we must be able to discern truth; a generous person must employ practical wisdom—akin to our notion of "common sense"—to see how, when, and to whom she should give. Though we can distinguish virtues in the abstract, they must come into union in the personality of any actual virtuous person.

Nevertheless, there's philosophical interest in classifying the virtues. For instance, Lester Hunt has suggested that they can be classified by their role or purpose:[10]

---

[10]Lester H. Hunt, "Generosity and the Diversity of the Virtues," in *The Virtues: Contemporary Essays on Moral Character*, eds. Robert B. Kruschwitz and Robert C. Roberts, (Belmont, CA: Wadsworth Publishing Company, 1987), 217–228. Hunt's choice of terms has been somewhat modified. This discussion also incorporates Robert's thoughts on "virtues of will power," which are presented in an article appearing in the same anthology. Robert C. Roberts, "Willpower and the Virtues," 122–136. Roberts' article is reprinted from *The Philosophical Review*, 93 (April 1984): 227–247.

- **Obligation virtues**—serve to fulfill our moral duties to act in certain ways (e.g., promise keeping, justice, truthfulness).
- **Good-promoting virtues**—serve to promote specific values or goods (e.g., sociability, generosity).
- **Limiting virtues**—serve to control or manage our inclinations and feelings (e.g., courage, temperance [self-control], loyalty, or faithfulness).

Each of these groups reflects a different moral emphasis. Obligation virtues, for instance, closely parallel the most established principles of deontological ethics (see Chapter Eight). These comprise the central core of morality, and are normally assigned the highest priority. Such obligations hold universally (or nearly so), and typically call for the highest degree of impartiality. It hardly seems to matter, therefore, whether we base the virtue of honesty on a principle of truth telling or base the principle on the virtue. For obligations, virtue and principle-based ethics appear roughly equivalent.

Good-promoting virtues seem to be of more limited moral importance. Although there is certainly moral value in being generous and sociable, for instance, one is not necessarily a moral failure for being weak in these areas. Virtues in this category have moral value because their effects are valuable (e.g., they meet people's needs and advance social interactions). Because we care about such things, furthermore, these virtues tend to engage our personal feelings more than obligation virtues. As these virtues promote effects that ultimately tie to overall utility, they parallel aspects of consequentialist ethics.

Limiting virtues, finally—or "virtues of the will"—seem almost morally *neutral* in themselves. Certainly, each is crucial for developing other sorts of virtues, especially when the behaviors called for by another virtue go against our own inclinations. The ability to say "no" to our desires (temperance), for instance, must constantly be exercised as we learn to give generously, and courage is usually needed when an obligation virtue requires us to act against our own interests. Limiting virtues can equally serve in the exercise of vice. To avoid getting caught, for instance, a burglar must learn to move in silence and with careful deliberation, a skill requiring much self-control. A more terrible illustration is of the terrorists who crashed airplanes into the World Trade Center. In steeling themselves to face injury and death, they certainly exercised great strength of will. Was this courage? Since the limiting virtues can strengthen both vices and virtues, maybe they are best viewed as amoral—having no *moral* value in themselves. Taking them this way, we could describe the terrorists as having courage. Many are very uncomfortable with this, however, seeing courage as a positive moral virtue—as taking risks for the good. Going this route (and not letting our everyday ways of talking confuse us), we would refuse to describe them as courageous. Either way, the limiting virtues have the fewest parallels to anything found in principle-based ethics, falling almost exclusively within the province of virtue ethics.

These thoughts about Hunt's categories support a couple of points made in the previous section. One is that virtue ethics extends beyond the normal reach of principle-based ethics. While there is a large amount of overlap regarding the first category's concerns (obligation), differences begin to appear in the second category (good promoting), and the differences become considerable in the third category (limiting). Because Ashley's case centers on the latter categories (compassion and loyalty), it reaches beyond principle-based theories. Hunt's categorization also suggests how virtue theory may help reconcile impartiality with the role of personal feelings (see §IV). Impartiality most strongly associates with obligation and duty—those aspects of morality where impartiality is most important. The subjective and partial nature of personal feelings brings them more in line with promoting good (compassion, for instance, usually acts to meet needs). Since they relate most strongly to different aspects of morality, impartiality and feelings may best be seen as complementing rather than conflicting with each other.

For Discussion

1. *Do you think that courage is a moral or amoral character trait?*
2. *What about loyalty or temperance (self-control)—are these moral or amoral character traits?*

Summary

Virtues can be placed into different categories. Obligation virtues reflect moral duties like keeping promises, telling the truth, and acting justly and closely parallel basic deontological principles. Good-promoting virtues like generosity produce desirable effects and so relate to consequentialist ethics. Limiting virtues are virtues of the will like courage and temperance. These can be considered moral values; alternately, these may be considered as amoral if viewed as serving both virtue and vice.

Key Terms

- **Obligation virtues**: *help us fulfill moral obligations to act in certain ways (e.g., promise keeping, justice, truthfulness).*

- **Good-promoting virtues**: *help promote specific values or goods (e.g., sociability, generosity).*

- **Limiting virtues**: *help us control or manage our inclinations and feelings (e.g., courage, temperance [self-control], loyalty, or faithfulness).*

VI. PROBLEMS WITH VIRTUE ETHICS

While much can be said in favor of virtue theory, it also has difficulties.

Attaining virtue: Principle-based ethics asks us to *do* what is morally right. Although this can be difficult, it at least lies within our power one act at a time. In contrast, virtue ethics asks us to *transform* our very characters to be virtuous persons. This is a much more holistic demand than just doing the next thing right.

Is this humanly possible? In addition to the questions about character raised by moral psychology (see Chapter Five, §II), there are two particularly interesting challenges to virtue theory's practicability (see Part II Introduction).

The first aims at Aristotle's assumption that we all begin life with a more or less neutral moral character. While many agree with this or even maintain that people are "basically good," others counter that human nature innately inclines toward selfishness, violence, lust, and other vices—just look at the news.[11] Add to this the conviction of many that while we have some power over ourselves, no amount of human ingenuity or effort can entirely overcome our undesirable tendencies. As they progress toward being more honest or kind, for instance, many report that they then find themselves becoming judgmental about the lack of honesty or kindness they perceive in others. Similarly, smokers who successfully "kick the habit" often become highly critical of other smokers. If a serious attempt to combat a failing in one area exposes some other crack in our character, then it may not be possibly to fully attain virtue.

A second challenge comes from Michael Slote. His argument begins with the observation that the entire ancient world—including Aristotle—accepted slavery as "natural and inevitable."[12] Even those who owned no slaves had no moral objection to slavery and would have had no qualms about having their own slaves if given the opportunity. But since slavery violates fundamental human rights, it is morally wrong. This makes its acceptance incompatible with having virtue since genuine virtue must *know* the right and good. This fact, Slote argues, precludes any of the ancients from qualifying as virtuous.

Slote then says that it is equally difficult for anyone today to attain genuine virtue. Although we don't accept slavery, Slote considers it overwhelmingly likely that we—no less than the ancients—are ensnared by one or more virtue-defeating moral errors of our own. To think otherwise, after all, would be to make the audacious claim that *our* moral beliefs are all perfectly correct. Yet if any such errors do grip us, then, like the ancients, we accept something that no genuinely virtuous person could accept. Generalizing this line of thought, it seems unlikely that *any* human being can ever achieve genuine virtue: virtue is unattainable.

Since these are challenges against the possibility of attaining *virtue,* they don't readily carry over as difficulties for other ethical theories. In contrast with virtue theory, other theories don't ask us to do what is not even *possible.* Yet the first challenge raises doubts about our having the power necessary to become different

---

[11]The view that human nature has natural inclinations toward vices is shared by such diverse perspectives as Christianity (original sin), Freudian psychology (libido), and versions of sociobiology (inherited aggressions). The latter two assume a determinism that may largely defy human correction; Christianity, meanwhile, insists that only God's supernatural power can adequately transform a person (i.e., the need to be "born anew").

[12]Michael Slote, "Is Virtue Possible?" in *The Virtues: Contemporary Essays on Moral Character,* eds. Robert B. Kruschwitz and Robert G. Roberts, (Belmont, CA: Wadsworth Publishing Company, 1987), 102.

persons; the second raises doubts that we can have the moral knowledge necessary to qualify as virtuous.

Explanatory power: The virtues are foundational moral values. But what makes *them* good? It would be helpful to have some account or explanation of these values too, since ideally an ethical account should shed some light on the nature of morality in total. Can virtue theory satisfy the criterion of *explanatory power?*

The least satisfactory possibility is for virtue theory to treat its foundational virtues as primitive, as admitting no more basic explanation. Although we might intuitively *recognize* the inherent goodness of honesty, for instance, there's nothing more to say about why it is good. This gives us very little insight into the nature of morality, other than that morality begins with these virtues.[13]

A better alternative would be for virtue theory to identify some basis for unifying the virtues. For instance, Aristotle tells us that virtues reflect our living in accordance with reason and that virtue falls at a mean between extremes. His most tantalizing suggestion is that virtuous living is necessary for human flourishing. But because Aristotle defines flourishing mainly in terms of exercising the virtues, this isn't much help in explaining virtue. Further, Aristotle is rather vague about just *how* reason reveals the nature of virtue. Yet even if a virtue theorist were to clear up these details, we would still need more explanation of what gives virtues their *moral* value.

The remaining alternative would be to explain the virtues in terms of some foundational non-moral value. For instance, we might explain virtue's goodness in terms of promoting human flourishing.[14] However, this line of thinking seems to present flourishing as a *consequence* of virtue, which makes it look like something a utilitarian might aim at. The more virtue theory resembles utilitarianism, however, the closer we come to effectively abandoning the distinctive nature of virtue theory.

Incompleteness: A common complaint against virtue theory is that it doesn't tell us enough about what we should do. Of course, if virtue theory is correct, then our yearning to be told what to do is just another symptom of our misplaced dependence upon moral principles. Take care over the kind of person you *are,* virtue theory says, and what you should *do* will become clear by itself. Further, virtue theory encourages us to look at outstandingly virtuous persons and, by watching how they consistently act, formulate rules of thumb to guide what we do. But how do we determine who is virtuous? If we can only identify virtuous people as those who *do* the right things, then we are stuck in a circle. This has led critics to

---

[13]The problem is similar to the lack of any explanation provided in Ross's account for his seven moral duties.

[14]Although Aristotle is often interpreted as taking this approach as well, a careful reading of Aristotle cannot support this. In fact, as previously noted, Aristotle leaves the origins of virtue largely unexplained except that virtue accords with reason. In treating human flourishing as the goal or basis of virtue, therefore, contemporary virtue theorists depart significantly from Aristotle (Simpson 1992).

conclude that virtue theory cannot be complete unless it appeals to some set of moral principles.

Virtue theory also seems ill-equipped to address certain moral problems:

- Is it right to invade a sovereign country to stop genocide?
- Is capital punishment wrong?
- Is it morally acceptable for a multinational corporation to enter a neighborhood and overwhelm the local competition?

These are clearly *moral* questions. Yet the kinds of acts these questions refer to cannot be carried out by individuals, and so cannot arise from *personal* character or virtue. Invasions are carried out by states, as is capital punishment. Even when individuals (e.g., a king or a judge) do make decisions about such things, they don't do so on their own *personal* authority but only because the state has granted them the necessary authority. Something quite similar normally holds true of corporate CEOs. But since these and other acts are not possible for mere persons on their own, they are not acts to which personal virtues pertain.

Virtue ethics even seems ill-equipped to furnish the kind of moral guidance an *individual* might sometimes need:

- What sorts of conditions, if any, could justify euthanasia (i.e., "mercy killing") or assisted suicide?
- Would having a late-term abortion be wrong?
- In what circumstances should I "blow the whistle" on my company?

These are also clearly moral issues, but what sorts of virtues are needed to deal with them? Becoming generous requires a series of opportunities to practice generosity. But few of us can get practice in dealing with euthanasia, abortion, or whistle blowing. The virtue theorist would reply that this is all confused—there is no euthanasia-oriented virtue that one needs for dealing with questions involving euthanasia. Rather, having developed ourselves into virtuous persons, we should be equipped to respond virtuously to *any* moral challenges, including such extraordinary ones. But *which* virtues do we most need to address such cases virtuously? More important, is there reason to think that having the *ordinary* virtues can adequately equip us to handle a truly *extraordinary* moral challenge?

Further, virtue theory isn't able to provide the *kinds* of answers these questions are looking for. These questions seem to ask about the specific conditions that must be fulfilled for such acts to be morally justifiable. For instance, a late-term abortion may *only* be justifiable if the mother would not otherwise survive. Whistle blowing might *always* be justified when it would avert great harm. As the words "only" and "always" strongly suggest, we may need universal principles to answer these sorts of questions. Since virtue theory doesn't generate such principles, it probably can't address these and other important moral questions, making it less than a complete moral theory.

* * *

There nevertheless remains a strong appeal in much of what virtue theory has to offer. Above all, its exhortation for each of us to work at achieving an integrated and morally good character speaks powerfully to the felt need of many who think that ethics must be more than just rules and rights. Further, Aristotle does us a valuable service in emphasizing the important moral influences of good leadership and good laws within a society. The notion of inculcating virtue by practice may also come as a revelation to parents and educators who have despaired of rules, punishments, and rewards as tools for shaping moral sensitivity in children. Even if virtue theory cannot stand as a complete ethical theory by itself, it's certainly worthwhile for us to keep exploring and thinking deeply about virtue and its moral implications.

For Discussion

1. *Are people innately good? What supports your view on this?*
2. *In what area(s) might we be getting things seriously wrong today, like people did with slavery?*
3. *Do you agree that serious moral mistakes in our beliefs can keep us from being virtuous?*
4. *Consider some virtue like kindness or honesty. How would you explain what makes these good? Does your explanation take you beyond virtue theory?*
5. *What would you say is needed to morally justify our invading another country, ignoring traffic laws, "blowing the whistle" where you work, or capital punishment (assume that it can be justified so you can discuss this)?*

Summary
There are several difficulties for virtue theory. On the practical side, there is the worry that no one can actually attain genuine virtue, since it might not be possible for us to overcome our natural inclinations toward vice. Michael Slote argues that people of every period are susceptible to serious errors in their moral beliefs, and such errors preclude the attainment of genuine virtue. On the theoretical side, virtue theory has little explanatory power since it can't explain what makes virtue good in the first place. Finally, virtue theory itself appears incomplete with its inability to address certain types of moral questions.

Chapter Assignment Questions

1. *Virtue theorists think that our personal and emotional involvement can be morally important. Defend or criticize this.*
2. *Explain the difference between the principle-based and virtue-based concepts to virtue.*
3. *Explain how virtue theory can lead to there being more than one right choice in a single situation. Can you give an original example?*

4. *If virtue theory allows for several right choices, why isn't it subjectivism?*

5. *In your own words, what is eudaimonia? Is Aristotle right in claiming that this is the thing we all ultimately seek?*

6. *How powerful are habits? What do you think of Aristotle's idea that moral virtues are habits that must be practiced?*

7. *How is developing virtue like improving your football throw or your guitar playing? How does it differ?*

8. *Is being an honest person essentially the same as obeying a principle like "People should be truthful with each other"?*

9. *Is being a generous person essentially the same as obeying a principle like "People should help others out with liberal amounts of time and money when they are in a position to"?*

10. *** Thinking about either a Kantian or utilitarian saint, what do you find most appealing and most unappealing about each?*

11. *Is there such a thing as "will power"? Discuss.*

12. *** How well do you think virtue theory addresses moral motivation?*

13. *Do you think virtue is attainable? Support your position.*

Additional Resources

Aristotle. *Nichomachean Ethics* (350 BCE), translated by W. D. Ross. Accessed August 28, 2016. http://classics.mit.edu/Aristotle/nicomachaen. See especially Books I and II for Aristotle's account. Books III–V offer detailed analyses of the various moral virtues.

Kraut, Richard. "Aristotle's Ethics." In *The Stanford Encyclopedia of Philosophy* (Spring 2016 Edition), edited by Edward N. Zalta. http://plato.stanford.edu/archives/spr2016/entries/aristotle-ethics/. This article provides a detailed discussion of Aristotle's ethics that parallels Aristotle's *Nicomachean Ethics*.

Kruschwitz, Robert B., and Robert G. Roberts. *The Virtues: Contemporary Essays on Moral Character* Belmont, CA: Wadsworth Publishing Company, 1987. A very good anthology on virtue, which includes the articles mentioned in the text by Slote, Wolf, and Hunt.

Latus, Andrew. "Nagel on 'Moral Luck.'" In *Internet Encyclopedia of Philosophy* (2008). Accessed August 8, 2009. ISSN 2161-0002. http://www.iep.utm.edu/moralluc/. This is a detailed discussion of moral luck, including Nagel's article and an earlier article by Bernard Williams. This reading applies to Case 4 of this chapter.

Wolf, Susan. "Moral Saints." In *Virtue Ethics*, edited by Robert Crisp and Michael Slote, 79–98. New York: Oxford University Press, 1998. This article was first published in *Journal of Philosophy*, 79.8 (August 1982): 419–439. This article also appears in a great many ethics anthologies.

Case 1

The Unlikely Rescue

On September 9, 1996, Daniel Santos, a twenty-one-year-old volunteer firefighter, dove off the Tappan Zee Bridge to save the life of a young woman. According to the *New York Times*, the woman just "slammed her Chevrolet Blazer into the railing,

Continued

Case 1 (Continued)

then got out and jumped into the Hudson River"[15] in an attempt to commit suicide. As soon as he saw this, Santos stopped his own car on the bridge and took a
140-foot dive over the bridge rail. According to Santos, "without thinking twice, I
just jumped and did what I had to do. I just prayed and closed my eyes."[16] A person
jumping from this height collides with the water at approximately sixty miles
per hour, so Santos was very lucky to survive the impact. Indeed, Santos suffered
from a broken rib and partially collapsed lung as a result of his dive. Nevertheless,
Santos managed to swim toward the woman. A nearby boat quickly came to their
rescue, and both Santos and the woman survived.

On first blush, it would seem that Santos behaved virtuously. He was certainly
celebrated as a hero after the incident. His story received coverage in the national
papers as well as in the evening news. But would Aristotle agree with this assessment? To be sure, Aristotle considered courage a virtue. But according to Aristotle, acting courageously in one instance does not show that a person is virtuous.
Second, Aristotle's doctrine of the golden mean makes virtue the mean between
excess and deficiency. A genuinely courageous act lies between foolhardiness and
cowardice. Thus, not every act that people call "courageous" would qualify as virtuous in Aristotle's sense.

THOUGHT QUESTIONS

1. Would Aristotle see Santos' actions as courageous or merely reckless? Why?
2. Santos wanted to become a full-time firefighter. If he were to succeed, do you
   think he would be an asset to the force? In terms of Hunt's categories, did Santos
   perhaps have some kinds of virtues while lacking others?
3. Did Santos meet all the conditions for a person having virtue?

Case 2

Video Games

As Aristotle noted a couple of millennia ago, human beings are creatures of
habit. How do we learn to tie our shoes, walk, write in good English, or drive, for
instance? Repetitive experience develops habits and skills that become *second
nature* to us—part of our very *selves*. Once established, habits are hard to change,
normally remaining part of us for the rest of our lives. What fifty-year-old couldn't
still manage to balance a bicycle—even if she hasn't ridden for thirty years? Of
course, not all habits involve *physical action*—we also develop *habits of mind*. For
instance, how often have you found your parents (or even yourself!) falling back
into the same old ways of thinking (e.g., prejudices), even after making a serious
effort to change?

Continued

---

[15]"Even Rescuer Admits It Seemed Crazy," *New York Times*, September 14, 1996, accessed August
28, 2016, http://www.nytimes.com/1996/09/14/nyregion/even-rescuer-admits-it-seemed-crazy.html.
    [16]Ibid.

Case 2 (*Continued*)

Aristotle emphasized that habits (whether mental or physical) also have important *moral* implications. This brings us to video and computer games. While many games are perfectly innocent (often employing the aforementioned principles of habit to develop some desirable skill, knowledge, etc.), some have gained notoriety. Take, for instance, *Grand Theft Auto*,[17] in which the player rises through the criminal ranks by committing crimes. As one player describes it, "I can steal cars, kill anyone in pretty much any way, have sex with hookers, take drugs, sell drugs, sell stolen cars, etc. If you can think it, this game does it. It is a world with no borders, which is very relaxing." This gamer also comments, "I have had trouble with playing hours of a driving game and then getting in my car and feeling like I was still in the game. . . . Games today look so real, it feels like the real world to a degree." (Disorientation upon reentering the real world—sometimes severe—is a documented effect of "full-immersion" virtual reality.)

So we must ask: if people indeed develop habits of thought and action—and ultimately their moral character—through repetition and practice, what is likely to happen to the person (especially an impressionable child) who spends day after day thinking through, choosing, and acting out virtual crimes, murders, and sexual encounters of immense immoral proportions? Is it possible for such continual immoral reinforcement to have no effect? The worry is not that playing such games will turn good people into criminals. But are such games promoting the kind of personal character that a morally good society values? This worry seems substantiated by studies that indicate a child is more prone to violent behavior if he simply *watches* a violent TV show that has characters the child relates to. If children can be significantly influenced by violence as simply *passive* viewers, how much more are they likely to be influenced by violence they participate in—as highly realistic, deeply absorbing video games make possible? It's also been shown that even adults become more accepting of violence after spending as little as a half hour watching a violent show on TV.

Thanks to the wonders of modern computing power, a ten-year-old, often with 3D sound, tactile feedback, and powerful graphics, can work her way through fifty bloody murders in an hour's time. Some argue that this isn't real life and that even children don't typically confuse the two. But as the adult gamer just quoted says, *realism* is what these games are all about, and the back-and-forth transition between such games and reality can become, at the very least, quite disorienting. The graphic portrayal of blood, exploding bodies, and shattered faces amid groans and shrieks may occupy a kid's playtime—and is likely to become still more absorbing and realistic as game programming progresses. Some games overflow with gratuitous violence, offensive language, perverse values, and explicit sexual exploitation. Again, it's important to remember that such games don't simply *expose* the player to such things (as in movies and TV)—rather, they *actively engage* the participant's mind, will, emotions, and senses. This is an entirely new phenomenon, and although it may be too early to assess the effects of such games and activities on individuals and society, Aristotle certainly suggests what directions these effects are likely to take.

---

[17]*Grand Theft Auto* (New York: Rockstar Games), creator Dave Jones, is a video game series begun in 1997.

THOUGHT QUESTIONS

1. Since we use (even in schools) a variety of video games to develop and reinforce skills in mathematics, spelling, typing, and other areas of education, is it consistent to maintain that violent video games have little effect upon their users?

2. It seems that if certain video games can have a bad influence on children or teens, they would likely have similar effects upon adults. What do you think, and why? Would you be willing to let felons play such games to while away their time behind bars?

3. Should children and teenagers be permitted to play violent video games? Apply Aristotle's account in answering that question.

Case 3

Compulsive Gambling and the Internet

According to some studies, up to 5% of American adults have a gambling problem. This problem is most prevalent among younger adults and can start as early as high school. For adolescents and college students, the figures average around 15%.[18] A survey of three thousand students in over fifty New Jersey high schools revealed that more than 30% of the students gambled at least once a week. Some of these students are already in serious debt to loan sharks.[19] And the problem of compulsive gambling is getting worse. Over the past twenty years, gambling has increased by 20% in the United States. In that same period, the amount of money spent on gambling has doubled.[20]

It seems safe to say that in coming years, the *main* contributor to the spread of gambling, especially among the younger population, will be the Internet. Gambling websites are readily available, which makes a trip to a casino unnecessary. Although a credit card is needed to play, many eighteen-year-olds already possess their own credit cards, and others have access to their parents' cards. Furthermore, it's impossible to verify a gambler's age over the Internet. Also, Internet gambling takes place anonymously and in an isolated context. This makes it hard to track or for authorities or other concerned persons to interfere. For these reasons, it's likely that even more people will become addicted to online gambling. This is confirmed by another study that suggests that the percentage of problematic and compulsive gamblers is much higher among Internet gamblers than with other forms of gambling.[21]

The effects of gambling on a person's habits, character, and ultimate well-being are often devastating. Since these effects are measurable, they give *prima facie* credibility to Aristotle's views on habits and on the formation of both virtue

Continued

---

[18]H. Shaffer, M. Hall, and J. Bilt, "Estimating the Prevalence of Disordered Gambling Behavior in the United States and Canada: A Research Synthesis," *American Journal of Public Health*, 89.9 (1999): 1369–1376.

[19]Ed Looney and Kevin O'Neill, "Adolescent Compulsive Gambling: The Hidden Epidemic," *Council on Compulsive Gambling of New Jersey*, accessed August 28, 2016, http://casinowatch.org/children_gambling/adolescent.html.

[20]Shaffer, Hall, and Bilt, "Estimating the Prevalence of Disordered Gambling Behavior."

[21]George Ladd and Nancy Petry, "Disordered Gambling Among University-Based Medical and Dental Patients: A Focus on Internet Gambling," *Psychology of Addictive Behavior*, 16.1 (2002): 76–79.

Case 3 (*Continued*)

and vice. To see this, consider the four phases of compulsive gambling described by the Arizona Council on Compulsive Gambling.[22] The first phase, the *winning phase*, is characterized by winning more often than losing. It may start with one big win. In this phase, the gambler gradually risks larger and larger amounts of money and gambles more often. As he starts becoming addicted to gambling, this decreases the amount of time he spends on other activities (e.g., time with family or friends or on working or studying). The gambler then transitions into the *losing phase*, when there are more losses than wins. This leads the gambler to need more money, both to cover losses and to continue gambling. He also will probably want to cover his tracks, so that others don't discover that he is losing more and more money and so try to stop him. This is when he begins to *lie*. He borrows money he can't pay back. Because of the time spent gambling, the steady loss of money, and the increased lying, the gambler's family life and friendships begin to deteriorate. The gambler next enters the *desperation phase*, in which his entire life becomes centered on gambling; depression may set in as well. At this point, the gambler has completely lost control—gambling controls him rather than the other way around. The addiction is now too strong to overcome. As others stop trusting the gambler, he may then be forced to obtain money illegally, perhaps telling himself that these are "loans" that he'll pay back as soon as he starts winning again. The gambler is now lying *to himself* in addition to lying to others. In the last phase, called the *hopeless phase*, the gambler gives up. If he has committed crimes to obtain money, he may have gotten caught. He may even commit suicide.

In rare cases, gamblers will seek help, usually because friends or family have intervened. Nevertheless, the recovery rate for compulsive gamblers is slim and when successful, recovery usually takes years. Once a person has become a compulsive gambler, he is unlikely to ever return to the person he once was.

THOUGHT QUESTIONS

1. What kinds of habits (including habits of mind) are developed by a compulsive gambler? What other vices can be associated with gambling?
2. How would Aristotle describe the process of turning into a compulsive gambler? How well does the Arizona Council's four phases agree with Aristotle's thinking ?
3. What particular issues/concerns does *Internet* gambling raise? What is there about Internet gambling that can make it particularly dangerous?
4. Could a virtuous person make (occasional) use of Internet gambling sites? Is this an instance of there being several right choices? In terms of Hunt's categories of virtues, which sorts of virtues can gambling undermine?
5. Hopes for a gambler's recovery are slim. Why do you think this is? What light, if any, does Aristotle's theory of virtue shed on this fact?
6. Suppose you or a friend have begun to do some online gambling—just once or twice a week for a couple hours. Occasionally, the betting has gotten up into the

---

[22]Arizona Council on Compulsive Gambling, accessed August 28, 2016, http://www.azccg.org.

$50–$100 range. How harmless is this activity? Take Aristotle's arguments into account in your response to this question.

Case 4

Moral Luck

Aristotle tells us that we develop virtues and vices by practice, by establishing behavioral patterns which, over time, become part of our moral character. Nevertheless, he also observes that it is much easier to develop into a virtuous person if the society one lives in is just and morally healthy. Thus, our moral characters are the products of both our own behavioral choices and our social environment. But while we have a great deal of control over our own choices, we have little or no control over our social environment, especially when we are young. The environment we are born into seems little more than a matter of luck.

Arbitrary factors beyond our control can also profoundly affect the success or failure of our everyday actions. Tom Nagel, in his essay "Moral Luck," observes, "[w]hether we succeed or fail in what we try to do nearly always depends to some extent on factors beyond our control. . . . What has been done, and what is morally judged, is partly determined by external factors."[23] For example, "there is a morally significant difference between rescuing someone from a burning building and dropping him from a twelve-story window while trying to rescue him."[24] Furthermore,

> What we do is also limited by the opportunities and choices with which we are faced, and these are largely determined by factors beyond our control. Someone who was an army officer in a concentration camp might have led a quiet and harmless life if the Nazis had never come to power in Germany. And someone who led a quiet and harmless life in Argentina might have become an officer in a concentration camp if he had not left Germany for business reasons in 1930.[25]

Clearly, each of us sometimes experiences good moral luck and sometimes bad moral luck. For most of us, do the good and the bad tend to average out? Since we know that much of what will affect our lives lies beyond our control, do we have a (moral) responsibility to plan ahead for such contingencies, prudently preparing, like a defensive driver, for the worst? Consider the following situations:

1. George is on his way home from work. While heading down the freeway, he sees a car smashed up against the guardrail. Although he first considers just calling the police, he then decides to pull over. Walking up to the car, George finds a woman sitting behind the wheel, unconscious. Not realizing that persons with neck injuries (a common effect of traffic accidents) can be paralyzed or even killed by movement, George pulls the woman from the car. Luckily, she had no neck injuries and so is not harmed by George's action. Just as he gets her a few feet away, the car bursts into flames. In less than a minute, the fuel tank explodes—but George and the woman are safe.

Continued

---

[23]Thomas Nagel, "Moral Luck," in *Mortal Questions*, ed. Thomas Nagel (Cambridge, UK: Cambridge University Press, 1979), 25. Note that moral luck is a problem for other ethical theories besides virtue ethics.
[24]Ibid.
[25]Ibid., 26.

Case 4 (*Continued*)

2. Janet, brought up in an upper-middle-class neighborhood by wise and loving parents, has enjoyed a wide range of opportunities and a good education. In her freshman year at college, away from home for the first time, her roommate invites her one night to try drugs. Although feeling slightly pressured—and even a bit curious—Janet nevertheless refuses after a moment's thought and never considers drugs again in her entire life. Meanwhile, in another part of town, Ed angrily heads out of the hot, smelly two-room apartment where his drunken mom and four siblings live. His mom has been screaming at him for the past hour, although, as usual, there doesn't seem to be any reason. A high school dropout because of poor grades, Ed has been working at the corner garage, but today the owner said something about not having any more work for him. As he walks down the hall, he encounters a sweet, acrid smell wafting from a cluster of people in a corner. In passing, he recognizes one of his street buddies, who looks up and yells, "Hey Ed—you want some? It's on me tonight—I just got paid." Shaking his head slowly, Ed walks on.

3. Mark is a successful businessman who regularly donates both his time and money to a homeless shelter in New York City. One evening, after leaving the shelter, he goes to a restaurant with some friends and orders one of the specials, which comes with a margarita. Although he doesn't much care for margaritas, he has the drink to be sociable. He also takes one of the allergy pills his doctor just prescribed him. He doesn't remember his doctor mentioning that the pills can cause drowsiness, and he doesn't notice the warning on the bottle to not mix them with alcohol. After dinner, Mark feels a bit light-headed but, without thinking much about it, gets into his car and drives home. Coming down a street with cars parked on both sides, he sees a truck on his left suddenly swerving out of its lane toward him. The truck straightens out, but Mark's attention has been so riveted on the truck that he doesn't immediately notice the child who just then darts out from the parked cars on his right. Mark tries to stop, but doesn't make it in time and feels the sickening thud as his right bumper collides with the child, who is badly injured. When the police arrive, they notice a hint of alcohol on Mark's breath. Even though he passes a breathalyzer test, they book him for driving under the influence.

THOUGHT QUESTIONS

1. What do you think of George's moral character? Did he act virtuously? Suppose that in moving the woman, George severed one of her nerves; as a result, his action saved her from a fiery death but also paralyzed her for life. Would that make any moral difference? Why or why not?

2. Think about Janet and Ed. Is either of them a more virtuous person than the other? What reasons can you offer?

3. Even though the effects of many external factors upon us seem to be just a matter of luck, we do have control over our thoughts and intentions. Although their luck differed, both Mark and George presumably meant well—neither had any evil intentions. How are a person's habitually good intentions relevant to their moral character?

4. Do you believe there is such a thing as moral luck? Some people think that a person's "luck" is often just the result of that person's consistently prudent or foolish choices. Maybe it was rare thing for Mark to do, but he put himself in a position of being more vulnerable to the "bad luck" he later encountered. Of course, George likewise made himself vulnerable to some very "bad luck," although he was luckier.

5. Many people talk about how things were "meant to be" and how "everything has a purpose"—although they are often quite vague about what or who is behind those purposes. What are your views on this, and how do they affect your thinking about moral luck?

6. Should Mark be blamed for harming the child in the accident? Did Mark do anything wrong? Do you think Mark could be called a "good" man? Discuss and evaluate his case with care, commenting on how Aristotle would assess it and the role of moral luck in the case.

Case 5

Democracy in Switzerland

The Swiss democracy is rather different from democracy in the United States (also see footnote 5 of this chapter). Switzerland has as direct democracy, which means that the people govern directly, not through a representative. Developed and re-fined for over eight hundred years (and in its current form for over one hundred years), the Swiss democracy has a long tradition. Opinion polls and referendums determine what decisions are to be made—for instance, on a draft of a new or amended law (the drafts are prepared by experts in the administration). In indi-vidual cantons (member states, of which there are twenty-six), budgets are set by referendum.[26] If the majority of the electorate agrees, even the constitution can be changed. Switzerland's system is considered extremely stable but it also requires more involvement from its citizens. Switzerland does have a parliament and politi-cal parties, but constitutional changes (changes in law) cannot take place without the expressed agreement of the people. The Swiss generally tend to vote conser-vatively, but it's noteworthy that they have also favored equal representation of women in parliament and voted against payouts for managers of failing compa-nies (golden parachutes).[27]

THOUGHT QUESTIONS

1. What kind of character would the ideal citizen have in the Swiss democracy? Answer this question from both your own and Aristotle's perspectives.

2. Do you think that the United States or other countries could profit from having a more direct democracy like this? What are some pros and cons?

---

[26]"Switzerland's Direct Democracy," accessed August 28, 2016, http://direct-democracy.geschichte-schweiz.ch.

[27]"Switzerland: The Ultimate Democracy," *The National Interest*, September 7, 2014, accessed August 28, 2016, http://nationalinterest.org/feature/switzerland-the-ultimate-democracy-11219.

3. In 2009 the Swiss voted against constructing any additional minarets on mosques. In 2004 it rejected a referendum to grant citizenship to foreigners who had grown up in Switzerland.[28] Do these facts suggest that a direct democracy could work in both just and unjust ways?

4. What advantages and disadvantages do you see with a direct democracy compared to a representational democracy? Include some of Aristotle's views as you answer this.

5. After the 2016 United States presidential election, many again pushed to remove the electoral college and allow the popular vote to determine each state's winner. Elections by popular vote are a long way from a direct democracy, but they do remove one small group of representational middlemen from determining election outcomes. Given the growing evidence that much of the popular electorate can be easily swayed by targeted advertising and other forms of manipulation, is dumping the electoral college a good idea? What would Aristotle say?

---

[28]Ibid.

CHAPTER TWELVE

Feminism and Care Ethics

I. INTRODUCTION

Jared was born at 3:09 AM on December 13, 1992.[1] Unfortunately, he was not wanted—especially not by his twenty-year-old father, the on-and-off boyfriend of Jared's eighteen-year-old mother. Nor did Jared's infant screams endear him to the neighbors, to his weary mother, or to the relative who, for fifty bucks, helped with the birthing. Why did Jared keep screaming? Probably because of the withdrawal symptoms he started experiencing soon after birth, the result of his mother's drug habit. Even after he got past that, he was always screaming. His mom had first thought it would be fun to have a baby, but she soon tired of Jared and left him alone most of the time after that. This neglect left Jared continually hungry, which fueled more screaming. He was crying when his father stopped by about six months later. An illegal alien, his father was often both verbally and physically abusive to Jared's mother who was too frightened and too dependent on his occasional financial help to move out.

On this night, his father was already on edge because, for reasons he wouldn't explain, he thought the police were on his trail. It didn't take long for Jared's screaming to throw him into a rage. Grabbing Jared, he started shaking and smacking him, yelling "Shut up, brat!" until Jared's mom ripped him from his father's hands. The neurological damage was one reason Jared later had trouble in school.

Although he preferred it to hiding in the closet from his father, Jared hated school. Learning to read took forever, and since this made him feel stupid, he compensated by demanding attention. By third grade, his behavior had become unusually disruptive, and he was constantly being punished. When his teachers grew tired of him, they sent him to the principal. As the principal got tired of him, Jared started being suspended. When he was assigned a social worker, she didn't like what she saw and decided he wasn't worth her time given the forty other kids in her caseload. This left Jared with a lot of time on the street, where he became the local gang's honorary ten-year-old member. Basking in this approval, Jared gradually became more dangerous. He got away with his first few crimes. Then, on his nineteenth birthday, he got into a screaming match with his mother, went

---

[1] This story is fictional.

into the bathroom, lit the paper in the wastebasket, and climbed out the window. He didn't show any remorse at his trial, so the judge had no choice but to slap him with twenty years—the mandatory sentence for what the prosecutor portrayed as drug-related manslaughter. In prison, he remains pretty much a loner.

*   *   *

Who *cares?* Jared's father didn't seem to care much for Jared, Jared's mom, or even himself. Maybe his mom would have taken better care of Jared if his father had treated her better. Growing up in such an environment, Jared experienced very little love and care. While justice may have been served at Jared's trial, would his story have turned out differently if he'd been handled in early life with more sympathy—at home, when he became difficult at school, and later as one more "case" in the child welfare system? Jared never cared much for anyone else either, except for one or two of his street buddies. Although most of us aren't as bad off as Jared, we would probably *all* benefit from more caring—from the friend who never calls, the boss who couldn't care less, or from the bureaucrat who just hit you with a big penalty because you filed your state tax return a few hours late. There's plenty of opportunity for each of us to start caring more as well—for family and neighbors, about the conditions in which people like Jared live, about child sex slaves, about genocides around the world, about environmental disasters—and that's just a start.

Justice is also a good thing, and the world could use more justice and caring both. But do they go together? Jared's punishments in school were probably well-earned, his trial verdict just, and your tax penalty exactly in keeping with the law. So there's justice. If Jared's teachers, his trial judge, or your bureaucrat had softened their responses and been more caring, would that have undermined justice? And if we were to make it a practice of caring for others, would that erode fairness or make us vulnerable to exploitation? On the other hand, does basing a society upon a strong foundation of justice tend to keep people from caring?

These are very difficult questions. The problems they raise are by no means new, however; people have struggled to balance justice with mercy and caring for ages. The difficulty particularly surfaces, however, as we consider the experiences of women in most societies up through to the present. How do such considerations relate to ethics? An answer requires that we trace the story of feminism and one of its most important outcomes—*care ethics*—over the last century.

For Discussion

1. *Morally assess the various people in Jared's story.*
2. *How would you describe caring?*
3. *Do you think Jared's life would have turned out differently if he had experienced more caring in his childhood? How?*
4. *Describe some ways the world would be different if government, businesses, and individual lives all included much more caring.*
5. *How can caring (including mercy) and justice conflict with each other? Offer some examples.*

II.** FEMINIST ETHICS

Concerns about the condition and roles of women, both morally and socially, have a long history. Their impact upon ethics, however, has grown considerably since about the middle of the twentieth century, paralleling the development of feminist thought over the same period. At present, feminist ethics is exploring a very large range of topics, and there has been a great proliferation of viewpoints. Although this makes feminist ethics impossible to summarize, it is at least possible to identify several of its defining themes. We begin with the broadest of its themes here.

- *The importance of women's experience:* The distinctive values, perspectives, and practices of women need to be studied and appraised with great care. Historically, societies have assigned women roles that have kept them from participating in the *public world.* Most "women's work" thus has taken place in the *private world,* often as some type of caregiving (e.g., for young children, the sick, and the elderly).
- *The existence of gender bias:* In several cases, the roles traditionally taken by women have both originated in and preserved sexist presuppositions. More generally, women, their work, their contributions, and their perspectives have been almost universally undervalued or even completely ignored. Women have suffered injustices and been made subordinate because of the ways male-dominated societies are structured, including even by widely accepted ethical systems.
- *The need for moral reform:* Nevertheless, the activities of women, especially in the private world, have nurtured perspectives and values that bring important new or neglected moral insights to light. These insights—especially having to do with caring—can be profitably applied in the development of alternate ethical viewpoints and theories. But these must not remain abstract; instead, they then need to be implemented with the ultimate goal of reforming the entire social system. Negatively, the main goal is to remove those structures within society that ground and preserve its injustices against women. Positively, the goal is to enrich and transform society by incorporating valuable feminine moral insights that it presently lacks.

Let's look at each of these themes more deeply. After millennia of neglect, women and their unique experiences have especially received more focused study since the "second wave" of feminism[2] started in the late 1960s. Women's studies gained academic acceptance, which greatly increased the awareness of social ineq-

---

[2]"First wave" feminism, as characterized by Martha Lear, dealt with *legal* inequities, focusing especially on voting rights and legal forms of discrimination. The "second wave" broadened feminism to address a wide range of *social* inequalities as well. Martha Lear, "The Second Feminist Wave," *New York Times Magazine,* March 10, 1968, in Linda Napikoski, "The Second Feminist Wave," About.com, accessed August 28, 2016, http://womenshistory.about.com/od/feminism-second-wave/a/Martha-Weinman-Lear-Second-Feminist-Wave.htm.

uities against women. As this awareness grew, more comprehensive and sophisticated critiques of society began to appear.

Useful as these critiques were, they did not break a great deal of new ethical ground; rather, they tended to apply established concepts of justice and of rights to the fight for social equality.[3] This was in keeping with the practical emphasis of second wave feminism: social reform. As a result, a number of major changes in both attitudes and practices—often enforced by the weight of law—began to take place in the areas of women's health, education, and employment. Although all contemporary feminists still see a need for continued social reform, concerns over justice and rights remain prominent especially among feminists who feel that only sweeping revolutionary changes in society's structure can give women the freedom from domination and control that they require.

Reform can't be accomplished solely by opposing all that is wrong; alternatives must also be made available. Further, social reform usually requires more than changes in law and even social practices. Thus, most feminists now think that reform requires human change as well: changes in how we think and how we perceive both the world and ourselves. This *third wave* of feminism focuses primarily upon our understandings of personal identity and gender.[4]

This latest wave includes concerns for other marginalized groups within our society and across the globe as well as with environmental issues and the larger issues of social justice. It has also led to considerable fragmentation and disagreement. For instance, feminists tend to agree about their dissatisfaction with the traditional male/female gender distinction, which they feel still fosters inequality and social polarization. The solution, many maintain, is to transcend this distinction and move toward a degenderized society. But other feminists embrace an opposite tact, proposing that the two genders be replaced by a multiplicity of diverse gender concepts. Either approach has profound implications for sexual ethics. Another major difference pits what some take to be male-oriented conceptions of justice against an ethics of caring. Many feminists consider caring to be both prior and theoretically superior to justice. Others object that an emphasis on caring only contributes further to the injustices women face. This returns us to the tension between justice and caring and particularly to that between justice and the novel concept of caring presented within care ethics.

For Discussion

1. *How have women's and men's experiences differed historically, and how do they differ even today?*
2. *What injustices and biases do women presently encounter in our society?*
3. *Are women in other parts of the world better or worse off than in our society?*

---

[3]These critiques also made use of several non-ethical accounts in novel ways—most notably, Marxism and psychoanalysis.

[4]The notion of "third wave feminism" originated with Rebecca Walker in her "Becoming the Third Wave," *Ms. Magazine*, 11.2 (1992): 39–41.

4. *How far has society actually progressed in making reforms that affect the standing of women? What changes are still needed?*

Summary

Feminism is not a single unified movement. Still, a few points can serve as defining themes of feminist thought: the uniqueness of women's experience, problems with gender bias, and the need for moral reform in our society. In addressing these themes, feminists first worked toward legal equality; it then broadened to address social in equalities. Third wave feminism focuses primarily upon our understandings of personal identity and gender and gave rise to the ongoing project of care ethics.

III. THE CARE PERSPECTIVE

The origins of care ethics can be found in one corner of feminism's story just preceding the third wave. In her groundbreaking 1982 book, *In a Different Voice*, Carol Gilligan argued that there is a feminine moral perspective distinct from the more familiar masculine perspective. Gilligan described the masculine perspective as the **justice perspective,** in contrast to the feminine **care perspective**. According to Gilligan, these perspectives reflect fundamentally different ways people think and talk about moral problems. For instance, Gilligan reports that in justifying a rejection of their parents' religious beliefs, one teenage boy declared that while he respected his parents' views, he nevertheless had a right to his own opinions, while a teenage girl worried about the "fear" her parents had of her new religious beliefs. What's interesting here is that the boy appealed to abstract principles of fairness and respect—which belong to the justice perspective. In contrast, the girl adopted the care perspective by empathizing with her parents' feelings and by taking on the moral responsibility to preserve her relationship with them. Gilligan's two perspectives are likewise demonstrated by two medical students who had to decide about reporting a proctor's violation of school drinking rules. While one questioned the school's authority to prohibit drinking (the justice perspective), the other worried that reporting the offender would not help him address his drinking problem (the care perspective).[5] Although members of either sex can understand and employ both perspectives, women tend to focus upon care considerations, while men focus more upon justice. In describing these perspectives, Gilligan's work clearly aligns with the third wave focus on human identity and gender differences.

---

[3]Both examples are from Carol Gilligan, "Moral Orientation and Moral Development," in *Women and Moral Theory,* eds. Eva F. Kittay and Diana T. Meyers (Lanham, MD: Rowman & Littlefield Publishers, 1987), 19–36. Selections reprinted in Mark Timmons, *Conduct and Character, Readings in Moral Theory,* 5th ed. (Belmont, CA: Wadsworth, 2006), 199–200.

Traditional moral theories—especially utilitarianism and Kantian ethics—strongly align with the justice perspective. This perspective has dominated our society for several hundred years, so it's no accident that our social institutions neglect moral considerations associated with care. Recognizing this imbalance, care theorists have constructed a new ethics that takes the distinctive moral perspective of care. Given that our society usually deals with moral problems in terms of universal principles, rights, and justice, care theorists offer a major alternative as their basis for social reform.

Care ethics – another instance of moral particularism (see Chapter Eleven, §II and Chapter Four, §V) – tends to resemble virtue theory much more than it does any principle-based theories. It's thus not surprising that it goes along with the virtue criticisms against these theories—that principle-based theories are incomplete, that they overemphasize impartiality, and that they present a distorted picture of human nature. Yet care theorists also extend these criticisms in ways more characteristic of their own perspective. According to Virginia Held, a prominent writer in care ethics, care theorists particularly decry the rigid universalism, abstract rationalism, and the exaggerated individualism of traditional theories.[6] What is striking is that these perceived faults touch those very aspects of traditional theories that have usually been regarded as their strongest points.

Universalism: Traditional principle-based ethics reflect **universalism** and its reliance upon universal moral principles. Kant's categorical imperative requires that any morally acceptable action falls under a maxim that is rationally universalizable. Rule utilitarianism likewise sees any rule that promotes overall utility as being universal, while act utilitarianism reduces all moral duties to the single universal duty to promote overall utility.

The moral point of universalism is to combat self-centeredness—to encourage impartiality. As we all learn through hard experience, self-centered attitudes can greatly hinder moral action and understanding. Universalism helps combat our thinking exclusively about ourselves. But if universalism has such great moral value, what about it do care theorists find so objectionable?

Like virtue theorists, care theorists reject the assumption that morality can be rigidly summarized by universal or "one-size-fits-all" principles. As particularists like to point out, morality is too complex for any set of rules to address all moral concerns. Unlike virtue theorists, however, care theorists are especially concerned about our moral responsibilities within relationships—between friends, between parents and children, and between spouses—which have been largely ignored by traditional theories.

Next, principles cannot lead us to think about relationships in the right sorts of ways. It's bizarre to speak of a mother's *duty* to love and cuddle her newborn or

---

[6]This set of objections reflect themes widely (but not universally) accepted by feminist ethicists. Virginia Held, "Feminist Ethical Theory," in *Conduct and Character, Readings in Moral Theory*, 4th ed., ed. Mark Timmons (Belmont, CA: Wadsworth, 2002), 237–243.

of the husband's *duty* to lend a sympathetic ear to his wife's story of her day. Yes, people *should* do these things. But they should just naturally do these things because they care for each other—not because their failing to do them violates some abstract principle.

One interesting claim arising out of the care perspective is that the moral responsibilities of particular relationships may sometimes override the ideal of impartiality demanded by universalism. While this is more controversial, it might be maintained, for instance, that an employer of a small business should hire a needy relative over an equally worthy outsider. Likewise, most of us feel that we normally ought to help our friends, relatives, and neighbors before we concern ourselves with strangers.

For all of these reasons, care theorists reject universalism, maintaining that the right act depends on each distinct situation, including not only the personal character traits involved (virtue theory) but also the *relationships* between the persons involved. More specifically, care ethics looks at particular *kinds* of relationships (e.g., friendship, marriage, parent/child), together with particular *aspects* of those relationships (e.g., a friendly acquaintance vs. a close friendship; being the parent of a young child vs. an adult child). The latter, especially, make it possible for certain moral obligations to exist for one relationship that do not for another. For these reasons, and because of its moral particularism, care ethics is another account to which the thinking strategy of *moral reflection* applies (see Chapter Four, §V).

Emotion: Traditional theories (even virtue theory) view morality as inherently rational. They thus have taken a dim view of emotion, which can run counter to the dictates of reason. Yet while reason can certainly help us when our feelings clash with morality, the rationalistic tradition has been mistaken, care ethicists maintain, in viewing emotions exclusively as obstructing moral action. Hate, anger, and selfishness can indeed move us to do wrong, but "sensitivity, sympathy, empathy and solidarity of feeling" can promote morally desirable attitudes.[7] Care ethicists thus urge us not to reject interpersonal emotions wholesale but to embrace the "moral" emotions as essential to morally healthy relationships. In fact, some care ethicists consider reason to be only a *secondary* determinant of morality. Although nothing in care theory goes so far as to discard reason entirely, it does seem to assign reason a more limited role than does any other theory.

Individualism: A third mark of traditional ethics—together with liberal social thought—is the conception of persons as self-sufficient moral agents. Individualism lies at the heart of what we have called *value-neutral* autonomy (see Chapter Three, §V), the notion that autonomy is only about freedom from everything beyond our direct personal control. This negative view encourages a "take it or leave it" attitude toward relationships, which should never be

---

[7]Ibid., 240.

allowed to affect or alter one's autonomy. In keeping with this, individualism conceives of interpersonal relationships as essentially *contractual:* as agreements freely entered into by autonomous individuals for the sake of sharing certain interests and for mutual benefit. In short, individualism portrays each of us as largely unaffected even as we interact in various relationships, just as billiard balls remain unaffected as they collide with or temporarily rest against each other on the table.[8]

In stark contrast, care ethics emphasizes interdependence and connectedness, basing morality upon *relationships* rather than *individuals.* As a *relational* ethic, care ethics sees us developing our personal characters, moral responsibilities, and even our personal autonomy through our relationships. Care theorists offer a host of reasons for making this shift. First, traditional individualism is unrealistic, especially given today's complex social networks. As essentially social beings, furthermore, most of our needs must be met within relationships, starting with often the most formative relation of all—the mother/child relationship. Because of its importance, care theorists often view this to represent the ideal model of care. The deep dependency that characterizes this relationship is also something many of us occasionally return to—in serious illness, disability, and often in old age. For these and other reasons, care theorists propose that we instead adopt *relational autonomy,* a version of *substantive autonomy* (see Chapter Three, §V).

For Discussion

1. *In separate groups of men and women, consider a moral issue (e.g., capital punishment, abortion, gun control, economic injustice). Is the justice or care perspective reflected as each group explains and supports its views?*
2. *Does your own moral thinking emphasize one moral perspective?*
3. *What are the strengths and weaknesses of moral particularism?*
4. *Which emotions seem to you to be morally helpful or harmful?*
5. *What are some similarities and differences between virtue ethics and care ethics?*

Summary
There is evidence that two different moral perspectives exist; while men tend to take the justice perspective, women more often adopt the care perspective. Attention to the care perspective has led to the ethics of care. This new approach to ethics rejects the universalism, rationalism, and individualism of traditional theories. Instead, it maintains that special responsibilities can arise within particular relationships (particularism), that certain relation-building emotions are no less important than reason, and that relationships rather than individuals are morally central.

---

[8]Most traditional ethics developed at the same time as mechanistic science, which treated all natural bodies like billiard balls regulated by the laws of nature. Paralleling this, traditional ethical theories viewed people as autonomous entities whose interactions are regulated by moral laws.

Key Terms

- **Justice perspective:** *a characteristically masculine moral perspective that focuses upon moral rights, principles, and justice.*
- **Care perspective:** *a characteristically feminine moral perspective that focuses upon feelings, relationships, and individual needs.*
- **Universalism:** *a view of ethics that rejects moral particularism and insists on the universalizability of moral claims.*

IV. FOUNDATIONS OF AN ETHICS OF CARE

Since the care perspective introduces assumptions and values quite different from those of most other ethical theories, it has great potential for enriching our moral understanding. As several approaches have been taken, it's still not clear what care theory will ultimately look like. Still, any acceptable care theory would agree with most of the following foundations.[9]

1. Caring Relationships: According to Nel Noddings, an important early care theorist, our most fundamental moral obligation is to interact with other persons as caring: "Whatever I do in life, whomever I meet, I am first and always one-caring or one cared-for."[10] In this sense, caring can never involve just one person; it can only take place within *relationships.*

Yet because there can be many different kinds of relationships, it may be useful to make a few further distinctions. With friends, co-workers, and spouses, for instance, many relationships remain **symmetrical**—each person depending upon the other to roughly the same degree. Depending on the situation, either person may act as the **carer** (the initiator of caring) or as the **cared-for** (its recipient), although neither occupies either role predominantly. In relationships between teachers and students, doctors and patients, and parents and children, meanwhile, one mainly depends on the other. In such **asymmetrical** relationships, the more dependent person typically remains the cared-for, whereas the other acts as carer. We should not assume, however, that persons occupy the same role in all their relationships. In one relationship a person may usually act as carer (e.g., a parent caring for a child), while also acting as the cared-for in another relationship (e.g., as a student). People normally fill both roles many times in their lives.

Relationships also vary in **closeness**. One of the closest human relationships is that between a mother and her child—although relationships between spouses, friends, or siblings can also be very close. Relationships with acquaintances,

---

[9]These are foundational themes to care ethics in general, though not to any specific care theory. These themes are *not* ascribed to by all feminist ethicists. Much of what follows is discussed by Virginia Held in her *The Ethics of Care, Personal, Political, and Global* (New York: Oxford University Press, 2007), although this section also draws from Nel Noddings, *Caring: A Feminine Approach to Ethics and Moral Education* (Berkeley: University of California Press, 1984).

[10]Noddings, *Caring,* 175.

neighbors, co-workers, and classmates are usually much less close but can still involve special responsibilities for caring. Even as relationships become yet more distant, we can still act as carer or cared-for. For instance, the ties of shared needs, mutual interests, or even just our common human experience can make us receivers of care in the form of welfare, protection, or help from strangers. We may also give care as charitable donors, as activists for the poor, and as guardians of the environment for future generations. Close or distant, symmetrical or asymmetrical, all relationships should exhibit most of the qualities (in differing degrees) found in the closest caring relationships.

Although the carer has the primary responsibilities within a relationship, the cared-for also has certain responsibilities. Noddings maintained that the cared-for must **complete** the act initiated by the carer by *recognizing* himself as the recipient of care and *acknowledging* that in a confirming way. Thus, the infant responds to the mother's caring with smiles and happy sounds, while students may react to the teacher by showing interest, involvement, and cooperation. Unless most acts of caring are completed, caring can become too burdensome for the carer.

What happens when it's not possible for a caring act to be completed as when one cares for a comatose patient or gives charitably to people in distant countries? Most care theorists grant that a response from the cared-for is not always necessary. Still, we should always be thinking in caring and relational terms, even if we can only imagine the cared-for making a response.

2. *Mutuality:* Again, caring relationships are to be modeled upon relationships that closely tie people together. Being "tied" to another is captured by the concept of **mutuality**. Ideally, a caring relationship ties people to each other in several ways.

First, both persons *value* many of the same things (e.g., they value certain shared interests, each other, and the relationship itself). Yet it isn't enough that both simply value these things on their own. Rather, they must share their valuing of these things as part of what constitutes their relationship. They would not value these same things in the same way if they didn't have that relationship.

Such mutual valuing naturally leads, second, to shared *feelings* in which they not only *care about* the things they mutually value but also feel affection toward and *care for* each other. This is where "moral" emotions like sensitivity and empathy become important. Because such feelings tie the concerns and well-being of each to those of the other, a hurt suffered by either is suffered by both. What parent, for instance, has not felt a desperate desire to *do something* in the midst of her child's pain or fear? On the more positive side, goods and satisfactions experienced by either is also shared by both.

Third, since it's not possible to care about something without knowing something about it, mutuality shares knowledge. Sharing an interest, for instance, requires that people know something about the subject of their interest and share that knowledge. Furthermore, mutuality requires that each learn something about the other person's feelings, concerns, and needs. Thus, each should constantly strive to gain a better understanding of the other, for this is how relationships deepen and grow.

There are other aspects to mutuality. One of the most important is the foundation of trust upon which relationships must be built. Just as the valuing, feeling, and knowledge of mutuality are essentially relational, trust likewise is essentially relational. It is a quality of relationships, not individuals within relationships. We shall return to this crucial part of mutualism shortly (see §V).

3. *Transformation*: Caring relationships can profoundly affect the individuals involved. Since caring begets caring, those involved grow as caring persons. It is thus necessary that both individuals actively participate within a caring relationship for caring to develop; this parallels the individual's practice of virtue (according to virtue theory) as being necessary for virtue to develop. More fundamentally, caring helps make us who we are as persons. Although relationships help create autonomy, they go deeper than this. As is revealed even in how we describe ourselves—"I'm her brother," "He's my child," "We're good friends"—our relationships largely define us and so are crucial to the formation of our very identities.

4. *Action*: Genuine caring results in action, since action is needed to fulfill people's needs. While specific caring acts don't all have to be aimed at specific needs, every act of caring must contribute to fulfilling some sort of human need. The nature of those needs can vary; in addition to life-sustaining needs, for instance, there are subtler psychological and emotional needs that we also all share. Meeting needs is essential to caring. It follows that when the carer fails to address the needs of the cared-for, she shows either that she doesn't genuinely care or that she is inept as a carer. Either way, there is a failure in caring.

5. *Caring as normative*: Having seen what caring involves, we mustn't forget that care theory is an *ethics* and is therefore intended to be *morally normative*. Care ethics has important things to say about aspects of relationships that can be morally good or bad (values) as well as about what we should or should not do (prescriptions).

Care ethics first identifies an ideal caring relationship as *the* fundamental good; it then proceeds to analyze those moral qualities that can contribute toward good relationships. For example, we can describe good relationships in terms of values like being respectful, trusting, open, and characterized by mutuality. Then there are relationships that lack such qualities or, worse, that are "dominating, exploitative, mistrustful, or hostile." [11] Whether good or bad, relational values can also be extended to individuals. Indeed, those personal qualities that help promote caring relationships can be treated much like "virtues." For instance, the character traits of sensitivity, compassion, and loyalty are morally desirable in individuals because they positively contribute to relationships. Naturally there are vices as well.

In addition, care ethics implies a number of moral prescriptive claims. Generally speaking, the good qualities just mentioned *ought* to be nurtured and

---

[11] Held, *The Ethics of Care*, 37.

encouraged. Factors that contribute to bad relational qualities, meanwhile, should be avoided. General claims like these can also support prescriptions for more specific kinds of actions (e.g., "I should not say things that express hostility to others" or "He ought to show more respect for his wife"). We must keep in mind, however, that care "virtues" and "prescriptions" never stand on their own; to the degree that they have moral worth, their worth depends entirely upon the degree to which they are supportive of caring.[12]

Care ethics considers it an important moral responsibility for us to promote and nurture caring in the relationships of others. This is best done by *modeling* genuine caring within actual relationships. For the most part, caring cannot be taught through rules or motivated by rewards or punishments (because of its particularism). Instead, individuals can learn about caring by being *shown* deeply caring relationships. They learn even more by actively *participating* in caring relationships, experiencing for themselves the range of qualities that make up healthy caring relationships. Participation nurtures caring in another way as well. Arguably, one cannot effectively function as a carer without having the emotional capacity needed for caring. Developing such a capacity requires that one feel genuinely loved and cared for, which requires being in caring relationships. It's especially important that children experience deep and consistent caring (unlike Jared), which then enables them to initiate and develop caring relationships with others.

Finally, care theory has moral implications for political, economic, and even global issues. Although our interactions at these levels are usually both distant and impersonal, we *are* still tied to each other by many shared interests and concerns and *can* still act in ways that affect others. We thus can still have obligations for caring even at these levels. We can help meet the needs of others by how we vote, invest our finances, or give to alleviate poverty. We also have a moral responsibility to restructure schools, businesses, and government programs so that these meet people's needs in more caring ways.

For Discussion

1. *When have you last acted as a carer? As a cared-for? Describe.*
2. *Discuss types of relationships that are close, not close, symmetrical, and asymmetrical.*
3. *Imagine yourself as a caring teacher, friend, parent, or counselor, but then add that your caring is seldom or never "completed." How would that affect you?*
4. *What aspects of mutuality are particularly important? Are there any you disagree with or consider unimportant? Why?*
5. *Describe a non-family relationship that has had a powerful and positive transforming effect upon you.*
6. *Do you agree that true caring must typically result in action?*

---

[12]For this reason, care ethicists consider their theory to be more fundamental than other ethical accounts, including even virtue ethics.

7. *What interests and concerns do you share with people in, say, Kenya, Taiwan, or Ecuador? How do these tie you in mutuality and make caring possible?*

Summary

Most versions of care ethics acknowledge the centrality of caring relationships; the ties of mutuality; the view that caring establishes and transforms us as persons; the importance of caring leading to action; and the fact that, as a normative theory, care ethics has important implications for people's relationships, for people as individuals, and for how we should promote and encourage caring values.

Key Terms

- **Carer/cared-for**: *the carer initiates an act of caring towards the cared-for, who receives the caring.*

- **Symmetrical/asymmetrical relationships**: *in symmetrical relationships each person depends upon the other to roughly the same degree; in asymmetrical relationships one person tends to depend upon the other.*

- **Closeness**: *a quality of relationships that depends on things like the amount of knowledge each has of the other and how often they interact with each other.*

- **Completing** *a caring act, according to Noddings, requires that the cared-for recognizes himself as the recipient of care and acknowledges that to the carer.*

- **Mutuality**: *a quality of relationships that "ties" each to the other and is built upon the sharing of knowledge, feelings, and trust.*

V.** CARE AND VIRTUE

Care theory and virtue ethics have a great deal in common. How far, then, do their similarities reach? For instance, since we can describe individuals as "caring," should we treat "caring" as simply another virtue? Many virtue theorists think that care ethics is merely a variant of virtue theory, maintaining that care ethics can be derived from virtue theory.

Despite their commonalities, however, care ethics and virtue theory are fundamentally distinct. Their main difference lies in the fact that care ethics makes *relationships,* not *individuals,* morally basic. When care theorists speak of caring, they conceive of it as a moral quality of *relationships;* in that sense, caring *cannot* be an individual character trait or virtue. Nor can this concept of caring be derived from the virtues. Caring is particularly characterized by mutuality—the various interpersonal ties that can only exist within relationships (see §IV). But since virtues comprise individual traits rather than relational properties, they cannot in themselves involve or support the sorts of relational qualities necessary to caring (in the care ethics sense). Although the presence of individual virtues can certainly contribute to caring relationships, it doesn't seem possible for the distinctive moral qualities of caring to derive from virtues alone.

This may become clearer by considering one aspect of mutuality—the quality of trust. It's true that an individual can exhibit the trait of "being trusting" (i.e., being willing to place himself at risk in reliance upon others). Nevertheless, indiscriminate and one-sided trusting is not even a virtue. If anything, it may be more of a vice. Being trusting is an appealing mark of childhood innocence, but it also indicates (for the same reasons) inexperience and immaturity. It can even be dangerous, as when a child is trusting toward a sexual predator or an abusive parent. In adults, it can be a mark of mental simplicity. Since being trusting—in this sense—is not even particularly desirable, it cannot be considered a virtue.[13]

Although indiscriminate trusting is neither virtuous nor wise for *individuals*, the trust of mutuality is necessary to *relationships*. It's indispensable to friendships, marriages, business relationships, and even to stable associations between nations. How should we understand this kind of trust? Since trust is always *trust in* someone, it is essentially relational. It cannot be created by individuals alone but must develop as a shared quality. Trust makes relationships possible; it's also partly a *product* of relationships. As people say, "trust must be earned." Trust can only develop as people interact with each other and grow in all the various aspects of mutuality (e.g., in increasing knowledge and concern for each other). It takes *two* to establish and build trust. Since other aspects of mutuality are no different, it can be seen that care ethics addresses relational components that individual virtues cannot adequately capture.

What about deriving virtues from care theory? Some care theorists take this to be a real possibility. Certain personal character traits—particularly those like compassion and loyalty—are morally desirable characteristics of people in caring relationships and positively contribute to relationships. Although these cannot in themselves create caring relationships, they are necessary to such relationships. In addition, caring relationships establish, nurture, and strengthen these individual traits; for that matter, caring relations may be *necessary* for these to develop. For instance, children first learn compassion by experiencing others acting compassionately toward them and by observing compassion being extended from one person to another. As a virtue, loyalty builds up out of the trust that is shared in relationships.[14] Thus, care ethics may indeed be able to support virtues. Understanding virtues in more relational terms, however, may not be satisfying to virtue theorists who particularly wish to emphasize the *individual* character of personal virtues.

For Discussion

1. *What is the difference between caring as a virtue and as a quality of relationships?*
2. *Why can't "being trusting" qualify as a virtue?*

---

[13]These points about trust are explored by Annette Baier, "Demoralization, Trust, and the Virtues," in *Setting the Moral Compass,* ed. Cheshire Calhoun (New York: Oxford University Press, 2005), 177, and are discussed in Held, *The Ethics of Care,* 57.

[14]One can be one-sidedly loyal to another, but as with "being trusting," this sort of loyalty is not necessary *virtuous.*

3. *Why do people, when they first meet, engage mainly in "small talk"? Discuss this in terms of trust.*

4. *Describe the several "give and take" steps people take as they gradually move from their first meeting into an ongoing and trusting relationship. Or, act out this process by "going through the motions."*

Summary
We can describe individuals as "caring" and "trusting," but this is not how care ethics understands these terms. In care ethics, caring depends upon mutuality and so is essentially relational. So is trust. Thus, neither of these (understood in the care ethics sense) can exist in individuals alone. Both involve important moral qualities that individual virtues (either alone or in combination) cannot adequately capture. Therefore, care ethics probably cannot be derived from virtue ethics, though it might be possible to define virtues in terms of caring relationships.

VI. A BLUEPRINT FOR REFORM

In a society where people clamor for their own rights even as they disregard the rights of others, where corporations seem bent on exploiting workers, and where even our schools are overly institutionalized and dehumanizing, the ethics of care feels like a breath of fresh air. What if daily human encounters began to take on a greater degree of caring? Instead of exploiting their employees, what if corporations showed them respect, caring about their well-being and that of their families? What if children could grow up in overlapping environments of caring?

According to care theorists, this moral vision is one our society urgently needs. In keeping with their feminist roots, care theorists also insist that our society's gender-biased structures must be replaced and that the values and perspectives of care ethics can provide the basis for doing just that. Justice-perspective ethical theories are inadequate; it's time for something different. The ethics of care is thus not just another ethical theory; it's also a call for reform, a deliberate attempt to alter fundamental moral values. It is, as Virginia Held describes it, revolutionary.

Being revolutionary, the care vision can only be completely realized by making fairly drastic changes in our society.[15] As most adults are already too conditioned to alter their ways, however, Noddings urges that the first steps in reform be taken with our children and how we educate them. With young girls, we should foster the inclinations and values of the feminine perspective. At the same time, girls should never be denied the opportunities that society has typically reserved for

---

[15]As feminists, most care theorists agree that society needs change. But not all—and certainly not all feminists—share Noddings's (an educator) vision for reform described here.

boys. The same values of genuine caring must also be developed among boys, even if society views these as "effeminate." More generally, caring should be integrated into every subject across the curriculum. The initial goal of such efforts is not to replace our society's masculine orientation with a feminine one but to bring the two more into balance.

For many feminists, however, the longer-range goal is to create a new moral perspective—to be shared by both men and women—that transcends our present gender conscious perspectives. Although such a transcendent morality might still incorporate elements of care ethics, it will undoubtedly need to supplant even present versions of care ethics. The hope is then that as this **degenderized morality** gradually becomes accepted it will ultimately lead to a completely degenderized society. Many care theorists see their present work in care ethics as comprising the first crucial step toward total social reform.[16]

For Discussion

1. *How could schools—including school schedules, classes, and activities—be redesigned so that both students and teachers would feel cared for?*
2. *Other than those closest to you, what and who else also needs more of your caring?*
3. *Do you agree that caring should be integrated across the curriculum? How could this be done?*
4. *How do you feel about the goal of degenderizing society and morality?*

Summary
Care ethics is undoubtedly right in criticizing our society as being too uncaring. In their vision for changing our institutions and practices, however, many care theorists also hope to change the way we view our identities and gender. The goal of transcending these ways of thinking is to reform and ultimately replace existing society and morality.

Key Terms

- **Degenderized morality**: *a morality that is intended to replace both the present masculine (justice) and present feminine (care) perspectives.*

VII. PROBLEMS

There is much about care ethics that is compelling. Furthermore, it's undeniable that care ethics has already illumined our moral thinking in places where traditional theories have never tread. But it still wrestles with problems like the following.

---

[16]As mentioned in §II, other feminists want to replace the simple two-gender categorization with a multitude of distinct genders. While not creating a degenderized system, this would still offset the biases they feel are preserved by the two-gender categorization.

Nature vs. nurture: This problem is the oldest and relates directly to care ethics as reform. Many care theorists want to see our present understanding of human nature replaced with a degenderized way of thinking. But this raises an important question: are our present genderized perspectives the products of society, or do they reflect the outworking of *innate* differences between men and women?

Suppose that today's genderized perspectives are the results of socialization (effects of **nurture**). Then both the present justice and care perspectives, together with the ethics of care itself, are products of a male-dominated social system and so are tainted by the oppressive values that feminism opposes. Further, as all of us have been deeply influenced by this genderized social system, it's not clear how any of us could achieve sufficient moral clear-sightedness to determine what ought to be preserved or rejected as we transcend these perspectives. How can we be sure that our reforms are aimed in the right direction? The problem is like trying to drive to a definite destination when each person sees the road differently and no one sees the road as it actually is.

Alternately, it may be that these two perspectives result from innately determined differences in the way men and women actually think and feel (effects of **nature**). If so, then our perspectives remain largely inevitable despite socialization, and no attempt to transcend them is likely to succeed. More seriously, attempts to "educate" children into new patterns of thinking might even harm them since such attempts would run contrary to each child's nature, thereby inhibiting or even damaging their development.

How can care theorists respond to this dilemma? Since the existence of innate differences would largely preclude reform, most care theorists take the "nurture" viewpoint and interpret both perspectives as products of a genderized society. It's for this very reason, they would add, that these need to be replaced by a new moral ideal. As for finding the moral clarity needed to guide us, care theorists respond that while genderized perspectives may *currently* cloud our vision, we can at least make a start by correcting those practices that are most clearly unjust and uncaring. Doing so should somewhat improve our moral vision, which can then help us identify the next most needed social changes, and so on. Via this back-and-forth process, we can ultimately achieve a moral ideal beyond what our present social system could otherwise attain.

This response has much to commend it; still, it adheres to the assumption that socialization causes and profoundly distorts our moral perspectives. If this is so, then there's still a chance that even our initial moral "corrections" could turn us *away* from the moral ideal we want. Unfortunately, if we must start out driving blind, we can never be sure that we'll arrive at our destination. Of course, if the assumption of *nurture* is itself mistaken, then we may be heading in the wrong direction already.

Caring and justice: Many early theorists assumed that caring should replace traditional emphases on justice and rights; now, most consider *both* perspectives essential to a complete ethics. This amounts to an admission that, up till now, care ethics has failed to adequately address important aspects of justice. More urgently, care ethics must squarely face the challenge of reconciling the values of caring with considerations of justice, rights, equality, and autonomy.

There are several aspects to the problem. To begin, Gilligan's studies suggest that the justice and care perspectives are mutually exclusive—it's not possible for people to adopt both perspectives at the same time.[17] Since the two can call for different responses to the same moral questions, we have the problem of determining which perspective we should take when considering any particular moral question.

Further, while the justice perspective emphasizes the universality of principles and rights, care ethics explicitly rejects universalism in favor of moral particularism. This makes it hard to see how the particularism of care ethics can be reconciled with the universalism essential to justice. Worse, although care theorists have offered important criticisms of universalism (see §III), particularism has its own problems. For one thing, it's rather vague, leaving us uncertain about how any specific moral problem should be resolved. It also downplays the objective impartiality that universalism champions, which at times can still be of great moral importance. And there's the fact that the particularism of care ethics (especially) makes so much depend on the characteristics of each relationship. This seems to make right and wrong too relative to specific relationships since they can vary from one relationship to another.

Care and justice seem to be pitted against each other practically as well. Feminists who oppose care ethics, for instance, complain that it neglects women's rights and even commends the traditional subservient roles that have subjugated women. Yet care theorists have long argued that the justice perspective is fundamentally contrary to the values and experiences of women.

How, then, can the most important aspects of both justice and care be combined? Care theorists maintain that justice should be based upon caring itself. How could this be done? Very roughly, the idea is that if we are to be caring toward others, we will need justice as well. For instance, Robinson maintains both of the care ethics claims that (a) relationships and caring must remain fundamental and that (b) abstract (universalist) concepts of justice are ineffective and inappropriate in addressing moral problems.[18] But she adds that we must also recognize how much relational caring is affected and even controlled by the larger social structures and systems within which it takes place. If a social system is not just, then caring will be hampered within that system, and relationships will be forced into forms that make the full realization of moral caring impossible. (This point parallels Aristotle's observation that personal virtue cannot thrive except within a larger social context of reasonable laws and virtuous leaders.)

As with any attempt to derive justice from caring, this approach is likely to yield somewhat softened notions of justice and rights compared to how our present justice oriented society employs them. This is nearly inevitable, given the

---

[17]Their exclusivity can be compared with interpreting a gestalt. In the familiar duck/rabbit gestalt, for instance, you can see either a duck or a rabbit but not both at the same time. In another, you can see either a vase or two faces but, again, never both at a same time.

[18]Fiona Robinson. *Globalizing Care: Ethics, Feminist Theory & International Relations* (Cambridge, MA: Perseus Books, 1999).

many tensions and apparent conflicts between caring and justice just considered. This is not to say, however, that justice would somehow become less important than caring. Since both represent core moral values, both would still have to be reflected in all facets of morality. A great deal of work is being done in the ethics of care, as well as in several other areas of feminist ethics, to address the nature of justice as it relates to many of the feminist themes we have previously discussed.

Exploitative relationships: A common reaction to the ethics of caring and a criticism often leveled against it by other feminists is that caring invites the cared-for to take advantage of the carer. Caring can be *enabling* to people who are perfectly happy to receive whatever they can but are never willing to give. We've all run into "sponges" like this—those who just soak up help and kindnesses from others but never reciprocate. In the worst cases, caring relationships may become *codependencies*— one-sided relationships in which those who are cared-for develop a nearly complete reliance upon carers to take care of them and meet their needs.

Care ethicists recognize this to be a very real practical danger, and they offer a fairly persuasive response. First, it's obvious to everyone that there are serious moral and emotional weaknesses in people who are inherently selfish (i.e., the "sponges"). It's also widely recognized that codependency is a dysfunctional emotional and psychological condition.[19] Any relationship in which there's an over-reliance of one person upon the other, therefore, is flawed. As care ethics is all about morally healthy relationships, it directly opposes all enabling behaviors, codependent relationships, and whatever else might promote these things. In one way or another, all versions of care ethics consider the exploitation of caring to be morally wrong and even take it to be part of a carer's moral duty to avoid allowing such relationships to develop or continue as they are. They also view the cared-for as having a moral obligation to not exploit or establish a dependency upon the carer.

The priority of relationships: Care theory is founded on the ideal of a close interpersonal relationship and so identifies relationships as morally basic. This can create difficulties for certain sorts of relationships.

Consider the impersonal relationships we have with fellow citizens in other parts of the country or with people in other parts of the world. None of these comprises an *interpersonal* relationship in the care ethics sense. Nor is there much opportunity for mutual knowledge, for interaction, or for any response to a caring act. Can care ethics extend moral responsibility to such "relationships"? As previously suggested (see the discussion of *closeness* in §IV), we do all share many aspects of the human condition, especially as members of the shrinking global community. Perhaps these commonalities provide some basis for caring even with such distant

---

[19]Originally noted in addicts, codependency is now seen as a more general problem, especially in family relationships, that can be handed down from one generation to the next. See "Co-Dependency," Mental Health America, accessed August 28, 2016, http://www.mentalhealthamerica. net/co-dependency.

and asymmetrical relationships. To better close the gap, we might also *imagine* the response of someone affected by our caring act (e.g., a charitable donation). A danger with this, however, is that a carer's imaginings might be so unrealistic as to lead her to act *against* the actual needs of the cared-for. Unfortunate illustrations of this abound in the useless or even harmful effects that are sometimes caused when well-meaning people act in ways they think will "help" others. At best, imagination may be a poor substitute for the accurate knowledge that effective caring requires.

Next, can we have moral obligations toward future generations? Since future people don't yet *exist,* it's not *possible* for us to have any sort of interpersonal relationship with them. It's hard to see, then, how care ethics could support our having any moral responsibilities to look out for future generations, although we often talk and think of ourselves having such responsibilities.

We also need to make sense of moral obligations towards *ourselves.* Surely there *are* such obligations (e.g., to maintain our own physical and emotional health, to develop our abilities, and to become morally better persons). But as moral obligations can only arise within relationships for care ethics, this seems to require that we each somehow establish a relationship with ourselves. This is psychologically awkward! One alternative might be to base my obligations of self-care upon obligations I have toward others. Thus, suppose that another person cares a great deal about me; this could then give me a duty *toward that person* to take good care of myself. This duty would not be for *my* sake, but for *theirs,* which is strange and which still cannot explain any duties of self-care I might have separate from others. There is clearly some work remaining in care ethics to make sense of the full range of moral obligations.

For Discussion

1. *Do you think that gender is the product of nurture or nature? Why?*
2. *If gender is largely determined innately, how could attempts to reeducate children harm them?*
3. *If gender is largely determined by nurture (socialization), how compelling is the argument that we can't be sure we are heading in right directions?*
4. *Have you ever had someone take advantage of you or of your caring for them? How can this be avoided?*
5. *Do you think that we have moral responsibilities toward ourselves or toward future people? Why or why not?*
6. *Could caring for future generations be supported by the moral duty to care for people of our present generation, and then, since their children matter to them, also for their children, and so on?*

Summary

There are several problems for the ethics of care. First, the nature/nurture distinc-tion raises concerns over the possibility of our ensuring that a reform of genderized ethics heads in the right direction. There is also the prior question of whether reform

is even possible if gender differences are innate rather than socialized. Second, prob-
ably the most important challenge has to do with reconciling caring and justice. Third,
many have also worried that caring invites and encourages exploitative relationships,
though care ethics seems to address this. Finally, care ethics is based upon relation-
ships, which creates difficulties for caring responsibilities to be extended to distant
people, future generations, and even ourselves.

Key Terms
- **Nurture**: *gives rise to those beliefs, personal traits, and so on, that are the pli-*
  able products of one's environment, particularly of social norms.

- **Nature**: *gives rise to those beliefs, personal traits, and so on that are innate and*
  so belong to one's unchangeable being, regardless of outside influences.

VIII. A CONCLUDING REFLECTION

The ethics of care highlights important moral values largely neglected by traditional ethics. Yet in attending almost exclusively to the care perspective, early care
theorists didn't adequately accommodate the equally important implications of
justice and rights. Recognizing this, contemporary care theorists are now attempting to reconcile both justice and caring within a single ethical theory. While the
challenge appears immense, a great deal of work is being done on this problem. It
will be interesting to see what this reconciliation looks like when it is completed.

Meanwhile, it's worth pointing out that achieving this reconciliation is not
only a challenge for care theorists. If caring relationships are as morally central
as care theorists maintain, then *no one* can avoid the conclusion that both justice
and care comprise essential components of morality. *Any* ethical theory will have
to work at reconciling them. The challenge therefore extends to all of ethics and
not just to care ethics. In offering us this realization, care ethics may have already
rendered its greatest service to ethics.

For Discussion
1. *Do you agree that moral caring must be part of any complete ethical theory?*
2. *It would probably be easiest to add caring to act or rule moral utilitarianism. How
   would you do that?*
3. *Adding caring to Ross's theory seems to require just a single step. But Ross's theory
   is universalist. Is that a problem?*
4. *Is it even possible to add caring to Kantian ethics? Would it help to first change Kantian
   autonomy into relational autonomy (see this chapter, §III and Chapter Three, §VI)?*

Chapter Assignment Questions
1. *Explain the justice and care perspectives. Can you offer examples of each?*
2. *What makes the justice and care perspectives masculine and feminine,
   respectively?*
3. *Explain why care ethics rejects universalism in favor of particularism.*

4. *What should be the role of emotion in our moral thinking and decision-making?*

5. *Individualism leads us to picture ourselves in certain ways. How realistic are those pictures?*

6. *Could you have developed your present autonomy without the many relationships that have affected your life?*

7. *In what ways have relationships shaped your personal identity?*

8. *Explain mutuality.*

9. *Why can't caring be taught through rules or motivated by rewards or punishments?*

10. ** *What are some similarities between virtue and care ethics? What is the crucial difference between these?*

11. ** *Many virtue theorists think care ethics is simply a variant of virtue theory. Do you think that care ethics could be developed from virtue theory? How?*

12. *Can you think of any way for care ethics to handle your moral obligations to yourself?*

Additional Resources

Gilligan, Carol. *In a Different Voice: Psychological Theory and Women's Development.* Cambridge, MA: Harvard University Press, 1982. This is an influential report of Gilligan's psychological research that helped stimulate the development of care ethics.

Gilligan, Carol. *Women and Moral Theory,* edited by Eva F. Kittay and Diana T. Meyers. Lanham, MD: Rowman and Littlefield Publishers, 1987. This is a more recent presentation of Gilligan's views.

Held, Virginia. *The Ethics of Care, Personal, Political, and Global.* New York: Oxford University Press, 2007. Provides a readable general review of care theory up to the present, while also presenting Held's own account of care ethics.

Noddings, Nel. *Caring: A Feminine Approach to Ethics and Moral Education.* 2d ed. Berkeley: University of California Press, 2003. This book presents Noddings's most developed care theory.

Tong, Rosemarie and Williams, Nancy. "Feminist Ethics". In *The Stanford Encyclopedia of Philosophy* (Winter 2016 Edition). Edited by Edward N. Zalta. Accessed March 23, 2016. <https://plato.stanford.edu/archives/win2016/entries/feminism-ethics/>.

Case 1

The International Gemstone Trade

Emily is excited to start her new job. She just finished her degree from the Gemological Institute of America (GIA) and is going to work for a New York gem dealer who specializes in goods from Africa. After her initial training, Emily will join the company president on some gem sourcing trips to Tanzania, something she has always dreamed about doing. She's also excited to work for a company that purchases gems from small miners in tiny African villages. These are hard-working poor people who live in very poor conditions, and she hopes to get to know some of them. Since Tanzania is one of the main gemstone suppliers to the United States, she's particularly pleased that some of the profit goes back to people who need it

Continued

Case 1 (Continued)

more than her. Having a strong sense of justice, Emily doesn't particularly like the idea of U.S. companies taking most of the profits.

A few weeks into her job, Emily is a bit disappointed to learn that the trips to Tanzania are only made once or twice a year. And, her boss Mukkesh explains, they don't actually visit the regions where gemstones are mined. Rather, they purchase their gems in the large city of Arusha where the main gem dealers reside. These dealers, in turn, pay the miners through brokers. The miners themselves never leave their villages in the bush, Mukkesh says. In fact, he's never met a miner himself, despite his many trips to Africa. Nor has he ever visited a mine.

What she next learns is even more disappointing. It turns out that the gem dealers take a cut of the profits, and so do the Tanzanian brokers. The return to the miners themselves is thus far less than Emily expected. When she expresses her dissatisfaction about this, Mukkesh responds: "Look, it's not like we're treating anybody badly. Like a lot of other businesses, we don't have much contact with the people we deal with. I'm glad that the miners get paid fairly—we pay them the same everyone else does. But I don't meet with these people. I don't know much about how they live or even where the live, exactly. Their problems aren't my concerns; after all, we're not some sort of family."

"I get it," Emily says; "but I'm still not very happy about it."

THOUGHT QUESTIONS

1. In this and other businesses, do you share Emily's concerns for the people who work "at the bottom of the food chain"? Or, like Mukkesh, do you feel that business is just business, and shouldn't become a personal matter? What are your reasons?

2. What values drive Emily's viewpoint and her reaction to what she learns about the workers?

3. Given the essentials of caring, do you think it possible for Mukkesh to pursue a more caring relationship with the miners? What are some of the barriers to doing this?

4. Why can't a business relationship be more like "family?" What could serve as a basis for mutuality between Emily or Mukkesh and African miners?

5. Who is taking a justice perspective, and who is taking a care perspective? Is one perspective better or more appropriate to the situation than the other? Which is harder to put into practice?

Case 2

Parent Responsibility Toward Their In Utero Child

The number of newborns affected by the drug abuse of their pregnant mother is on the increase. About 5% of newborns are exposed to drugs prenatally. As a result, many of these babies end up in intensive care, and often they are brain damaged. It's also estimated that nearly 15% of women consume alcohol while

Continued

Case 2 (Continued)

pregnant.[20] Some of the effects of fetal alcohol syndrome are permanent, including retardation and facial malformations. Studies suggest that even just three or four drinks a week can harm the fetus. Various attempts have been made to prosecute such cases. For instance:

1. *The case of Pamela Rae Monson* (1985, California): Twenty-seven-year-old Pamela Rae Monson, a married mother of two, was pregnant. Toward the end of her pregnancy, she experienced some vaginal bleeding and went to see a doctor. The doctor diagnosed her as having placenta previa and advised her to stay home and immediately see a doctor if it happened again. She was also told not to have sexual intercourse and not to take any amphetamines. Monson ignored all these instructions: she began to bleed again but didn't seek medical treatment. She took amphetamines that she had obtained illegally and had sex with her husband. Later on the same day she started to have contractions. This finally prompted her to go to a hospital, where she gave birth to a child with massive brain damage. The boy lived for only six weeks. Although the police wanted Monson prosecuted for homicide, the district attorney only charged her with not providing her child with medical attendance. In court, even this charge was thrown out—the judge argued that an unborn child is not a person and so does not fall under the scope of the child abuse law.[21]

2. *The case of Tiffany Michelle Hitson* (2006, Alabama): Tiffany was arrested the day after delivering her baby because she and her baby tested positive for cocaine. She pled guilty to child endangerment and was sentenced to one year in prison as well as rehab. Two years later, both Hitson and her child were fine. While Hitson admitted that her taking cocaine was the biggest mistake of her life, she said that what she really needed was the rehabilitation, not prison. She regrets missing the first year of her child's life. The Alabama district attorney maintained that prison sentences are necessary to prevent pregnant women from using drugs. Arguably, however, the fear of prosecution might instead push a woman to get an abortion or avoid all prenatal care.

In recent years, many U.S. states have amended their laws to allow for the prosecution of pregnant women who abuse alcohol or illegal drugs. Punishments include jail time, forced confinement, and termination of parental rights. However, no U.S. court has upheld a murder conviction against a pregnant woman. Punishments largely consist of short or suspended sentences and community service.

THOUGHT QUESTIONS

1. Explain the reasoning behind the first court ruling. What is the difference between the moral and the legal? Is there any legal or moral basis for the judge's claim that a child near birth is not a person?

---

[20]Marvin Wang, "Perinatal Drug Abuse and Neonatal Drug Withdrawal," EMedicine Medscape, accessed August 28, 2016, http://emedicine.medscape.com/article/978492-overview.

[21]The case of Pamela Rae Monson was obtained from the book by Ronald Munson, ed. *Intervention and Reflection: Basic Issues in Medical Ethics* (Belmont, CA: Wadsworth, 2000).

2. Suppose that a pregnant mother *does* have certain moral responsibilities toward her unborn child. Would such responsibilities simply be negative—to not harm the fetus—or should the mother also take positive steps to ensure the child's well-being? Does the father have any rights or responsibilities in these matters?

3. Can a woman have a caring relationship with her unborn child? How, and what implications would this possibility have for care ethics?

4. What moral obligations do you think a pregnant woman has to protect her unborn child? How might a care ethicist answer this?

5. Do you think that a fetus should be protected by law and, if so, how? If yes, should the fetus's development be considered by such laws?

Case 3

The Nestlé Boycott

According to reports by the World Health Organization (WHO) and UNICEF, "about *1.5 million babies die every year because they were not breastfed.*"[22] Breast-feeding can be essential to the survival of babies because infant formula should not be used in countries where the water is unsafe to drink. But why would women opt out of breastfeeding when they can't use the local water to prepare infant formula? The Infant Feeding Action Coalition Canada (INFACT Canada) answers that this is at least partly due to the aggressive way breast milk substitutes have been marketed. Notoriously, Nestlé provided infant formula samples to healthcare workers around the world (not to mention calendars, pens, and other marketing gifts). The infant formula was intended for distribution to new mothers, including those living in areas where the water was not safe (e.g., Bangladesh, Brazil, Mexico, Zimbabwe, Chile, Columbia, etc.). If a mother starts using formula and never starts breastfeeding her newborn, then she will stop producing her own milk. Once this happens, the mother is forced to use the formula, which also means she must begin purchasing formula for her baby. Since many poorer mothers can't afford to buy either the formula or safe water, they may both dilute the formula and keep mixing it with unsafe water, which can cause malnutrition, illness, and often death.

INFACT, which was established in the 1970s when these marketing practices first became public, called for a boycott against Nestlé. Since the company has not changed its practices very much (it does now educate mothers on the proper use of breast milk substitutes), the boycott continues to this day.

Nestlé continues to give out free samples in developing countries. In doing so, Nestlé violates WHO guidelines, which among other things, "prohibit the promotion of infant formula to the public . . . [and] through health care systems." The WHO guidelines also call for "proper labels on all products describing the benefits of breastfeeding and the dangers of bottle-feeding."[23]

---

[22]All the facts for this case were obtained from "Boycott Nestle," INFACT Canada, accessed August 28, 2016, http://www.infactcanada.ca/Nestle_Boycott.htm.
[23]Ibid.

THOUGHT QUESTIONS

1. Imagine you are a nurse working in a hospital in a developing country. Your job includes advising new mothers, training them to breastfeed, and teaching them how to care for their baby. Your doctor suggests you give out the free samples of infant formula that a company has "donated" to the hospital. From an ethics of care perspective, what should you do and why?
2. Does the care ethics answer to the previous question differ from, say, a Kantian or act utilitarianism answer?
3. You are a recent college graduate and have invested in the stock market. You own a fair amount of Nestlé stock, which is doing quite well, but have just learned about Nestlé's formula marketing practices. Should you sell the stock or hold it and complain to the company about its practices? What would care ethics say you should do?
4. Do you believe that Nestlé has a moral obligation to comply with the WHO guidelines? How would care ethics answer this? Would a Kantian or a rule utilitarian give a different answer? How would they reason?

Case 4

Absolute Poverty

According to Princeton philosopher Peter Singer, the term "absolute poverty" was coined by Robert McNamara when he was president of the World Bank.[24] Absolute poverty is "the lack of sufficient income in cash or kind to meet the most basic biological needs for food, clothing, and shelter."[25] Those in absolute poverty suffer from malnutrition and disease and have no access to healthcare or education. It's not an overstatement to say that absolute poverty is the main cause of suffering today since up to 20% of the world's population experiences it. In contrast, most people living in the United States enjoy what Singer calls "absolute affluence." Not only do we have enough to eat, a place to live, and basic healthcare, we even spend money on clothes, food, and other items purely out of preference. Such wealth is unimaginable for billions of the world's population.

Singer argues that those who are relatively well off have a moral obligation to help those in absolute poverty. He argues that refusing to help these people is as immoral as not saving a child drowning in a nearby pond because you don't want to ruin your clothes. He offers a simple and powerful argument in support of this:

> *First premise*:　If we can prevent something bad without sacrificing anything of comparable significance, we ought to do it.
> *Second premise*: Absolute poverty is bad.
> *Third premise*:　There is some absolute poverty we can prevent without sacrificing anything of comparable moral significance.
> *Conclusion*:　　We ought to prevent some absolute poverty.[26]

Continued

---

[24]Peter Singer, *Practical Ethics* (Cambridge, MA: Cambridge University Press, 1993), 218.
[25]Ibid., 220.
[26]Ibid., 230, 231.

Case 4 (Continued)

Although he's a utilitarian, Singer believes that this argument can be endorsed by any moral theory. It seems obvious to him that those in absolute poverty need more help than anyone else in the world (including even the poor in the United States). To those who say our own poor should take first priority, he replies that we should not discriminate against people on the basis of where they've had the bad luck of being born. Also, Singer argues that we don't sufficiently meet our personal moral obligations in these matters by simply leaving them to the government (although he does maintain that governments, too, have an obligation to assist). Lastly, Singer claims that nearly everyone living in the United States is in the financial position to help at least in some way.[27]

Is it true that *any* moral theory supports Singer's position? What would a care ethicist say? Certainly, the relationships we have with people in absolute poverty are very indirect and distant since we have no personal interaction with the cared-for. The way we engage with the Third World needy when we give them money is clearly not the way we engage in ordinary caring relationships. Some care ethicists have even maintained that since a caring relationship between us and those in absolute poverty is not possible, we have no moral obligation to help them at all.

THOUGHT QUESTIONS

1. Does a maxim against our helping those in absolute poverty create inconsistency when universalized in accordance with Kant's principle of universal law? Compare the Kantian analysis with Singer's argument. What similarities or differences are there?
2. What utilitarian elements do you see in Singer's argument to assist? Can you think of any objections to Singer's argument?
3. Do you agree that it's discriminatory not to help those born in poorer countries? What do you think of his argument that individuals have an obligation to assist over and above what the government can do to help?
4. Can *you* have a caring relationship with someone in absolute poverty? Discuss this by considering the elements of closeness and mutuality that a caring relationship involves.
5. It seems extraordinary that some care ethicists have asserted that we have no obligation to care for people suffering horribly in other parts of the world. How much of a problem does this pose for care ethics, particularly as the theory has developed? (Noddings has since deserted her earlier position on this.)

---

[27]Ibid., 232–246.

CHAPTER THIRTEEN

Ethics and Religion

I. INTRODUCTION

About 380 BCE, the Greek philosopher, Plato, wrote a philosophical dialogue that portrayed Socrates (Plato's teacher) conversing with a conceited religious "expert" named Euthyphro. Socrates, who would soon be executed partly because of his religious beliefs, had lived a life that could well be described as a deeply pious and exemplary moral life. Euthyphro tells Socrates that he is taking his own father to court, an act that most Greeks considered extremely impious. Because Euthyphro nevertheless believes this act to be morally justified, Socrates asks Euthyphro what a pious or morally justified act amounts to.

In the following excerpt, Euthyphro has just defined a pious act as an act that the gods all love and approve. But this is ambiguous. Here, Socrates hones in on the problem by stating the two different ways Euthyphro's definition might be taken.[1]

> **Soc.** ... The point which I should first wish to understand is whether the pious or holy is beloved by the gods because it is holy, or holy because it is beloved of the gods.
> **Euth.** I do not understand your meaning, Socrates.
> **Soc.** ... is not that which is beloved distinct from that which loves?
> **Euth.** Certainly.
> **Soc.** ... And what do you say of piety, Euthyphro: is not piety, according to your definition, loved by all the gods?
> **Euth.** Yes.
> **Soc.** Because it is pious or holy, or for some other reason?
> **Euth.** No, that is the reason.
> **Soc.** It is loved because it is holy, not holy because it is loved?
> **Euth.** Yes.

---

[1]Plato, *Euthyphro,* trans. Benjamin Jowett, Internet Classics Archive, accessed August 28, 2016, http://classics.mit.edu/Plato/euthyfro.html.

Euthyphro's view is that the gods love or approve pious acts precisely because those acts *are* morally right. That is, something isn't made right by the gods approving it; rather, the gods are moved to approve something because it *is* right. Thus, the moral standard is something that exists *autonomously;* it stands on its own, independent of any deity. The moral standard would still exist even if there were no deity. Of course, this leaves open the question of where the moral standard comes from, but that's not something Socrates and Euthyphro pursue.

In contrast to Euthyphro's **autonomy thesis**, many religious thinkers have instead thought that God, being the infinitely perfect creator of all things, must be the source of the moral standard. This view maintains that morality originates entirely in God and depends upon God—the **dependency thesis**. There could be no moral standard if there were no deity.

Given the dependency thesis, there are two important views on just *how* morality depends upon God. According to natural law theory (see Chapter Nine), morality arises out of the goals toward which things aim. For instance, since the human body strives to maintain life, this makes human life a good that we have a moral duty to preserve. Likewise, humans desire love and relationships with each other, which implies that society and friendship are goods and ought to be promoted. If we then follow Aquinas by adding that a good God purposely designed all of creation with these natural goods embedded within it, then these goods along with their moral implications (i.e., all of morality) *ultimately* originate in God. This makes the moral standard *indirectly dependent* upon God as its source.

The main alternative to this is traditional **divine command theory.** This view maintains that morally right acts are made right by God commanding or willing us to do them. The moral standard thus originates *directly* with God. For instance, the Ten Commandments include the following: "You shall not murder. You shall not commit adultery. You shall not steal."[2] According to divine command theory, murder, adultery, and stealing are therefore wrong since they violate God's will.

The following diagram summarizes the options just described:

The moral standard

/ \

Autonomy thesis   *Dependency thesis*
(Morality is independent of God)   *(Morality depends upon God)*

/ \

Natural law theory   *Divine command theory*
(Morality depends indirectly   *(Morality depends* directly
on God the creator)   *on what God wills)*

---

[2]The story of Moses meeting with God on Mount Sinai appears in the Bible in Exodus 19–20; these specific commands appear in Exodus 20:13–15. Bible quotations are from the New American Standard Bible, updated 1995, The Lockman Foundation.

For Discussion

1. *What do you think is the relationship between many people's moral beliefs and religion?*
2. *Given your present perspective (regardless of whether you believe God exists), which seems more likely: the autonomy or dependency thesis? Why?*
3. *Again, regardless of your present beliefs, would you prefer a natural law or divine command version of the dependency thesis? Why?*

Summary

There are two possible views about the origins of morality: (a) that morality depends upon God or (b) that morality is autonomous—independent of God. Among the dependency views, there are two further alternatives. Aquinas's natural law theory maintains that morality indirectly depends on God, because God is the ultimate source of all those natural goods that make up the immediate basis of morality. The alternative—divine command theory—maintains that morality depends directly upon God, whose will determines what is morally right.

Key Terms

- **Autonomy thesis**: *the moral standard is something that exists autonomously—on its own, independent of any deity.*
- **Dependency thesis**: *morality originates in God and so depends upon God for its existence.*
- **Divine command theory**: *a traditional dependency theory that maintains that morally right acts are those that God commands or wills.*

II.** KANT ON AUTONOMY AND RELIGION

Of those advocating the autonomy thesis, Kant provides one of the most carefully developed accounts. According to Kant, morality depends on reason and so stands by itself. It depends on no other authority, not even God. Like Euthyphro, therefore, Kant would say that God loves or approves pious acts precisely because those acts *are* morally right—the autonomy thesis.

For Kant, the **Principle of autonomy** is simply another version of his categorical imperative, equivalent to the other versions (see Chapter Eight, §IV–§VI). Specifically, because reason exists in persons and because reason (in persons) is what "makes" the universal moral law, it follows that the moral law is "made" for each person by their reason. Since God is a person, the moral law is "given" to God, then, just as it is for the rest of us. Because it resides in every person, it cannot be imposed by any outside authority: not by government, by church, by religion—not even by God. Rather, God is bound by the same moral law that we are.

Given Kant's rejection of the dependency thesis, you might expect him to see little relation between morality and religion. However, Kant thinks that there's a very close relationship between the two. For one thing, God's knowledge and understanding far exceeds ours. God must thereby arrive at a deeper and more accurate understanding of morality than we ever could. Since God is perfectly good, furthermore, God could never violate any moral principle nor could God command another to do so. Thus, true religion and true morality can never conflict.

In fact, Kant thinks that morals argue in favor of certain important religious claims. Kant's thinking on this begins with a problem he sees in ethics: although the moral law is rationally necessary, are its demands *realistic* or *fair?* After all, no matter how hard we try, none of us is able in this life to satisfy the entire moral law. Why then should we struggle to do what we can't do anyway? And how could our having to struggle with such an impossible task ever be fair? Worse, what if the universe were neither good nor fair: what if it ultimately allowed wrongs to stand, justice to be left undone, and right acts to never achieve any good? Kant knew as well as anyone that doing right isn't always to our advantage; sometimes we'd be better off by lying, cheating, or stealing. If neither morality nor immorality makes any difference in the ultimate scheme of things, what reason can there be to do the right thing?

Kant answers that we can lay these worries aside; since the demands of the moral law *must* be realistic, we can be sure of two things. First, death cannot be the end of our existence; as persons we must be immortal, continuing forever. Why? Because, the only way we can attain moral perfection is to have an infinite series of opportunities to achieve it. Being immortal, no moral effort we make in our present lives is wasted, for we can continue to build upon those efforts even after death. There must be immortality, then, for any efforts we make now to achieve moral goodness would otherwise be pointless.

Furthermore, the demands of ethics are only just if good can ultimately prevail. Thus, there must exist a good and just God who will repay all that is right and redress all wrongs. Despite any present appearances, there can be no ultimate divergence between the universe and its moral law. No matter how much evil and wrong may triumph at the moment, God's universe will prove otherwise. Since the moral law will be satisfied in full, its demands are therefore both realistic and fair.

Kant's theory is not the only one to imply that morality stands autonomously from God. In fact, the autonomy thesis has dominated ethics for the past several centuries. For instance, it was a desire to break loose from both civil and religious authority that motivated act utilitarianism. Today's versions of both act and rule utilitarianism likewise attempt to establish their autonomy by appealing to empirical experience as the sole means for determining what is morally right. Contemporary virtue theory likewise appeals to individual character and concepts like human flourishing, while care ethics is based upon the dynamics of human relationships.

Despite the predominance of *secular* (nonreligious) ethical theories, it remains hard to separate religion from morality in the minds of most people. Many people's moral convictions are first formed by religious instruction. Even those with no religious training still internalize the moral values of their culture—and no culture exists today that has not been deeply influenced by some religious tradition. Religious beliefs also give many their primary motivation for acting morally, whether that be a desire to please God, to avoid punishment, to accumulate "good" karma, or whatever. In fact, many worry that our ongoing drift away from religion is fueling an increasing moral indifference already evidenced within our society.

Finally, it's worth commenting that, whatever the relation between God and morality, a great deal of both good and evil has been perpetrated throughout human history in the name of religion. Just as the Crusaders were once encouraged by religious leaders in their march to war, some religious leaders today encourage people to blow themselves up (along with as many others as can be managed) for the sake of gaining God's favor. On the other side, religious belief bears tremendous fruit in the United States in the form of charitable giving. In one study, giving by individuals with religious commitments was shown to be more than three times, on average, what those who practice no religion gave.[3] If religion can have such an overwhelming effect upon the moral or immoral activities of real people, could the autonomy thesis be harmful to the moral good of society?

For Discussion

1. *If the universe were completely amoral (not immoral), do you agree with Kant that morality would be unreasonably and unfairly burdensome? Why?*
2. *How compelling is Kant's argument from ethics to an afterlife?*
3. *How compelling is Kant's argument from ethics to God's existence?*
4. *Morality is rather strange; for example, it has no physical basis and it overrides other normative realms. Does any of this argue for God's existence?*
5. *To what degree do your religious (or non-religious) beliefs affect how you act and charitably give and/or volunteer?*

Summary
Kant's third version of the categorical imperative is not exactly a practical guide to determining what is right or wrong. Instead, it emphasizes that each person—as a rational being—"makes" the moral law for herself. Thus, morality is autonomous: it arises purely from reason itself and so is not something made or given to us by anything outside of ourselves. Despite his rejection of the dependency thesis, nevertheless Kant thinks that true morality and true religion must completely agree with each other. Kant also sees morality as the basis for inferring both that we have an immortal existence and that there is a just God who will ensure that good prevails in the end.

---

[3]According to Arthur C. Brooks, associate professor of public administration at the Maxwell School of Citizenship and Public Affairs, Syracuse University, "The average annual giving among the religious is $2,210, whereas it is $642 among the secular. Similarly, religious people volunteer an average of 12 times per year, while secular people volunteer an average of 5.8 times." Brooks defines "the religious" as those who participate in services once a week or more. Arthur C. Brooks, "Religious Faith and Charitable Giving," *Policy Review* 121 (October–November 2003).

Key Terms

- **Principle of autonomy**: *the third version of Kant's categorical imperative, this principle states that every person is equally a creator of the universal moral law—that is, that each person makes the moral law for herself.*

III. DIVINE COMMAND THEORY

It is widely held that God is good. If God is good, then God must not only always *do* good but must also always *intend* or *will* good. But, to restate Socrates's question to Euthyphro, is what God wills and approves right because God already agrees with some autonomous moral standard, or is something made right because God wills and approves it? Does the moral standard exist independently of God (the autonomy thesis), or does it depend—directly—upon God (divine command theory)?

There are problems with either answer. If we accept the autonomy thesis, then there exists a moral standard independent of God. While God no doubt perfectly fulfills that standard—and so deserves our praise and admiration—this nevertheless places God *under* that standard. That is, there is a standard, independent of God, which sits in judgment, so to speak, over God. But as a judge exercises authority over the one who is judged, this implies that the autonomous standard somehow has authority over God and so is greater than God. This makes God something less than the greatest possible being—something less than what God is usually conceived to be. The autonomy thesis thus conflicts with a widespread concept of God.

If we instead accept traditional divine command theory—that whatever God wills is, by definition, morally right—then we have other problems. First, this empties the claim that God is good of any real significance. Given divine command theory, whatever God does or wills simply *has to be* right because whatever God does or wills is *defined* as right. Similarly, we can say that whatever Congress enacts (and the Supreme Court upholds) is *legal*—although again, this tells us nothing about the quality of Congress or its laws. Yet when people ascribe goodness to God, they usually intend to say something more significant; they mean that God is good in ways that *we* understand to be good.

More seriously, divine command theory seems to allow *anything* to qualify as morally okay. Suppose that God wills what seems to us to be some terribly immoral thing, for instance, the torturing of innocent persons. Then torturing innocents would be right since God wills it. *Anything* could thus be made right just as long as God wills or commands it. But since we *know* that certain things can't be morally right, this alternative seems unacceptable.[4]

---

[4]Some would reply that God's goodness would preclude his willing anything evil. But this isn't a possible argument assuming divine command theory, which defines the good as what God wills.

So we have a dilemma: the autonomy thesis reflects an inadequate concept of God,[5] while divine command theory, among other problems, seems to grant the possibility of *anything* counting as morally okay. Is there an account that can both preserve a strong concept of God and still draw a line against any evil being okay? The next section considers a possible answer.

For Discussion

1. *Whether or not you believe God exists, what is your concept of God—that of the greatest possible being or of something less? If less, how much less?*
2. *What are some other things implied by the greatest being concept of God?*
3. *Given the dilemma posed by the autonomy thesis and divine command theory, have you changed your view from what you held after just section 1?*

Summary

Euthyphro's alternatives present a dilemma. By the autonomy thesis, God falls under a moral standard that does not originate with God, making God less than all God conceivably could be. Alternately, divine command theory trivializes God's goodness and seems to allow for even the most terrible evils to count as morally okay.

IV. AN ALTERNATE DEPENDENCY ACCOUNT

Assume that a superlative God—the greatest being possible—exists. Then, arguably, God must set the moral standard, because God cannot be under any independent standard. Furthermore, since God must be the origin and sustainer of *all* things, nothing can exist independently of God. Again then, God must be the ultimate origin for the moral standard. Traditional divine command theory takes whatever God wills or commands to thereby be good by definition. The present account changes this to the following:

1. *The moral standard of good consists of all that fully conforms to God's essential nature or character.* Anything that *conflicts* with God's nature is evil. Whatever is *neutral* with respect to God's nature—which neither conforms nor conflicts with God's nature—is morally permissible.

To understand this, we can find help in the notion of virtue. Consider a person of impeccably virtuous character—Socrates, say. Socrates sought to understand and live by the truth at any cost. As the virtue theorist would say, virtues like truth-seeking, sincerity, and honesty were parts of Socrates's very nature. One day, Socrates meets Euthyphro, who claims to fully understand what righteous living (piety) amounts to. Inevitably, then, Socrates asks Euthyphro to talk to him

---

[5]This concept is inadequate even for those atheists who start with the "greatest being" concept of God and then argue that such a perfectly good God cannot exist.

about piety, for this is clearly in keeping with Socrates's nature as a seeker of truth. It would be nearly impossible for Socrates to pass up such an opportunity to investigate Euthyphro's claim. Suppose, next, that Socrates is hungry. Passing some vendors selling foods, he can either buy some bread or some grapes. Here, he may choose either, for neither choice is called for by Socrates's essential nature and neither conflict with it. Finally, imagine that while Socrates buys his lunch, the vendor forgets how much Socrates paid him and whether it was ten denariis or just one. It would be totally "out of character" for Socrates to lie in his reply to the vendor.

We now consider a second claim:

2. *God never wills or acts in ways that conflict with his essential nature.* Thus, God always acts and wills in a way that is consistent with the moral standard.

God is not schizophrenic; furthermore, God is not disingenuous. Although you and I may try to conform to what we think are our essential natures, we sometimes fail. God, being the greatest being possible, would never act against his nature. Doing so would be inconsistent, and the greatest being possible must remain wholly consistent. Furthermore, God could not even *will* or *desire* anything that conflicts with his nature. Statement 2 thus claims that all of God's acts and intentions (God's will) must be consistent with his nature, which in turn precludes any of God's acts or intentions from being evil.

Another widely held claim is that God must be *unchanging*. In fact, Plato provided an argument for this. He reasoned that, if God is perfect, then any change in God could only be a change from perfection to something less. Since a perfect being cannot be less than perfect, God, who is perfect, cannot be changed by anything. This has often been taken to say that God cannot even be *influenced* by anything (thus, God could not even be influenced by prayer), but this may be unnecessarily strong. So let's consider a somewhat weaker claim:

3. *God's essential nature cannot change.*

Although God is free to act as he chooses, God's character—and thus the moral standard (given Statement 1)—cannot change. Taken together, these three statements present the following picture. First, Statement 1 makes the account a version of the dependency thesis. It does this by making the moral standard depend on God's essential nature. It thus preserves the fundamental intuition behind divine command theory—the familiar concept of God as being under no other authority. Statement 2 then says that anything that God wills or does must be consistent with his character. Because God's character is the basis of the moral standard, this guarantees that everything God wills or does must be either right or morally neutral. This keeps God's goodness from being a mere triviality, for it can now be intelligibly said that God, in both will and action, *does* measure up to the moral standard (i.e., the standard that has its origin in God's nature). By distinguishing what God wills from the basis of the moral standard, Statements 1 and 2 also remove some of the arbitrariness from divine command theory, which implied that *anything* could count as right. This arbitrariness is further reduced by Statement 3, which ensures that since God's nature is unchanging, the moral standard must remain unchanging. If torturing innocents were *ever* to qualify as morally evil, then it would *always* have to be morally evil (e.g., it can't suddenly become okay because God changes his mind). In these ways, the alternate dependency account appears to sidestep the main objections against both the autonomy thesis and traditional divine command theory.

But doesn't this alternate account merely put off the main objection to divine command theory? Granted, there's no longer the worry that God might will something against the standard of good, for God cannot go against his nature and that nature defines good. But how do we know that some terrible evil couldn't turn out to conform to God's nature? Or putting this more simply, how can we know that God *is* good? Suppose you conclude that God is good by comparing what you think about God with what you understand about goodness. To do this, don't you have to appeal to a standard that stands independently from God? And wouldn't that conflict with the idea that the moral standard originates in God? Alternately, suppose you conclude that God is good by appealing to a standard that depends directly on God. Then isn't your determination that God is good circular and thus empty? To address these sorts of worries, the account adds one more claim:

4. *The means by which we initially form our knowledge of the moral standard need not appeal directly to either God or religion.*

What we need to keep clear is this: even if the moral standard depends directly upon God, it doesn't follow that we can only learn about morality directly from God. Certainly, God *could* be a source for our moral knowledge. We might gain moral knowledge directly from God by revelation (e.g., the Ten Commandments) or by, for instance, a conscience through which God speaks to us. But we might also gain moral knowledge through reason (Kant's theory), by discovering what is most fulfilling to us (natural law or virtue theory), or through observing what promotes well-being (utilitarianism). Maybe *all* of these contribute to our moral knowledge. Since this knowledge is so important, it would certainly not be surprising for a good God to provide multiple means for us to obtain moral knowledge.

Once again (see Part II Introduction), *how* we obtain moral knowledge has little or nothing to do with what *makes* something good or right. Thus, the alternate account could be true without our needing to appeal directly to either God or religion to gain moral knowledge. Similarly, a parent's discovering that her child is ill (by observing symptoms) need have no particularly immediate connection to what is actually *causing* that illness—even though the symptoms ultimately do depend on that virus.

Armed with even an independently acquired knowledge of good and right, therefore, one can then employ this knowledge to evaluate God's goodness by considering how God is portrayed in a given religion or how God has appeared in one's own spiritual experiences and that of others. This introduces no circularity even if we accept the alternate account. Nor does it imply that any moral standard exists other than that (according to the alternate account) which originates in God.

Suppose next that God *does* appear to be good; this can then provide support of the alternate account with a defensible basis for believing that God *is* good—and even for maintaining that various terrible evils like torturing innocents could not conform to God's nature. Thus, the alternate account can talk of God being good as most us understanding "good," without appealing to some empty concept of "good."

For Discussion

1. *How does the statement that good conforms to God's essential nature differ from the divine command claim that good is what God wills or commands?*
2. *What do you think of Plato's argument that God must be unchangeable?*
3. *Some theologians hold that nothing can even influence or affect God. Others think that God is unchangeable but can be influenced (e.g., by prayers). Which view do you take, and why?*
4. *Can you give other examples of how the origin of something and how we come to know about that thing can differ?*
5. *The alternate account argues that we can talk of God as "good" in the way we understand "good." Could God's goodness largely match our understanding of "good" but also extend beyond that?*

Summary

The alternate dependency account may manage to avoid the problems that both the autonomy thesis and divine command theory encounter. It preserves the greatest being concept of God by having the moral standard originate in God. By holding that God is consistent and unchanging, it also avoids the worries that anything could count as morally right and that God could will anything whatsoever. The account then makes a distinction between the basis of morality itself and how we can come to know what is morally right or wrong. This makes it possible to talk of God's goodness in the sense that people normally understand goodness.

Key Terms

- **Alternate dependency account**: *a dependency account that bases morality in God's nature and that avoids the objections to both traditional divine command theory and the autonomy thesis.*

V. OBJECTIONS AND ELABORATIONS

Different beliefs: What if my beliefs about God differ from those assumed by the alternate account? After all, there are many religions and conceptions of God. But while this is true, the alternate account avoids specific religious portrayals of God and instead employs the philosophical concept of God as *the greatest being possible*. This has certain advantages. For one thing, it doesn't necessarily reflect any particular religion.[6] Yet it still captures the intuition that whatever God may be like, God must be superior to all other beings. If there could be a being greater than what we call God, then *that* being would be more deserving of the title "God" than the one we have been talking about. If, furthermore, there could be more than one deity, then the greatest of these deserves the name "God," being the one of greatest importance. Although this concept allows some leeway regarding the precise attributes the greatest being must have, it offers a concept of God that most could agree to.

Someone might still object, "But what about the fact that some people don't believe that God exists?" After all, both divine command theory and the alternate account assume that God exists. Neither, therefore, has much appeal for those who don't believe in God. Nevertheless, it's important to recognize that whether someone *believes* that God exists is not really relevant to what the account claims, because its claims are about the objective basis of morality, not people's beliefs. Similarly, what people may believe about some physical fact – for instance, about climate change - isn't relevant to what actually holds true in the objective world. Of course, if there is compelling evidence against God's existence, that will also count against any account that affirms the dependency thesis.

At this point, a questioner might press yet further and ask what evidence there could be for or against God's existence in the first place. But *this* question is no longer a question about ethics—rather, it raises questions about human knowledge and, more specifically, about knowledge of God's existence. While these sorts of questions are certainly important, the considerations and arguments that address them lie outside the field of ethics.

Practicability: Although the alternate account may provide an *explanation* of what makes something right or wrong, its adequacy as a practical guide to moral living is much less clear. It's fine to be given the ultimate basis of morality, but we also need a theory to tell us what we should do in specific situations. How does the alternate account do this? For that matter, what *are* the moral claims implied by this account?

The alternate account answers that morally right actions are ones that conform to God's character. This makes it resemble virtue theory, which says that we determine right actions by asking what would be done by someone who has a virtuous character. Given the alternate account, then, we should ask questions like: "If my personal moral character closely conformed to God's character, what would I do in this situation?" Just as with virtue theory, this approach probably won't yield any precise rules about what we should or shouldn't do. Still, if virtue theory is on the right track, then such rules may be more than what ought to be asked of any ethical theory.

---

[6]It can be readily embraced by Jewish, Christian, and Muslim believers. It is also widely referred to by nonbelievers when considering arguments for and against God's existence.

In the present case, however, the character in question is *God's*. To be practicable, then, we must be able to know something about God's character! In terms of sheer *practicability*, is this possible? How might one go about discovering what we need to know about God's character?

Philosophically speaking, the best starting point would be to appeal to the greatest being concept of God. This and related resources should allow us to gain some information, at least, about God's character. For instance, God must surely be just. In addition, since God must always act in conformity to his own character, the results of God's creative acts (including human nature) should presumably reflect God's character, much as an artist's work reflects something about the artist. This is also in keeping with natural law theory's claim that we can gain important moral insights simply by studying the laws and natural ends of nature. Further, since the greatest being possible must surely create a *moral* universe—a universe that reflects and upholds the demands of morality—we should expect morally right actions to often yield good and desirable consequences (utilitarianism), to satisfy the constraints of reason (Kantian ethics), to contribute to personal fulfillment and human flourishing (virtue ethics), and so on. Given the alternate account's Statement 4 and the greatest being concept of God, therefore, a supporter of the account could reasonably argue that much initial knowledge of God's character can be attained in all of these ways. In short, the alternate account places the problem of learning some of the most important facts about God's character on a par with the problem of our assessing the major claims of any or even all of our best moral theories.

Still, this is only a starting point and so leaves many important questions about God's character—or equivalently, the moral standard—unanswered. This is especially true of those areas where our best moral theories and intuitions conflict. To achieve a complete moral theory, then, a believing supporter of the alternate account can't stop there, nor would she want to. In particular, if the believer desires to conform herself more and more to God's character, then she will want to acquire a deeper and more intimate knowledge of God than can be obtained from purely secular and philosophical resources. But if God is indeed the greatest being possible, then it's only reasonable to expect God to love his creatures enough to also communicate more directly about his character. The believer will thus naturally look to the clearest and most dependable claims religion can offer about God—including religious *revelations*—to learn more about God's moral character. To do this, however, the believer must first answer the question, "To which religions and religious revelations should I turn?"[7] This brings us to a final problem.

Moral confirmation: Since a complete version of the alternate account requires supplementation by religious revelations, its supporter must sooner or later face

---

[7]Here, "revelation" refers to the words of an established prophet or religious scriptures through which God has allegedly communicated to humanity. While individuals sometimes claim to receive private revelations, those are *not* under consideration here.

the problem of determining which *religious "theory"* (i.e., which religion and its accompanying revelations) could truly be from God.[8] This problem has two sides. On one side, the criterion of moral confirmation requires that a theory's moral implications not clash too severely with our firmest moral convictions. If a particular religion's implications were to clash *quite drastically* with our moral convictions, then that would provide a good reason to not accept that religion.

On the other side, it also seems that if there indeed is a God, then we should expect some tension to exist between *our* moral convictions and the moral perfection of God. Similarly, a young child's moral understanding normally cannot compare with the moral knowledge of his parents. Once a believer has good reason to believe that certain religious revelations *are* from God, therefore, consistency requires that she be willing to allow those revelations to influence her moral convictions. In particular, if a believer were to discover a conflict between her moral convictions and the moral implications of such revelations, it would not be unreasonable for her to begin making adjustments to her own moral convictions.

Given the preceding considerations, we are thus brought to the following fundamental problem: how can a religious believer *rationally* (a) maintain an appropriately critical stance toward a particular religious theory's moral implications, while (b) also remaining appropriately open to adjusting her moral convictions in the light of her religion's revelations?

Any adequate defense of a religion-supplemented alternate account must face this problem head on. Yet again, how different are the issues involved in confirming a religious "theory" from those involved in confirming any moral theory? The believing supporter of the alternate account would probably answer that they are no different. For any moral theory, the initial steps toward moral confirmation require that we compare the majority of a theory's implications to our deepest and most considered moral convictions. If we find a severe enough clash between these, then we probably should reject that theory. The same can be said about rejecting a religious theory if many of its implications clash too severely with our most considered moral convictions.

But what if a religion's implications do *not* clash so severely with our moral convictions? Then again, we should proceed just as when we are dealing with a moral theory (see the discussion on moral confirmation in Part II Introduction). In particular, we further develop and elaborate an ethical theory to bring its implications into closer agreement with our moral convictions. When we can do this successfully, the result is a better confirmed moral theory. Similarly, the believer can pursue a deeper knowledge of God's character through further clarifications and elaborations of her religious theory and its moral implications. If doing so enables her to resolve several initial conflicts between her religion and her moral convictions, then she has reason to consider her religious theory better confirmed.

---

[8]For simplicity, we will consider any particular *religion*, which we will treat as a particular *religious theory*, to be essentially equivalent to its central *revelations* since religions usually are based on the revelations preserved in their scriptures or traditions.

By further clarifying and elaborating either an ethical or religious theory, new moral questions may arise, which may call for further adjustments to the theory, and so on.[9] As this process continues, the theory's supporter (whether religious or ethical) may gradually become justified in letting his continually more refined theory start influencing his moral convictions. This back and forth adjustment of theory and moral convictions can lead to yet deeper insights, continuing toward ever-increasing moral confirmation.

For Discussion

1. *Applying the text's artist analogy, in what ways would you expect God's creation of the natural world to reflect God's character?*
2. *Do you think that the greatest being possible would create a world that reflects morality in human reason, in the consequences of our actions, and so on?*
3. *Applying the greatest being concept of God, would you expect a good God to also reveal truths about himself and his character (i.e., the moral standard)?*
4. *The text compares the process of confirming a religious theory to that of confirming an ethical theory. What similarities and differences do you see?*

Summary

Having morality dependent upon God's character inevitably raises questions about what can be known about God. Although some of these questions reach beyond ethics, the concept of the greatest being possible can help. The greatest being possible presumably loves his creatures and so would reveal aspects of his character to them in possibly many different ways. This would allow people to learn important things about God's character and thus the moral standard. But what if some of that information clashes with our moral convictions? On one hand, we would have reason to reject claims made about God that clash too severely with our strongest moral convictions. On the other, it's not likely that every one of our moral convictions would perfectly agree with such an authority as God. Sorting this out requires that the alternate account be supplemented by the claims of a specific religion.

VI. COMPLETENESS

Among dependency accounts, traditional divine command theory is too problematic to accept as it stands. As for the alternate dependency account, it seems that this must reach beyond ethics and appeal to some specific religious tradition. By supplementing the alternate account with the richer resources of a particular religious theory, the account's believing supporter may then begin to address the

---

[9]A nice example of this process is seen in the historical clarification of Christianity's rejection of slavery. While this was not appreciated initially or even for some time, it now is quite clear to the Christian world that Christian principles forbid slavery—something Christian abolitionists began to realize a century or two ago.

issues of practicability and moral confirmation. Yet this also shows that the alternate dependency account, taken by itself, cannot comprise a *complete* ethical theory without supplementation with some particular religion. This result is no surprise to many religious believers who are already persuaded that *no* ethical theory can be fully adequate except as supplemented by religious insights. This is the challenge that proponents of the dependency thesis bring against those who approach morality via secular moral theories. Of course, this returns us to the questions of God's existence and of which religion might best represent the genuine character of God. While the foregoing discussion is meant to be suggestive regarding how to approach these questions, we must again observe that investigations into these latter questions lie largely outside the scope of ethics. For this reason, they are offered as an exercise to the reader.

For Discussion

1. *Do you agree with many religious thinkers that no ethical theory can be fully adequate except as supplemented by religious insights? Why or why not?*

Summary

Since the alternate dependency account must appeal to religion, it is not a complete moral theory. Supplemented by religion, it may become complete. Many religious believers maintain that the same is true of any moral theory—that no moral account can be adequate unless it appeals in some way to religion as well.

Chapter Assignment Questions

1. *Explain the difference between something being good because the gods approve it and the gods approving something because it is good.*
2. *** *What does Kant mean when he talks about rational beings "making" the moral law for themselves? Why isn't this just subjectivism?*
3. *How does the autonomy thesis conflict with the concept of God as the greatest being possible?*
4. *How does traditional divine command theory allow for anything to count as morally right?*
5. *Explain in your own words how something can conform with, conflict with, or remain neutral with respect to a person's nature or character.*
6. *How could moral knowledge be gained from sources other than God or religion if morality depends directly on God (apply the alternate dependency account)? Explain.*
7. *Why aren't people's beliefs about God relevant to God's existence, to God's actual character, or to a morality dependent upon God?*
8. *Practicability—particularly our coming to know facts about God's character and thus what is right—poses a problem for the alternate account. Explain and assess the text's response to this problem.*

9. *Explain and assess the text's discussion of how to determine what religion, and its accompanying moral claims, may be confirmed.*

Additional Resources

Burnor, Richard. "Murphy, Mark C. *God and Moral Law: On the Theistic Explanation of Morality*" [book review]. *Reason Papers* 37.2. https://reasonpapers.com/wp-content/uploads/2016/02/rp_372_17.pdf. Murphy's book is a difficult read, but this review provides a summary. Murphy defends a theistic basis of morality that combines a dependency account with natural law theory.

Plato. *Euthyphro*, translated by Benjamin Jowett. Internet Classics Archive. Accessed August 19, 2016. http://classics.mit.edu/Plato/euthyfro.html.

Kant, Immanuel. *Grounding for the Metaphysics of Morals*. 3d ed. Translated by James W. Ellington. Indianapolis, IN: Hackett Publishing Company, 1993. See especially section 2 for his discussion of the principle of autonomy.

Case 1

By Divine Command?

In a *Law and Order* episode entitled "Under God,"[10] a priest, Father Hogan, confesses to murdering a drug dealer. His justification? He believes that God told him to do it. The drug dealer had sold drugs to one of Father Hogan's parishioners, who subsequently died of an overdose, leaving behind a bereaved father. In explaining his actions, Hogan states, "A man was destroying my community, poisoning my neighbors. I prayed for guidance, and the guidance I received was that I should kill him."[11]

Father Hogan's lawyer, Wheeler, files a defense based on Father Hogan's claim that he received direct guidance from God. Wheeler argues that if the jury accepts the existence of God, then they cannot deny a defense that is predicated on that existence. McCoy, the prosecutor, objects that "if a layperson tries to exert a 'God Told Me To' defense, the court would render him incompetent to stand trial." Wheeler retorts: "So, if you talk to God, you're pious; and if he talks back, you're crazy?"

A psychological exam later confirms that Father Hogan is perfectly competent and not at all crazy. And Father Hogan is fully convinced about the authenticity of the instructions he received.

THOUGHT QUESTIONS

1. Instead of committing murder, imagine that Father Hogan starts a ministry to both drug dealers and victims to heal and revive the neighborhood. He does this—at great risk to himself – because he believes that this is what God has told him to do. How does this alter the situation and your thoughts about it?

---

[10]Muzio, Gloria, dir. and Marc Guggenheim, writer. "Under God," *Law and Order,* season 13, episode 12, first broadcast February 5, 2003, National Broadcasting Corporation.

[11]Quotations for this case were obtained from Dan W. Clanton, "These Are Their Stories: Views of Religion in Law and Order," *Journal of Religion and Popular Culture*, IV (Summer 2003).

2. Assume that God exists. Do you think that God could have told Father Hogan to kill the drug dealer? Why or why not? How can we evaluate guidance purported to be from God?

3. Would it make any difference to our conclusion about Father Hogan's case if we apply the alternate dependency account rather than simple divine command theory?

4. What role, if any, might the Bible or Church teaching play in our determining if God actually commanded Father Hogan to kill the drug dealer? Until now, Father Hogan has been a sincere and sensitive man who deeply cares about people. How relevant is that?

5. If the moral standard were autonomous and so exists independently of God, would that affect your evaluation of Father Hogan's claim that God told him to commit murder?

6. Given that Father Hogan is a sincere priest, that he truly believed that he received a divine command, and that he was indeed in his right mind, could his act be morally justified, as the defense implies?

Case 2

Religious Symbols and Public Schools

In early 2004, the French senate approved a controversial new law. In a vote of 276 to 20, the senate decided to prohibit the wearing of "conspicuous" religious symbols in public schools. While this law was primarily aimed against the headscarves worn by Muslim women, it also addressed the wearing of large crosses, the Star of David (if it's big enough to be seen), and the Jewish Yarmulke.[12] This law touched off a debate in other European countries (e.g., Germany and Belgium) about whether to pass similar laws. So far, none has followed suit, although a British poll from 2007 showed that 56% in the United Kingdom would favor a law banning the veil in public places, and 60% would be for a law prohibiting the veil in airports and at passport controls.[13]

In a speech, French President Chirac argued as follows for the new law:

> All of France's children, whatever their history, whatever their origin, whatever their beliefs, are the daughters and sons of the republic. They have to be recognized as such, in law but above all in reality. By ensuring respect for this requirement, by reforming our integration policy, by our ability to bring equal opportunities to life, we shall bring national cohesion to life again. We shall also do so by bringing to life the principle of secularism, which is a pillar of our constitution. It expresses our wish to live together in respect, dialogue and tolerance. Secularism guarantees freedom of conscience. It protects the freedom to believe or not to believe.[14]

Chirac's expressed goal is for the law to promote equality by encouraging the assimilation of various cultural/religious subgroups into mainstream French society

Continued

---

[12]Bootie Cosgrove-Mather, "France Bans Head Scarves in School," CBSNews.com, accessed August 28, 2016, http://www.cbsnews.com/news/france-bans-head-scarves-in-school/.

[13]"Survey Finds Support for Veil Ban," BBC News, accessed August 28, 2016, http://news.bbc.co.uk/2/hi/uk_news/6194032.stm.

[14]"Chirac on the Secular Society," BBC News, accessed August 28, 2016, http://news.bbc.co.uk/2/hi/europe/3330679.stm.

Case 2 (Continued)

(immigrant groups, especially). His view is that removing distinctive religious tokens from the public schools would help promote respect and tolerance for all. The strategy, one might say, is to promote equality in uniformity as opposed to equality in diversity. Unmistakably, Chirac's words and his emphasis on secularism also tell religious believers that they may believe as they choose, but not necessarily do what their beliefs require. Although many believers interpret the law as opposing religion, French lawmakers didn't think that the law interferes with religious freedom.

Others worry, however, that there's more to this law than meets the eye. France has the largest Muslim population in Europe—about 5 million. Could the new law have been an attempt to discourage Muslim practices in France? Some think that the government may have perceived the Muslim headscarf requirement as being oppressive and discriminatory and so was attempting to protect women's rights. Yet the law might instead discriminate by keeping devout Muslim women (who feel they must wear a headscarf) from ever going out in public.

For many Muslims, the headscarf also serves as a *political* symbol, signifying more than just membership in a particular religious group. Interestingly, French law also prohibits *political* symbols to be worn in public schools. Indeed, proselytizing of any sort, religious or political, is prohibited.

For nearly all Muslim women, the headscarf is an important piece of religious identity. Hiding the face also helps protect the woman's personal identity because the headscarf makes it harder for a random passerby to form any judgment of a Muslim woman merely by her looks. For a Muslim woman, not wearing the headscarf may feel like going naked. Of course, the yarmulke is also an extremely important mark of Jewish identity, just as a cross is for many Christians.

THOUGHT QUESTIONS

1. What do you think of the reasons Chirac offered for this new law? How well do they justify the law? What reasons, moral or otherwise, might be brought against such a law? What do you see to be at stake here?

2. Someone may wear a religious symbol because she believes that God has commanded her to or because she thinks that this is a way she can please God. Should such a person's submission to God override her obedience to the state? Why or why not?

3. Do you think that this law was likely to help promote national unity as Chirac seemed to think it would? Why or why not?

4. How would you react if a similar law were proposed in the United States?

5. Philosopher Dianne Gereluk argues that permitting students to wear symbolic clothing provides them the opportunity to reflect on their own values and the values of others. What do you think of this, and what bearing does this have on the French law?[15]

---

[15]Dianne Gereluk, "Children's Autonomy and Symbolic Clothing in Schools: Help or Hindrance?" in *Philosophy of Education in the Era of Globalization*, eds. Yvonne and Gerhard Preyer (New York: Routledge Taylor and Francis Group, 2010).

Case 3

A Question of Authority

In 1995, Robert Eliot Harlan was found guilty of the rape and murder of Rhonda Maloney, as well as of shooting Rhonda's friend, Jaquie Creazzo, when Jaquie attempted to help Rhonda. As a result, Jaquie Creazzo was paralyzed for life. The prosecution sought the death penalty, and the jury had to decide whether that penalty was appropriate. As a jury makes this sort of determination, it's important that it not be "under the influence of passion, prejudice, or any arbitrary factor."[16]

Although the jury did decide to impose the death penalty, the court set this verdict aside and imposed a sentence of life in prison without parole. Apparently, one of the jurors had brought a hotel Bible into the jury room and had read biblical passages to make a case for the death penalty. As a result, the "court concluded that there was a reasonable possibility that use of the Bible ... would have influenced a typical juror to reject a life sentence for Harlan."

One of the biblical passages used was Leviticus 24:20–21: "fracture for fracture, eye for eye, tooth for tooth; just as he has injured a man, so it shall be inflicted on him. Thus the one who kills an animal shall make it good, but the one who kills a man shall be put to death." Another was Romans 13:1: "Every person is to be in subjection to the governing authorities. For there is no authority except from God, and those which exist are established by God."[17]

According to Justice Hobbs, these passages speak directly to the question of whether murder should call for the death penalty. In addition, many people view biblical documents as "codes of law." In his opinion, Justice Hobbs also noted that the Papal Edition of the Holy Bible describes the first five books of the Bible as "almost entirely legislative in character." The judge stressed that "the text is written in the first person voice and commands death as punishment for murder." In addition, "[t]he Romans text instructs human beings to obey the civil government."

It is admissible (as well as unavoidable) for jurors to be influenced by religious and moral beliefs as they make a "reasoned judgment" about a case. However, the judge objected to the use of a written document (the Bible) when that document had not been introduced as evidence. According to the judge, "[t]he written word persuasively conveys the authentic ring of reliable authority in a way the recollected spoken word does not. Some jurors may view biblical texts ... as a factual representation of God's will. The text may also be viewed as a legal instruction." In short, the judge felt that the one juror's use of the Bible unduly influenced the rest of the jury to favor the death penalty.

In a dissenting opinion, Justice Rice pointed out that the jury was never instructed *not* to refer to the Bible. In his view, furthermore, these biblical passages—especially Leviticus—are widely known and may even function as a "cultural precept" within our society. They should thus be counted as part of the jury members' religious and moral beliefs—beliefs that cannot be separated from the overall set of background beliefs and attitudes that inevitably influence jury members as

Continued

---

[16]*People v. Harlan*, Colorado Supreme Court Opinion, March 28, 2005, Docket No. 03SA173. All quotations for this case (except biblical quotations) are taken from this document.

[17]Bible quotations are from the New American Standard Bible, updated 1995, The Lockman Foundation.

Case 3 (Continued)

they make their judgments. The fact that *written* passages were consulted, he said, would not alter their influence upon the jury.

Justice Rice also argued that jury members are usually selected for their capacity to "make reasoned judgments based on their respective backgrounds and beliefs. To presume that jurors who have a religious background cannot distinguish between written biblical passages and written jury instructions ... is to underestimate their intelligence and to belittle their participation in our legal system."

THOUGHT QUESTIONS

1. Which viewpoint seems more reasonable to you: that of Justice Hobbs or of Justice Rice? Do you think the jury *was* unduly prejudiced by the written passages? Why? To what degree would these passages influence you?
2. Suppose that a juror is sincerely persuaded after considering these passages that God does indeed command the death penalty for a crime like Harlan's. Would that make this juror's support of the death penalty for Harlan inappropriate or unwarranted?
3. Suppose that God has commanded the death penalty for murder. Could God have commanded a different punishment instead, given the divine command theory? Could God have commanded a different punishment according to the alternate dependency account? Explain.
4. Although some Christians support the death penalty in view of passages like these, others think that God has now suspended the death penalty, in view of Jesus' teachings. For instance, Jesus' Sermon on the Mount includes the following statements: "You have heard that it was said, 'an eye for an eye, and a tooth for a tooth.' But I say to you, do not resist an evil person; but whoever slaps you on your right cheek, turn the other to him also. ... You have heard that it was said, 'you shall love your neighbor and hate your enemy.' But I say to you, love your enemies and pray for those who persecute you, so that you may be sons of your Father who is in heaven" (selections from *Matthew* 5:38–45). In view of this, how should we determine what God wills regarding the death penalty? Does context play a role here?
5. What is your view on whether Harlan ought to have received the death penalty? Why?

PART III

Ethical Pluralism

INTRODUCTION

Ethics offers us a rich choice of viewpoints. But does it also offer us any hope of finding a successful account of morality? Every theory sheds valuable light on morals, but there is none we can accept without reservation. What good is a set of problematic theories?

We might try melding a couple closely related theories into one that captures the advantages of each. For instance, the affinity between virtue and care ethics suggests that we might try supplementing care ethics with justice-oriented virtues. Combining virtue and care ethics, however, risks preserving and reinforcing problems from *both* theories – a risk that arises with most attempts to combine theories.

More adventurous mixtures are even less promising. DDE attempts to bring deontology and consequentialism together (see Chapter Nine, §IV). Unfortunately, DDE doesn't stand as a theory by itself, though it has its own problems. Or, it might seem like a great idea to apply act utilitarianism to tell us what to do whenever Kant's theory encounters a dilemma, but this makes no theoretical sense. Because Kantian ethics assigns foundational moral value only to the Good Will, it can't grant any moral standing to utility. Nor can utilitarianism make sense of Kant's refusal to consider consequences. How about using natural rights to add justice to care ethics? But rights are universal and apply to individuals, while care ethics rejects universalism and makes relationships basic. In most cases, the differences between theories are irreconcilable.

Could the attempt to find a single complete ethical theory itself be mistaken? **Ethical pluralism** says that it is and that no single comprehensive ethical account exists.

A particularly clear example of pluralism is Ross's ethics (see Chapter Eight, §II), which lists several distinct moral duties (e.g., justice, beneficence, non-maleficence). Each of these duties is foundational—there's nothing more basic that can explain any particular duty or link these duties together through some underlying, unifying account. This contrasts with non-pluralist theories like Kantianism and utilitarianism, which see all of morality as unified—as following from a single foundational value or principle. Next, each of Ross's foundational duties supports a corresponding set of derived duties; for instance, justice supports duties like "Don't discriminate," "Pay fair wages," and "Wait your turn." Let's say that every duty and moral claim that can be derived from the foundational duty of justice together comprise one *branch* of morality. Each of Ross's other foundational duties likewise give rise to its own distinct branch. The resulting picture, then, portrays morality as consisting of several separate branches, each largely distinct from the others, though every moral duty and claim within each branch derives from that branch's one foundational duty.[1]

Beside Ross's ethics, there are other ethical accounts that adopt the pluralistic approach as well. All of these demonstrate the nature of ethical pluralism in moral *theorizing*. But at the start of this book, we emphasized the *practical* value of ethics. How useful have our various ethical theories shown themselves when applied to specific moral problems? Some indication of this can be gained from considering how these theories have dealt with the book's many case studies. For instance, act utilitarianism does indeed seem useful for evaluating the morality of torture lite, while Kantian ethics has definite implications for organ donation. In addition, natural law has much to offer regarding warfare, social contract theory and rights regarding gun control, and care ethics regarding poverty. While helpful, however, can these theories provide fully adequate analyses and solutions to these and other practical problems? Not quite. For instance, act utilitarianism doesn't consider whether torture lite violates basic moral rights. Nor is it clear that natural law theory is fully able to handle the problems posed by covert warfare, by new technologies such as drones and robots, or by the sorts of conflicts that remain undeclared or that are taking place internationally (by ISIS and other terrorist organizations). Meanwhile, the knotty issue of gun control itself seems to result from multiple conflicts between rights; poverty, finally, is a multi-faceted problem that care theorists themselves have divided over.

Specific theories may not be that successful at resolving specific practical problems completely. Fortunately, pluralism looks like it's able to help us out here. As demonstrated by the newer field of *applied ethics*, it turns out that substantial

---

[1]There's nothing here to prevent some specific situation bringing two or more branches of morality into play at the same time or even deriving additional "composite" duties from more than one branch.

responses to many moral problems can be provided by combining the resources and insights of several theories. Why not use whatever insights we can, regardless of their theoretical underpinnings, if they can help us address today's most complex moral problems?

In this Part III of our ethical studies, we will give a bit more consideration to ethical pluralism as it pertains to theories and examine some pluralistic applied ethics analyses as well. We take up the first in the next section.

For Discussion

1. *If you were to try combining a few of our ethical theories to create a new account, which would you choose? What pros and cons would your new account have?*
2. *Do you think that ethical pluralism may be a good strategy for solving problems in applied ethics? Why? Could pluralism be something we ultimately have to use?*

Summary

Ethical pluralism *(e.g., Ross's ethics) gives up the attempt to find a single unifying theory for all of ethics. Instead, it views morality as consisting of several unrelated branches. We can also take a pluralistic approach to problems in applied ethics.*

Key Terms

- **Ethical pluralism**: *maintains that morality consists of several distinct branches that are largely unrelated to each other.*

CHAPTER FOURTEEN

⤴

Pluralism in Theoretical and Applied Ethics

I.** KINDS OF ETHICAL PLURALISM

In the introduction to Part III, we described Ross's theory as an instance of *ethical pluralism*. But there are at least two different kinds of pluralism. Ross's ethics reflects one version which we can call *foundational pluralism*. This kind of pluralism divides morality into several distinct branches, each deriving from its own foundation (in Ross's case, a foundational duty). As a pluralist, Ross rules out the possibility of there being any underlying or unifying theory that accounts for all (or even some) of the separate branches. In addition, he rules out any explanation that accounts for any particular branch's foundational duty; each branch's foundation exists on its own and with no further explanation. For instance, Ross's ethics refuses to answer questions like "Why is justice a foundational moral duty?" and "What makes benevolence morally important?" As a result, foundational ethical pluralism can feel rather unsatisfying since it tends to have little explanatory power. In fact, foundational pluralism largely rejects our desire for explanations in ethics.[1]

A different approach to ethical pluralism might be called *explanatory pluralism*. This approach still divides the moral realm into several distinct branches, but all the claims, values, and principles belonging to a given branch are at least tied to each other by some more fundamental account. To see one way this might go, let's return to Hunt's classification of the virtues (see Chapter Eleven, §V). Hunt distinguishes three types of virtue: *obligation virtues* (e.g., promise-keeping; these require right actions), *good-promoting virtues* (e.g., generosity; these promote others' good), and *limiting virtues* (e.g., courage; these call upon us to discipline our inclinations and feelings). Borrowing Hunt's types for our own purposes, let's divide the moral realm (no longer thinking only of virtues) into distinct branches, each reflecting one of Hunt's types. Thus, one branch would consist of all moral

---

[1]This discussion greatly simplifies Ross's actual theory.

claims relating to moral obligations, another relating to human goods, and another to personality traits like self-control. We might even add a branch relating to caring—or to something else entirely.

Following Hunt's classifications, this differentiates branches of morality by the particular purposes each play in morality (e.g., promoting good)—rather than by their content (e.g., having to do with justice). For instance, justice, honesty, and promise-keeping would all belong together in the branch of moral *obligations*. But in contrast to Ross, we might then provide a deeper unifying account of everything that belongs to a given branch (but only to that branch) by appealing to an explanatory theory that naturally allies with that branch. Kantian ethics or rule utilitarianism, for instance, might do well at explaining universal obligations. To address *good-promoting* considerations, we might appeal to some version of act utilitarianism or even natural law theory. Still other accounts would be employed to explain and unify moral *limiting* values or the values of relational *caring*.

Explanatory ethical pluralism thus divides the moral realm into several branches and allows for distinct theoretical explanations of each distinct branch. This may help with the problem most of our theories have with achieving theoretical completeness. For instance, Kantian ethics handles obligations well but can't promote consequences or make sense of particularistic moral concerns. This makes it incomplete as an account of the entire moral realm. Utilitarian accounts appear incomplete in their accounting for justice and rights, a weakness that care ethics also shares. And so on. But if each of these accounts is only used to support one particular branch of morality rather than all of morality, then each might at least achieve completeness for all of the moral phenomena belonging to its own particular branch. That would greatly diminish the problem with theoretical completeness for ethics overall.[2]

By the way, this is just like the way we've dealt with the natural sciences and its distinct branches or fields (e.g., chemistry, geology, and biology). It's made things vastly more manageable to develop satisfactory theories for limited scientific fields rather than for all of science as a whole. What is so interesting is that after treating the sciences pluralistically for centuries, we are now finding them increasingly interconnected. In fact, many scientists expect that we will someday arrive at a single comprehensive account of all natural phenomena—a grand unified theory. But if we do, that will be the *end* result of our scientific efforts, not their *starting* point. Curiously, we've taken the reverse tact in ethics and aimed almost exclusively at finding a single comprehensive account of ethics. Yet finding satisfactory theories for distinct branches of morality would surely be easier than finding a single account for all of morality as a whole. By applying this "divide and conquer" strategy, perhaps we would someday arrive at that single comprehensive account of the moral realm that has eluded us for so long.

---

[2]This discussion is to illustrate explanatory pluralism, not to argue for this use of Hunt's classification or for any form of ethical pluralism.

Whether ethical pluralism is the best way to go theoretically, a pluralistic approach to ethical *practice*, as we have previously mentioned, has proven value. There needn't be a single comprehensive ethical theory for us to apply various theories' insights to handle the moral difficulties that business, medicine, and the environment all place before us. The following sections provide a sampling of how *applied ethics* can help us with important problems in each of these areas.

For Discussion

1. *Do you prefer to keep searching for one single, comprehensive ethical theory that can explain the entire moral realm? Or would you go with some type of ethical pluralism instead? Why?*

2. *How satisfying do you find the explanatory power of a* foundational pluralism *(like Ross's)?*

3. *Which do you prefer and why:* foundational *or* explanatory pluralism?

Summary

With respect to theories, there are at least two kinds of pluralism. Foundational pluralism *derives each distinct branch from its own unique foundation but offers no further explanation of any branch or foundation.* Explanatory pluralism *ties everything within a branch together by appealing to that branch's own explanatory account. We have sketched an illustration of explanatory pluralism that has four branches, each explained by a different ethical theory.*

II. MEDICAL ETHICS: FUTILITY

A. *At eighty-six years old, Martha firmly believed in the "old school" rule: never complain about how you feel. Living in a retirement home with mid-level medical care because of a weak heart and progressive arthritis, Martha always attended dinner in the dining room, making her way back and forth using her trusty walker. The nurses loved her: Martha often made little jokes, always knew what was going on, and never complained. One Thursday, Martha felt a little under the weather and skipped dinner; she had a slight cough as well. When a nurse asked if she was okay, she smiled, saying "I'm fine as usual, thanks." By the next day, however, she had a fever and her cough was worse. The doctor later confirmed pneumonia. Martha started antibiotics, but by Saturday, her fever had skyrocketed. She was transferred to the hospital, where she was switched to a stronger antibiotic. She suffered a stroke Monday afternoon, which paralyzed her right side and made breathing difficult. She was put on a respirator and a mild sedative to help her sleep. Over the next week, her kidneys began to fail. Martha would occasionally wake up and even understand much about her situation. Nevertheless, it was quickly becoming clear that Martha was dying. Although the doctors could aggressively treat her infection, keep her on the respirator, and start kidney dialysis, everything now indicated that these medical interventions were medically futile.*

Medical futility involves a situation when further medical interventions serve little or no purpose. Futility doesn't mean that all treatments are useless and should be suspended; efforts should still be made to ease Martha's suffering and maintain some quality of life. But no further "extraordinary" or "heroic" interventions are likely to do her any good. More formally, a treatment is **medically futile** for a *specific patient and situation* if it is highly unlikely to bring any *overall benefit* to the patient. "Overall benefit" isn't merely physical; it also includes mental, emotional, and spiritual well-being. Medically futile situations are more common now than ever because of our increased ability to prolong life. What moral considerations, then, apply to futile interventions for a dying patient?

1. The first considerations relate to autonomy. Martha still seems able to act as a moral agent (See Chapter Three, §IV). We thus have a duty to show her moral deference, informing her of her condition and offering her the choice of accepting or refusing treatments. The right to *refuse treatment* is widely recognized in medical practice and places important limits on what medical caregivers may do.[3] But why would anyone refuse a treatment that could be provided for them? Martha might refuse dialysis or antibiotics because she sees no point to making a negligible extension to her life (even a futile treatment can extend life slightly, and sometimes for quite a while). Another patient may have just learned that his cancer has returned and not want to endure another bout of chemotherapy. Refusing treatment in such situations is not the moral equivalent of suicide, even if it leads to death. Rather, patients choose against undergoing treatments that are neither desirable nor beneficial. While they understand that they may die sooner, they view death as a result of their condition, not of their choice. Such choices therefore, are not *for* death, but *against* treatment. Given the right of moral agents to control what is done to them, there is ordinarily no moral wrong committed in such situations.[4]

B. Suppose we change the story a little:
Martha continues to deteriorate, especially mentally. She now only rarely wakes and just for a few moments; also, she no longer recognizes anyone, nor does she know what has happened. Because the respirator makes her uncomfortable, she is kept asleep most of the time. She had previously told a close friend that she had no desire to be kept alive in such situations, and she had also appointed this friend as her medical proxy. As family members start to visit, they initially urge that Martha be kept alive as long as possible. However, the friend convinces them that the situation is largely hopeless and that Martha herself would not want anything more done. The friend asks the attending physician to just keep Martha comfortable, and the rest of the family agrees.

---

[3]The right of a moral agent to refuse medical treatment is the *negative* right to keep others from doing things *to us*. It's not about what someone may choose to do to herself (a *positive* right).

[4]Something closer to suicide may be involved if a patient refuses a non-futile treatment that could improve life for a time. But our interest here is only with futile treatments.

1. Martha has now lost capacity (see Chapter Three, §II). But she had previously expressed her wishes to her friend, whom she had also appointed as her *proxy* to make treatment decisions for her (a *proxy* makes medical decisions for a patient when the patient is unable to make them for herself). Martha has entrusted her friend, who understands Martha and her desires, with legal and moral authority to make choices in her place. Clearly, one's choice of a proxy is a matter of great importance. But if this friend fulfills her trust carefully and responsibly, then her choices will provide a good substitute for the patient making her own choices. It would be even better if the patient had also made out a *living will*—a document that specifies what interventions and treatments the patient wants and does not want done once she can't make her own choices (see Chapter Three, Case 4). The will could help provide additional guidance to the proxy and medical caregivers. With or without a will, the proxy can exercise agency in ways similar to the way the patient would have—by becoming as informed as possible, by sympathetically considering the patient's desires, and by making choices aligned with those desires and the actual situation. Under such conditions, there's good reason to take the proxy's choices—even a choice to reject futile treatments—as reflecting the patient's own choices.

2. Let's now suppose that Martha has *only* established a "living will." This may not be as effective for fulfilling the patient's wishes. For one thing, unless the patient has periodically reviewed and updated her will, it may not adequately represent her current values since people's values evolve over time. Further, living wills can't anticipate every aspect of a situation. Despite these drawbacks, a will might still represent a patient's values and desires better than could some people. With neither a living will nor a proxy, decision-making usually falls next upon family. But some family members may be too traumatized by the situation to make reasonable decisions in keeping with the patient's wishes. Things can become even worse when all options are futile since refusing such treatments for the patient can feel like causing the patient's death. Unless the family is capable of some emotional and mental objectivity, a living will may be the best guide for the difficult choices that must be made.

3. In actual situations, living wills are often not followed with exactness. Even with a living will, close family members—particularly a spouse or one who knows the patient well—are also usually consulted, especially about end-of-life choices. If the family member cannot be objective and clear-headed, this *can* lead to the sorts of problems just discussed. An objectively minded and sympathetic family member, however, can represent the patient's interests as well as a good proxy. As with a proxy, this family member's choices should be well-informed, reasonable, and remain largely in keeping with the living will (if there is one). The main advantage with including family in making decisions, even when they've not been legally appointed, is that family members usually know the patient best.

So far, our versions of Martha's story have included no significant conflicts. However, the issue of futility is important mainly because conflicts often develop. To consider possible conflicts, let's proceed with a somewhat altered version of Martha's story:

C. *Martha has neither a medical proxy nor a living will, so the doctors consult the family. Several family members want to "do anything" that might keep Martha alive a little longer. After watching Martha's condition steadily deteriorate, the attending physician has concluded that any further interventions would be futile and that treatment should focus solely upon keeping Martha comfortable. At her age, Martha could never fully recover from the stroke, and everything also points to her requiring dialysis indefinitely. In addition, she will soon need a feeding tube installed. Yet when the physician meets with the family to recommend that Martha simply be allowed to die without further treatment, several vehemently disagree.*

1. This sort of thing often occurs, as family members can have all sorts of motives for wanting to put off death even if only for a little while. Some motives can be reprehensible (e.g., the family wants a few more months of the patient's social security checks—this has actually happened!). More often, not every family member is prepared to lose his loved one. Still, nothing can improve the patient's well-being, so it cannot serve her interests to be kept alive. The conflict, then, is between the patient's interests and those of some family members.

   Because their interests *are* being affected, family members cannot simply be dismissed as morally irrelevant to decisions regarding the patient's situation. But a compromise can sometimes resolve such conflicts. As long as the patient is not suffering, and her life isn't prolonged more than a short while, even futile treatments may be justified (e.g., maintaining Martha's respirator and antibiotics) to, say, allow family time to reconcile themselves to the impending loss. This is because the family's interests will often outweigh the limited interests of an unconscious patient. For instance, patients are often maintained long enough so the closest family members can arrive to "say goodbye." This raises no moral problems. However, if the patient *is* suffering, then her interests (avoiding suffering) begin to rival those of the family.

2. Conflicts can become more serious when family members refuse to "let go." The problem might be that family or friends don't fully grasp the reality of the situation. Then the attending physician, with sensitivity, should lead the family into greater understanding. One common misconception is that suspending futile treatment amounts to abandoning the patient completely. In response, the physician should make it clear that futile treatments cannot benefit the patient in any way. They also need to realize that the patient can still receive ***palliative care***—care that supports the patient and relieves discomfort. Once they understand these things, family members often abandon their objections for the sake of the patient.

3. The most serious conflicts arise when family adamantly insist on treatment in the hope that some degree of recovery may still occur regardless of all they've been told. They may cling to this hope as their only source of comfort. Such hopes are encouraged by reports we've all heard of miraculous recoveries despite all odds. Further, hopeless cases don't always *appear* hopeless as when the patient occasionally seems to be aware or responsive. Even PVS (permanently vegetative state) patients make movements that can be misinterpreted as intentional (see Chapter Nine, Case 4).

In such situations, the overall moral situation expands beyond just the patient and family. For instance, if many of the patient's medical caregivers have been involved with her for some time, they may have developed an attachment to the patient. Over time, they may also have developed relationships—good or bad—with some of the family members. These caregivers can suffer the emotionally draining effects of providing medical care that they know is futile. They also may be forced into a moral dilemma between their duty to ensure the patient's well-being and their responsibility for the effects of continued treatment. Others can be affected as well. Medical care—especially for the dying—is very expensive. Insurers, hospitals, and families usually all bear some part of these costs. Even the needs of unrelated patients become relevant if a hospital bed, medical equipment, lab resources, and the time and energy of many caregivers are all devoted to this patient instead of to others. A protracted conflict over futile treatment thus takes its toll, both directly and indirectly, on a great many people and resources.

This heavy toll can make it morally right—even *obligatory*—to suspend futile treatment. In addition to harming caregivers and denying needed resources to others, futile treatment arguably doesn't even serve the interests of those demanding it. If it keeps the patient alive a little longer, then the painful process of "letting go" is lengthened; it can encourage false hopes that must later be disappointed. If she is in any discomfort (even with palliative care), then even the slightest extension of the patient's life wrongs her by prolonging her discomfort to no purpose. Worse, keeping the patient alive in such a helpless and hopeless state commits a moral offence against the patient by diminishing her personal dignity. Unless a patient or her representative specifically requests such treatment, therefore, many reasons add up against continuing futile treatment.

Are there any arguments *for* continuing futile treatment? As previously mentioned, it can buy time for family and friends to be present at their loved one's death. Denying them such an opportunity can be hurtful and disrespectful to them. But more seriously, isn't the suspension of life-extending treatments (even if they only extend life for a short time) equivalent to killing by neglect? It certainly would be *if* the treatments were *not futile*. But again, we need to understand that suspending futile treatment doesn't cause death but only allows the patient's condition to proceed on toward death. In fact, when the death process can only be temporarily slowed but not halted or reversed, it seems morally preferable to let it proceed without our interference. Attempting a futile struggle against impending death somehow seems "unnatural"— an attempt to deny death as the inevitable closure to being a living person—thereby diminishing the dignity of being a person.

Suppose the patient herself, or her living will and/or proxy, has requested that futile treatments be continued. How do the many reasons for suspending such treatments weigh against the moral duty to show deference to these requests? Could the costs of futile treatment ever outweigh even the value of moral agency? Probably not in ordinary cases, though they could if an ongoing futile treatment came into direct conflict with our meeting the serious needs of others. For instance, in wartime or natural disasters, medical resources might become so scarce that maintaining one patient's futile treatment would make it impossible to save another patient's life. This would create a moral obligation to suspend the one's futile treatment for the sake of the other.[5]

Medical futility can bring a large number of moral values, concerns, and principles into play. Let's summarize these:

- **(a)** There is a moral responsibility to show deference toward the choices of moral agents, which can extend to choices made by a living will or suitable proxy.
- **(b)** There's disutility in unnecessary, unproductive suffering, BUT
- **(c)** There's utility gained by respecting grieving family members and their needs.
- **(d)** Medical caregivers have moral duties to care for their patients and to be truthful.
  - Virtue ethics calls upon caregivers to be fully honest and open with family decision-makers about a situation and to avoid encouraging false hopes.
  - Care ethics require care to be given in appropriate ways, which can include suspending futile treatment if it reduces dignity or causes suffering.
- **(e)** The general right to life doesn't necessarily require treatments that can offer nothing beyond a negligible extension of the patient's life.
- **(f)** The utility of constructively using valuable medical and financial resources can weigh heavily against their misallocation, especially when conflicting needs are great.
- **(g)** The moral value of human dignity may begin to be undermined by futile treatment.
- **(h)** There may be moral force in the idea that death's inevitability should be accepted as part of what it is to be a human person.

Although this list is not complete, it makes clear that the issue of medical futility draws into consideration a wide variety of moral concerns, the distinctive insights of different moral theories, and important facts about the patient's

---

[5]In such situations, *Triage* assigns priority to those who can benefit the most when many needs and lives are at stake and medical resources are too limited to adequately treat everyone.

condition, family concerns, and the judgments of established medicine. It should also be clear that each case of potential futility is more or less unique, depending a great deal on the relevant facts, concerns, and judgments. These circumstances largely determine *which* moral concerns apply to each case, *how* they apply, and thus, what is morally right in that particular case.

For Discussion

1. *Consider the concept of a patient's overall benefit; what, in detail, should that include?*
2. *Nowadays, it's considered best for a patient to have both a living will and an appointed proxy. Why?*
3. *What characteristics would you want your own proxy to have?*
4. *Describe situations in which a family member (a) effectively serves an incapacitated patient's interests, and in which (b) she acts against those interests.*
5. *Enact a scene in which a physician meets with family members to explain why futile treatments ought to be suspended for their loved one.*
6. *What hopeless hopes do people sometimes have for their dying loved one? Discuss why people hold these hopes and how hopeless they actually are.*
7. *What theoretical accounts and insights does this discussion of medical futility draw upon?*

Summary

Cases of medical futility and the conflicts they produce have become common in recent years. When a competent patient refuses futile treatment, there's usually no moral problem. Nor is there usually a problem when the patient's medical proxy or a living will refuses futile treatment. The value of moral agency is so strong, in fact, that it can also justify continued futile treatment if that is requested by the patient or proxy (though this doesn't often happen). Conflicts can develop, however, when family members want to continue treatments that can't benefit the patient but that may be costly to others. These conflicts might be resolved by some compromise or by bringing the family to a better understanding of the actual situation. When families cling to hope in medically hopeless situations, however, there can be moral reasons for suspending futile treatment, particularly if the patient is suffering or when the costs of continuing futile treatment are too great.

Key Terms

- **Medically futile:** *a treatment for a specific patient and situation that is highly unlikely to bring any overall benefit to the patient.*

- **Proxy:** *a person who makes medical decisions for the patient when the patient can't make decisions for herself.*

- **Living will:** *a document specifying what interventions the patient either does or does not want done for her when she cannot make choices for herself.*

- **Palliative care:** *care that supports the patient and relieves discomfort.*

III. ENVIRONMENTAL ETHICS: ANTHROPOCENTRISM AND ECOCENTRISM

Alex enjoys working on his car; it's a nice break and it saves him money. He recently bought a used car, knowing it needed an oil change. With an hour to spare one Saturday, he drained the oil, replaced the filter, and added fresh oil. After putting things away, he drove to a nearby garage to dump the used oil. To his surprise, they said they didn't take oil drop offs any more. Alex asked if they knew of another place to take his oil, but they didn't. He went back home and stuck it in his garage for a couple months, but it started eating through the container. Not knowing what else to do, he waited till dark one night and poured it all down a nearby storm drain.

William Baxter's controversial book, *People or Penguins: The Case for Optimal Pollution,* came out in 1974. According to Baxter, it's just plain wrong for us to try to stop polluting our world. For one thing, it's impossible for us to meet our most basic needs, much less meet our important interests, without producing pollution. Nearly everything humans do creates pollution. Instead, we should aim at producing an *optimal* level of *pollution.* Since it's important that we not be harmed by pollution, this level mustn't be set too high. We shouldn't set it too low either, for that would require sacrificing too many human needs and interests. An *optimal* level would appropriately balance all of these factors.

Unfortunately, human needs and interests tend to conflict with each other. Fulfilling one need often reduces our ability to fulfill some other need. For instance, we have an increasing need for new medicines, and tropical rainforests can be abundant sources of new drugs. But people also need food, and cleared rainforests make fertile farmlands. Thus the dilemma: using rainforests to develop needed medicines will limit food production, but if we turn these forests into farms, we won't get medicines we need. We can't have both.

One particularly important conflict is that between ensuring a safe and healthy environment and fulfilling *most* of our needs and interests. If we are to have cars, we must accept the pollution caused by their manufacture and use. If we burn fossil fuels, we can't avoid adding carbon monoxide (CO) and particulates to the air. Manufacturing puts pollutants into the land, water, and air, and disposing of these products later causes further environmental damage. Still, we need and want cars and many other products. Further, our economy depends on our constantly inventing new products and expanding manufacturing. On the other side, none of us wants our food, water, and air teaming with carcinogens and other hazards. Minimizing these threats, however, requires that we cut back in our overall production and consumption of goods. Being a bit simplistic, there's a conflict between protecting our health and well-being, and our need for economic and technological development.

Another sort of conflict exists: meeting the needs and desires of some people often places serious burdens upon others. For instance, environmental harms are not distributed equally across the globe. To obtain cheap labor and avoid restrictive environmental laws, multi-national corporations have manufactured many of their First World consumer products in Third World countries. Even in the United States, mining and drilling operations are most often located in or near poorer communities. As a result, large tracts of land around the world now have standing pools of oil, water sources have been contaminated, whole communities have been poisoned by mercury, children die from brain cancers, and important fisheries have been damaged or destroyed.[6] Many of the world's worst environmental disasters have affected the poor more than any others.[7] Meanwhile, wars, political and financial fraud, and weak infrastructures continue to create major inequalities in how the crucial needs of different people groups are met.

How should choices be made so that everyone's most important needs—including the need for a safe environment—are satisfactorily met? Again, there are conflicts between people and people, between meeting one set of needs and meeting other needs, and between meeting all of these needs and interests while ensuring a reasonably safe and healthy environment. Since these conflicts are all unavoidable, we must respond by trying to balance all of these needs and interests at once. The ideal balance would more or less address the needs of all but would also impose various kinds of costs upon all (including unavoidable environmental damage). This ideal balance of benefits and harms entails Baxter's optimal level of pollution.

Baxter views our determining this ideal balance as essentially an economic problem. Economists study competing forces and interests, including intangible and monetary goods. Using tools like cost–benefit analyses (which resemble utilitarian analyses), we can evaluate how different choices affect different interests. With this understanding, we can then determine how to impose various market controls to achieve a more ideal balance. In achieving and maintaining this balance, we will inevitably produce a modest level of pollution—more than the false hope of no pollution at all but less than what would seriously harm our health and welfare.

The economic tools for achieving balance are already in our hands. In keeping with pluralism, several ethical theories also speak relevantly to aspects of the problem. For instance, Baxter's account employs cost–benefit analyses, but these can be given moral import by relating them to utilitarian evaluations. Social contract and Kantian principles of justice call for a fairer distribution of both goods and pollution. Care ethics encourages us to take the poor and disadvantaged more into account in our social systems. Having both the tools and numerous moral motivations, why then are we still so far from achieving balance?

Two issues particularly stand out. The first involves a widely recognized economic barrier: the *Problem of the Commons*. Returning to Alex's story, Alex wants

---

[6]Oil production in Ecuador by Texaco and later by an Ecuadorian national company harmed indigenous peoples by creating literal swamps of oil; Midwest fracking has turned water wells into potent sources of flammable gas; a Unilever thermometer factory in Kodaikanal, India, spread mercury everywhere; run-off from coal strip mining at Coal River Mountain in West Virginia led to an unusually high incidence of cancer in a local community, and Alaskan and gulf fishing was badly damaged by the Exxon Valdez spill and the BP gulf oil spill, respectively.

[7]The Bhopal India chemical plant explosion in 1984 killed thousands and injured about half a million people.

to keep his newly acquired car in good shape. He thus has strong reasons for re-placing and maintaining its oil. Why? People have interests in taking care of what is theirs. We also have moral, legal, and prudential incentives to respect the prop-erty of others. Taking or damaging others' things is wrong, it can get us into legal trouble, and when we act irresponsibly toward others' property, they may act the same way toward ours.

But what about **common property**—things shared by all? Neither you nor any other person actually *owns* your town's storm drains or roads; these are parts of the town's shared or common property. Thus, everyone uses Main Street, but no one has direct responsibility for it like we have, say, for our own driveways. Thus, none of us has much incentive to care for Main Street or the storm drains, though both are cer-tainly useful to us. This is the problem with common property: everyone has strong incentives to get the most we can out of it, but we have little or no incentive to take care of it. So people litter the road and spray graffiti on signs, and Alex pours his oil down the storm drain. The temptation is especially strong for us to use and abuse environmental commons like air and water. You do everything you can to take good care of your car but probably think nothing about the CO and particulates it pumps into the air each day. Alex carefully looks after his car's oil but probably doesn't lie awake at night worrying about his dumped oil washing into a nearby river.

When Alex buys new oil for his car or new plugs and an air filter, he obviously has to pay for these things. But that's okay since they are all part of what it costs to own a car. The blobs of oil in the river, however, and the CO and particulates in the air are also costs created by his owning and maintaining a car. Called *externalities*, these sorts of things cost us little or nothing at the time and maybe not even very much in the long run (though the next generation may pay substantially for them). Rather, their cost is spread out throughout the commons.

That's the **Problem of the Commons**. It's largely responsible for our pres-ent environmental problems, since manufacturers and consumers have long had strong incentives to *take* and to *dump* but never to *pay*.[8] Only recently have we begun to realize how much our past cost-free exploitation of these commons are now hurting people. But again, there are inequalities. The accumulated damages of unpaid externalities have affected the world's poor more than anyone else. Now poor nations want to improve their condition but hardly have any more of an incentive to pay for the externalities than we did. Thus, they too become pollut-ers (e.g., Beijing's dense smog is a direct result of China's rapid industrialization). Clearly, unless the incentives to carelessly use up the environmental commons are largely removed, it's unlikely that the world will ever attain the balance Baxter wants us to aim at.[9]

---

[8]Baxter calls it the "Problem of the Commons." William Baxter, *People or Penguins: The Case for Optimal Pollution* (New York: Columbia University Press, 1974). Garret Hardin calls it the "Trag-edy of the Commons." Garret Hardin, "The Tragedy of the Commons," *Science, New Series*, 162.3859 (December 13, 1968): 1243–1248, accessed August 30, 2016, http://www.geo.mtu.edu/~asmayer/rural_sustain/governance/Hardin%201968.pdf

[9]Much of Baxter's book is dedicated to this problem and to proposing a complex of solutions.

The commons is not simply an economic and social problem; it's also a moral problem. Naturally, it would help if individuals and nations started shouldering more of their environmental responsibilities. That is simply a requirement of justice, and theories like Kantian ethics, Ross's ethics, and Rawls's international social contract account would certainly support it.

But there's a more fundamental issue. Returning to Baxter, his entire project is based on the assumption—called **anthropocentrism**—that *only people* have foundational or intrinsic value. In attempting to achieve ideal balance (and optimal pollution), he only wants to consider *human* needs and interests. The non-human world has only instrumental value and so should be considered only as far as it affects human beings. This is what Baxter means by the other provocative part of his title: "People or Penguins?" He says, "My criteria are oriented to people, not penguins. Damage to penguins, or sugar pines, or geological marvels is, without more [factors to consider], simply irrelevant. . . . I have no interest in preserving penguins for their own sake."[10]

It's important to understand this correctly. Anthropocentrism entails that the needs of people always takes precedence; when these conflict with those of the natural world, the natural world should normally be ignored. If a city needs low-cost housing for its homeless but can only build in a wetland habitat, there is no moral duty to protect the wetlands. If the insecticide DDT effectively controls mosquito-borne diseases, we may be morally obligated to use it even though it threatens penguins. We must not exaggerate this, however. Although we lack any *direct* responsibilities toward the natural world, we nevertheless ought to keep the natural world in decent condition. This is because it still has instrumental value, and its condition can affect people. Thus, if the wetland is essential to the city's water supply, then the city probably should build elsewhere. Penguins have no intrinsic value but should still be counted in our plans as far as they affect human interests (even if we simply find them cute). As already seen, harmful levels of pollution are not acceptable in an ideal balance of human needs and interests. In this way, then, the natural world still is morally important to anthropocentrism—not for its own sake but for the sake of the people it affects.

Anthropocentrism is one of several positions one can take regarding the natural environment. Another is called **ecocentrism**, which largely opposes anthropocentrism. All versions of ecocentrism—and there are several—agree that the natural world and its parts have intrinsic (foundational) value. Creatures and things, local environments, whole species (both people and penguins), and even the entire earth ecosystem—these all have value in their own right. In this view, our moral considerations must include the needs and interests of both people and the natural world whether or not the latter serves any human purpose.[11]

Let's call the weakest version of this position *mild ecocentrism*. Its main goal is to correct our long-standing neglect of the environment by shifting attention from

---

[10]Baxter, *People or Penguins*, 5.

[11]It's worth noting that the extension of utilitarianism to animals already makes it ecocentric.

humans to non-humans. In practice, ecocentrism calls us to consider the needs of the non-human world along with those of human beings. This does not require that the natural world be assigned greater value; in attempting to balance human and non-human needs, mild ecocentrism could still assign greater value to critical human goods than to some goods of the natural world. But it can also sometimes favor non-humans instead. For instance, it might maintain that the moral importance of protecting a species from extinction outweighs the potential profits of building a luxury high rise.

Even in its mildest form, ecocentrism can give us moral responsibilities that anthropocentrism might not. We might have a moral responsibility to preserve a wolf habitat even though wolves pose some threat to domesticated animals and, more rarely, to humans. It might be morally wrong to build a road through virgin forest land. Most important, ecocentrism has implications for the Problem of the Commons. With anthropocentrism, there's a strong incentive for people to use up common resources but only a rather weak and indirect incentive to care for and renew the commons. Ecocentrism, in contrast, adds the moral incentive that the commons has intrinsic value in itself. This gives us all a prima facie obligation to care for the commons, regardless of its immediate usefulness to ourselves. Even if this obligation may sometimes be overridden, ecocentrism at least gives us reason to value the commons, counterbalancing the incentives to exploit it.

There are stronger ecocentric viewpoints; the most important claims that at least some non-humans have moral rights. If dolphins, wolves, and even domesticated animals like poultry and cattle have intrinsic value, then shouldn't they also have rights—at the very least, a right to life and a right not to be caused unnecessary suffering?

Despite the intuitive connection between having value and having rights, we can't conclude that something has rights simply because it has intrinsic value. A mountain ecosystem may have intrinsic value, but we don't think it can have any rights. To assign rights, we need to appeal to an account of rights; not surprisingly, different accounts disagree over what can have rights. For strict accounts like Locke's or one based on Kantian principles, moral rights are limited to moral agents or at least to what has the *capacity* or *potential* to become a moral agent. Since animals lack even the potential to become moral agents, they cannot have moral rights.

There are less strict accounts of rights. Utilitarians, for instance, often observe that the "higher" animals experience pain and suffering. Since suffering is part of any concept of utility, consequentialists can unapologetically include sentient animals (those capable of suffering) in their moral calculations. This, in turn, supports moral rights for animals.

If the less strict accounts can extend moral rights, how far do they extend moral responsibility? For humans, shared rights support equally shared responsibilities. If you have property rights to something, those give me certain responsibilities regarding how I treat your property. If I have similar rights, that gives you similar responsibilities as well. So suppose we grant rights to some non-humans: does that give them responsibilities as well?

We certainly don't think of non-humans as having responsibilities. Further, we ascribe rights to human infants, young children, and comatose adults, though none of these have any corresponding moral responsibilities. Being a bit simplistic, only moral agents can have moral responsibilities, and neither non-humans nor some humans can function as moral agents. But as they can still have rights, there's no reason to worry that if we confer rights to animals, they must also have moral responsibilities.

It's possible, then, to grant rights to non-humans, but are non-human rights a necessary part of morality? Animals needn't have rights for us still to have moral responsibilities toward them. Kant holds, for instance, that humans have moral duties toward animals, though he would never have thought of animals having rights. These duties are *indirect*: we should not abuse animals because doing so makes us more likely to abuse humans as well.[12] Nevertheless, indirect duties are not always very strong. In contrast, even mild ecocentrism can give us *direct* duties toward animals, plants, species, and even ecosystems, since it assigns them intrinsic value. Since mild ecocentrism can already support such duties, many consider it unnecessary to embrace a stronger ecocentrism to also give animals rights.

There are much more drastic varieties of ecocentrism. Of these, the most important, **deep ecology**, branches into several further variations. All variations of deep ecology agree, first, that humans and non-humans have *equal* value; no species has priority over any other. This contrasts with milder ecocentrism, which can grant value to all the earth's components while still giving preference to the most pressing human concerns. Second, deep ecology views people as simply one part of the earth's total ecological system. Humans and nonhumans, various species, and even nonliving things all have their own roles, all are important, and all belong to a single, dynamic, ecosystem.

What are the moral implications of deep ecology? Since the complete earth ecosystem cannot continue without the contributions of most of its components, all living and even non-living things have intrinsic value. This certainly helps with the Problem of the Commons, though its other moral implications can be shocking. For instance, the earth ecosystem may require the sacrifice of human interests, needs, or even individual lives for the sake of its greater needs.

The most radical view of all would be that *only* the complete earth system has intrinsic value: no component, not even the human species, has any value in itself.[13] Each can still have instrumental value, however, and so can be important or not, depending on the circumstances, for preserving the complete earth system. How could this affect humans? The answer may be up to us. If humanity stops harming the earth and instead works to care for and preserve it (which would require sacrifices on our part), then we could take on considerable instrumental

---

[12]Kant's view here parallels anthropocentrism.

[13]Note that this still adheres to deep ecology's claim that humans and non-humans have equal value; instead of assigning positive intrinsic value to all, however, it assigns all zero intrinsic value.

value. This could make our survival morally essential to the earth system. If we instead continue to undermine the earth system, then that system would probably be better off without us. In the worst case, the annihilation of humanity could become a moral necessity.

For Discussion

1. *How much non-recyclable waste do you think you create each day? How could you cut back on this? Should you try to cut back on this?*
2. *What are some commons that people use regularly?*
3. *Which position do you take: anthropocentrism or ecocentrism? Why?*
4. *Discuss: Do any animals have rights? If you think so, what are those rights?*
5. *What moral responsibilities do we have toward some animals?*
6. *Discuss: Do humans have a moral responsibility to protect other species? What sorts of species? Do we also have a responsibility to protect some non-living natural things (e.g., waterfalls, canyons, forests)?*
7. *At what point (ranging from mild ecocentrism to deep ecology) do you think that ecocentrism becomes indefensible (if ever)?*

Summary

Baxter observes that we can't meet human needs without producing pollution; we must therefore apply economic methods to balance the needs of all humans. The best balance would produce an optimal level of pollution. One barrier to achieving balance is the Problem of the Commons, which especially encourages us to exploit environmental common property like air or water. The result is environmental damage that affects all (e.g., polluted water—an externality). Even if Baxter's economics can solve this problem, there remains a possible moral weakness to his approach—namely, anthropocentrism, which assigns only instrumental value to non-humans. Another approach, ecocentrism, includes several versions. All of its versions assign foundational value to non-humans thereby adding a moral incentive to care for other things in the environment. Stronger versions of ecocentrism extend this by adding animal rights or treating humans and non-humans as equals (deep ecology).

Key Terms

- **Common property:** *property that is shared by all.*
- **Problem of the Commons:** *the problem that everyone is motivated to use and exploit common property but not to care for it.*
- **Anthropocentrism:** *holds that only humans and human interests have foundational value; everything else has instrumental value.*
- **Ecocentrism:** *holds that both humans and non-humans have foundational value.*
- **Deep ecology:** *assigns humans and non-humans equal value.*

IV. BUSINESS ETHICS: WHISTLE-BLOWING

Roger Boisjoly was an engineer with Morton Thiokol, the contractor that supplied rocket boosters for NASA's space shuttle program. Months before the January 1986 Challenger disaster, Boisjoly analyzed a previous launch and found that the O rings intended to shield one booster section from another didn't work, particularly at cold temperatures. In reporting this to his managers, he predicted a likely "catastrophe of the highest order—loss of human life" unless the design was changed. Getting no response, he kept submitting memos. Finally, a task force was appointed to study the problem, but even with Boisjoly on it, the task force accomplished little. The night before the Challenger launch, he and other engineers requested that it be delayed, as it was expected to be very cold the next morning. Under pressure from NASA, however, their concerns were set aside as inconclusive, and the launch went forward as planned. Within moments of ignition, the O rings failed as Boisjoly had predicted, and the remaining rocket boosters and shuttle blew up a little over a minute later, killing all seven crew members.

President Reagan appointed the Rogers Commission shortly afterwards to investigate the disaster, and Boisjoly served as one of the key witnesses. After the commission report cited problems with how NASA and Morton Thiokol made decisions, Boisjoly found himself blamed for damaging the company's reputation. Concerned with how official statements misrepresented the actual events, Boisjoly tried to set the record straight by commenting on the commission's report and through testimony that often contradicted NASA and Morton Thiokol's claims. As his work environment became increasingly hostile, Boisjoly took a leave of absence and later resigned.[14]

Whistle-blowing—the act of exposing illegal, immoral, or dangerous practices occurring within an organization to those who can address the problem—has received more attention than ever in the past decade. Whistle-blowers have often helped correct wrongs. Unfortunately, they also often harm the organization. Profits, projects, and reputations can suffer, jobs may be lost, and legal actions may result. Companies sometimes go out of business, hurting the entire economy.[15] Given such effects, we might ask if the good that whistle-blowers accomplish is worth the costs. Since whistle-blowers are normally "insiders," furthermore, they have access to facts that were never intended to be known outside the organization. By revealing such information, do whistle-blowers betray their own organizations and co-workers? Finally, whistle-blowers themselves usually suffer backlash from their own organizations and are often denied employment by other businesses in their fields.

---

[14]Because the Challenger crew included Christa McAuliffe, a New Hampshire high school teacher, the launch was widely viewed on television, including by her own students. McAuliffe was to become the first teacher in space. The disaster was traumatic to the entire nation and led to the Shuttle program's suspension for nearly three years.

[15]Enron and WorldCom are examples.

Given the many problems and risks of blowing the whistle, potential whistle-blowers need to think hard about the moral implications of their actions. Yet whistle-blowers have lately been more accepted and admired by the public than ever before. This may be due to the many recent government and corporate scandals that have badly hurt even the general public. Increasingly, ordinary people have come to distrust the government and corporations; they have also come to feel they have a "right to know" as consumers, stakeholders, and citizens. Just as government and business vilify whistle-blowers, the public treats them as heroes, as the few who willingly put themselves on the line for the public good.

How should whistle-blowing be viewed ethically? That depends a great deal on the circumstances. To sort out the relevant issues, business ethicists have argued that *ethically justifiable* whistle-blowing must fulfill the following conditions:[16]

1. *Motive:* The whistle-blower's motives for acting should be morally right.
2. *Proper channels:* The whistle-blower has unsuccessfully pursued all available *internal* means to overcome the problem within the organization.
3. *Severity/urgency:* The problem is serious and poses a pressing threat that can only be adequately addressed by whistle-blowing.

These three conditions constitute the most widely accepted analysis of whistle-blowing, though the *proper channels* and *severity/urgency* conditions were initially considered most important. Later, Norman Bowie added the *motive* condition. This list is motivated particularly by the view that potential whistle-blowers have a prima facie duty (see Chapter Eight, §II) of loyalty to their organizations. The accepted analysis, then, sees whistle-blowing as *morally justified* only when the potential whistle-blower first takes well-intentioned and appropriate steps within an organization to counter some truly serious threat in a timely manner.

The accepted analysis further acknowledges a *moral obligation* to expose the organization's problem *externally* when the situation also fulfills the following two conditions. The thinking seems to be that the first list of conditions establishes the gravity of the situation while these latter conditions support going outside the organization:

4. *Evidence:* The whistle-blower has objective and compelling evidence that the problem exists.
5. *Success:* There is good reason to expect the whistle-blowing will succeed at overcoming the problem and any related threats.

Much can be said about each condition. Starting with the *motive* condition, the whistle-blower should not act to get attention, "get back" at someone, or for personal gain. Still, this condition can be challenged. When a situation is extremely serious, it seems that personal motivations become greatly outweighed

---

[16]Drawn from Norman Bowie's and Richard T. De George's analyses of whistle-blowing. These analyses appear in their business ethics texts, respectively. Norman Bowie, *Business Ethics* (Englewood Cliffs, NJ: Prentice Hall, 1982), 140-43; Richard T. De George, *Business Ethics*, 7th ed. (Upper Saddle River, NJ: Prentice Hall, 2010).

by the need to blow the whistle. Imagine yourself as a company engineer who has found a product design flaw that endangers thousands of customers, but your supervisor tells you to sign off on the product so production can be started. You already dislike this supervisor and realize that his attempt to suppress the flaw could get him fired. So what? If lives can only be protected by your exposing the flaw, shouldn't you expose it? On the other hand, you would really love to see this supervisor fired. Wouldn't your petty hostility make it wrong for you to blow the whistle? There are two separate considerations here. First, heading off a serious threat may be the morally right *act*, regardless of your feelings. But, second, that doesn't excuse your bad *motives*. You thus may fail as a *moral actor*, even if your *act* itself is morally right. We can do right things for wrong reasons. It thus seems that motive may not be of much importance. Failing as an actor is morally wrong, but it isn't relevant to the act, which is our concern here. Acting in the right way seems just as important whether one's motives are pure, contemptible, or mixed.

The accepted analysis requires going through *proper channels* out of its concern for loyalty. As long as an organization has established internal procedures (as most now do) for resolving problems, potential whistle-blowers should surely pursue these before taking the problem outside. There's a duty to act loyally toward an organization and its people before airing its dirty laundry before the rest of the world. It also seems wrong to bypass those responsible for a problem without giving them any opportunity to correct their mistakes. Following proper internal channels thus is called for both as a matter of loyalty and because we ought to respect persons and their autonomy.

Yet even the accepted analysis grants exceptions to this condition. Pointing out problems or resisting other people's decisions may be interpreted as personal attacks or as interference with others' jobs. The reaction may be to bully or "punish" the whistle-blower in return. Thus, when the backlash becomes too great, the duty to keep following internal channels ceases. Second, this duty is also suspended if the whistle-blower comes to realize that no one is going to do anything no matter how far she goes up the ladder. Finally, there sometimes is simply not enough time. Problems of extreme urgency call for immediate action, and if the only adequate solution requires notifying external authorities, that's what must be done. As morally important as the proper channels requirement can be, the accepted analysis adds that it may be dropped in any of these three special cases.

There is yet another worry regarding this condition, however, even with these exceptions. It used to be taken for granted that employees owe their employers loyalty. In return, employers took care of their employees all the way into retirement. Joining a company was a long-term commitment on both sides. For better or worse, this is no longer true; again and again, businesses "downsize" or "outsource" employees to save money. Adding insult to injury, many sectors traditionally cut jobs just before Christmas. Few organizations feel they have responsibilities toward employees of twenty, thirty, or more years. Worse, a company may fire an employee just before retirement to avoid paying retirement benefits. It's not surprising, then, that today's workers respond in kind, taking jobs with the attitude that "If a better opportunity arises, by all means, take it!"

In such a work climate, employees may not have a moral duty of loyalty—except perhaps to organizations that take exceptional care of their employees. Even with the duty of loyalty much reduced, however, the *proper channels* condition still seems to have some importance. The moral obligation to respect others remains; employees also commit themselves, upon hiring, to follow their new organization's procedures. There is also great value in whistle-blowers taking the moral "high ground," avoiding susceptibility to any possible accusations of disloyalty, disrespect, or the like. Taken with its exceptions, therefore, the *proper channels* condition remains a condition for justified whistle-blowing.

Severity and urgency: These are distinct, and severity is the more important of the two. Think of severity along utilitarian lines: what would be the expected scope, intensity, and duration of the harms if the problem was not dealt with? The worse the effects, the more severe the problem. Urgency—how quickly the problem will produce its effects—is different. For instance, polluting underground aquifers by fracking[17] could be very serious if it destroys critical water sources. Since the damage accumulates over time, however, this problem isn't so urgent. Depending on the aquifer, continued fracking for months or even years may not cause irreparable damage. Meanwhile, better ways to map aquifers and predict pollutant flow, new methods of containment, and safer chemicals may be found to protect water supplies. In contrast, the Challenger involved both severity (loss of life) and urgency (a launch the next morning). Although situations can involve one without the other, however, severity and urgency do often coincide. Most often, greater severity adds to the urgency.

The accepted analysis maintains that whistle-blowing is morally justified as long as the first set of conditions are satisfied, though our considerations suggest that *severity/urgency* is the most important of the three. If the next two conditions are also satisfied, then whistle-blowing becomes a moral duty. Starting with the *evidence* condition, we need to distinguish two separate requirements. First, without a doubt, the whistle-blower must have definite evidence of a serious problem that needs addressing. The whistle-blower should be personally and directly acquainted with this evidence, and it should convince him beyond doubt. Boisjoly had such evidence from his own careful study of the previous launch. This is important because whistle-blowing can cause terrible effects if it turns out to be mistaken. Indeed, how could a whistle-blower be *justified* in even raising questions *within* the organization unless he has this kind of evidence? Thus, this part of the evidence condition really belongs among the first set of conditions: there must be such evidence for whistle-blowing to be justified at all.

---

[17]Fracking is environmentally controversial. It is done by forcing water and chemicals at high pressure between underground layers of stone to break them up and release natural gas and oil. These are then pumped to the surface. Fracking has added substantially to American gas and oil supplies, thereby reducing prices. It has also contaminated ground water and increased the number of earthquakes in nearby areas.

Even when a whistle-blower knows about a problem with personal certainty, however, it still remains for her to convince others of the problem. Thus, second, the whistle-blower must ultimately obtain evidence that can *substantiate* the problem for others. Often, the facts that have convinced the whistle-blower of a problem are also available to others *within* the organization; what's remains needed, then, is substantiation sufficiently convincing to people outside the organization. This second part of the evidence condition, which we will call *substantiation* to distinguish it from the first part (still to be called the *evidence condition*), best applies as a requirement to whistle-blowers exposing a problem *externally*.

The *success* condition has impressed some people as exceedingly important, while others see nothing to it. This is probably due to their interpreting "success" in different ways. Directly averting a serious threat is unquestionably a "success." But when this isn't possible, whistle-blowing might still "succeed" in putting a stop to some pattern of wrongdoing or some developing threat. Maybe an act of whistle-blowing merely draws attention to a wrong practice or serves justice by leading to punishment. Do these looser interpretations stretch the notion of "success" too far? Contrary to the accepted analysis's interpretation, most people today consider the accomplishment of any sort of valuable good to be a "success."

Putting these considerations all together yields a *modified analysis* of whistle-blowing:

For an act of whistle-blowing to be morally justified, the following conditions must be met:

1. *Severity/urgency:* There must be a *severe* threat of harm with some degree of *urgency*.
2. *Proper channels:* The whistle-blower should first attempt to address the problem by following the organization's *proper channels*. But this requirement is suspended if
   (a) the whistle-blower herself increasingly risks harms due to her action;
   (b) no appropriate response will likely occur within the organization; or
   (c) the threat is too urgent to work through ordinary internal channels.
3. *Evidence:* The whistle-blower must be convinced by strong and compelling evidence that there is a genuine problem;

For whistle-blowing outside the organization to become a moral duty, the additional conditions must be met:

4. *Substantiation:* The whistle-blower must be able to convincingly demonstrate to outsiders that the problem exists.
5. *Success:* The whistle-blowing will likely *succeed* in achieving some constructive and morally valuable effect.

Before leaving the topic of whistle-blowing, let's briefly examine just one very different justification for whistle-blowing. This is found in Michael Davis's **complicity theory**, which may capture the thinking of many recent whistle-blowers better than the accepted or even modified analyses. Complicity theory appeals to the moral principle that one should not be a knowing and willing *accomplice* in wrongdoing. Davis argues that many actual cases of whistle-blowing have been motivated by this principle and have seemed both justified and commendable even when they have not fulfilled every condition of the accepted analysis.[18]

Knowing of a wrong, being able to resist that wrong, and then doing nothing creates complicity—a sharing in the wrong. This is obvious when one has direct responsibility over a problem; for example, if Boisjoly had said nothing about the rocket boosters he was responsible for, he would share moral guilt for the explosion. But one can also be complicit without having any direct responsibility. Suppose you notice someone shoplifting a valuable item. If you remain silent and offer no warning about this to anyone, you have become an accessory to the shoplifting, having enabled the shoplifter to get away with her theft. If the shoplifter were to realize that you observed her crime but said nothing, she would be thankful for your help! Although it's not as bad as shoplifting itself, not doing anything about a shoplifting still deserves moral blame. In general, then, complicity is morally blameworthy and should be avoided. In this view, an act of whistle-blowing can become morally justified—and even a moral duty—simply because we shouldn't share in or participate, even indirectly, in a wrong.

For Discussion

1. *What distinct theories do the various conditions of the modified analysis most closely relate to? (e.g., Bowie's earlier "motive" condition was clearly Kantian in nature).*
2. *How relevant are the whistle-blower's motives, if at all, in justifying whistle-blowing?*
3. *People still take showing loyalty to their school(s) very seriously. If you became aware of some serious problem at your school, how much should loyalty affect how you proceed as a potential whistle-blower?*
4. *Do you consider all the conditions of the modified whistle-blowing analysis to be equally important? Why or why not?*
5. *Would you add or remove anything from the modified analysis?*
6. *Imagine that you could blow the whistle about some very serious and urgent situation. You realize this would create many enemies for you and hurt your career. Would you act as a whistle-blower?*

Summary

Starting with the widely accepted analysis *of whistle-blowing, we moved to a* modified analysis, *which maintains that ethically justifiable whistle-blowing must fulfill the following conditions:*

1. Severity/urgency: *There must be a severe threat of harm with some degree of urgency.*

---

[18]See the Case 6 of this chapter on Edward Snowden as an example of a problem that put no one at risk of physical injury or death.

2. Proper channels: *The whistle-blower should first attempt to address the problem by going through the organization's proper channels. But this is suspended if:*

   (a) *the whistle-blower increasingly risks harms due to her action;*

   (b) *no appropriate response will likely occur within the organization; or*

   (c) *the threat is too urgent to work through ordinary internal channels.*

3. Evidence: *The whistle-blower must be convinced by strong and compelling evidence that there is a genuine problem;*

For whistle-blowing outside the organization to be a moral duty, the following conditions should also be satisfied:

4. Substantiation: *The whistle-blower must be able to convincingly demonstrate to an outsider that the problem exists.*

5. Success: *The whistle-blowing will likely succeed in achieving some constructive and morally valuable effect.*

A quite different alternative to justifying whistle-blowing is complicity theory.

Key Terms

- **Whistle-blowing:** *the act of exposing illegal, immoral, or dangerous practices occurring within an organization to those who can address the problem.*

- **Complicity theory:** *Maintains that whistle-blowing is morally justified when the whistle-blower acts to avoid becoming an accomplice or sharing in the responsibility of a wrong.*

V. THE PERSONAL DIMENSION: HOW CAN I MAKE MORALLY RIGHT CHOICES?

Ethical theories, while imperfect, can provide insight on the nature of morality, draw our attention to moral phenomena we might otherwise have missed, and have practical value, as the preceding illustrations show. But can they help you and I as we face our own personal problems? Many of the cases in this book involve personal problems, and you may have applied a few ethical theories to some of them. But let's get *really* down to earth and personal. Three questions usually come to mind when we find ourselves in the midst of a moral problem. Our theories can help us answer each.

1. *Why should I do what is morally right?* What motivations are there for acting morally, particularly when doing right is much less in my interest than acting immorally? Telling the truth, keeping a promise, or refusing to compromise on integrity can be costly. But our ethical theories and concepts suggest many reasons for acting ethically, regardless of the cost, and at least some of these are bound to resonate with anybody:

- Right acts usually contribute to the overall good (or at least avoid doing harm), and most people want their lives to leave a positive mark upon the world (act and rule utilitarianism).

- Acting immorally is ultimately irrational; there's often a conflict between what I'd like to do and what would happen if others did the same thing (Kantian universalization).
- Not treating others as valuable also devalues myself since my moral value is the same as theirs (the Kantian Good Will).
- Acting immorally might add to my short-term pleasure, but it won't contribute to my genuine happiness (Aristotle's virtue ethics).
- Acting immorally goes against who I am and what I want to be as a person (virtue ethics).
- To act immorally is to act against human nature (natural law theory).
- A morally good person loves and cares for others, wants to become more caring toward them, and never wants to act in a completely uncaring way (care ethics).
- I want to practice my faith and please and obey God, thereby coming to know God better (Alternate dependency account).
- I should minimize my negative impact upon the environment and promote its care and protection since it has value in itself (ecocentrism).

2. *What is the morally right thing to do?* The many theories we've looked at in this book highlight plenty of values and perspectives worth considering whenever you must answer this question. There's also a formal procedure presented in the Guidelines for Case Study Analyses (preceding Part I) that can be followed when addressing nearly any moral problem. To help you make moral choices in everyday life, here's an adaptation of that procedure that's shorter and more informal:

1. **Clarify the problem.** What is the problem, and what led to it in the first place? Who is affected, and what's at stake? Ask others for their "take" on the problem.
2. **Possible responses?** How could you address the problem? Try to think "out of the box" but stay realistic.
3. **Picture each response's *moral* implications.** *Imagine* carrying out the responses you've just considered, and ask questions like these: What are the likely effects of each response? How does each response treat those involved? Is each caring or virtuous?
4. **What's best?** Use moral reasoning or moral reflection to figure out which of your possible responses is best.
5. **Compare alternatives.** What makes your choice better than the other responses?

3. *How can I do the morally right thing?* The most difficult challenge for many of us is simply to do *right*, especially when it's painful, embarrassing, or costly. Sometimes we just don't seem to have the inner resources to do what we know we should. Do we have what it takes, particularly when it seems we could "get away with it" instead? This takes us back to Gyges (see Chapter One, §1). Gyges clearly lacked the moral character needed to act rightly once he found the

ring. The same may be true of many of us, but it's best to recognize that now, while we can still do something about it.

So what can we do now, before we face our next test of fire? Virtue and care ethics seem to suggest the best answers. We won't find much help from pure "will power" (if there even is such a thing). But we can invest ourselves—for the long run—in building up our personal characters. This means ongoing practice, which we can get by choosing right options moment by moment, day by day, even in small things. Think of today's self making you into tomorrow's self. We probably also all need the help and support of others. This may require breaking off bad relationships and spending time with people we can respect. Those caught in abusive relationships or who carry deep emotional scars from the past may need to seek out even more help.

Ultimately, the answer to this last question is up to you. As an autonomous person, you have the power to make choices of moral significance—some small, some great. Whether you view that power as a blessing or as the curse of the human condition, none of us can escape the responsibility it places upon us.

For Discussion

1. *Since starting your study of ethics, have you found anything you've been able to apply directly to your life?*
2. *Has your study of ethics helped you to better distinguish right and wrong?*
3. *Is there a moral question you now feel you can answer thanks to your study of ethics?*
4. *The text lists several reasons for acting morally. Which are most compelling to you?*
5. *Can you think of other reasons for acting morally besides what the text lists?*
6. *Have you ever found doing the morally right thing particularly hard? Give some examples.*
7. *Are you committed to living morally? Why? How will you work at this goal?*
8. *As a parent, how would you go about equipping your child to become a moral person?*

Summary

The thing we might most want from ethical theories is practical help in facing our own personal moral problems. Ethical theories are pretty good at giving us reasons for doing what is morally right. They also can contribute a great deal toward our figuring out what is morally right. In combination, meanwhile, our theories' insights can help guide us through the multi-layered problems that medicine, the environment, business, and other areas of life can hand us. But this still leaves the most difficult problem: How can I do the morally right thing? Working through some of this book's cases gives you practice with solving moral problems. But what's more important is what you learn from dealing with the problems you encounter in your own life. The rest is up to you!

Chapter Assignment Questions

1. *Which of our ethical theories looks best to you? Why?*
2. *** Compare and contrast foundational and explanatory pluralism.*
3. *** If you were to set up a explanatory pluralism using the four branches proposed in section 1, what theories would you use to explain each branch? Would you add or remove any branch?*
4. *How might a seriously ill patient's refusal of treatment* not *be a choice for death? Under what circumstances might such a refusal* be *a choice for death?*
5. *When futile treatment is continued to keep a patient alive for the family's sake, how should patient discomfort or even suffering be balanced with family's needs?*
6. *Imagine and evaluate a couple situations in which continuing one patient's futile treatment interferes with providing care for others.*
7. *Research some other environmental commons that have or are now suffering damage (e.g., ocean pollution, aquifer damage from fracking, etc.). Describe and discuss the moral aspects of the commons you have researched.*
8. *Determine your carbon footprint (you can do this online; there are many sources). Discuss your reaction. Do you plan to change any of your habits or activities? If so, which ones and why?*
9. *Non-humans can't vote or express any views. Baxter thinks that this raises serious difficulties for including their interests in determining an optimal level of pollution, particularly when non-human and human interests conflict. How would you answer him on this?*
10. *How do the rights of future human generations affect our environmental responsibilities and considerations? (See the OUP online ancillaries for this book, which include a supplementary chapter about future generations.)*
11. *Both the accepted and modified analyses of whistle-blowing distinguish between justified and obligatory whistle-blowing (roughly matching the distinction between internal and external whistle-blowing). Is it right to make this distinction, or should there just be one analysis for whistle-blowing (being both justified and obligatory)?*
12. *Our presentation of complicity theory needs supplementing. What would you add to it?*
13. *Read online about a whistle-blowing case (there are many!) that you find interesting. Discuss it, applying either the modified or complicity analysis.*

Additional Resources

Baxter, William. *People or Penguins: The Case for Optimal Pollution.* New York: Columbia University Press, 1974.

Boisjoly, Roger M. "Ethical Decisions—Morton Thiokol and the Space Shuttle Challenger Disaster—Index." Online Ethics Center for Engineering and Science, May 15, 2006. Accessed August 30, 2016. http://www.onlineethics.org/Topics/ProfPractice/PPEssays/thiokolshuttle.aspx.

Boisjoly, Roger. "The Result Would Be a Catastrophe." WebCite, October 27, 2009. Accessed August 30, 2016. http://www.webcitation.org/651nnfKDv. This is a copy of Roger Boisjoly's original July 31, 1985 memo warning about the O rings on the Space Shuttle.

Bowie, Norman. *Business Ethics.* Englewood Cliffs, NJ: Prentice Hall, 1982.

Burns, Ken and Dayton Duncan. *The National Parks: America's Best Idea*. WETA and The National Parks Film Project, 2009. Accessed August 30, 2016. http://www.pbs.org/nationalparks/. This is a six-episode documentary film for television. It is also available for purchase on DVD.

Davis, Michael. "Some Paradoxes of Whistle-Blowing." *Business and Professional Ethics Journal*, 15.1 (1996): 3–19. Accessed August 30, 2016. http://philosophia.uncg.edu/media/phi361-metivier/readings/Davis-Paradoxes%20of%20Whistle-Blowing.pdf. This article critiques the accepted analysis and presents Davis's complicity theory. It was part of a symposium sponsored by the Centre for Professional Ethics, University of Central Lancashire, Preston, England, on November 12, 1996.

De George, Richard T. *Business Ethics*. 7th ed. Upper Saddle River, NJ: Prentice Hall, 2010.

"Edward Snowden: Leaks That Exposed US Spy Programme." BBC News, January 17, 2014. Accessed August 30, 2016. http://www.bbc.com/news/world-us-canada-23123964.

"Enron Whistle-Blower Tells of 'Crooked Company.'" NBCnews.com, March 15, 2006. Accessed August 30, 2016. http://www.nbcnews.com/id/11839694/ns/business-corporate_scandals/t/enron-whistleblowerwhistle-blower-tells-crooked-company/#.VnxQuxUrLIU. This article summarizes the whistle-blowing story of Sherron Watkins at Enron.

A Ghost in the Making: Searching for the Rusty-Patched Bumble Bee. Day's Edge Productions, August 2016. Accessed August 30, 2016. https://vimeo.com/149689195. This is an HD video on the rusty-patched bumblebee and was the "Best Short" at the G2 Green Earth Film Festival in August 2016.

Hardin, Garrett. "The Tragedy of the Commons." *Science*, new series 162.3859 (December 13, 1968): 1243–1248. Accessed August 30, 2016. http://www.geo.mtu.edu/~asmayer/rural_sustain/governance/Hardin%201968.pdf.

Homer, Julia and David M. Katz. "WorldCom Whistle-blower Cynthia Cooper." *CFO Magazine*, February 1, 2008. Accessed August 30, 2016. http://ww2.cfo.com/human-capital-careers/2008/02/worldcom-whistle-blower-cynthia-cooper/. This article summarizes the whistle-blowing story of Cynthia Cooper at WordCom.

Jecker, Nancy S. "Medical Futility." Ethics in Medicine, University of Washington School of Medicine. Accessed August 30, 2016, https://depts.washington.edu/bioethx/topics/futil.html.

Kasman, Deborah L. "When Is Medical Treatment Futile? A Guide for Students, Residents, and Physicians." *Journal of General Internal Medicine*, 19.10 (October 2004): 1053–1056. Accessed August 30, 2016. http://www.ncbi.nlm.nih.gov/pmc/articles/PMC1492577/ .

"*The Last Mountain*: Trailer." Uncommon Productions, March 2, 2011. Accessed August 30, 2011. https://www.youtube.com/watch?v=c5wmUkpOCKE. This is a trailer for the documentary about the story of Massey Coal and the local community.

Mason, Elinor. "Value Pluralism." In *The Stanford Encyclopedia of Philosophy* (Summer 2015 Edition), edited by Edward N. Zalta. Accessed August 30, 2016. http://plato.stanford.edu/archives/sum2015/entries/value-pluralism/.

"My Old Lady." *Scrubs*, Season 1, Episode 4," NBC, October 16, 2001. Accessed August 30, 2016. https://www.youtube.com/watch?v=0uuCYzUjWik. This episode contains a short clip from a story of a dying patient.

Plungis, Jeff and Dana Hull. "VW's Emissions Cheating Found by Curious Clean-Air Group." *Bloomberg Daily Newsletter*, September 19, 2015, updated September 20, 2015. Accessed on August 30, 2016. http://www.bloomberg.com/news/articles/2015 09 19/volkswagen-emissions-cheating-found-by-curious-clean-air-group. This link is to an article and short news video.

Schiermeier, Quirin. "The Science Behind the Volkswagen Emissions scandal." *Nature: International Weekly Journal of Science*, September 24, 2015, updated September 25, 2015 and September 30, 2015. Accessed August 30, 2016. http://www.nature.com/news/the-science-behind-the-volkswagen-emissions-scandal-1.18426.

"The Snowden Leaks Explained: Video." BBC News, October 30, 2013. Accessed August 30, 2016. http://www.bbc.com/news/world-24737793.

Case 1

Infant Medical Futility

One controversial case of medical futility began in October 1992 with the birth of a baby girl. (Futility issues are not limited to end of life situations.) "Baby K" was anencephalic: she was missing portions of her brain's cerebral hemispheres as a congenital defect. Normally such babies die soon after birth. In this case, however, the physicians placed her on a ventilator when she first had difficulty breathing. Wanting the baby to stay alive, the mother asked that a ventilator be used again, each time the baby had breathing problems. This use of the ventilator kept her alive for more than two years. Because the child was anencephalic, there was no chance that she could ever achieve consciousness. For this reason, the physicians in the case had come to consider these treatments medically futile. They asked the hospital to seek a court order that at the next episode of difficult breathing, the ventilator be refused. Two courts successively rejected this request, maintaining that the law required the ventilator to remain available as needed.

  While refusing treatments in cases of futility can often be morally justified, physicians and caregivers have embraced futility as a compelling reason to allow for death, though in this case that was resisted.[19]

THOUGHT QUESTIONS

1. Did the mother have a moral right to keep the baby alive like this?
2. Did this baby have a right to be kept alive? What moral obligations did various people have to the baby herself?
3. Was keeping the baby alive morally right? How would various ethical theories answer this?
4. Is there a danger that medical caregivers may become too ready and willing to end life by suspending futile treatment?

Case 2

Climate Change and Oil

According to the Energy Information Administration, a U.S. government agency, the United States currently uses 25% of the world's oil supply. But the United States makes up only 5% of the world's population. Also, the United States uses fifteen

Continued

[19]This case is discussed in Mark A. Bonanno, "The Case of Baby K: Exploring the Concept of Medical Futility," *Annals of Health Law*, 4.1 (1995): article 9, accessed August 30, 2016, http://lawecommons.luc.edu/cgi/viewcontent.cgi?article=1333&context=annals.

Case 2 (*Continued*)

times more energy per person than developing nations but produces only 10% of the world's oil. Even with an uncertain economy, world oil demand is only likely to increase, especially in China and India.[20]

Most of the oil is used in transportation and heating, but oil has many other uses as well: some clothes, computer parts, and all plastics require oil for their production. Of course, it also takes energy—mostly from oil—to manufacture just about anything. Once goods are manufactured, they must be transported to the end user, which again requires oil. The demand for oil is everywhere.

Unfortunately, burning oil produces carbon dioxide (CO_2). About 60% of this CO_2 is absorbed by oceans and plants. The residual CO_2 stays in the atmosphere and warms up the planet by what is called the "greenhouse effect." Oil isn't the only fossil fuel that releases CO_2; coal does as well. Climate change from atmospheric warming is also fueled by other factors, including deforestation (since fewer trees exist to absorb CO_2, and there's more surface reflection of heat).

We can expect the following effects if, as the Environmental Protection Agency predicts, global temperatures rise at least 3 degrees Celsius in the next one hundred years:[21]

- Melting ice caps, which would raise sea levels, displacing millions of people presently living on islands and in coastal regions. Given current trends, summer sea ice is likely to disappear completely by 2030.

- Major weather pattern changes, including more severe hurricanes, torrential rains and flooding, heat waves, and droughts.

- Loss of biodiversity.

- Water and food shortages.

Already, northern permafrost is melting and the polar caps are losing ice masses the size of entire countries. This is reducing land mass on many islands and coastal areas, forcing people to move. In the tropics and subtropics, droughts are reducing crop yields, making famines more common. In all parts of the world, more people are dying from heat stroke, sun stroke, malaria, and cholera. There were more and stronger hurricanes in 2005 than any other year on record (twenty-eight total), closely followed by 2012, 2011, and 2010 (nineteen each).

Can we do anything at this stage to prevent further climate warming? Unfortunately, the short run answer, at least, is negative. Because effects are cumulative, reducing the burning of fossil fuels today won't do much to reverse the greenhouse effect until at least about 2050. Still, we *can* take steps that could help slow and ultimately reverse the present trends; taking these steps now could save millions of lives near the end of this century and later. In the meantime, we need to figure out how to adapt our lives to the coming changes. Adapting will be costly; for instance, New York City is currently considering what steps need to be taken to

Continued

---

[20]Energy Information Administration, "International Energy Outlook 2014," U.S. Department of Energy, accessed August 30, 2016, http://www.eia.gov/forecasts/ieo/pdf/0484(2014).pdf.

[21]"Future Climate Change," U.S. Environmental Protection Agency, accessed August 30, 2016, http://www3.epa.gov/climatechange/science/future.html.

Case 2 (Continued)

protect the city from rising sea levels and future hurricanes. More urgently, Holland needs to start projects to raise its dikes.

More generally, what must humanity do about these issues? Most important, we need to replace our use of fossil fuels with alternative energy resources, such as wind and solar energy. Although much of the necessary technology already exists, sizable investments will be required to bring about the needed restructuring of current industry. As for individuals, people can do several things to reduce our dependency on oil—for example, by buying Energy Star appliances, better insulating our buildings, using less air conditioning, and replacing incandescent lighting.

We Americans (especially) need to rethink our relationship to our cars since auto emissions are one of the main contributors of greenhouse gases. We need to change our agricultural practices, which produce other greenhouse effects due to their heavy reliance on nitrogen fertilizers. We also ought to cut back on our consumption of meat since its production generates a great deal of methane and nitrous oxide (methane, a by-product of meat production, is an especially powerful greenhouse gas).

Each of these steps will profoundly affect our lives. The price to be paid will likely include limitations upon our prized freedom of mobility (driving cars and air travel), reductions in the variety of available foods, higher consumer costs (as industry begins to bear the environmental costs of manufacturing), and increased government regulation (of industry and even of private households). Many of us may find such changes very difficult, but, then again, nothing less than the future of humanity is at stake.[22]

THOUGHT QUESTIONS

1. Analyze this case in terms of the sorts of conflicts discussed in the text— between environmental welfare and what people want, between richer and poorer, and so on.
2. In view of climate change, is there still an optimal level of pollution? What do you think this optimal level would look like?
3. In what ways does this case illustrate the Problem of the Commons?
4. The problems listed in this case are important even if we just apply anthropocentrism. What additional problems become important when we apply ecocentrism instead?
5. What sorts of sacrifices probably need to be made by people today to reduce air pollution and climate change?
6. Suppose you are born forty years from now and must struggle with disease, famine, and severe weather because the present generation made no effort to change. Would you be justified in blaming today's generation for your suffering?

---

[22]Some insist that climate change has not been caused by human activity. Even if this is true, it's irrelevant. We know without a doubt that climate change is occurring and that air pollution can accelerate global warming. Regardless of how we've gotten where we now are, we will still share a responsibility in what happens next.

To what degree may we justifiably blame our present climatic problems on our predecessors and the past 150 years of unrestrained industrial growth?

7. How much of a moral responsibility do you think we have to ensure the welfare of future generations (our children's grandchildren and beyond)? How should their interests be balanced with our present needs and interests?

8. Pick one or two of our ethical theories. What do these theories say about what we ought to do in view of climate change?

9. Should you be willing to alter your present lifestyle to help ensure the existence and well-being of future generations? If so, what should you do?

Case 3

National Parks

The year 2016 celebrated the U.S. National Park system centennial. The park system protects huge tracts of land, a great number of cultural and historical artifacts, important natural resources (especially clean water for California), and many species, including some on the endangered list. It not only protects these now, but it preserves them for the good of future generations. It also provides countless citizens and visitors with opportunities for all kinds of wilderness experiences. These range from staying at a park hotel and taking a quick tour of some natural wonder to hiking for days or weeks in pristine wilderness. Recent studies have indicated that people can experience health benefits simply from spending time in a natural environment.

Still, the National Parks have been repeatedly put into peril from the very start by threats of cut-offs in funding, by damages caused by too many visitors, by poaching, and, among other things, by a never-ending string of attempts by businesses and Congress to develop and use park land and resources. What is surprising about the latter is that much larger swaths of land, overseen by the U.S. Forest Service and the Bureau of Land Management, are conserved and managed for government, commercial, and private use. With so much already available, why are the park lands still targeted?

One of the most notorious (and still contested) threats to a national park was actually realized in the early twentieth century. The Hetch Hetchy Valley in California is a large tract of land that had originally been part of Yosemite National Park. John Muir commented, "[N]ext to Yosemite, Hetch Hetchy is the most wonderful and most important feature of the great park."[23] Yet this valley, by a special act of Congress, lost its protected status in the park and was later dammed and converted into a reservoir to serve San Francisco's pressing water needs. Of course, San Francisco still stands today and has grown considerably. The Hetch Hetchy reservoir also still exists, although most of the valley was destroyed when it was flooded to create the reservoir.[24]

---

[23]John Muir, The Hetch Hetchy Valley, *Sierra Club Bulletin*, 6.4 (January 1908), accessed August 30, 2016, http://vault.sierraclub.org/ca/hetchhetchy/hetch_hetchy_muir_scb_1908.html.

[24]See this superb PBS 2009 documentary film for television that elates the entire history of the National Parks system, including the Hetch Hetchy story. Ken Burns and Dayton Duncan, dirs., *The National Parks: America's Best Idea*, Public Broadcasting System, 2009.

THOUGHT QUESTIONS

1. Analyze this case in terms of the sorts of conflicts discussed in the text— between environmental welfare and what people want, between richer and poorer, and so on.

2. In what ways does this case illustrate the Problem of the Commons? (Both water resources and parks are commons: most of the National Parks are free to visitors; when they do charge admission, those charges go toward park maintenance.)

3. The environmentally valuable Hetch Hetchy valley was sacrificed to help meet San Francisco's need for water. What conflicts were involved in that? Was the right choice made? Defend your answer.

4. Apply anthropocentrism and then apply ecocentrism to the Hetch Hetchy valley case. Do these different value systems support different conclusions about what should have been done?

5. Suppose you are born forty years from now, and there are no longer any national parks since all of today's parks have been converted to mines, farms, roads, water supplies, and other sorts of resources. How would you feel about that after you had learned that there had once been an extensive park system protecting those areas?

6. How much of a moral responsibility do you think we have to ensure the preservation of the National Parks and their resources for future generations (our children's grandchildren and beyond)? Who has a greater interest in their preservation—those living now or those living in the future?

7. Pick one or two ethical theories: rule utilitarianism or care ethics, for instance. What do these say about our moral duties involving the parks?

Case 4

Surfer, Sailor, Whistle-Blower[25]

When competitive surfer Aaron Ahearn joined the Navy, he probably didn't expect to become a folk hero. He was assigned to the *Abraham Lincoln*, one of the U.S. Navy's largest nuclear aircraft carriers. One of Ahearn's first duties was to dump the ship's garbage (wrapped in plastic bags). In addition to dumping the garbage generated daily by the nearly six thousand people aboard ship, he was also ordered to help dispose of things like desks, computers, paint cans, and diesel fuel. All of this went directly into the ocean. Raw sewage was also sometimes released, even within the vicinity of San Diego. At this time (the early 1990s), the Navy was dumping an estimated 28,000 tons of garbage each year from its ships at sea. Of that, about five hundred tons were plastics. (For comparison, a 1990 Coast Guard study reported that over 421,000 tons of garbage were being dumped each year

Continued

---

[25]This case is based on the article by Tom Alibrani, "Surfer Takes on the Navy—Environmental Protester Aaron Ahearn," *The Progressive*, October 1993, accessed August 30, 2016, http://www.thefreelibrary.com/Surfer+takes+on+the+Navy.-a013290565. It also draws from an August 13, 1993, radio show transcript, Steve Curwood, "Navy Trash Dumping," Living on Earth and World Media Foundation, August 13, 1993, accessed August 30, 2016, http://www.loe.org/shows/segments.html?programID=93-P13-00033&segmentID=1, and from an article by Doug Fine, "Going AWOL For the Earth," *Village Voice*, 1993.

Case 4 (*Continued*)

into the ocean by commercial and private interests.) Plastic refuse is of particular concern since it doesn't break down; it alone kills thousands of dolphins, whales, birds, and other ocean animals every year. Sewage, meanwhile, damages beaches, harms wildlife, and creates health hazards for swimmers.

Ahearn was sickened by what he was forced to do. In talking later about the dumping, Ahearn said, "It goes against everything I stand for as a surfer." Feeling that others needed to know about the dumping, Ahearn tried to take photos, but an officer grabbed his camera and threw it overboard. He also discussed his concerns with the ship's chaplain. When Ahearn submitted a written request for a transfer of duties, the commanding officer tore the request up right in front of him.

While sea dumping can do a lot of damage, most of the Navy's dumping, strictly speaking, had been legal. Although environmental laws prohibit most of these kinds of dumping, the Navy had long been exempt from many of these restrictions. The Navy *is* prohibited from dumping within fifty miles of shore—a rule it seems to have stretched near San Diego. But what particularly bothered Ahearn was that the Navy was being *allowed* to harm the environment in these ways.

After about six months, Ahearn took matters into his own hands and went absent without leave (AWOL) when his ship stopped at Alameda, California. After spending ten weeks living and surfing with his girlfriend in Santa Cruz, Ahearn turned himself in to the Navy. On that same day, he held a press conference to publicize his situation and his environmental concerns. As his story spread, some environmental groups and local government officials began supporting his cause. He started becoming popular as a hero—the young man who took on the entire U.S. Navy. Gradually, a few more sailors came forward with similar stories, confirming Ahearn's reports about the dumping. The Navy responded by insisting that it had acted responsibly and broken no laws. Indeed, the Pentagon has claimed that the Navy is a leader at adopting progressive environmental policies. Some people, meanwhile, suggested that Ahearn jumped ship just to spend time with his girlfriend and was using the environmental issue to sidetrack attention from his own irresponsible behavior.

At his court-martial trial, Ahearn pleaded guilty to taking an unauthorized leave. He could have been sentenced to two years and a dishonorable discharge. Thanks to his plea bargain, however, Ahearn got off with a sentence of just thirty days in the brig, a $500 fine, and a reduction in rank. What did the Navy get? Some mixed publicity, certainly; the Navy also expressed a commitment to stop most of its dumping at sea. In addition, it announced plans to introduce trash compactors onboard its ships. This pleased some environmentalists, though others worried that the Navy's careless attitude toward the environment would not change so easily. At about the time Ahearn began serving his sentence, the Navy submitted to Congress a request for a five-year exemption from the environmental regulations that prohibited dumping plastics at sea.

THOUGHT QUESTIONS

1. From an act utilitarian perspective, did Ahearn do right when he jumped ship and went AWOL? How about from a Kantian perspective? Virtue ethics?

2. What do you think were Ahearn's motivations for acting as he did?

3. How well does Ahearn's act of whistle-blowing satisfy the modified analysis guidelines? Explain and support your claims.
4. Do you think that Ahearn, among other things, wanted to avoid being complicit with the Navy and its dumping?
5. Would you have acted as Ahearn did? Why or why not?

Case 5

The Diesel Dupe

A little-known organization, the International Council on Clean Transportation (ICCT), had noticed conflicting results from emissions tests done in Europe on diesel Volkswagens. They decided to carry out further tests in the United States. They expected that with the stricter U.S. emissions laws, American VWs would test more consistently and, if anything, cleaner. Working with West Virginia University, they instead uncovered what is now called "the diesel dupe:" VW was selling cars in the United States that emitted ten to twenty-five times more nitrogen oxides (which contribute to smog and respiratory problems) than the U.S. emissions standard allows. VW had installed sophisticated "defeat devices" in their diesel cars that would cut back on emissions during testing but would switch back to releasing higher emissions whenever the car was being driven normally. Just when climate change was becoming a matter of world concern, VW, the world's second largest auto company, was cheating on emissions. With millions of their cars on the roads, VW's diesel dupe was badly harming the environment as well as giving the company an unfair advantage over competing manufacturers. Once these facts were made public by the ICCT in August, 2015, defeat devices were found in other VW cars. Volkswagen had to recall millions of cars, its stock value plummeted, its plans for expansion had to be shelved, and many market watchers have wondered about VW's long term survival.

THOUGHT QUESTIONS

1. What do you think of VW's actions?
2. What would act utilitarianism, Kantian ethics, and other theories say about VW's actions?
3. Was the ICCT justified in blowing the whistle on VW? Apply both the modified analysis and complicity theory.
4. Why do you think that no one working for VW ever came forward to blow the whistle on VW? If you had been working for VW and came to know about the diesel dupe, what would you have done?

Case 6

The Snowden Leak

On June 6, 2013, the *Guardian*, a London-based newspaper specializing in investigative reporting, first disclosed that the U.S. National Security Agency (NSA) had been violating U.S. privacy laws by collecting citizens' phone calls for at

Continued

Case 6 (Continued)

least a year. The next day, both the *Guardian* and *Washington Post* reported that, in addition to forcing Verizon to hand over its daily telephone records for analysis, the NSA had also been obtaining the online communications records of several large Internet companies like Facebook, Google, and Microsoft. Further disclosures followed daily, including reports of an even more massive interception of fiber optic messages by British intelligence. A little later, it came out that U.S. agencies had been spying on embassies and even on the leaders of several European and Latin American allies as well as carrying out a huge number of hacking operations in China and elsewhere.[26] Media finally indicated that all this information came from a series of top-secret leaks provided by Edward Snowden, a former CIA systems analyst who later worked for a contractor with the NSA. Snowden was charged with theft of government property, disclosure of classified intelligence, and espionage. Stating that he could not obtain a fair trial in the United States, Snowden fled to Hong Kong. As pressure rose to extradite Snowden back to the United States, he fled to Russia, where President Vladimir Putin confirmed that Snowden had been granted temporary asylum for a year.

The U.S. government wants to do whatever it can to arrest and prosecute Snowden, whom it views as an enemy to national security. According to the director of the NSA, the surveillance programs that Snowden exposed had "helped thwart 50 attacks since 2001."[27] Further, FBI Director Robert Mueller said that Snowden had "caused 'significant harm'" by leaking this information.[28] More recently, British and American intelligence agencies claim that the leaks have done incalculable damage, including placing field operatives in danger – though these claims remain largely unsubstantiated. Why did Snowden initiate the largest leak of secret U.S. documents in history?

Snowden was identified as the source of the leaks at his own request. His proclaimed intention was to serve the public interest and expose unlawful abuses of power. He never released many other documents, he says, "because harming people isn't my goal. Transparency is." In fact, he stated, "I carefully evaluated every single document I disclosed to ensure that each was legitimately in the public interest." His leaking this information certainly has not occurred without cost both to Snowden and his family. Still, he maintained, "I will be satisfied if the federation of secret law, unequal pardon and irresistible executive powers that rule the world that I love are revealed even for an instant."[29] To many, Snowden should be hailed as a hero. According to others, he is a traitor who has not yet paid nearly the price he owes for his crimes.

---

[26]"Edward Snowden: Leaks That Exposed US Spy Programme," BBC News, January 17, 2014, accessed August 30, 2016, http://www.bbc.com/news/world-us-canada-23123964.

[27]"Edward Snowden: Timeline," BBC News, August 20, 2013, accessed August 30, 2016, http://www.bbc.com/news/world-us-canada-23768248.

[28]Ibid.

[29]Barton Gellman and Jerry Markon, "Edward Snowden Says Motive Behind Leaks Was to Expose 'Surveillance State,'" BBC News, June 10, 2013, accessed August 39, 2016, https://www.washingtonpost.com/politics/edward-snowden-says-motive-behind-leaks-was-to-expose-surveillance-state/2013/06/09/aa3f0804-d13b-11e2-a73e-826d299ff459_story.html.

THOUGHT QUESTIONS

1. Do you view Snowden as a hero or a villain? Why? Is your view based on facts or feelings?
2. The NSA and other government agencies were breaking the law. They were also violating the privacy rights of countless Americans, though this was all intended to serve a good cause. Were they morally wrong in what they did? (Compare this to Chapter Six, Case 5, Torture Lite.)
3. Among other things, the U.S. government spied on the leaders of its own allies. What do you think of its doing this? (The NSA apparently tapped German Chancellor Angela Merkel's phone, which greatly angered Germany and the chancellor.) Apply virtue theory or care ethics to the United States and Germany as if they were individuals.
4. Did Snowden's whistle-blowing satisfy the modified analysis's requirements?
5. What were Snowden's motivations for doing what he did? Discuss Snowden's actions in terms of complicity theory.
6. Edward Snowden has suffered a great deal for his actions, though he apparently would do everything again. Does this make any difference regarding whether he should have blown the whistle? Does this reveal anything important about his motivations? Do you feel that he has "paid the price" he owed, if any?

Glossary

Absolute poverty: A condition in which persons lack resources needed to meet their most essential needs, of food, clothing, and shelter.

Acts, principle of (rule utilitarianism): Maintains that a morally right act obeys a morally right rule or practice (compare: **Rules, principle of**).

Act utilitarianism: Defines the morally right *act,* for a particular situation, as that which produces the greatest overall utility (compare: **rule utilitarianism**).

Actual moral duty (Ross's ethics): The one prima facie duty that is more important than any other in a particular situation and so is the duty that ought to be fulfilled.

Alternate dependency account (ethics and religion): A theistic account that attempts to avoid the objections against traditional divine command theory by basing morality on God's nature rather than God's commands or willing.

Alternate dilemma principle (rule utilitarianism): Requires that when a situation places rules in conflict, the right act obeys the rule that creates the greatest overall utility; an alternative to the **dilemma principle.**

Altruism (moral psychology): A concern for the well-being of others as a value in itself, independent of any self-interest.

Anthropocentrism (environmental ethics): Holds that only humans and human interests have **foundational value**; everything else has **instrumental value** (compare: **ecocentrism**).

Apply (ethics and values): Something applies for a person if it calls for some response in that person's particular circumstances; for example, "I should study my chemistry book" applies to me if I am taking chemistry and want to do well (compare: **hold**).

Authentic choice (autonomy): The third level of moral agency. This is a choice in which a moral agent exercises his capacity to choose (a) without constraint or compulsion, (b) by rationally deliberating, and (c) by assessing his own values (compare: **independent choice, competent choice**).

Authenticity condition (autonomy): Requires that an autonomous person have the capacity to discern and freely assess or choose her own values.

Autonomous person (autonomy): One who is able to make free choices as a self-determining individual; an autonomous person fulfills the (a) **independence condition**, (b) **competency condition**, and (c) **authenticity condition**.

Autonomy, principle of (Kantian ethics): A version of Kant's **categorical imperative**: every person is equally a creator of the universal moral law; that is, each person "makes" the moral law.

Autonomy thesis (ethics and religion): Maintains that morality exists on its own, independent of any deity (compare: **dependency thesis**).

Beneficence (Ross's ethics): The duty to act so as to improve the condition of another or of others, for example, acting kindly or generously.

Care perspective (care ethics): The characteristically feminine moral perspective that emphasizes relationships, feelings, and individual needs (compare: **justice perspective**).

Cared-for/Carer (care ethics): The carer initiates an act of caring toward the cared-for, who receives the caring.

Categorical imperative (Kantian ethics): A binding principle that holds unconditionally for everyone regardless of their desires or situation. The categorical imperative has several formulations, including the **principle of universal law** and the **principle of ends**.

Closeness (care ethics): A quality of relationships that depends on how much persons share their lives; close relationships can yield special responsibilities for caring.

Common property (environmental ethics): Property or resources held by all within a given society (e.g., air, water, parks).

Commons: Common property.

Commons, problem of (environmental ethics): The tendency of people to exploit common property to their own advantage, making it of less value to all.

Competency condition (autonomy): Requires that an autonomous person have the capacities necessary to rationally deliberate when making choices.

Competent choice (autonomy): The second level of moral agency: a choice in which a moral agent exercises his capacity to choose (a) without constraint or compulsion and (b) by rationally deliberating (compare: **independent choice**, **authentic choice**).

Completeness: A criterion of theory assessment: a theory must support everything that the theory is supposed to be about; a complete ethical theory supports all meaningful moral claims and values.

Completing a caring act (care ethics): Noddings's requirement that the **cared-for** recognize and somehow acknowledge that he is receiving care from the **carer**.

Complicity theory (business ethics): Maintains that **whistle-blowing** may be morally justified when a whistle-blower acts to avoid being an accomplice or accessory in committing a wrong (compare: **modified analysis**).

Consequentialist ethics: A general approach to ethics for which only consequences determine what is morally right or wrong (compare: **deontological ethics**).

DDE: see **double effect, doctrine of.**

Decision frame (moral psychology): The entire context of a problem or choice, including the set of possible choices, their consequences, and whatever else influences the actor.

Deep ecology (environmental ethics): An **ecocentric** viewpoint that assigns non-humans and humans equal foundational or intrinsic value (if any) independent of their **instrumental value**.

Deficiency (virtue ethics): For Aristotle, the point where an act or feeling is not enough and so counts as vicious, not virtuous (compare: **mean, excess**).

Degenderized morality (care ethics): A gender-neutral morality that is intended (by some feminists) to replace both the **justice perspective** and the **care perspective**.

Deontological ethics: A general approach to ethics that rejects consequences as a basis for moral right or wrong and instead focuses upon duties and right acts (compare: **consequentialist ethics**).

Dependency thesis (ethics and religion): Asserts that morality originates in or somehow depends upon **God**.

Dependent effects (natural law theory): Includes two ways by which the good and bad effects can relate to each other for the **means/end condition** of DDE; while a bad effect may depend on the good, the good may not depend on the bad.

Derived principle (making moral judgments): A value or prescriptive principle that is inferred from a more basic principle along with at least one **descriptive claim** (compare: **foundational principle**).

Descriptive (ethics and values): Relating to the world as it is, was, will be, or could be, but not to how it should or ought to be (compare: **normative**).

Difference principle (social contract theory): Adds certain social and economic inequities within a Rawlsian society for the benefit of all but never so as to suspend the **equality principle**.

Dilemma principle (rule utilitarianism): A defining principle that says that when a situation brings two or more rules into conflict, the morally right act is that act that will produce the greatest overall utility (compare: **alternate dilemma principle**).

Direct democracy: A political system in which the people make laws and establish policies directly and not through a representative (compare: **representational democracy**).

Direct duty (Kantian ethics): A moral obligation one can have directly to another person regardless of any other duties one might also have (compare: **indirect duty**).

Divine command theory (ethics and religion): An ethical theory that maintains that the **moral standard** depends directly upon God's commands or will:

morally right acts are commanded or willed by **God;** wrong acts are forbidden by God.

Double effect, doctrine of (natural law theory): A set of four conditions—the **moral principle, means/end, right intention,** and **proportionality** conditions—that must all be fulfilled for an act to be morally right when that act is expected to cause both a good effect and a bad effect.

Duration (act utilitarianism): Used in utilitarian calculations, that aspect of an effect that reflects the period of time over which that effect lasts.

Ecocentrism (environmental ethics): Holds that both humans and non-humans have foundational value (compare: **anthropocentrism**).

Ends, principle of (Kantian ethics): A version of Kant's **categorical imperative:** Act so as to treat every person affected by your action as an end and never as a means only.

Equality principle (social contract theory): Assigns equal liberties, rights, and duties to members of a Rawlsian society (compare: **difference principle**).

Ethical egoism: An ethical theory that defines a morally right act for a particular situation as that act that most benefits oneself (compare: **psychological egoism**).

Ethical pluralism: Maintains that no single comprehensive ethical account exists; rather, morality consists of distinct branches that may be largely unrelated to each other.

Ethical theory: A theory that typically attempts to explain the moral realm on the basis of just one or a few foundational values or principles.

Eudaimonia (virtue theory): Aristotle's notion of human flourishing (happiness); to achieve this, one must live in accordance with reason (virtuously) thereby fulfilling one's human function.

Excess (virtue ethics): For Aristotle, the point where an act or feeling is too much and so counts as vicious, not virtuous (compare: **mean, deficiency**).

Expected utility (act utilitarianism): Our best assessment, given our limitations and knowledge at the time, of the overall utility that a given choice or act will produce.

Explanatory pluralism (ethical pluralism): This kind of pluralism divides morality into distinct branches, but all the components of a given branch are tied to each other by some more fundamental account (compare: **foundational pluralism**).

Explanatory power: A criterion of theory assessment: a theory should give us explanatory insight as to what makes something morally right or wrong, good or bad.

Female genital mutilation (FGM): A culturally based practice in which the woman's clitoris is removed to reduce the woman's sexual pleasure and thus to help ensure her faithfulness; also called female circumcision.

Fidelity (Ross's ethics): The duty to speak truthfully, keep promises, pay debts, and so on.

Fine-tuning (rule utilitarianism): Introducing qualifications to a rule or practice that makes it more limited and precise; fine-tuning is intended to generate more utility.

Forfeiture, principle of (natural law theory): A principle that says that by deliberately attacking or threatening an **innocent**, an individual (or a nation) gives up the moral right to live (or exist).

Foundational principle (making moral judgments): A value or prescriptive principle that serves as the basis for deriving other moral principles but is not itself derived from other moral principles (compare: **derived principle**).

Foundational pluralism (ethical pluralism): This kind of pluralism divides morality into distinct branches, each deriving from its own foundation (compare: **explanatory pluralism**).

Foundational values (ethics and values): Goods that are intrinsically valuable in themselves, these are not derived from other values (compare: **instrumental values**).

Futile treatment (medical ethics): A treatment that, for a *specific patient and situation,* is not likely to bring to the patient any improvement in her physical, mental, emotional, and spiritual well-being.

Good and bad (ethics and values): The **normative** concepts having to do with values.

Good-promoting virtues (virtue ethics): Virtues that promote specific values or goods, for example, sociability and generosity (compare: **limiting virtues, obligation virtues**).

God: The supreme being, conceived in this book as the greatest being possible.

Good Will (Kantian ethics): The only thing of foundational moral worth according to Kant; the Good Will freely chooses to do something because it is one's moral duty.

Grade inflation: The trend toward giving out higher grades, which thereby tends to reduce the value of high grades (since so many students have them).

Gratitude (Ross's ethics): The duty to express thanks, return favors, and so on.

Gyges: A mythical character mentioned by Glaucon in Plato's *Republic* who finds a ring that makes him invisible, allowing him to commit moral wrongs without getting caught.

Hedonism: A tradition that maintains that there is just one foundational good—pleasure (or happiness)—that may serve as the basis for any action.

Hold (ethics and values): Something holds for a person if it is true or morally binding, regardless of what that person believes or practices; for example, "The earth is round" holds for all (compare: **apply**).

Human rights (rights): Rights that extend to all human beings, either (a) as given by Rawls's theory or (b) by the United Nation's list of human rights.

Hypothetical imperative (Kantian ethics): A conditional principle that prescribes how to act if you satisfy some condition or hope to achieve some goal (compare: **categorical imperative**).

Impartiality: A moral attitude of detachment from one's own feelings, desires, and interests.

Imperfect duty (Kantian ethics): An obligation that can depend upon one's circumstances and may be fulfilled to varying degrees (compare: **perfect duty**).

Inalienable right (rights): A right that cannot morally be given up or transferred to another (e.g., life, liberty).

Independence condition (autonomy): Requires that an autonomous person have the capacity to make a choice without being under the control of an external constraint or inner compulsion.

Independent choice (autonomy): The first level of moral agency; a choice in which a moral agent exercises his capacity to choose without constraint or compulsion (compare: **competent choice, authentic choice**).

Independent effects (natural law theory): A way by which the good and bad effects can relate to each other for the **means/end condition** of DDE. When independent, neither effect depends upon the other, but both depend directly upon the act.

Indirect duty (Kantian ethics): A moral obligation one person can have to another person regarding a third party; for example, I have a moral obligation to an animal's owner not to harm her animal, even if I have no moral obligation to the animal itself (compare: **direct duty**).

Innocent (natural law theory, principle of forfeiture): A person or nation that has not attacked or threatened another and so has a moral right not to be threatened by others.

Instrumental values (ethics and values): Goods that are useful for attaining something else of value; a *purely* instrumental value has no genuine worth in itself (compare: **foundational values**).

Intensity (act utilitarianism): Used in utilitarian calculations, that aspect of an effect that reflects the degree of strength or force of that effect.

Intuitionism (Ross's ethics): Maintains that we can discover our general moral duties and determine our actual duty in a given situation by consulting our inner selves honestly and thoughtfully.

Justice (Ross's ethics): The duty to act fairly to distribute goods to people according to their due.

Justice perspective (care ethics): The characteristically masculine moral perspective that emphasizes moral rights, principles, and justice (compare: **care perspective**).

Just war theory (natural law theory): Attempts to determine under what conditions a state may justifiably wage war and how that war should be waged.

Limiting virtues (virtue ethics): Virtues that help us control and manage our inclinations and feelings, for example, courage (compare: **good-promoting virtues, obligation virtues**).

Living will (medical ethics): A document previously prepared by a patient that specifies what sorts of medical treatments the patient either does or does not want when the patient is unable to make decisions for herself.

Manifesto right (rights): A "right" that Feinberg doubts is a genuine right but that is intended to emphasize the moral importance of some pressing human need or concern.

Maxim (Kantian ethics): A general rule or pattern of behavior that one can act in accordance with. A Kantian maxim also expresses the intention of acting that way; for example, I will lie to get someone to do what I want.

Mean (virtue ethics): For Aristotle, the point between **excess** and **deficiency** where an act or feeling achieves the proper balance and so counts as virtuous (compare: **deficiency, excess**).

Means/end condition (natural law theory): One of the conditions of **DDE**, this requires that the bad effect not be the cause of the good effect or be necessary for it to occur.

Modified analysis of whistle-blowing (business ethics): The set of conditions that must be fulfilled for whistle-blowing to be morally justified or even become one's moral duty.

Moral agent (autonomy): A person who satisfies all three conditions of autonomy (see **autonomous person**) and is able to appropriately apply these capacities to specific choices.

Moral capacity (autonomy): Fulfilling all three conditions for autonomy (see **autonomous person**); when one's state precludes autonomy for a period of time, one lacks capacity over that time.

Moral confirmation: A criterion of theory assessment: a theory should yield results that fit with our deepest, clearest, and most widely shared moral intuitions.

Moral deference (autonomy): Respecting another person's choices without interference.

Moral judgment (making moral judgments): A moral claim that is limited to specific people or situations; for example, "I should keep my promise to her" (compare: **moral principle**).

Moral luck: Factors beyond our control that affect, to some extent, our ability to act morally in a given situation.

Moral particularism: Maintains that universal moral principles are not useful for determining what is right or wrong; instead, moral judgments must normally be made on a case-by-case basis.

Moral principle condition (natural law theory): One of the conditions of **DDE**, this requires the act not violate any moral principle.

Moral principle (making moral judgments): A moral claim that holds in general and so is not limited to particular people or to a situation; for example, "People should keep their promises" (compare: **moral judgment**).

Moral psychology: An empirical field that investigates psychological aspects of moral motivation and behavior.

Moral realm (ethics and values): Taking "moral" in one of its senses, this is the subject matter of ethics; more generally, this **normative** realm contains the entire range of moral phenomena, including people's moral beliefs and practices.

Moral reasoning (making moral judgments): A pattern of moral thinking that infers a moral judgment from one or more **moral principles** and **descriptive** claims (compare: **moral reflection**).

Moral reflection (making moral judgments): A pattern of moral thinking that does not infer a moral judgment from explicit principles but instead arrives at a moral judgment by considering the individuals and relationships involved in a particular setting (compare: **moral reasoning**).

Moral reformers (moral relativism): Persons who, on moral grounds, work to change some of their own society's accepted beliefs and practices.

Moral responsibility (autonomy): Being morally accountable to others for one's own choices and actions, thus deserving blame or praise.

Moral saint (virtue ethics): A moral saint, for a specific ethical theory, fulfills the requirements of that theory (e.g., a Kantian saint).

Moral standard (ethics and values): A complete set of moral value and prescriptive claims; together, these dictate what is morally good or bad, right or wrong.

Mutuality (care ethics): A quality of relationships that "ties" persons to each other and that is built upon the sharing of knowledge, feelings, and trust.

Natural function (natural law theory): The role or purpose of something in nature; a natural function ultimately aims at achieving some end or goal that has natural value.

Natural value (natural law theory): Some desirable non-moral good; an end or goal toward which nature aims.

Nature (care ethics): Gives rise to those beliefs, personal traits, and so on that are inborn or innate and so remains largely unchanged by environmental influences (compare: **nurture**).

Negative rights (rights): Allow us to make claims on others regarding what they should *not* do to us, for example, my right to property (compare: **positive rights**).

Non-maleficence (Ross's ethics): The duty to avoid harming others.

Normative (ethics and values): Relating to some norm or standard; moral values and claims are normative (compare: **descriptive**).

Nurture (care ethics): Gives rise to beliefs, personal traits, and so on that are not inborn but are developed as products of one's environment (compare: **nature**).

Objectivism (moral relativism): Maintains that there is one universal moral standard that holds for all cultures, social groups, and persons regardless of their particular moral beliefs or practices (compare: **subjectivism, relativism**).

Obligation virtues (virtue ethics): Virtues that help us fulfill our moral obligations to act in certain ways, for example, truthfulness (compare: **good-promoting virtues, obligation virtues**).

Original position (social contract theory): A hypothetical situation in which free and rational persons negotiate a Rawlsian social contract under the **veil of ignorance**.

Override (making moral judgments): To take precedence or priority over other values or prescriptions; moral values and claims may be characterized as overriding the values and claims of other **normative** realms.

Palliative care (medical ethics): Care provided to seriously ill patients in an attempt to relieve pain and discomfort and support their quality of life as far as is possible.

Paternalism (autonomy): Overruling another person's choices for her own good.

Perfect duty (Kantian ethics): An absolute obligation that cannot be obeyed by degrees and does not depend on circumstances (compare: **imperfect duty**).

Permanent vegetative state (PVS): A state in which a patient has been largely unresponsive for three months or more; PVS usually involves irreversible damage to at least one of the brain's cerebral hemispheres.

Pluralistic relativism (moral relativism): David Wong's version of **relativism**, which maintains that different societies can have different but equally valid moral standards, although all share a common moral core.

Positive rights (rights): Allow us to make claims on others regarding what they should do for us, for example, a right to education (compare: **negative rights**).

Practicability: A criterion of theory assessment: a theory should be useful to us in actual applications by (a) being clear and precise, (b) furnishing helpful moral guidance, and (c) not generating irresolvable conflicts.

Prescriptive (ethics and values): A type of **normative** statement that tells us what we should or should not do.

Prima facie duty (Ross's ethics): A duty that I ought to fulfill unless some more important moral duty overrides it.

Probability (act utilitarianism): Used in utilitarian calculations, that aspect of an effect that reflects the chance or likelihood of that effect actually taking place.

Proxy (medical ethics): A person who makes medical decisions for the patient when the patient can't make decisions for herself.

Prudential realm (ethics and values): The non-moral **normative** realm of claims reflecting what is in one's interest; prudential claims are best expressed in an "if/then" (conditional) form: if some value or goal is important and relevant to you, then you ought to act in a certain way.

Psychological egoism (moral psychology): The thesis that we can only choose what we think is in our interest as a matter of psychological necessity.

Psychological situationism (moral psychology): Maintains that various non-moral aspects of a person's situation—their **decision frame**—can strongly influence how a person thinks and behaves.

Quality (act utilitarianism): For use in utilitarian calculations, a proposed aspect of an effect that reflects Mill's distinction between higher and lower pleasures; higher-quality pleasures are to be given more moral weight.

Realm of etiquette (ethics and values): The non-moral **normative** realm that defines acceptable social behavior or "good manners" for a given culture.

Realm of law (ethics and values): The (strictly) non-moral **normative** realm determined and enforced by a given civil authority; many laws reflect moral claims.

Relational autonomy (autonomy): A type of **substantive autonomy** that rejects individualism and emphasizes the role of human interdependencies especially in establishing self-identity and developing autonomy.

Relativism, popular (moral relativism): Maintains that there is no universal objective **moral standard** but that there can be different moral standards for different social groups (compare: **objectivism, subjectivism**).

Reparation (Ross's ethics): The duty to make up for any wrongs you have previously done to another (e.g., to apologize).

Representational democracy: A political system in which people elect representatives to make laws and establish policies on their behalf (compare: **direct democracy**).

Right and wrong (ethics and values): The **normative** concepts having to do with actions.

Right intention condition (natural law theory): One of the conditions of **DDE**, this requires that the actor intend only the good effect, even if she still anticipates the bad effect.

Right (rights): A right allows its holder to validly make a claim upon another; most often, a right confers a privilege to protect, use, or exercise control over something or to act in certain ways without interference from others.

Rules of thumb (act utilitarianism): Informal rules that tell us how to act, based on what usually best promotes utility in similar situations.

Rules, principle of (rule utilitarianism): Maintains that morally right rules or practices are those that promote significantly greater overall utility than if they did not exist (compare: **Acts, principle of**).

Saint: see **moral saint**.

Scope (act utilitarianism): Used in utilitarian calculations, that aspect of an effect that reflects how many individuals are affected.

Self-improvement (Ross's ethics): The duty to invest in one's well-being and growth (e.g., to exercise, to learn new things).

Social contract (social contract theory): An agreement established by a set of people (usually theoretically) to set up a social system that fairly benefits all.

State of nature: (social contract theory): A moral and social condition of people for which no government or formal civil society exists.

Subjectivism (moral relativism): Maintains that there is no universal objective **moral standard** but that there can be different moral standards for different persons (compare: **relativism, objectivism**).

Substantive autonomy (autonomy): The view that we can only be truly autonomous as long as our basic values are consistent with human fulfillment and flourishing, including the foundational values of morality (compare: **value-neutral autonomy**).

Symmetrical/Asymmetrical relationships (care ethics): In a symmetrical relationship, each person depends upon the other to roughly the same degree; in an asymmetrical relationship, one person tends to depend upon the other.

Tacit consent (social contract theory): The idea that people born into an existing contract effectively consent to that contract by participating as adults in the state and accepting its benefits.

Proportionality condition (natural law theory): One of the conditions of **DDE**, this requires that the bad effect not be greater than the good effect.

Tolerance (moral relativism): A moral value that calls upon us to respect the beliefs and practices of others but doesn't preclude expressing disagreement or even taking action in certain cases.

Torture lite: Interrogation techniques that cause no visible physical harms (e.g., sleep deprivation, isolation, water boarding).

Truth claim (making moral judgments): Any statement that asserts something true or false; moral claims may be characterized as truth claims.

Universalizable (making moral judgments): Something that can commonly be generalized so that it holds for anyone; moral values and claims may be characterized as universalizable.

Universal law, principle of (Kantian ethics): A version of Kant's **categorical imperative**: act only in accordance with a **maxim** that you can at the same time (rationally) will to be a universal law or principle.

Utility (utilitarianism): Whatever makes consequences desirable; disutility, then, is undesirable.

Value (ethics and values): The **normative** concept of a good or an end that is worth acting to obtain, either as something desirable in itself or as a means to some other value.

Value-neutral autonomy (autonomy): The view that we can only be truly autonomous as long as we are able to choose our values without constraint and that any set of values can serve equally well as the basis for a person's choices (compare: **substantive autonomy**).

Veil of ignorance (social contract theory): Makes those in Rawls's **original position** equal by removing from them any knowledge of the place or condition that any of them will occupy within society.

Vice (virtue theory): A specific character trait, like dishonesty, that is the opposite of **virtue** and is morally bad: a vicious person has many vices.

Virtue (virtue theory): A specific character trait, like honesty, that is morally good: a virtuous person has many virtues.

Whistle-blowing (business ethics): The act of exposing illegal, immoral, or dangerous practices occurring within an organization to others who can address the problem.

Index